Sex Changes with Kleist

Sex Changes with Kleist

Katrin Pahl

NORTHWESTERN UNIVERSITY PRESS
EVANSTON, ILLINOIS

Northwestern University Press
www.nupress.northwestern.edu

Printed in the United States of America

10 9 8 7 6 5 4 3 2 1

Library of Congress Cataloging-in-Publication Data

Names: Pahl, Katrin, author.
Title: Sex changes with Kleist / Katrin Pahl.
Description: Evanston, Illinois : Northwestern University Press, 2019. | Includes bibliographical references and index.
Identifiers: LCCN 2018058160 | ISBN 9780810140110 (paper text : alk. paper) | ISBN 9780810140127 (cloth text : alk. paper) | ISBN 9780810140134 (e-book)
Subjects: LCSH: Kleist, Heinrich von, 1777–1811—Criticism and interpretation. | Sex (Psychology) in literature. | German literature—19th century—History and criticism.
Classification: LCC PT2379.Z5 P34 2019 | DDC 838/.609—dc23
LC record available at https://lccn.loc.gov/2018058160

CONTENTS

ACKNOWLEDGMENTS

This book was written in many places and nurtured by several communities. In Baltimore, I benefited tremendously from the vibrant intellectual community that forms around the program in Women, Gender, and Sexuality as well as from the conversations with my colleagues and students in the German program and the larger German and Romance Languages and Literatures context. For helping to create an intellectual environment where my research could thrive, I would like to thank, in particular, Rüdiger Campe (for the initial encouragement), Jane Bennett, Jennifer Culbert, Bernadette Wegenstein, my WGS codirector Todd Shepard, Bill Connolly, Shane Butler, Drew Daniel, Veena Das, Laura Di Bianco, Márton Dornbach, Bill Egginton, Naveeda Khan, Chris Nealon, Rani Neutill, Leo Proietti, Eugenio Refini, Rochelle Tobias, Noelle Dubay, Jo Giardini, Nathan Gies, Katherine Glanz, Christina Hinz Speach, Christiane Ketteler, Maya Nitis, Sarah Ross, Elisa Santucci, and Jason Yonover, as well as those who shared their expertise as invited speakers, among them Karen Barad, Mel Chen, Astrid Deuber-Mankowsky, Annamarie Jagose, Raquel Gutiérrez, Jack Halberstam, Sharon Hayes, Birgit M. Kaiser, Dana Luciano, Jan Mieszkowski, Camille Robcis, Gabriele Schwab, Joan W. Scott, Kathrin Thiele, Karen Tongson, Trinh Minh-ha, and Juliane Vogel. I am grateful for the various opportunities I have at JHU to invite inspiring scholars and for the freedom to teach difficult and controversial ideas.

Parts of this book were presented at the Department of Comparative Literature at the University of California, Berkeley; the Kleist Museum in Frankfurt an der Oder; the Germanistische Seminar at the Universität Hamburg; the Heinrich-von-Kleist-Gesellschaft; the Division of Literatures, Cultures, and Languages at Stanford University; the German Studies Department and Humanities Center at the University of Pittsburgh; the Department of German at Princeton University; the Department of German, Russian and Eastern European Studies at Vanderbilt University; and the Internationale Kolleg für Kulturtechnikforschung und Medienphilosophie (IKKM) in Weimar. I thank everybody who invited me and offered their feedback.

In Berlin, the friendship and the many stimulating conversations I had with Mohammed Bamyeh, Elena Blum, Gabriele Brandstetter, Simon During, Juli Gudehus, Randall Halle, Masayo Kajimura, Kader Konuk, Vanessa Agnew, Christoph Menke, Eva Meyer, Lisa O'Connell, Eran Schaerf, and Leander Scholz made writing this book more pleasant.

I am grateful that I can spend days, sometimes weeks, with the collective of the Gutshaus Mesendorf, who jointly restore and maintain an ample estate while also working on their texts or other academic and artistic projects. I appreciate their distinct kind of hospitality, which consists in inviting their friends to care for the flourishing of the house in addition to the intellectual and creative projects of the people who live in it. I want to thank, in particular, Lucy Duggan, Aurélie Herbelot, Matthias Mader, Eva von Redecker, and Sophie von Redecker.

I have grown very fond of my house community in Witzenhausen and want to thank my housemates for welcoming me and for the friendships that have built over the years. They have taught me that age difference doesn't need to matter and that a group can give room to the needs and proclivities of every participant.

I thank my mother and my mother-in-law for letting me write at their places whenever I wanted to, for giving me warmth and a sense of abundance while also allowing me to withdraw into concentration.

I wrote most of this book while trying to spend as much time as possible with Sophie von Redecker, setting up desk wherever she was. I thank her for the many conversations we had—about theater, queer theory, political theory, farming, ecology, and Agrarian Humanities—for the important advice she gave me at many stages of this project, and for the sense of home I feel with her.

Sincere thanks go to Lucy Duggan, who, with a light touch and capacious grasp, improved my prose in English, and to Amelia Clarke, Rahel von Minden, Brandon Pelcher, and Johannes Schade for their assistance in preparing the manuscript for publication.

The artist, filmmaker, and curator Masayo Kajimura created the artwork for the front cover. It is a paper cut that layers differently textured papers and motives. Her technique echoes the mackles that I discuss in this book. Titled "Les Fleurs Somnambules," the work overlays Penthesilea, the Amazon, and Katie, the swan, with their variously queer breast_s. It was an extraordinary pleasure to continue our conversations about her artwork, which I deeply admire, with chats about my work via Kleist and her visual response to it.

ABBREVIATIONS

The titles of works by Kleist are cited throughout the text and notes using the following abbreviations:

A — *Amphitryon*
BH — *Die Herrmannsschlacht* (*The Battle of Herrmann*)
G — *Robert Guiskard, Herzog der Normänner* (*Robert Guiscard, Duke of the Normans)*
J — *Der Zerbrochne Krug* (*The Broken Jug*)
K — *Das Käthchen von Heilbronn* (*Katie of Heilbronn*)
P — *Penthesilea*
PH — *Prinz Friedrich von Homburg* (*Prince Frederick of Homburg*)
S — *Die Familie Schroffenstein* (*The Schroffenstein Family*)

When citing or referencing passages from these plays, I provide the page number from the translations below, followed by act (where existent), scene, and verse number (e.g., *K* 236/4.2.2129, or *P* 134/24.2787):

A — 2004. *Amphitryon*. In Heinrich von Kleist, *Selected Writings*, translated by David Constantine, 66–134. Indianapolis: Hackett.
BH — 2008. *The Battle of Herrmann*. Translated and with critical apparatus by Rachel MagShamhráin. Würzburg: Königshausen und Neumann.
G — 1990. *A Fragment of the Tragedy of Robert Guiscard, Duke of the Normans*. In *Heinrich von Kleist: Five Plays*, translated by Martin Greenberg, 351–73. New Haven, Conn.: Yale University Press.
J — 1982. *The Broken Pitcher*. Translated by Jon Swan. In *Heinrich von Kleist: Plays*, edited by Walter Hinderer, 1–90. New York: Continuum.
K — 2000. *Ordeal by Fire (Das Käthchen von Heilbronn oder Die Feuerprobe)*. In Heinrich von Kleist, *Three Plays*, translated by Noel Clark, 159–259. London: Oberon Books.
P — 1998. *Penthesilea: A Tragic Drama*. Translated by Joel Agee. New York: HarperCollins
PH — 1982. *Prince Frederick of Homburg*. Translated by Peggy Meyer Sherry. In *Heinrich von Kleist: Plays*, edited by Walter Hinderer, 269–341. New York: Continuum.
S — 1916. *The Feud of the Schroffensteins*. Translated by Mary J. Price and Lawrence M. Price. *Poet Lore* 27, no. 5: 457–576.

I modified these translation where necessary to stay close to the original signifiers. It is indicated in parenthesis whenever I altered a translation or provided my own.

When altering the translation of *Katie*, I have often drawn on

> 1927. *Kaethchen of Heilbronn or The Test of Fire*. Translated by Frederick E. Pierce. In *Fiction and Fantasy of German Romance: Selections from the German Authors, 1790–1830*, edited by Frederick E. Pierce and Carl F. Schreiber, 248–344. New York: Oxford University Press.

When altering the translation of *The Broken Jug*, I have often drawn on

> 2004. *The Broken Jug*. Translated by David Constantine. In Heinrich von Kleist, *Selected Writings*, edited by David Constantine, 3–65. Indianapolis: Hackett.

Sex Changes with Kleist

INTRODUCTION

Kleist responded in a unique way to the change in the organization of sex and gender described by Claudia Honegger (1991) and more explicitly identified by Thomas Laqueur (1990) as a shift from the one-sex or one-flesh model to the two-sex and oppositional or complementary gender system. This change developed in tandem with and partially as a reaction to a whole complex of crises, revolutions, and changes that culminated in the emancipation of the European bourgeoisie or middle class, brought about by the French Revolution. Quite at odds with historical development, Kleist lingered in the interstices of these enormous shifts, overlaid the new with the old, elaborated a poetics of incongruity—or of mackles, as I call it—and dared to generate a logic of confusion and to experiment with alternative symbolic structures, all the while developing a distinctive humor.

His work inhabits a broken temporality and, for that reason alone, cannot be integrated into a narrative of historical development. Kleist (and any study of Kleist's take on sex, gender, and sexuality) cannot escape anachronism. Given this situation, this study will, prudently, embrace the risk of presentism, of anachronistically applying ideas and terms that were forged much later (e.g., homosexual, gay, lesbian, queer, trans) to the work of an author who wrote during the first decade of the nineteenth century and thus could not have known them.

While, as Robert Deam Tobin (2015) emphasizes, the modern discourse of sexuality (including the terms "homosexual" and "heterosexual") was developed in the German language, it was so in the second half of the nineteenth century.[1] In addition to scientific and political discourse, literature played a significant role in shaping and disseminating the lexicon and the repertoire of images and thought patterns that constitute modern sexual culture.[2] The initial circulation of a variety of creative new terms was settled with the decisive appearance of Richard von Krafft-Ebing's *Psychopathia Sexualis* in 1886, and Krafft-Ebing's terminology was introduced into English with the book's translation, by Charles Gilbert Chaddock, in 1892.[3]

We have already seen a wave of scholarship challenging Foucault's (1990, 43) dating of the "birth" of homosexuality to the invention of the word around 1870. These studies trace the emergence of same-sex culture and identity into the eighteenth century, specifying places, rituals, role models, and idioms for (mostly male) same-sex desire.[4] In particular, they provide evidence against the accepted notion that the eighteenth-century cult of friendship was asexual. They also sometimes appreciate—somewhat at cross-purposes with the goal of proving the existence of a homosexual culture avant la lettre—that this not entirely asexual, enthusiastic friendship allowed for queerness (i.e., nonbinary and antiessentialist indeterminacy), for feelings and desires to come out without any demands for identification.[5] In *Warm Brothers: Queer Theory and the Age of Goethe*, Tobin (2000, 6) calls attention to the fact that, in addition to the birth of homosexuality around 1870, Foucault also speaks of the "birth" of "man" around 1800 and similarly historicizes the rise of the "author." It is quite apparent that the use of the words "man" and "author" in contexts referring to a time prior to enlightened humanism, the emergence of the public realm and its legal regulation is not similarly policed for ahistoricism as the use of the word "homosexual" or other modern terms of sexuality is. We have to ask whether such selective eagerness doesn't contribute to an unfortunate silencing of same-sex or queer desire and its culture.

In any case, it is not my purpose here to describe Kleist as a precursor of or an early participant in modern (homo)sexual culture. Nor do I find it sufficient to build on Heinrich Detering's (1994, 117–56) argument and further expand his analysis of the effects of Kleist's legible but presumably suppressed same-sex desire on his writing and his aesthetics.

Rather than preparing modern homosexuality, Kleist puts an end to modern gender norms before they take hold and refuses the oppositional organization of sexual desire into homosexual and heterosexual that sprouts from these norms. With the Napoleonic Wars, and especially after the Prussian defeat in 1806, sex changes (for everybody in the German lands) when German nationalism combines with the new ideas about gender complementarity based on sexual difference to produce the man with same-sex desire as a figure of treason and use him as a scapegoat.[6] As Alice Kuzniar (1996, 17) explains, "A distinct sign that a radical shift had occurred can be observed in the case of the eminent Swiss historian Johannes Müller, whose known penchant for men was generally accepted until 1806, when it was almost universally condemned once he was perceived to have betrayed his country in his admiration for Napoleon. . . . Here we have an example, perhaps the first of its kind in the modern period, of personality being assessed in terms of homosexuality, which is to say that homosexuality becomes imbricated in such other issues—as it is today—as moral virtue, social interaction, national defense and patriotism."[7]

Johann Wolfgang von Goethe reacts naively to this shift in sexual mores: unfazed by the acute increase of bourgeois moralizing, he continues his quest to develop a metaphorics of moderately fluid desire.[8] The Romantics are spooked and begin to pitch their stories of gender ambiguity and transgression in an ominous key, thereby contributing to the ostracizing of the deviant.[9] But Kleist aggressively proliferates the sex changes, undoing both gender norms and the separation of homo- from heterosexuality.

Time

Kleist writes at the beginning of the nineteenth century (from about 1799 to 1811) in response to several revolutions and far-reaching changes.[10] Central among these was the Kantian revolution of thought, which severely curtailed metaphysical authority and led to a destabilizing of objectivity. Immanuel Kant's answer to his most fundamental concern—"What can we know?"—barred access to the supersensible realm while also pulling the rug out from under empiricism with the far-reaching insight, which Kant himself likened to the Copernican revolution, that the mind plays an active role in structuring reality. Kleist staged his personal "Kant crisis," which has received much attention in scholarly literature.

The Enlightenment, including Kant's philosophy, effected a radical change in how subject formation works. Matthias Waltz (1993) describes the shift, drawing on Jacques Lacan, roughly as follows. In the pre-Enlightenment world, the subject is given its place in the social order by inheriting a name. Everyone is part of a lineage and there is no strong investment in individuality. A person's freedom lies in accepting their symbolic endowment, which comes with a charge—with the responsibility to act, speak, and think a certain way. In the modern world, all subjects have to make a name for themselves or to fashion themselves. They are thus in the paradoxical situation of serving as creator and created at once, with the considerable increase in freedom but also in anxiety that this brings. The modern subject experiences the names it might be given as either aggressive (as name-calling) or empty (as interpellation—an abstract address that forces them into a subjectivity without specificity) or otherwise inadequate (not true to their being). The symbolic order has thus become problematic. Whereas the old order was firmly rooted in a cosmology where everything was meaningful and concrete, the new order has bought its claim to universality with abstraction and revolves around an empty center.

In Lacanian psychoanalytic terms, this historical shift is registered by putting the big other (who anchors the symbolic order) under erasure: from A to Ⱥ. The modern symbolic seeks new legitimization in narcissistic ideals like welfare and happiness and, given that these ideals are rooted in the imaginary order (which involves deceptive self-images), the big other is filled with the aggression that the imaginary produces. In addition, the lack of symbolic legitimacy creates its own compensatory aggression. As if the big other under erasure were jealous, the modern symbolic only castrates; it doesn't empower. Nevertheless, the modern subject clings to the tenuous link between the phallus and masculinity as the only, if illusive, promise of power or status left and vigorously defends it against those who cannot so easily claim this link for their benefit. At the fringes of the imaginary fulfillment of the symbolic, the big other is experienced as unable to bind or hold the subject and the individual falls into what Lacan calls the experience of the real—isolation, loss of world, and inability to participate. In the old order, this was known to those who did not or could not accept their name, and it becomes a pervasive but also more lighthearted mode with postmodernism.

At first Kleist bends to the pressure of the imaginary symbolic and the modern demand for self-realization, as is evident in his very early essay "On the Surest Way to Find Happiness and Enjoy It Undisturbed—Even Amid Life's Greatest Tribulations" (1799). But then he begins to counteract the narcissistic and aggressive weight of the imaginary (which stems from the deceptive appeal of the well-defined mirror image) by blurring contours or mackling forms, and to corrode the compensatory aggression of the phallic by devising alternative symbolic orders. He also anticipates (or offers an identificatory vessel for) our postmodern experiences of the real.[11]

The shift from the old order of established social differences to the new order of presuming equality while requiring singularity has also produced a new notion and experience of love. Whereas social stratification and the grammar of names and properties regulated the choice of a partner in the old world, modernity constructs love as a miracle (cf. Luhmann 1998, chapters 9, 12). According to the modern value of social equality, everybody could be a potential partner—especially since objective reasons for love have fallen into disrepute—yet modern or romantic love is imagined as unique, exclusive, and eternal. This tension makes for an intense experience of falling in love—an overwhelming feeling and a sudden recognition (the coup de foudre): true love is supposed to be inexplicable, as one loves the other not for specific properties or signs of status but for who they are, that is to say, for everything they are. The beloved means the world to the lover (ibid., chapter 13). While in the old order lovers participated in and contributed to a public world by trading names and properties, romantic love forms a private world that removes the lovers from the public realm. Since each love is unique, the lovers have to invent from out of their felt but unspecified congeniality of souls—out of thin air, one could say—the language and the rituals of their love. Romantic love is an art and requires a "genius of love," who can create without being given rules (Neumann 2007, 57). While infinite, its creativity is confined to the private realm, to interiority, to the dyad of lovers who are caught in the imaginary sphere of their mirror relation. The more intense and fulfilling their love, the more isolated the dyad becomes, which can result in social death (often figured in novels, and even in real life, as biological death) (ibid., 58–64). The danger of social death is particularly high for women (in fact, it was all but designed for them), since the discourse of romantic love constructs woman as a figure for love and teaches women to live exclusively for love (cf. Fichte 2000, §§4–6). Interested in liberating female sexuality, Helga Gallas (2005) argues that Kleist harks back to the old notion of love that is supported by the old symbolic order. I don't think Kleist tries to reestablish the outdated, but he does overlay the new with the old in order to disturb one with the other and to allow something altogether different to emerge. In claiming that the notion of romantic love atrophies sexual desire, Gallas operates with a heteronormative notion of passion.[12] She thus inadvertently feeds the new heterosexual matrix of gender complementarity back into the old system of symbolic love and mobilizes Kleist for a sensibility (not to say, an ideology) that, I argue, was not his concern.

This brings us to the historical sex change that is central to this study. As already mentioned, a fundamental shift in the conception of gender difference and in the study of sexual anatomy occurred in the wake of the Enlightenment.[13] Before the shift to the modern sex-gender system, bodies and their properties functioned as signs indicating a place and determining relations in a metaphysical order. The reproductive organs were but one sign among many and the body but one articulation (and not the most significant one) among others that conveyed a person's position. The break with the old metaphysical order in favor of a new scientific paradigm based on the natural sciences led to the biological determination of gender. Anatomical difference moved center stage, one began to observe mutually exclusive, complementary features, and sexual difference became one of the most important and ideologically entrenched differences (along with racial difference).

For the second-century Roman physician of Greek origin Galen of Pergamon, the only physiological difference between men and women was a difference in the degree of what he called "vital heat." Men were men because they were hotter than women. Men's higher body temperature had driven their sexual organs from inside the body to the outside and allowed them to cook their blood into foaming white semen. Those human bodies that seemed to have less energy and appeared colder and more humid were called women—they had the same sexual organs as men (only still somewhat dormant inside the body) and they periodically released red (uncooked) blood. In this paradigm, only one physical sex exists but it comes in different stages of perfection, which can be roughly divided into two categories—male and female. All flesh is fallen, heavy, and sluggish—but the more energized or spiritualized a body appears, the more perfect, as in able to transcend the material realm, it is. Men have achieved a higher degree of perfection than women, but transitions from one stage to the other are definitely possible. This view of sexual anatomy is informed by a metaphysical, cosmic order that predates Galen and remains influential in Europe at least until the Enlightenment. Laqueur (1990) calls the old system the "one-sex model." Consequently, one can say that the historical sex change consists in the invention of a second sex. For the first time, woman was considered not a lesser version of man but a different being with a value of her own. Modernity thus establishes the sexual binary. But modernity also links gender to the biological sex, thus coercing sex identification or the assignment of each individual to one of the two sexes. Gender characteristics and gender roles become naturalized—Honegger (1991, ix) speaks of the "positive legend of the mere observation of nature"—and pseudoscientific evidence is produced to show that men and women must take different positions in society because their reproductive organs and other body parts are different in size, structure, or function (see also Weckel 1998, 265). The emancipatory potential of a second, female principle with its own authority is quickly lost when womanhood is relegated to the status of a minority.[14] This study will analyze how Kleist reacted to the historical sex change.

The decisive changes mentioned so far combine and culminate in the French Revolution, which radically restructures society based on the idea of equality and reorients politics around the ideal of freedom. The bourgeoisie establishes itself as the political force and reorganizes the public and private spheres based on its distinctive values (informed, to a large extent, by the structure of the nuclear family with its regulation of gender, emotion, and sexuality).[15] Napoleon's colonization of Europe disseminates some of these changes. In particular, as Rebecca Comay (2001, 137) recounts, after the decisive Prussian defeat near Jena in 1806 Napoleon "imposed a dramatic reorganization of the legal, fiscal, political, military, agricultural, educational, and administrative fabric of German life." If the German experience of the French Revolution can be described as a missed experience on the order of a traumatic event,[16] the heteronomous imposition of autonomy, the colonizing delivery of freedom, and the imparting of reason through brute violence followed a no less self-defeating logic and broken temporality. Whether one considers his reign to have advanced or perverted the ideals of the revolution, Napoleon did, "by forcing an accelerated modernization upon a state long regarded as moribund and beyond resurrection," induce "a temporal short-circuit that leaves Germany breathlessly suspended between two epochs. He confronts Germany with the specter of its own noncontemporaneity" (ibid., 137–38). The reaction from German poets and thinkers is mixed. While the proponents of Weimar Classicism smooth over the rupture with an aestheticizing interest in the harmonious whole, and the German Romanticists, after having jumped ahead by celebrating fragmentation, turn to folk and children's literature, Kleist, whose relatively short writing life spans the period of the Napoleonic Wars and the Napoleonic restructuring of German society, responds to and intervenes in this situation drawing creative energy from its broken temporality.[17] His stories and plays dramatize the overlay of the two epochs. Kleist is the author of noncontemporaneity.

He intimately understands the bizarre temporality of revolutions, which breaks the chain of experience, of causality, of the law. Robespierre used the image of the thunderbolt during the trial of Louis XVI not only to express his impatience with due process but also to articulate the absolute novelty of the situation (while ironically having to rely on an ancient topos) and the impossibility of process for a creation ex nihilo: "A people does not judge in the manner of courts of law; it does not hand down sentences but hurls down thunderbolts" (Maximilien Robespierre, speech of December 3, 1792, quoted in Comay 2001, 41). The image of the thunderbolt meant to cut through the twisted logic of inaugurating a new law while having to rely either on the old one in order to abolish its own authority or on the new one before it is authorized. Kant had already grappled with the related problem of bringing about what is posited as universal and thus atemporal. The conversion to autonomy must itself be timeless, that is to say, instantaneous. And in the *Anthropology*, Kant compares the transition to an explosion: "Education, examples, and teaching generally cannot bring about this firmness and persistence in principles *gradually*, but only, as it were, by a kind of explosion which happens *one* time [*auf einmal*]" (Kant 2006, 194).

Revolutionary moral rigor and Enlightenment universalism thus rely on the violent temporality of the explosion or of thunderbolt and lightning. Kleist uses both images in abundance and often sets his plots in revolutionary times or uses ancient stories as allegories for the revolutions of his time, running the gamut from the Protestant Reformation (*Michael Kohlhaas* and *Saint Cecilia, or the Power of Music*), the Enlightenment (*The Earthquake in Chile* and *The Broken Jug*), the French Revolution (*Penthesilea*), and the Haitian Revolution (*The Betrothal in Santo Domingo*) to the Napoleonic Wars (*The Battle of Herrmann*). He does so while staunchly breaking with the common narrative of progress. His revolutionary eruptions never inaugurate a permanent new order. Instead, Kleist explores the twisted logic of revolutionary change and perfects his experiments in instantaneity and repetition with his daily newspaper *Berliner Abendblätter*.

Theater

If the Enlightenment emphasizes the intellect and champions the rules of logical reasoning against dogma and caprice, it also requires intuition (despite the perceived danger of intuition corrupting intellectual reasoning). In 1787, Kant (1990, 45) offers the formula "Thoughts without content are void; intuitions without conceptions, blind" and, injecting a dose of empiricism into pure reason, adds, "hence it is necessary for the mind to make its conceptions sensuous." Even Christian Wolff, the most rationalist of the German Enlightenment philosophers, acknowledges the superior liveliness and hence pedagogical usefulness of intuition.[18]

The two mental faculties have distinct characteristics and involve different temporalities. The intellect is rule-governed, sequential and abstract; it relies on arbitrary signs to represent the thoughts that it infers one from the other according to the laws of logic. Intuition is a concrete form of knowledge that happens all at once. It is inherently visual (the word derives from the Latin *intuēri*, "to look at") even if it doesn't always involve visual sense perception. The synoptic, sudden (all at once) and immediate (not based on deduction) quality of intuition is well captured in the figure of the *Augenblick* or blink of an eye.

In their efforts to educate the citizens in a morality based on the proper use of reason, Enlightenment authors turn to the theater (*Schaubühne* or "showstage") as the art form most apt to place thoughts, as it were, before the eye and to make reason sensible (see Graf 2010, 36). Johann Christoph Gottsched's reform of the theater around 1730 draws on Wolff's logocentric philosophy. For Gottsched, it is the task of the theater to make intuitive and show by example the truths or maxims that one could also arrive at by reasoning. Because not everybody is willing or able (yet) to reason logically, and because lessons have a much stronger impact when experienced with the senses, theater fills a crucial need.

In the long run, the theater reform institutionalizes bourgeois theater in Germany. Before, traveling theater troupes used makeshift stages to produce more or less improvised plays based on sets of well-known characters and plot components, where each actor tried to draw the attention of the spectators with witty and showy extemporaneous responses, sometimes (especially when they traveled across linguistic borders) relying more on pantomime than on verbal communication. Now cities demand and create playhouses for their citizens, and as the theater reform bans improvisation, developing German theater into a literary art form, the new playhouses allow for the introduction of the proscenium stage (*Guckkastenbühne*). These two innovations—the creation of a repertoire of dramatic literature in German and the proscenium stage—define the reformed theater as a (not always harmonious) interplay of the verbal and the visual. Whereas theatrical production is henceforth governed by the literary text (and thereby susceptible to a wide array of regulations), the proscenium arch architectonically frames the scene as an image (adding the *Bild* to *Bildung* while stabilizing and distancing the scene from the spectators).

The theater reform thus mirrors the rise (but also the restraint) of the citizen as spectator, commentator, and critic of politics. The emergence of the *Publikum* (in both senses: audience and public) leads to a culture of critique in which public opinion serves as quasi political action and reality is haunted by its own virtuality. "There is no experience that is not already its own interpretation, no action that is not already its own representation, no revolution that is not already theater, spectacle, imitation" (Comay 2001, 150). Wary of engaging in phony or possibly disastrous action, the modern subject invests its energies for self-improvement in becoming a more disciplined spectator and a sharper critic. The subject gains autonomy, the sense of superiority that accompanies it, and, as Waltz (1993, 217) argues, the "pleasures of 'feeling' " that correspond to it. The price of this autonomy, though, is the ascetic withdrawal from the scene of "actual" life to a seat in an unlit auditorium—the spectator's body unseen and immobile.[19]

When Waltz emphasizes the pleasures of feeling or sentiment, he refers to the new, distinctly bourgeois phenomenon of inner life. This decidedly inward increase in liveliness has been described by Kant as aesthetic pleasure: an inner movement (the pleasurable play of the mental faculties) that is sparked by the contemplation of an external object or scene by an outwardly inactive and disinterested person. Bourgeois "feeling" is inherently vicarious. As Waltz puts it, "The subject of feeling is the invisible, disembodied subject, who lives on letting himself be drawn into the lives of others, but only 'in play' and without having skin in the game" (1993, 221, my translation). In theater terms, such feeling requires the strict separation between the scene and the auditorium—between those who act and suffer and those who observe. While the theater reform (in its various incarnations from Gottsched, Neuber, and Gellert to Lessing to Goethe) stimulated German theater culture and led to an increase in respect and compensation for the profession of the actor, this did not mean that a bourgeois subject couldn't find plenty of opportunity to enjoy feeling outside the confines of the theater and free of charge. Children, simple folk, and, to a certain extent, women served as the unknowing objects of his sentimentalizing and aestheticizing gaze. "Love for those who are immature . . . is not just paternalism but also motivated by the fact that children and simple folk provide the only place where the autonomous subject can live" (219, my translation).[20] The autonomous subject feels vicariously and does so proportionately to his ability to separate the scene of sentimentality from his anesthetized spectator position: "because the autonomous subject is, by definition, disembodied and indifferent to the gaze of others, he can be completely absorbed in the spectacle" (221, my translation).[21] At this theater of bourgeois self-formation, all feeling comes down to the same: the feeling of being alive. Given that the autonomous subject cultivates suspended animation by suppressing his impulses to (re)act and arresting himself in the spectator position, his need to feel alive is quite pronounced. At the same time, he can disavow such need by discrediting the scene of sentimentality as emotionality, theatricality, and hysteria. If the beautiful increase in vitality is threatened by unruly and overwhelming forces, the subject may switch gears to the sublime. The experience of the sublime likewise receives support from the reformed theater and its strict separation of the scene from the beholder.[22] Educated in the auditorium, German intellectuals watch the terror of the French Revolution from a distance, sublimely uplifted by the spectacle for a more or less emancipatory philosophy, without the urge to come to the aid of the self-massacring people on the world stage. "The vicarious experience of bloodshed beyond its borders helps Germany forget its own history of atrocities as well as the territorial and confessional schisms that continue to torment it," Comay (2001, 23) argues, referring to the violent suppression of the peasants' uprising in 1525. The projection effects a virtualization; it renders actual atrocities unreal or theatrical to the point that it seems inappropriate to intervene: only children, who cannot tell play from reality, shout out to Kasperle when a crocodile lurks behind his back. The *Bildungsbürger* waits until the tragedy has run its course to draw his lessons (not realizing that his behavior is based on the reverse ontological mistake to that of the child).[23] Thus, virtualization shifts the stage inward. "The real theater is within," where the conflict of the faculties is dramatized and resolved in the superiority of reason over sense-perception and intuition (32).[24] "It is in the invisible theater of the self that I come to acknowledge" the self-scrutinizing, self-producing and self-annihilating formalism of the Kantian moral will (89).

Given the tremendous importance of the theater for subjectivity around 1800, this study focuses on Kleist's theater and Kleist's theatricality. It will show how radically Kleist subverts the function of the theater at the time. I use the term "theater," instead of "dramatic literature," which is more commonly employed in the field of literary scholarship, for several reasons, of which one should be obvious by now—namely, that the significance of theater for subjectivity exceeds the confines of the dramatic genre. Another reason is that Kleist mobilizes nonliterary forms of theater in his plays. At the same time, it must be said that Kleist's theater lets itself be disturbed by the intrinsic logic of textuality and that there is a pronounced and distinctive theatricality to Kleist's texts, including the nondramatic ones. Finally, it is important for my analysis of Kleist's dramatic texts to attend to the various possibilities and impossibilities of staging them.

The Beginning and Ending of Modern Gender Norms

Kleist's at times indirect, at times violent unsettling of subject positions (whether they manifest as social standing or epistemic viewpoint) makes him exceptionally interesting for us today. But his rage against identities also betrays a wound or trauma. Joachim Pfeiffer (1996) has pointed out a conspicuous similarity in Kleist's aesthetics to that of a certain strand of late twentieth-century gay literature. Both show a destructiveness that, according to Pfeiffer (1996, 222), stems from the experience of "social homelessness" (one could also speak of social death or of a fall into what Lacan calls the real).[25] Drawing on scholarship by Tomas Vollhaber and Dirck Linck on Hubert Fichte and Josef Winkler, Pfeiffer discusses Kleist's style and notes that his "threatened identity does not save itself through integration, but celebrates literarily the homelessness to which it has been damned" (224). Like some of the homosexual, queer, or trans outcasts of the twentieth century and of today, Kleist, he argues, does not use literature to forge a self and to emancipate his kind, but engages in a "contra-phobic writing," by which he means "the blasphemous outbidding and destruction of [that] reality" that destroys the author who is unable to find a place in it (224).

Like Pfeiffer, I detect in Kleist the experience of profound abandonment and lack of belonging, which are familiar from the context of sexual and gender deviance and their cultural expression. I also think that contra-phobic writing can provide inspiration for a critique of normativity. But Kleist interests me first and foremost because his experience is not mediated, like ours, by two hundred years of naturalizing the symbolic order of gender and minoritizing and ostracizing the homosexual. Kleist lives and writes as the modern gender polarity is being cemented and the grounds are laid for the development of modern, scientifically substantiated, heteronormative sexuality. While Pfeiffer points to an individual trauma, typical for a certain group (the gay outlaw), I argue in this book that Kleist uniquely responds to a historical trauma that Europe underwent around 1800 and that radiated from there across the globe, producing the gay outlaw in the first place and still affecting the modern subject today.[26]

The trauma consists in the production of a second sex. For millennia, only one body was known. It appeared sometimes more, sometimes less perfect but no one concluded that these differences constitute sexual dimorphism (Laqueur 1990, 25–113). Then a new paradigm emerged: the female body. Its entrance onto the stage of history was both inevitable and shocking. The frantic production of anatomical studies, theories, and opinions concerned with and about sexual difference, which is well documented for the early nineteenth century, bespeaks the shock. The scrutiny was spurred on not only by the goal of emancipating the still budding new sex but also by the will of the male sex (which, logically, emerged together with the second sex) to dominate this new female sex.[27] With every contribution to the fervor of inquiry, the traumatic sex change is belabored, repeated and consolidated. Eventually, the complementarity was organized hierarchically and the new system of two incommensurable genders tied to two distinct anatomies was seen as providing stability in a world that had been profoundly shaken by so many revolutions.[28] While the sex change was gradual and contested, to be sure, the new paradigm nevertheless, in typical revolutionary temporality, appeared timeless as soon as it became hegemonic and its birth then seemed as if it had happened in the blink of an eye.[29] When exactly the change occurred escapes our knowledge (Laqueur has received criticism for locating the change in as broad a timeframe as the eighteenth century and evidence for the existence of a second sex before the eighteenth century has been supplied), which means that we cannot have closure but still live in the shadow of this trauma.

The main literary schools of Kleist's time—Classicism and Romanticism—fall into line with history and—their gender experiments and affirmations of desire notwithstanding—add to the developments that confirm sexism and establish what today we call heteronormativity. The Romantics elaborate on the nascent gender polarity and thereby contribute to the emergence of the hetero/homo binary. The novel idea of the complementarity of the sexes reinforces opposite-sex desire to the point of requiring it. Even the transgender experiments of Romanticism are games played within the framework of this gender polarism. Friedrich Schlegel's *Lucinde*, for example, while celebrating sexual gender-play, does not explore same-sex desire but seeks to perfect opposite-sex desire with the fantasy of completing what it means to be human by cultivating the traits of the other sex within each (cf. MacLeod

1996, 203–8). And even homo sex is viewed as being based on the heterosexual paradigm as the notion of gender inversion is invented for same-sex desire (see Tobin 2000, 11–12). The Romantics toy with transsexuality but the gender binary organizes life and thought so powerfully that it colors their perception of same-sex desire, and that their ideal of perfection in turn contributes to the abjection of the homosexual.[30]

Goethe, as Susan E. Gustafson (2002, 70) shows, was chiefly concerned with developing a language for desire. While his explorations and poetic articulations of desire do not furnish sex scenes, Goethe staunchly maintains an unabashed and guiltless affirmation of desire as fluid. This includes the unproblematic interchange of what will later be separated into homo- and heterosexual desire (ibid., 39). But Goethe embeds this kind of fluidity in a narrative of individual and historical development, where male same-sex desire is cherished but relegated to the carefree time of personal youth and associated with ancient Greek culture, which is figured as the youth of humanity.[31] He also largely ignores female same-sex desire, which puts him in line with, rather than at the avant-garde of, his age with its gendered ideas about sexual desire.[32]

However, as Elisabeth Krimmer (2004, 36) notes with respect to the binary sex-gender system, "it is not the ultimate triumph of this model that is interesting. Rather, it is the failure to achieve complete dominance that is so fascinating to modern readers; the fact that within the mold of a natural gender is hidden the knowledge of the instability of both nature and authenticity. It is in this sense that the late-twentieth-century deconstruction of sex and gender already exists within the late-eighteenth-century creation of a natural gender."[33] Krimmer argues that the beginning of the gender polarity mirrors its ending in that both are a time of relative fluidity and both know of the constructedness of gender and desire. She also thinks that an awareness of fluidity and constructedness is preserved, from beginning to ending, in the folds of naturalized heteronormativity. I propose that Kleist puts an end to the model before it became hegemonic. This might make Kleist noncontemporaneous with the developments of history, but, from a different vantage point, a history that continuously and obsessively repeats what was already put to rest must be deemed anachronistic.

Kleist steps out of line with history. He refuses the stability that the hierarchical two-sex model promises and, instead, makes sex and gender the focal area of his proliferation of revolutions. He multiplies the sex change on every level: when he mixes and assaults literary genres, when he doubles the drama, when he perverts the culture of sensibility with male swoons and the revolutionary celebration of *fraternité* with the Amazon sisterhood, when he destabilizes identity and amplifies drag, when he mingles high and low forms of theater and troubles the line between earnest and playful. Kleist's work features strong heroines who do not join the ranks of the virtuous, passive, and sexually anesthetized bourgeois woman often depicted in the literature of his time. His heroines are driven by desires that offend social conventions—including same-sex sexual desire.[34] Generally remaining elusive and difficult to recognize, these desires invite names such as "lesbian" (that figure for the inconceivability of female and deviant sexuality) or "queer" (that epithet indicating the refusal to straighten out desire).[35]

By multiplying the sex changes, Kleist puts an end to the binary system before it becomes hegemonic. Yet history has chosen to cement the gender norms, sexual norms, and reproductive norms that Kleist nipped in the bud. The blurry pictures Kleist produces force us to participate in his theater, to contribute our interpretations, to make sense of it in light of our concepts, our horizon of meaning, and our interests. So far we have mostly opted for heteronormative readings of Kleist's texts. It is time to bring out the other layers of his work and to realize, for the first time, how profoundly sex changes with Kleist. His work calls for an ethics of reading that resists hegemonic notions—an ethics of conscious anachronism.

Approach

As might have already become apparent in the previous section, I draw from Kleist's texts the leads for my approach to reading his work. In addition to his unique exploration of anachronous temporality—his mixing of incongruous times, orders, and logics, I pay particular attention to his peculiar and unusually concrete language use, which also involves the conflictual overlay of the visual and the verbal. With the emphasis he places on the literal—which, as we will analyze under the heading of metalepsis, doesn't oppose the figurative but stretches it to the point of abstruseness and bad taste—Kleist's poetics offers an intriguing and useful counterweight to the focus on the rhetorical and the theatrical in queer theory and politics.

My network of theoretical affiliations relies (in a critical and revisionary vein) on psychoanalytic thought for a variety of arguments and investigations. Waltz builds on Lacan's system of the three psychoanalytic orders—the symbolic, the imaginary, and the real—to describe a historical development where first the symbolic is foregrounded (in feudal society), then the imaginary (in modern capitalist bourgeois society) and then the real (in the postmodern condition). Most, if not all, of the queer theorists I engage with here use psychoanalytic theory of Freudian, Lacanian, or Kleinian origin for their critique of heteronormativity and their elaborations of homo aesthetics and queer structures of kinship, desire, and emotionality. Other theorists (like Comay) are informed by the rich and vastly influential psychoanalytic conception of the noncontemporaneity of experience. While it would be an exaggeration to describe my work here as predominantly psychoanalytic, I will—especially when I contextualize Kleist's work with the help of these scholars within a larger argument—assume familiarity with the basic thought patterns and the most influential terms of psychoanalysis, especially of the Lacanian persuasion (such as the symbolic, the imaginary, the real, the phallus, the name and no of the Father, sexual difference, and the absence of sexual relation). For my critique of Lacanian assumptions, I will sometimes draw on the work of Melanie Klein. Since psychoanalysis has been criticized as one of the fields of medicine (in addition to sexology) that contribute heavily, together with literature and law, to the shaping of modern ideas about gender and sexuality, it might feel counterproductive to adopt its tenets here. But I hope that this study will serve as a case in point that a psychoanalytically informed reading of Kleist can be used to subvert the heterosexual norms of psychoanalysis because Kleist is already queering the literary discourses out of which sexual science and psychoanalysis both develop.

Sex Changes with Kleist builds on and resumes my research on emotionality. It examines the unusual performance of feelings in Kleist's theater and explores, sometimes more explicitly (for example, in chapter 5), sometimes within a discussion of either sexuality or dramaturgy, what Kleist might have to contribute to the theory of emotion. Emotional and sexual sensibility are correlated in the social cultivation or *Bildung* of the bourgeois subject. Kleist subverts one while also troubling the other, and thereby exposes the constructedness of both.

Chapter Overview

The first chapter, "Mackles, Mess, and Metalepsis," makes an argument for incoherence. With Kleist, it advocates for relaxing the imperative of logic that demands clean resolute distinctions, and the aesthetic principle that requires harmonious unified wholes. Kleist isolates, doubles, and then improperly overlays the elements of the theater, which in the conventional theater of his day complement and mutually enhance one another. He thus creates dramaturgical mackles. With apparent mistakes, inconsistent characters, character doubles, and porous composition, he creates confusion and offers an education in tolerating mess. Furthermore, he literalizes language in a mannerist way, which I describe as metalepsis.

The second chapter, "Double the Drama (Transorgasmics)," favors the queer model of the drive as repetitive, pulsating, or trembling insistence over the idea of the goal-orientedness of drives and shows how Kleist unleashes shivers with a dramaturgy that overlays at least two dramas. Focusing on the example of *The Broken Jug* and reading the three versions of the narrative climax of this analytic play as three orgasms, I argue that reception so far has only seen one drama (that of Eve) but not the other (the drama of Adam). I show that Adam, rather than wanting to have Eve, wants to be Eve and is made a scapegoat by an audience community invested in enforcing the proper linguistics of national normative gender and sexuality.

Chapter 3, "Mammalogic and Analgrammar," recognizes the possibility of multiple (queer) symbolic orders. This chapter probes Kleist's experiments with language drawn from and shaped in the image of the breast and with a symbolic (dis)organized by the anus. Both of these additional privileged signifiers function in genderqueer ways. Mammalogic offers a logic of ambivalence and analgrammar dissolves identities and ties.

Taking its cue from the current renaissance of comedy against minoritization, the fourth chapter, "Camp (Drummer Boys)," explores Kleist's camp humor. It treats one of Kleist's anecdotes from the Napoleonic Wars in dialogue with two plays that respond to Napoleonic imperialism, *The Battle of Herrmann* and the fragmentary tragedy *Robert Guiscard, Duke of the Normans*, examining the irony of Kleist's seemingly warmongering and nationalist poetry. I analyze instances of physical comedy (including slapstick, the melodramatic gestures of drag queens, and defiant mooning) intertwined with verbal wit and textual jokes, and discuss the ambiguous implication of this complex form of comedy in isolation, despair, grace, and care.

Chapter 5, "Offstage Onstage, or How to Crack an Emotion," contributes to Emotion Studies by analyzing what I call "teichoscopies of feeling." Unsettling the interiority-exteriority divide, Kleist uses the Classical dramatic device of teichoscopy in novel ways and thereby demonstrates that emotions are constructed in the moment. This simultaneity of construction and experience, I caution, renders feelings susceptible to ideology (to the extent that it has to rely on available, most likely normative or hegemonic, scripts), but it is also this simultaneity which makes transformation possible.

The final chapter, "Obscene Lesbians and Lost Queers," addresses how sex might change if we learn, with Kleist, to see what has long remained invisible and to speak to what could still remain unintelligible: queer female sexuality. It reads Katie and Kunigunde, the rivals for the knight's attention in *Katie of Heilbronn*, as lesbian lovers and reminds us of what has been all but lost in the reception of *Penthesilea*, namely the queerness of the Amazon queen Penthesilea, of Achilles, and of their relationship.

Chapter 1

✦

Mackles, Mess, and Metalepsis

Awr/ay. I propose this neologism that oscillates between "awe," "awry," and "away" to render the German particle *ver*, which pervades Kleist's texts with its devastating ambivalence and its confusing polysemy while succinctly capturing the spirit of Kleist's entire work. Penthesilea's *Versprechen*, the family Schroffenstein's *Versehen*, Alcmene's *Verzeichnen*, and the many *Verhöre* we encounter in Kleist's plays are but the most conspicuous examples of Kleist's work with the prefix.[1] In one of its uses listed in the major dictionaries, the prefix *ver-* changes nothing in the meaning of the verb it is attached to.[2] For example, when Kleist prefaces his novella *The Marquise of O* with the comment "Based on a real event with the place shifted [*verlegt*] from the north to the south," he could have used the same verb without the prefix (*gelegt*) and it would have meant the same thing: *deren Schauplatz vom Norden nach dem Süden gelegt worden* (Kleist 2004, 281, translation altered). Here the particle means nothing; its strange insistence vanishes in the meaning of the sentence. It thus enacts another one of its uses, listed as "one of the first and oldest meanings" of the word, namely to express a shift or a movement away.[3] *Ver-* goes away. But both the redundant and the largely value-free spatial uses of *ver-* have a tendency, in Kleist, to turn malign. His scenarios hinge not just on innocuous vanishing, but on awe-inspiring destruction. This brings us to another sense of *ver*: it can indicate the thorough or emphatic completion of the action expressed by the verb.[4] *Versprechen*, for example, can mean "pledging," which is an emphatic form of speaking complete with real-life action. While *ver-* may be used to add intensity to the verbal action or to express that the action is being carried out to the end, it can also indicate its perversion: that the action is going awry. *Versprechen*, in *Penthesilea*, designates both an intense speaking, that brings about the completion of what it says, and a misspeaking. The many scenes of *Verhör*—of questioning or interrogation—in Kleist's oeuvre also carry the sense of mishearing. What is more, they are often performed in such a forceful fashion that the hearing corrupts the search for truth, overshoots the mark, or even exhausts itself so completely that nothing is (left to be) heard in the end.[5] Awr/ay.

The Grimm brothers' authoritative dictionary bundles the various meanings of *ver-* into an opposition between completion and perversion.[6] But in Kleist's use the poles of the opposition overlap: carrying the action to completion perverts the action.[7] Kleist uses the particle *ver-* to spread the sense that the more thoroughly an action is performed and the more seriously it is taken, the more likely it is to be perverted. A thorough look—a *Versehen*, if you will—exposes the epistemological conditions that render mistakes (*Versehen*) inevitable. Or, to raise the issue of *Vertrauen*, which we will discuss in a different chapter: the more keenly one demands trust, the more problematic trust becomes.

Against the dramatizing and constricting momentum of the opposition, Kleist's serial aesthetic, his use of repetitions, reiterations, and replications, brings the full polysemy of the particle *ver-* to the fore. In the next section I will discuss this practice as "mackle." Kleist's mackles mobilize the spatial meaning of *ver-* and leave room for a less awe-inspiring insistence/vanishing of the prefix that changes (close to) nothing and might change everything.

Ver- also keeps close connection to metalepsis. I have already muddled ontological levels and linguistic registers in my presentation of the various uses of the prefix *ver-*. I mixed up sign and referent as well as descriptive and enacting language. Metalepsis has thus already affected my discourse before I will make it my topic in the last section of this chapter. The metaleptic transgression of ontological modes, narrative levels, and medium-specific universes echoes the working and the (il)logic of *ver-*. There is also a kind of rhetorical metalepsis that misspeaks and overstates, or *verspricht*, in that it takes a figure too seriously and, in doing so, speaks badly or in rather bad taste. Kleist employs this (non)figure extensively.

Mackles

Kleist repeats and layers slightly different images (or scenes) of the same event, conflict, character, thought, or feeling, and thus produces a multiple impression or—to use a technical term from printmaking—a mackle.[8] Mackles result from a small shift—*Verrücken*—of plates during the printing process and present a blurred picture that might create the impression of movement in place—a slight jiggle or wiggle. In addition to the small spatial shift, the prefix *ver-* in *verrücken* indicates a mistake (the less than ideal shift of printing plates), which under normal circumstances renders the product useless (produces wastepaper). *Ver-* here also suggests an intensity that easily overshoots the mark and extends the movement (*rücken*) beyond its singular occurrence to the ongoing jiggle of blurry contours (cf. Nessel and Pauleit 2004). Kleist's theatrical mackles shake the spectators' sense of what exactly they are beholding to the point of rendering them quite mad (*verrückt*). Even in the shift from the North to the South (*verlegt*) that we have encountered in

The Marquise of O, *ver-* cannot maintain its innocent appearance. The more we read (Latin: *legemus*) or the more we lay (*legen*) one version of the picture, the story gives, upon the other, the more we witness or, rather, produce the marquise's slip from the upright (or northward) position to a compromising recline (*legen*). This should make us quite embarrassed (*verlegen*), so we ourselves slip and can be sure that something is forgotten (*verlegt*) as we get lost.

The mackle might seem an overly mechanical figure for a literary poetics but it fits in this case. It is a defining characteristic of Kleist that he develops more or less mechanical procedures for the creative process, which rely on chance rather than inspiration or genius. When Kleist, in *Katie of Heilbronn* (*Das Käthchen von Heilbronn*), has a weeping Count vom Strahl evoke the "rhyme-smith [*Reimschmidt*]" as he is trying to express his feelings, this is not only mockery but also method (*K* 184/2.1.676). Penthesilea also acts as a wordsmith when she forges a feeling with words into a dagger, in her great final monologue. I read her, through this monologue, as a figure for the playwright, whose task it is to produce feelings in the audience, to touch the spectators, perhaps even to hurt them. For Kleist, poets are craftspeople, but funny and clumsy ones. They commit forgery in their smithies and produce mackle in their print shops. Their creative process involves dogged insistence as well as haphazardry. The resulting artwork is neither the masterstroke of *Sturm und Drang* nor the perfectly crafted harmonious whole of Classicism but a conglomeration of different layers of the same.[9] I will discuss a structural example of the artwork as mackle and elaborate on Kleist's notion of procedure in the next chapter. For now, we can gain a better understanding of what is meant by "mackle" by looking closely at a passage from *Penthesilea*, which I will read as an interpolated critique of the dominant, antimackle poetics.

In the first scene of *Penthesilea*, Antilochus cuts short the detailed description Odysseus offers of the first encounter the Greeks had with Penthesilea, interjecting: "So, word for word, your messenger reported" (*P* 8/1.103). Beyond feeling impatient with a story he has heard before, Antilochus implies here a critique of a certain notion of art. Odysseus is so proud of his well-crafted portrayal that he does not want to change even one word. Antilochus is irritated that Odysseus rehearses a speech apparently written in advance (how else would the messenger be able to verbatim replicate what spans more than a hundred lines). Odysseus's recital shares in the model of the literary theater, where no improvisation is allowed and no room for chance left. Despite his proverbial cleverness, Odysseus anxiously clings to every word and proves no more eloquent than the messenger. Hence, Antilochus concludes that he lacks originality.[10] The passage also shows that rehearsing doesn't help understanding: "So, word for word, your messenger reported; / But no one in the entire Grecian camp / Could comprehend it" (*P* 8/1.103–5). Antilochus insists on a lack of comprehension across repetitions and suggests that repetition communicates incomprehension rather than information.[11]

While Kleist explores the stultifying effect of repetition by mimicking, in his dramatic texts, the rehearsals and replays that are constitutive of the literary theater, his writerly mackles do not only repeat the same. They also function as technologies for analysis: separating or fanning out the component parts of the whole. Like Andy Warhol prints that make visible the different colors that are overlaid, Kleist isolates the component elements of theater with his mackles (cf. Klotz 1996, 63).

The theater is an art form that allows the audience to see, hear, and feel. In the conventional European theater around 1800, the audience gets to see scenes, hear a literary text, and feel the pain of a tragic fate or the silliness of a comic confusion, for example, and these elements of the theater complement and mutually enhance one another. Kleist instead isolates these elemental activities of the dramatic art—showing, speaking, and touching—and presents them onstage or exhibits them in his texts at times in the physical and at others in the mental or emotional sense in sometimes literal and sometimes figurative fashion (Klotz 1996, 77, 80). For example, he isolates the visual elements of theater in his unusually frequent pantomimic scenes, he foregrounds the verbal element in his excessive use of narrative,[12] and he thematizes touching in the physical sense (alluding to the emotional sense), for example, when he has the Prince of Homburg reach for the wreath through the fourth wall of the scene the Elector stages for him.[13] Our readings of various passages from different plays across the chapters of this book will play through the gambit of these modes of analysis.

But separation is not all there is to Kleist's mackles either. They wouldn't be mackles if they didn't involve overlap, blur, and "error."[14] Once isolated, Kleist doubles the elements of theater with one another. Overlaid replications or juxtaposed repetitions allow for the contamination or mutual affection of these elements. Often one element plays the role of another or they are confused with one another.[15] *Versehen*, *versprechen*, and *vergreifen* get mixed up. Hypotypotic speech paints a scene. An image touches. A glance speaks volumes. Words cut through the surface of the body. Feelings speak. These are but a few examples of the doubling and mackling of registers and component elements of the theater; we will develop them and discuss others in the chapters to follow. For now, I find it important to point out that Kleist's way of combining the elements of the theater by isolating, radicalizing and then confounding them differs profoundly from more Classical forms of theater where these elements are arranged hierarchically such that they complement and support one another to form a quasi-organic aesthetic whole. The component pieces, shreds, and shards that Kleist's "analysis" produces are not and cannot be pieced back together—as the fate of the jug in *The Broken Jug* clarifies in exemplary fashion.[16] The apposition instead of subordination and the replication instead of complementation of the pieces allows for mutual affection, affectation, and transformation. I would even say that it allows for mutation—for unmotivated changes that don't make any sense within the presumed logic. Kleist's texts include distortions that cannot be fit into the puzzle. Hence his theater "relies even more on a showing to which no seeing can correspond"—or of which no seeing can speak (Harst 2012, 182, my translation).

Against the backdrop of the intense gendering not only of bodies but of every aspect of cultural life—including, perhaps most emphatically, looking, speaking, and feeling—by the bourgeois culture that is taking hold in Germany around 1800 and of the fact that this process constructs the gendered activities and characteristics as opposed and complementing one another, Kleist's poetics of "superpositions, not oppositions" strikes one as unconventional and even dissident (Barad 2014, 176). I argue that his theatrical repetitions, reiterations, and replications actively engage with and contest the newly forming bourgeois culture of gendered bodies and minds. Since that cultural gendering became increasingly dominant and eventually resulted in the heteronormative regime we know today, it makes sense, from the current perspective, to describe Kleist's aesthetic concerns as queer and/or transgender. Queer theory has elaborated on the transformative potential of iteration and demonstrated that "the reiteration, the echoes, the reflexivity, the cadences, the automatic self-parodies and the self-monumentalising," which constitute identity formation and gender performance rely on a provisional, dispersed, and unsettled temporality, in which "for good or ill the possibilities of politics constantly arise."[17] Rather than acceding to one preestablished way of relating, Kleist's mackles create wiggle room for sexual politics. They instigate an ongoing jiggle, shiver, or shake, an ever-new *Verrückung*.

Mess

"Philosophers have always aimed at cleaning up the litter with which the world apparently is filled," and they have produced "economical and orderly conceptions," which, "whether . . . morally elevated or only intellectually neat, . . . were at any rate always aesthetically pure and definite," according to William James (1977, 26). Kleist, I argue, encourages a mode of rationality that tolerates mess. In particular, his work explores what kind of sense it might make when we join the apparent messiness of the world with messy thoughts and messy utterances—that is, when we relax the imperative to produce clean distinctions. Acknowledging and embracing that things, feelings, and perceptions are entangled with language and thought, Kleist champions the muddle-headed utterance as an example of uneconomical, disorderly, impure, unaesthetic, and indefinite conception.

As long as we don't have a strong paradigm of messy thought in place, messy speech will look like a mistake of the uneducated or like the production of a confused mind. Accordingly, in this section we will discuss instances of apparent mistakes. It will soon emerge that the condition of possibility for a mistake lies in the availability of the correct answer and of criteria for differentiating right from wrong. The more we advance in the messy mode of thought, the more these criteria and this distinction go missing.

Undisentangled

Kleist's comedy *The Broken Jug* (*Der zerbrochne Krug*) is a messy play about mess that leaves one muddled.[18] On the diegetic level, we find a jug in shambles, a nighttime ruckus in Eve's room, a disheveled village judge, a broken axle, dubious bookkeeping, sausage in the files, a nest of cats in a wig (supposedly), a flooding creek, incontinence, bad smells, and so on and so forth. On the level of the play's structure, mess functions as the driving force—perhaps one can even say, as the organizing principle. It involves the mutual interference of at least two dramas (which we will discuss in the next chapter), improvisation paradoxically shaping a literary piece of theater, incompatible intertextual references, incoherent tempo, and a text that claims to be both complete and constitutively supplementary. The action of this analytic play largely consists in determining who violated Eve's private sphere and broke the jug in her room. It takes place as a court trial with Eve's mother, Marthe Rull, as plaintiff and Ruprecht Tümpel, Eve's fiancé, as defendant. The play also features the meta–legal action that, as the village judge Adam hears the case, he is being inspected by the assessor Walter from the high court in Utrecht and regarded with suspicion by his own clerk Licht. This meta-action gets entangled with the primary action as it quickly becomes obvious that Adam was involved in the breaking of the jug. The jumbled stories judge Adam makes up on the fly both encumber and advance the analysis of the case as well as the development of the play. Mistaken correlations, misalignments of words and things, and mismatched phrases do the same by both obfuscating and revealing what happened. Often such misunderstandings prove more productive than orderly ratiocination. The buildup and denouement of the dramatic arc follow the same jumping, leaping temporality as the court proceedings, which are sometimes hopelessly stalled, before hastily speeding up again. The play serves as a parodic commentary on several foundational myths of Western culture and several canonical moments in the history of European theater. The most prominent of them are Genesis and *Oedipus Tyrannos*. The two references are indissociably confounded in Adam's clubfoot, which allows him to figure as both Oedipus and the devil. Finally, the dramatic text presents a recalcitrant and unperformable mess in that Kleist publishes an abbreviated version together with an appended variant.[19] The extended version offers more or less the text that flopped in Goethe's production at his Weimar theater, only that Kleist now echoes Goethe's forced division into three acts with a cut into the penultimate scene. The short version is more truncated than abbreviated and cannot quite stand on its own (even though it has been published and translated independently). As if to show that cutting is a crime and, in any case, impossible, the abbreviated version features remarks that make no sense without knowledge of the variant, and it scandalously reduces Eve's account of the events to nothing but one sentence. The variant contains Eve's extended statement plus an exchange between her and Walter. While Eve's account seems to offer the resolution of the plot, Walter's intervention at the end raises new questions and substantially alters the meaning of the play. We get the impression that the assessor Walter is also deceiving Eve and that there is thus no higher authority of justice to appeal to when one runs into problems with the lower one. But this impression remains as inconclusive as the structure of the play: the final scene (in both versions) sets the stage for the (absent) sequel when it has the plaintiff, Marthe Rull, asking for directions to the higher court. The reader closes the book without a clear picture of what happened, and the spectator leaves the theater amused but puzzled and vaguely alarmed.

I want to single out one specific moment of disarray in this text, which will lead us to a larger argument about Kleist's poetics of mess. The passage of interest immediately follows the orgasmic moment in Ruprecht's account of the breaking of the jug when, all at once, Ruprecht crashes into Eve's chamber, the jug falls from the window sill into the room, and the unidentified perpetrator jumps out the window:[20]

RUPRECHT: And since I've got the handle [*Klinke*] in my hand still
From busting down the door I fetch
Him with the metal end, a pound-weight, one on the nob,
For there, Judge Adam, I could reach him.
ADAM: Was it a handle [*Klinke*]?
. . . .
LICHT: You probably [*wohl*] thought it was a sword [*Degen*]?!
ADAM: A sword? Me, why?
RUPRECHT: A sword!
LICHT: Easy enough
To mishear, I should say. A door handle
Is very like a sword.
ADAM: I think . . . !
RUPRECHT: Sure as I live! The shaft of it, Judge Adam?
ADAM: The shaft!
RUPRECHT: The shaft! But that's not what it was.
It was the end, the handle's turned round end.
ADAM: The turned round end of the handle's what it was.
LICHT: Well, well.
RUPRECHT: But where you hold it was a lump of lead,
Much like, that's true, the pommel of a sword.
ADAM: Yes, like a pommel.

LICHT: Good, like the pommel of a sword.
A treacherous sort of weapon, whatever it was,
It must have been. That much I knew already [*wohl*].
WALTER: The point, gentlemen, please, keep to the point!
(*J* 34–35/7.978–96)

I will pass over the obvious pleasure with which the three men linger with the phallic thing, handing it around, exaggerating its heft (pound-weight: *pfundschwer*) and trying out different names as if they needed an excuse to take it in their mouth (a German turn of phrase figures speech as taking words in one's mouth: *ein Wort in den Mund nehmen*). Against the postclimactic confusion and its retarding force, I am happy to heed Walter's (on the second take rather ambiguous because also possibly lewd) call ("to the point [*zur Sache*]!") and get down to business. The point is that the mess the men commit and indulge in here is identified as a mistake, specifically a mishearing: "Easy enough to mishear, I should say [*man kann sich wohl verhören*]."

The assessment that there was a mistake seems in itself to involve a mistake. There is very little phonetic similarity between the words *Klinke* and *Degen* and it is therefore rather unlikely that one could be misheard for the other. In any case, Adam doesn't mishear: Ruprecht says *Klinke* (door handle) and Adam repeats *Klinke*. Only Licht, rather forcibly, introduces *Degen* (sword) and then accuses Adam of mishearing by way of excusing him for it: "Easy enough to mishear, I should say [*man kann sich wohl verhören*]."

Already in the next sentence, Licht's rationalizing efforts shift from the similarity between two words to the similarity between two things: "A door handle / Is very like [*hat sehr viel Ähnlichkeit mit*] a sword." This might make more sense.[21] Did Licht misspeak when he said, "easy enough to mishear"? Did he want to say "easy enough to mistake" or "mis-see"? Did he actually mean to propose that the two things, the door handle and the sword, look or feel alike when he suggested that the two words sound similar? Did he confuse the sign with the referent? Or is his apparent misspeaking, rather, a precise and faithful rendering of the situation: the thing and its name overlap. The name has a materiality that can be orally enjoyed or aurally confused. And the thing shifts shape in experience and memory, thus highlighting a disconnect between experiential trace and thing that might not be qualitatively different from the arbitrary character of the link between signifier and signified. Whether thing or name, the effect is unmistakably one of both pleasure (in the hand or on the nob) and pain.

There is much more to say about this passage and about the way it leaves or creates things, that is, issues, undisentangled, but I want to turn now to another instant of an apparent mistake, in a different play, that gives us another figure for Kleist's poetics of mess.[22]

The Hobgoblin Way

Sosias, Amphitryon's servant in Kleist's *Amphitryon*, is bewildered. His master, the commander of the Theban army, has sent him back to Thebes to announce their victory over Athens and to let Amphitryon's wife Alcmene know that her husband is on his way home (see *A* 67/1.1.24–26). After a strenuous nocturnal hike through the forest, Sosias bumps into his double. This second Sosias keeps watch at the gates of Amphitryon's palace and refuses to let him deliver his message to Alcmene. He claims that husband and wife are enjoying each other's company inside. Sosias tries to talk his way in but gets beaten up by the other Sosias. So he eventually turns around and reports back to Amphitryon, who becomes angry with Sosias because his story seems to him a preposterous excuse for not complying with his orders. Sosias replies:

> It's not set in stone nor pin sharp [*gehauen nicht und nicht gestochen*],
> An incident, of the hobgoblin kind [*koboldartig*], like a fairy tale,
> And yet there it *is*, a fact, unarguable as sunlight.
>
> (*A* 86/2.1.701–3, my translation)[23]

Sosias is confounded by an incident (*ein Vorfall*).[24] Something has "fallen before him" that does not make any sense. A second Sosias fell before Sosias and confused him so that from now on he is at odds with himself.[25] Nevertheless, he feels confident. As if he didn't just lose his integrity, he is sure of what happened just as he is sure of himself—"because I am" (*A* 73/1.2.230): "It's not set in stone nor pin sharp, . . . And yet there it *is*." His reaction shows not only a healthy sense of self but also an unusually agile ability to understand things. He doesn't deny the incident, even though he has never seen anything like it and no such incident has ever had the honor of being represented in sculpture or engraving (*gehauen* can mean "chiseled" and *gestochen* can mean "etched" or "engraved"). Instead, he accepts that what happened to him lays the same claim to reality as the sunlight does. The comparison with the factuality of the sunlight is interesting because it implies the existence of an alternative medium of perception. Bright daylight lets things appear, and so does the way of hobgoblins, although it works very differently. Beyond the limits of common sense and conventional logic, we find not only darkness and madness, but something that is.

Yet Sosias cannot give Amphitryon a more satisfying story because he has no clear picture of the incident. It is difficult for him to get a picture or form an idea, not because he is a simple-minded servant who lacks the means of linguistic expression—Sosias certainly has his way with words[26]—and not because his memory fails him—one can be sure that the incident is actually etched into his brain (in this sense, it is *gestochen*)—but because the facts are neither pin sharp nor set in stone. The incident comes in the manner of hobgoblins—*koboldartig*, erratic, volatile, and capricious. Rather than standing still for thorough inspection, it falls before, *fällt vor*, tumbles, and turns somersaults—*kobolzt* or *schießt Kobolde*.[27]

Hobgoblins, or *Kobolde*, play tricks on us. According to German folklore, they are household sprites who cavort and romp about so that one can barely catch a glimpse of them. But they also like it cozy: they love a warm oven and the food that's being cooked there. Most of the time kobolds prove benign and even helpful. They might whisper smart ideas into the ears of the humans they associate with and if they are so inclined they do chores for humans or bring them riches overnight (see "Kobold" I.2 in Grimm and Grimm 1984, 11.1548). But they also have a quick temper (see "Kobold" in Bächtold-Sträubli and Hoffmann-Krayer 1933, 5.39). Kobolds are easily angered and turn on their human companions without apparent cause. They suddenly transform from angels into devils, throwing dishes and making a racket (see ibid., 40; Grimm and Grimm 1984, 11.1549). Sometimes they take rather violent revenge, even tearing those who offend them limb from limb.[28] Kobolds hate it when humans try to observe their nocturnal life (cf. Bächtold-Sträubli and Hoffmann-Krayer 1933, 5.36, 5.37). They become furious when someone takes their food. And they fly into a rage when they feel mocked (see Grimm and Grimm 1984, 11.1549). Some kobolds will tear themselves apart in anger—like Rumpelstilzchen.[29] But usually they are full of laughter, slightly mischievous, and extremely loyal. Once they have picked a human to live with, it is impossible to shake them off (Bächtold-Sträubli and Hoffmann-Krayer 1933, 5.44). In Freudian terms, one would call them *unheimlich*. Hardly visible or intelligible, they can nevertheless not be denied. The nightly succor they bring, their pranks and somersaults are facts—unarguable as sunlight.

The hobgoblin way of the incident that Sosias reports makes unequivocal categorizations and clear distinctions impossible. Hobgoblins refuse capture. They don't want to be seen, to be seen as something, to be put into a category (they like to sleep in pigeonholes, but they always climb out again) (Bächtold-Sträubli and Hoffmann-Krayer 1933, 5.38–39). They apparently experience every identification as an accusation.[30] Hobgoblins are queer creatures who do not fit social norms. Like the *bêtise*, as Derrida (2009, 151) has shown, the hobgoblin manner functions as a predicate that escapes (or quasi-transcends, as Derrida puts it) predication. Hobgoblins confound the rigid syntax of judgments with their somersaults and are difficult to grasp for the kind of thinking that is stupid enough to rely on definitions and to demand they be clear as day.[31] What makes hobgoblins so astute is that they are always game for folly.

The passage from *Amphitryon* throws a hobgoblin kind of light on some of the other characters and situations in Kleist. Sudden changes from playful harmony to deadly discord are the order of the day. Temperamental characters abound and they do not keep to the realm of minor, supporting, or contrasting figures.[32] Kleist introduces hobgoblin moodiness into the upper echelon of dignified protagonists. He blends the comic with the tragic,[33] the lighthearted with the serious, the queer with the straight—cobalt and nickel with iron and gold (cf. Bächtold-Stäubli and Hoffmann-Krayer 1933, 5.40). Count Wetter vom Strahl, whose name already speaks of his temper fits, throws tantrums and proves otherwise "inappropriate/d," but holds onto the idea that only a daughter of the Emperor can be a match appropriate for his status—"like a fairy tale," indeed (Trinh 1986–87; *A* 86/2.1.702). Count F in *The Marquise of O* changes abruptly from angel to devil (Kleist 2004, 311). One moment Penthesilea and Thusnelda are more or less pleasant, even loving, companions and the next they are wild animals mauling their mates. Even constant Katie can be read as hobgoblin: she proves thoroughly elusive, and at the same time Strahl has a hard time getting rid of her.

Doubles

Another source of apparent mistakes or another way in which Kleist produces confusion is that he creates character doubles—sometimes explicitly, as in the case of Sosias, sometimes almost imperceptibly so. Kleist's doubles function very differently from the antagonists of German Classicist theater. Whereas the Weimar Classicists use antithetical characters to build a dialectic of concepts,[34] Kleist replicates visual and verbal material and thereby pluralizes and blurs identities. Kleist's doubles are neither clearly opposed nor obviously copies of one another. His characters do not represent (or render tangible) a concept but dynamically present a verbal or visual image to create an effect that affects the audience.

Kleist uses specific tools (which often seem clumsy in the context of aesthetic expectations produced by Classical theater) to diffuse the relations between such character doubles. For instance, in his narratives, Kleist sometimes slightly changes the name of a protagonist during the course of the story, thus introducing an uncertainty or confusion about character identity. In the theater, where the physical presence of characters onstage renders their names less important for identification, this strategy might be more difficult to pursue. Nevertheless, Kleist finds ways to also make his stage characters' names uncertain and to undo or, at least, call into question their identity. In *Prince Frederick of Homburg* (*Prinz Friedrich von Homburg*), for example, the Elector and the Prince share the same first name—Frederick. In the first act, their names appear in direct address with exclamation marks. First the Elector is addressed by the Prince with "Frederick!" (*PH* 273/1.1.67). Then the Prince by a friend with "Arthur!" (*PH* 275/1.4.92). The expectation created by the title is confused first by the emphatic use of the same name for a different character and then by the equally emphatic use of a different name for the eponymous hero. Kleist's name troubling couldn't be more dramatic, yet it is so excessively strange and at the same time so easily rationalized

(Arthur is the Prince's middle name) that his maneuver leaves only a slight confusion—an unease that remains palpable in the fact that the first name is regularly excised from the title, which, in common parlance and academic discourse, is often reduced to *The Prince of Homburg*.

In *Penthesilea*, to give a different example, Achilles has so many names that their designating force wears off. Among them we find Aegenet, Prince of Aegina, Hero of the Dolopes, Son of the Nereid, Peleid, Peleïd, Son of Peleus, and Son of Thetis. It takes mental effort to keep applying all these names to one individual, especially since they are often used in reports or other narrative passages where there is no body onstage that serves as identifiable and stable referent. Sigrid Scheifele (1992, 3) argues that the different names (or groups of them) refer to different aspects of Achilles's character. Whether we follow Scheifele's taxonomy or not, Kleist's proliferating names certainly pluralize identity. The lack of a one-to-one relation between name and person undermines the common sense of individuality.

Even beyond the disorienting use of names, there is no strong character identity in Kleist's works. Mood swings and sudden changes in conduct often render characters virtually unrecognizable, as we saw when we discussed the hobgoblin way. Protagonists are frequently beside themselves, or they faint and come to completely changed—as a different person, so to speak. Kleist's unsettling of character identity also means that sometimes figures that present themselves as two different dramatis personae might with equal justification be read as twin manifestations of one person, as is the case with Sosias and Mercury, as well as with Amphitryon and Jupiter. The organization of the plays also creates doubles. The symmetrical structure of *The Schroffenstein Family* (*Die Familie Schroffenstein*) and *Penthesilea*, for example, duplicates the expository scenes in the two warring camps.[35] This technique produces doubled characters—Rupert and Sylvester, Eustache and Gertrude, as well as Ottokar and Agnes in *The Schroffenstein Family*, and Achilles and Penthesilea in *Penthesilea*—showing that the two camps and protagonists in each case are not only intensely opposed to one another but also strikingly similar.

In other plays, the doubles seem to be hierarchically organized: the authentic and the fake beauty (Katie and Kunigunde) in *Katie of Heilbronn*; the young enthusiastic Prince and the seasoned draconic Elector in *Prince Frederick of Homburg*; judge Adam and simpleton Ruprecht in *The Broken Jug*. But a closer look reveals similarities that disturb this hierarchy and present the characters as versions of the same. Katie, for example, quite willfully breaks both her legs right below the knee when she jumps out the window (*K* 167/1.1.181–87). This troubles the image of the natural beauty and brings her body, which grows back together, closer to the mosaic of a body that Kunigunde cultivates (*K* 249/5.3.2446–52). I read Eve's two main suitors, Adam and Ruprecht, as echoing the standard constellation in Spanish comedies of the *siglo de oro*, which couples a chivalric hero with his comedic double.[36] Only that Adam is no chevalier. The hierarchy of the honest and honorable over the mimicking and laughable is disturbed right from the start when the hero trips over his own feet as he gets out of bed.[37] The clear contrast between good and evil, which characterizes the world of *capa y espada*, is smudged.[38] There is no saint here whom Knecht Ruprecht could serve.[39] The double doubles the double, and soon there is nothing but doubles.

All this is to say that Kleist's protagonists are rarely one with themselves. As already indicated, this self-incongruity has an emotional valence; it manifests as moodiness. Gilles Deleuze and Félix Guattari (1987, 356) have argued that affect is completely exteriorized in Kleist and that his figures oscillate between "catatonic freezes" and "flights of madness." Without an inner life integrating or holding together these two aspects of character, individuals double and fall apart. Klotz observes a somewhat different doubling of emotional gestures along the inner to outer vector. He gives the example of Penthesilea's reported blushing at the beginning of the play, when she encounters Achilles for the first time, and reads it as an internally motivated show of affect which is repeated in completely exteriorized form at the end of the play when Achilles's blood shows on her face and neck (Klotz 1996, 83). Such repetition of the emotional gesture can train the audience in perceiving bodily changes differently. Even in the first instance Penthesilea's blushing must not necessarily be read as a straight expression of feeling, but may give us an example of a rather queer feeling. Read from the ending, her flushed skin in the beginning also appears like a "bib of blood," as Klotz calls it—something put on, something theatrical, that is to say, something somewhat external (83, my translation). Rather than referencing an inner agitation, the first blush then refers to the bloody ending. Beginning and end echo one another. The scenes double according to aesthetic rather than psychic principles. Gestures remain emotional but emptied of interiority. Leo Bersani (1986) has argued that aesthetic replications diffuse violence; I would add that they diffuse pathos.

Character doublings and multiple impressions (or mackles) not only teach the spectators a different mode of seeing, they also demonstrate diegetically the ethical effects of such seeing.[40] *Katie*, for example, ends with an unfocused organization of kinship. It remains unclear who Katie's "true" father is. In fact, she has at least two fathers: Theobald, who raised her, and the Emperor, who claims her symbolically (and secretly acknowledges his biological paternity).[41] Strahl recognizes this doubleness when he asks the fathers in the plural for permission to kiss Katie: "Let me imprint a kiss, fathers [*Väter*], one kiss only / Upon those lips of hers" (*K* 5.11.2578–79). This new organization of kinship might initiate a different economy of desire and sexuality and of emotionality and sensibility, as well: an economy based on dispersal. The fact that Strahl's request semantically claims singularity ("one kiss only") and syntactically performs repetition ("a [*einen*] kiss, fathers, one [*einen*] kiss only"), suggests that it does.

Kleist uses doubles to undermine character identity (in the quantitative and the qualitative sense, i.e., as numeric identity and as character consistency). The various doubling techniques and constellations produce an uncertainty regarding the identity of individuals and the difference between them. I therefore think it better, in Kleist's case, to abandon the habitual expectation that the dramatic action present individuals onstage. Kleist's characters function differently. They consist of variations of themselves and are only parts in a larger network of copies. At the same time, his characters easily fall apart and the coherence of the network readily disintegrates, leaving behind pieces that may be treated as identities in themselves.

Echoes

Not only the identity of individual characters is rendered uncertain in Kleist's work, even the boundaries of the individual texts are unsettled by echoes of certain formulations and variations on particular motifs, scenes, and characters. Kleist's corpus does not so much consist in a number of individualized masterpieces as it forms a net or texture of texts, with parts of each weaving into others, mutually mending one another. Such correspondences can also be traced between plays that would usually be considered as belonging to the opposite genre; in this case they form an overlay of tragedy and comedy.

The passage from *The Broken Jug* that we discussed earlier, which creates a confusion between door handle and sword, finds its echo, for example, in *Penthesilea*. Before going into further detail, here first a brief synopsis of the play: *Penthesilea* dramatizes the increasingly desperate struggle of Penthesilea, queen of the Amazons, to subdue the invincible Greek warrior, Achilles. Penthesilea leads her army into battle to procure the regular supply of male sex partners for procreation while she is still mourning the loss of her mother. As queen, she also seems to carry the foundational trauma of the "nation of women": the genocide (of the male members) and mass rape (of the female members) of her original people (the Scythians). As somewhat of a love story develops between Penthesilea and Achilles, she ends up brutally killing him by mauling him with her own teeth together with her hounds and then commits suicide. Penthesilea's explanation for her fatal mauling of Achilles has become infamous: "—So it was a mistake [*Versehen*]. Kisses, bites [*Küsse, Bisse*]. / The two rhyme, and one who truly loves / With all her heart can easily mistake them [*das eine für das andre greifen*]" (*P* 145/24.2981–83). Here we have two words that sound alike: *Küsse* and *Bisse* (kisses, bites). A mishearing is quite possible—"easy enough to mishear, I should say" (*J* 34/7.985). But there is no mention of mishearing. Instead, the lapse is termed a *Versehen*, literally a mis-seeing. In addition, Penthesilea describes it as a literal mis-taking, as grabbing one instead of the other (*das eine für das andre greifen*). Again, the elements of theater—hearing, seeing, and feeling—are brought into play and used interchangeably. And again, there is an additional confusion that concerns the difference between sign and referent, word and body: Achilles's body passes through Penthesilea's mouth just as his name does. And Penthesilea's biting into Achilles continues her devouring of the *Iliad* or her eating up of the infamous stories that circulate about Achilles (*P* 102/15.2194–2202).

Rather than considering them as parallels, I mean to suggest that these two passages quite literally speak to one another. They are two incomplete subjects in an open conversation. They don't say to each other things that are well formed and perfectly articulated (as actors do when they speak previously written speech at the audience); they engage in an exchange in which each contribution is faulty and messy, yet constitutive to the meaning and the understanding of the other. As the passage in the *Broken Jug* describes the physical grasp of exchangeable things, the passage from *Penthesilea* provides the phrase for it: "das eine für das andre greifen." As *Penthesilea* evokes the consonance of two words and deals with mistaking one for the other, *The Broken Jug* has the word for it: *verhören* (mishearing).

The textual material resists our constructing a linear temporality of development from one work to the next.[42] In *The Broken Jug*, the words *Klinke* and *Degen* are placed at the end of the lines as if to underscore the fact that they don't rhyme:

> Man kann sich wohl verhören. Eine Klinke
> Hat sehr viel Ähnlichkeit mit einem Degen.
>
> Easy enough to mishear . . . A door handle
> Has very much similarity with a sword.
>
> (*J* 34/7.985–86)

But we probably only notice this arrangement if we are primed by Penthesilea's reasoning based on rhyming. The earlier work, *The Broken Jug*, responds to the later work, *Penthesilea*, and the later work retroactively shapes the earlier work.[43]

The two passages—one from the comedy *The Broken Jug*, the other from the tragedy *Penthesilea*; one organized around the odd coupling and doubling of a door handle and a sword (*Klinke/Degen*), the other around the dynamic antagonism of kisses and bites (*Küsse, Bisse*)—communicate despite their unequal standing. *Küsse, Bisse* carries a good deal more weight. It is spoken by the protagonist toward the end of the play as part of the anagnorisis after an arresting peripeteia. *Klinke/Degen*, coming somewhere in the middle of the play, is spoken by a minor character, and has little to no impact on the further development of the plot. Penthesilea's quote has become canonical, and often functions as synecdoche for the play. Licht's quote is probably barely ever cited. Penthesilea's confusion is momentous; the mix-up that Licht projects onto Adam is downright silly. As these two passages begin to converse and converge, though, *The Broken Jug* contaminates the tragedy with its silliness, and *Penthesilea* infects the comedy with its violence.

As more or less naive readers of Kleist's perplexing scenarios, we tend to invest in the idea that the protagonists simply misinterpret the situation. This allows us to take a firm stand against mess. But, indeed, Kleist ruins any hope that the realities he creates can be sorted out.[44] He mixes (up) the senses—sounding or hearing is being confused with feeling and with looking. He loses the hierarchical organization of the characters and thereby the contrast between good and evil. Instead of a comic double subordinated to the melodramatic hero, we see the doubles proliferate and play on par with one another. This structure allows the simple, the comic, and the dark to tip over, at times, into the sophisticated, the serious, and the splendid, but it also presents the tragic as risible. With the mess that he cultivates in his theater, he twists out of the Oedipal regime, but does this mean that innocence is regained (cf. Harst 2012)? Or does this turn every hope for justice into a farce? Kleist shows the despair in the ludic—we get trapped in these structures and nothing really changes. At the same time, he also shows that one might have to fight to the finish for the power to determine the rules of the game. Then again, his work articulates autonomy and mastery as highly dysfunctional ideals that do not lead to the desired outcome. Instead, Kleist thematizes and draws considerable creative energy from the overlap of mistake, intention, and chance (or seized occasion).

In the first passage we discussed in this section, the adverb *wohl* functions as a node in the net of confusions (between the subjective and the objective, between mistake, intention, and chance). If it weren't such a trivial member of the lexicon, one could describe *wohl*, in its adverbial usage, as a speculative word in Hegel's sense. It can mean both "possibly" and "surely" and thus combines incertitude with confidence. Licht uses it three times in this passage, not accidentally to modify phrases that include verbs of knowledge and perception: "You probably [*wohl*] thought . . . ?!" (*J* 34/985), "Easy enough [*wohl*] / To mishear, I should say" (*J* 34/987), and "That much I knew already [*wohl*]" (*J* 35/995).

We might hear Kleist respond to interpretations and perspicuous subjective clarifications of his texts by saying "That much I knew already." But in what sense would we have to take this response? Kleist not only stages, as in this passage, the overlap of mistake, intention, and chance, but he also advocates for it—in particular, in the essay "On the Gradual Fabrication of Thoughts While Speaking" ("Über die allmähliche Verfertigung der Gedanken beim Reden")—and invites it into his practice as a writer, for example, with his daily newspaper project.[45] As part of a defense against mess, critics have accused Kleist of making mistakes unworthy of his talent, or they have shored up the author's omniscience and purpose. Both strategies strike me as ill-advised. Of course, it is always possible (to say) that Kleist made a mistake. But such a judgment gives him both too much and too little credit.

By the same token, it makes little sense to uphold authorial autonomy when the author engages in experiments designed to weaken authorial autonomy. If Kleist says "Das wußt' ich wohl," it oscillates between confidence ("That much I knew already") and incertitude ("That much I probably knew"). Someone who works with chance and with mistakes cannot draw the line between intention and accident without trembling. We might call this Kleist's authorial version of the intentional fallacy. For the reader of Kleist, a certain looseness (verging on silliness) in response to the mess he creates can be more productive and insightful than rigor and precision.

Metalepsis

The term "metalepsis" has a long history, dating back to Ancient rhetoric, and has undergone some changes in meaning and application, notably Gérard Genette's reconfiguration for narratology and the current transmedial approach. In an antipatriarchal argumentation informed by queer theory, Eva von Redecker has recently championed the figure for a praxis-oriented theory of radical social change and I have argued that metalepsis, with its oscillating between thing and word, renders things self-incongruous and thus emotional (Redecker 2018; Pahl 2011, 183–84).[46] In all its uses, metalepsis involves contamination and confusion. Its disregard for the boundaries of domains is transgressive, if sometimes only minimally so, and it tends to skid down the road of bad taste. It combines complexity with simplicity in that it relies on sophisticated distinctions and an often lengthy series of implicit deductions to produce a silly or muddled effect.

The rhetorical figure can take three forms—the distant metonymy, the cause-and-effect substitution, and a form of synonymy involving the (often derogatory) use of one (often lesser) trope for another trope (including mistakenly taking nonliteral speech at face value).[47] Narrative metalepsis consists in the deviant (usually temporary) merging of narrative levels (for example, frame narrative and embedded story), fictional universes (the worlds that different works of art establish), or ontological domains (for example, reality, representation, and virtuality) through *in verbis* or *in corpore* transgression. It can also be effected across different media. This use of metalepsis raises ontological questions concerning alternate universes and the status of fiction.

For her theory of social change, Redecker (2018) harnesses the series of gradual transfers that characterizes rhetorical metalepsis. Her argument accentuates the rhetorical structure of real life and of revolutions in the political and scientific realm, in particular. The metaleptic exchange of end and means serves her argument especially well. It captures the nonlinear processes of "uneventful revolutions" and paradigm shifts. Here Redecker describes the revolutionary tactic of practically anticipating a better future in the interstices of the present in order to trigger transformation (261). As an example from the scientific realm, she discusses the experimental fumbling required for a paradigm shift, which, according to Margaret Masterman's take on Thomas Kuhn, requires a "trick" or "device," chosen intuitively to serve as a placeholder for the new structure to come and to enable its operations before the theory is developed (223–38). As a political example of metaleptic substitution of one (lesser) trope—here a mistaken literalness—for another trope, she uses the lists of complaints (*cahiers de doléance*), which, requested of the *bailliages* (district courts and caucuses) by the king, helped bring about the revolution of 1789 because the peasants represented by the *bailliages* presumed that their complaints would have legislative power (i.e., would be taken literally) and rose up in protest when nothing changed (see 264–65).

For my reading of Kleist and his theatrical diffusion of the historical sex change around 1800, certain qualities of metalepsis prove more generative than others. I am particularly interested in metalepsis as a lame joke, in the metaleptic echoing of the new order in the old order and vice versa (which both the rhetorical figure of cause-effect substitution and the narratological figure provide), in the confounding of representation and reality or the "mistaken" literalness that brings about real change, and in the contamination of different media—the body, language, the visual—in Kleist's theater. The queer syntax, structure, and logic of Kleist's dramatic texts are crucially effected by metalepsis.

In the next chapter, we will discuss Kleist's poietic procedure, which anticipates—with political reach—the use of a trick in the realm of science to bridge the gap to what will have been a paradigm shift. In that chapter, we will discuss what Redecker captures with the figure of metalepsis by the name of a different rhetorical figure, proposed by Rüdiger Campe—*hysteron proteron*. In a somewhat metaleptic move, I will use "preposterous" as a translation for *hysteron proteron*, which will eventually bring us to Kleist's campiness (in chapter 4). In that context, I will mostly draw on the narratological version of metalepsis.

For now, I want to take a closer look at a specific version of rhetorical metalepsis, what I call prosopopeic literalization. It participates in the mammalogic or language from the breast that I will further develop in chapter 3. Altogether, I will discuss three modes of rhetorical metalepsis as instances of parodic fullness: "prosopopeic literalization" here and "hypotypotic text swell" as well as "metapenetrative speech" in a section of chapter 3 entitled "Full Breast Speech Emptied."

Prosopopeic Literalization

The indistinction of sign and thing is frequently thematized and practiced by Kleist. With his vibrant—often drastic—pictorial descriptions and with his use of syntax that materially enacts his meaning, Kleist ceaselessly pushes the normative boundary between language and reality. The fact that Penthesilea can kill herself with words, in Kleist's tragedy, serves as a barely exaggerated image for the strikingly concrete quality of Kleist's language. After Ilse Graham (1977), Carol Jacobs (1989) and Bettine Menke (1997) have noted that Kleist actively unsettles the usual distinction between literal and figurative language use.[48] Always overdoing things, Kleist misspeaks and overstates, "journeying into the physical regions of his medium" (Graham 1977, 243). With almost unsavory insistence—be it by way of repetition or via an abstruse detour—his metaphors tend toward the literal, but also push the literal and the concrete to the point where they fabulously blur with the figurative and the abstract.[49] I find that, with the emphasis he places on the literal—in bad taste and while mobilizing a fanciful and often ludicrous metaphoricity—Kleist offers an interesting and important corrective to the prevalence of the figurative in queer theory and politics.

As one specific form of such metaleptic scenarios of word become flesh, I would like to discuss his oddly physical figures of emotional life. In these cases, a conventional figure for a more or less abstract idea from the emotional realm (for example, the heart figuring love) is taken literally, or is reified as a body or organ, and then, in a second rhetorical operation that is incongruous with and almost opposite to the first (refiguring the literalized), the body or body part is anthropomorphized. The heart is turned into a homunculus with human expressions.[50] Such prosopopeia allows for theatrical interactions between characters and emotional tropes (in the shape of organ homunculi) that draw these operations into the realm of parody and camp. By taking seriously certain ideas deposited in symbols and tropes, Kleist shows their absurdity, erodes seriousness, and disperses emotional intensity.

In *Katie*, for example, we find the following:

> VOM STRAHL: You whose young soul, as it stood bared before me in the court today, dripped with sensuous beauty, like the bride of a Persian shah, anointed all over with oils, sprinkling the carpets as they lead her to his chamber!
>
> (*K* 185/2.1.691–94, translation altered)

The idea of the "beautiful soul" is presented here physically as a full female body: young, naked, and voluptuous. Kleist doubles and mixes excessively what the bourgeois ideology of feeling with its discourse of interiority wants to but cannot separate: inside and outside, body and soul. Katie's soul enters the virtual stage—doubling Katie—not only as beautiful but also completely naked and, furthermore, oozing oil, while this sentence, likewise, barely stops dripping. Descriptive and performative speech are twisted together in this comparison ("like the bride of a Persian shah, anointed all over with oils" does what it describes) that Kleist appends to the hypotyposis ("as it stood bared before me").[51] Against modern convention, Kleist proposes wetness or a lubricant (oil) as the quasi-allegorical attribute of the virtuous (beautiful) soul, and passivity (being led) as the quasi-allegorical posture of the soul (since Aristotle conceived as self-motion or life-force).[52]

Similarly, when Theobald tells the court that he went to find his runaway daughter hoping "to offer her lips the breast of his love," he reifies his feeling of love (and literalizes the trope of motherly love) by giving it a body with breasts and letting it engage in the gesture of giving the breast to Katie (*K* 1.1.334f, translation altered).[53] Thus we find Theobald's Love and Katie in theatrical interaction. The mannerism of the scene is increased by the inverted word order and the excessive mediation when Love and Katie interact via (or as if represented by) breast and lips.

We find prosopopeic reification differently mixed up when Penthesilea confesses to Achilles that "the feelings of this breast, oh youth, / Are just like hands, and are caressing you" (*P* 87/15.1772f, translation altered). Feelings are here rendered as hands. This might stage the linguistic association of feeling and touch. The hands are anthropomorphized in turn and attributed with the agency to caress the beloved. While this odd scene—which features hands, personifying Penthesilea's feelings, in interaction with Achilles—allows Penthesilea to keep a certain distance, the distancing effect is counteracted by the demonstrative pronoun (*dieser Brust*) that refers and attaches the hands/feelings back to her breast. In the end, the whole awkward arrangement might communicate the perfectly conventional pseudo-organic trope of feelings in the bosom expressed by hand gestures. Much ado about nothing.

The full-fledged camp of prosopopeic literalization appears—and it is particularly humorous that Kleist sends this example of bad taste to Goethe—when Prothoë addresses Penthesilea as she "to whom my heart bows down on bended knee" (*P* 135/24.2800).[54] Or when Strahl invites Theobald to live with them, insisting, "In the hands of my heart I receive him! [*In meines Herzens Händen nehm ich ihn!*]" (*K* 255/5.11.2574, translation altered). The heart, symbol for interiority, is exteriorized by way of personification. It enters the outside world and with its theatrical gestures, its prostrations and embraces, it remains exterior to itself. In the reconciliation scene at the end of *Katie*, from which the last example is taken, one certainly expects an intimate gesture from the Count. Once he has made it clear that taking Theobald into his home would not be intense enough of a gesture, one imagines he will take him to his heart. Yet this clinch is avoided. The lengthy series of gradual transfers that characterizes metalepsis disperses pathos. Not Strahl but his heart, and not the heart (as the literalized symbol of love) but the extensions of the heart, its hands, receive Theobald. As the Count sends his heart onstage as his double, the pathos of the moment is foiled and the subject loses its definition, its idealized shape. But all this ironically intimate distance and metonymic oozing out of line certainly does not mean that any of these characters are less emotional for it.

Theatrical Metalepsis

By way of another kind of metalepsis, Kleist comments on the theater of his day. This theatrical metalepsis also disperses pathos while at the same time, perhaps ironically, adding vehemence, if not force, to his plays. Kleist uses expressions from critical or poetological discourse and takes them literally or in a bodily rather than aesthetic sense, thus misspeaking by overstating or overdoing the referential link (*versprechen*). Then he transfers them *in verbis* or *in scaenis* into the universe of his plays.

In the eighteenth century, stage acting developed into a respectable profession and theaters evolved into tasteful and taste-shaping institutions.[55] Lessing introduced a return to questions of affect and sympathy, reinterpreting Aristotelian catharsis as refinement and moderation of fear and pity. So the critical or poetological terms that Kleist addresses often involve the idea of taste or revolve around the feelings that the work is supposed to arouse in the audience. Kleist renders both issues in the bodily register as appetite and as (often violent) touch. When Kleist's characters seize, devour, tear apart, pierce, or hit each other—as they frequently do—I read this (not exclusively but also) as scenic enactments of critical or aesthetic discourse.

With his plays, Kleist literalizes and dramatizes the phrase *ein ergreifendes Schauspiel* (a poignant spectacle, an emotionally moving spectacle, a spectacle that touches, pierces, or stings). The Prince of Homburg, for example, literally reaches through the fourth wall of the scene the Elector stages for him (*PH* 274/1.1.70). Fischer-Lichte reads this first scene of Kleist's last play as settling the scores with the dominant conceptions of the dramatic art of his time.[56] First the Prince presents a spectacle that is illegible to an audience that operates with Enlightenment notions of the passions and their physical expression, then he refuses to sit still and arrest his body in the spectator position as the stage director Goethe would demand of him.[57] Homburg physically touches and is touched. Kleist metaleptically integrates into the action a scene that acts out a metatheatrical idea—his notion of a participatory theater, where the audience, for better or worse, has a vested interest in the action and even in the bodies onstage, and contributes (with interpretations) to the shaping of the work of art.[58] The frequent observations and interpretations of the action by characters onstage could also be counted as theatrical metalepses because, even if they don't literalize a trope of theater criticism, they anticipate audience reaction, thus merging different temporal and ontological levels.

We find another version of this kind of theatrical metalepsis in the ninth scene of *Penthesilea*, when the wounded and possibly hallucinating Penthesilea calls out "Take me—," as she discovers the sun—which, a moment ago, she wanted to seize from the sky and draw down to her—at her feet, in the river (*P* 64/9.1388). About to sink into the water like a doubly twisted Narcissus (in love not with her own but with the sun's reflection and yearning not to embrace but to be embraced), she loses consciousness in the arms of her sisters who rush in. Enraptured, Penthesilea falls prey to a visual misperception. She sees the reflection of the sun in the river and takes it for the actual object. Her misperception or mis-seeing, Penthesilea's literal *Versehen*, comes across as rather silly. As Chaouli (1996, 137) puts it, "Mistaking the sun's reflection for the thing itself is already an act of stupidity . . . , but then attempting to embrace the reflection to be closer to the original is worthy of a Kaspar Hauser." Or, let's say, worthy of the *Kasperletheater*, for it is again the theater—Kleist's theater—that is at stake here. Like the commedia dell'arte, from which it derived, the *Kasperletheater*, or Punch and Judy show, is a participatory form of theater, where the actors or puppeteers react to the mood of the audience and the audience intervenes in the action with shouts. In the interplay between her action(s) and the audience reaction(s), Penthesilea's tragedy turns comical: Kleist makes us laugh at her *Kasperletheater*.[59]

When read as aimed beyond the scene at a virtual audience in the hope that it might receive her and build her fame, the words that accompany Penthesilea's *Versehen* or visual mistake, "Take me—," produce a transgressive literalization of the element of touching or feeling and a perversion of tact. If the German reform theater of the eighteenth century established the fourth wall and chased the Harlequin out of the new literary theater and if Goethe's Classicism aestheticized the stage and established a reflective distance by disciplining the bodies of actors and spectators, Penthesilea messes with the lines between stage and auditorium, representation and reality, as well as aesthetic form and brute force, by thrusting herself upon an antipathetic audience. The feelings that the play seeks to arouse are not only rendered physical but also sexualized in this lewd request.[60] Here we have not a character in the position of an audience member trying to touch the scene and grasp what s/he sees (as Homburg tries) but a character wanting to be held, penetrated, enjoyed by the spectator. Penthesilea's demand evokes—while blatantly breaking its rules—the discourse about tact (*Zartgefühl*) and taste (*Geschmack*) furthered by playwrights involved in the theater as dramaturgs, theater directors and theater critics, like Lessing, Schiller, and Goethe.[61]

In addition, Penthesilea breaks out of the discipline of the literary theater by consuming literature. She ruins the *Iliad* as she devours Achilles. Not only is there a continuity between her figuratively devouring the stories of the *Iliad* and literally devouring the body of Achilles, the literal sense also affects the figurative sense: by killing Achilles, Penthesilea eats away at the *Iliad* and its values, especially the gender roles that the *Iliad* so vigorously (re) produces.[62] With her grotesque appetite, she forces herself into the picture of the heroic epos. Like the comical figure who raises his head among the great characters in parody, Penthesilea interferes between Greeks and Trojans and between Achilles and Hector.[63] She insists on her place in the foundational narrative of Western civilization. But it is the tragedy of Penthesilea and of the Amazons that she and they are not being taken seriously—that she looks like a fool.[64] Her confusion of name and body, and Kleist's literalizing of language in Penthesilea's name (I am referring to the suicide monologue) have a powerful effect and create an extraordinary dramatic force. But there is also something ludicrous about it when Kleist pitches the literal against the literary. His critique of the newly dominant aesthetic and literary theater remains indistinguishable from the stupidity of literal-mindedness.

As already mentioned, metalepsis itself is in rather bad taste. Its use was certainly not encouraged by the teachers of rhetoric, and theatrical metalepsis has the dubious distinction of engaging low forms of theater. A particularly silly example, which we will discuss in a later chapter, is Kleist's enactment of a literalized standard of the Classical poetics of tragedy: in *Penthesilea*, he renders the tragic collision—an absolute requirement of the genre—as a physical clash between the protagonist and Achilles. This example will lead us to ask whether theatrical metalepsis can diffuse pathos and defer or even avoid tragedy. For now, it only remains to point out that theatrical metalepsis, in that it takes literally the talk of taste and of touching and stirring the audience, adds a rather graphic note to Kleistian aesthetics.

Chapter 2

✦

Double the Drama (Transorgasmics)

Each of Kleist's plays features several superimposed dramas. This does not mean that his plots are episodic. Kleist constructs seemingly unified aesthetic wholes, but nevertheless, each one is many. Some commentators have noticed this double play of unity and duplication. Employing their particular interpretative approaches, they each see two dramas in one. If we combine these angles, the dramas multiply and the picture becomes even more dazzling, or, indeed, blurry.

Allemann has comprehensively demonstrated the overlay of the plot-based drama with an intruding stationary drama. Campe (2012a) has described the inverse temporality: the peripeteia from a stalling story to the sudden incursion (*Einfall*) of an idea, which retrospectively pervades the story from the beginning and thus doubles the new with the old. Klotz has observed, using the example of *Penthesilea*, that the drama of the protagonists is supplemented by the drama of the intradiegetic spectators who struggle to understand the protagonists. In addition, Kleist extends the boundaries of the theater by playing with his audience, trapping his readers in inadequate interpretations, and manipulating audience (re)actions and development to unfurl a drama of interpretation parallel to but often diverging from the actions and motivations inscribed in the text. It has also been remarked that Kleist tends to twist together a tragedy and a comedy in one play (Müller-Seidel 1971, 114). All of Kleist's plays identify the main character in their title and yet this announcement is usually misleading because Kleist tends to construct parallel character dramas, each organized around a different protagonist.[1] *The Battle of Herrmann*, for example, also dramatizes Thusnelda's struggle, *Amphitryon* is often read as the tragedy of Alcmene, and *Katie of Heilbronn* likewise foregrounds the romantic tribulations of Count vom Strahl. Throughout this study, I argue, providing different examples, that Kleist tends to combine in one a drama that is driven by the values of the old order (premodern or prerevolutionary, feudal, authoritative, one-sex, symbolic) with a drama that grapples with the values of the new order (modern, bourgeois, deliberative, two-sex, imaginary). Finally, I would add that Kleist layers a same-sex, sinthomosexual, or lesbian economy of desire on top of a straight drama. I will call "queer" the fact that, in these superimposed economies and approaches, the straightforward and the homostatic are not distributed along the lines of two clearly distinguishable plotlines, dramas, or conflicts.

Zany Time

"Either the clock's gone mad, or you have"

(*J* 49/9.1399)

Allemann (2005) deserves credit for providing the most thorough and consistent analysis to date of Kleist's technique of superimposing two (or more) dramas. He shows that alongside with or on top of the conventional drama, which more or less follows Aristotelian poetics in that it offers the mimesis of an action and the development of a plotline (exposition, buildup, turning point, denouement) and which Allemann calls the "drama of action [*Handlungsdrama*]," Kleist layers a "stationary drama" (also termed *Über-Drama*, counterdrama, and secondary drama by Allemann). This stationary drama undermines the development of the action. Instead of carrying the plot forward, it brings things back again and again to the same fixation, the same knot. It thus poses an obstacle to the advent of the critical discovery or anagnorisis and counteracts the turning point or peripeteia even after it has already taken place in the drama of action. Allemann (2005, 139–41) sees this technique as coming to fruition with Kleist's adaptation of *Amphitryon* (1807), where, despite clear suggestions of a divine deception in the second act (scene 5), Alcmene in the third act falls behind her dawning insight and back to her initial absolute trust in the divine splendor of her husband. At the cost of incongruity, the stationary drama stages the insistence of a fixed idea, an obsession, or a dream image when an insight, a new discovery, a change of heart, or a plot resolution is either expected or actually takes place in the conventional drama.

Drawing on gay-theoretical elaborations of Lacanian psychoanalytic theory, we might see in this insistence the repetitiveness of the drive, as opposed to the goal-orientedness of desire. "Automatic reiterations" and "meaningless pulsions" characterize the drive, while libidinal energy pressed into the arch of a teleological and meaningful narrative produces desire (Edelman 2004, 143). With its senseless and counterproductive recurrence even after the character could have learned something, the fixed idea, dramatized in Kleist's plays, nevertheless provides the stuff the character is made of. "The subject's singularity depends" on this "senseless compulsion" or on what Edelman, demarcating it from the discursively organized symptom, calls "the repetitive insistence of the sinthome" (38, 56).

Isolated and pushed to its extreme, the superdrama would reduce theater to one scene—a nonmoving image. Indeed, Allemann traces each static drama back to a vision to which the character falls prey (Alcmene daydreams about Amphitryon, Penthesilea inherits a storied image of Achilles, Katie and Strahl share the vision of their supernatural encounter on New Year's Eve, and Homburg is led by his somnambular vision of glory, power, and romantic conquest). Allemann (2005, 36) argues that visions captivate the protagonists and render them as determined as they are unteachable. In line with Edelman's position that the sinthome constitutes the singularity of character, he maintains that the stationary drama revolves exclusively around the protagonist and knows no development but runs idle in high gear.

The drama of action, on the other hand, moves along a chain of words that allows the action to unfold in time. It dramatizes the power of logos to structure thought, to motivate action, to furnish stories, to convince, to provide insight, and to organize desire as oriented toward the future.

With the technique of the double drama, Kleist thus breaks down theater into two of its basic elements—letting us see an image and letting us hear speech—and explores them separately. Then he combines them in a distinctly nonorganic and imperfect way, by overlaying them. The incongruity of stasis and action makes a mackle of the superimposition and allows at some times the static image, and at other times the progressive line of words to come to the fore at the edges. In these moments, we get scenes that offer nothing to see but speeches (the teichoscopies of feelings, for example, that we will discuss in chapter 5) or, again, speeches that give us nothing to hear but the doubling of figures (as we will see in chapter 6). Most of the time, the static drama and the action drama blend and act upon one another. For example, repetition gives stasis its own dynamic—not a linear movement but a pulsating, stuttering one. And the progressive chain of words is affected by the obsessive return to the insistent idea, which results in Kleist's characteristically spluttering syntax. Either way, Kleist's experiments with the interaction of the isolated elements render markedly nonorganic results.

If one reads what Allemann identifies as progression and stasis through the lens of Bersani's (1986) elaborations on aesthetic relationality, the two structures reverse valences. Narrative progress comes to mean arrest, fixation, catastrophe, and death, whereas replications of the same can afford mobility, excitement, beneficial dispersion, and liveliness. Bersani (1986, 70) argues that "catastrophe is produced when violence *stops*, when the dislocations provoked by desire's mobility seek, as it were, to *take place*, to have a place, to become attached to particular objects and, in so doing, to destroy them."[2] Formal replication or structural doubling can counteract—disperse or blur—the will to fix. Bersani submits his argument by way of analyzing, for example, Assyrian palace reliefs: "These sculptors play, in risky fashion, with what appears to be almost identical repetitions. Indeed their work suggests a compulsive fascination with at least two versions of the same object or activity. But even such double images mobilize perception instead of arresting it" (ibid., 73). Kleist's play with doubles and with the insistence of the same shows remarkable similarities in this regard with the Assyrian reliefs, the paintings by Caravaggio, and the films that Bersani analyzes often together with Ulysse Dutoit.[3] Whether Kleist doubles the drama that comes to a certain end with the unending drama of recurrence with similarly optimistic hopes of preventing disaster as Bersani entertains, or whether he celebrates disaster and devises methods to bring it about, is more difficult to decide and will occupy us again in the fourth chapter.

The two kinds of drama produce two distinct temporalities and a third, rather queer one, results from their overlap. The drama of action creates a relatively simple temporal coherence: the line of progress, the succession of words, the deduction of thoughts, and the consequence with which the protagonists can walk the talk, as it were. The vision that determines the superdrama appears instantaneously (cf. Bohrer 1994). In the twinkling of an eye (*Augenblick*) the vision exists, immediately perfect, without the need for gradual development and without the causality that can lead to it.

Allemann describes the vision as "anticipatory image" (2005, 98), considers anticipation a "fundamental theme" (12) in Kleist, and speaks generally of the "Kleistian principle of anticipation" (105). This shows that he evaluates the vision from the perspective of linear time. Violating the principle of gradual and coherent progression, the concept of anticipation nevertheless relies on the existence of linear development. To my mind, the sudden completeness and yet repetitive insistence of the counterdrama entertains no relation to the teleology of anticipation. The interaction of the two temporalities—development and instantaneity—produces not only anticipatory but also paralyzing and retroactive effects in the drama of action.[4] As already indicated, protagonists return again and again to the same thought when a critical discovery would be in order, and even after the turning point the action in some way returns to previous conditions. We will discuss the retroactive effects of instantaneity in more detail in relation to *The Broken Jug*. Here it is important to emphasize that the static drama and the drama of action mutually interfere with one another. The static drama disturbs the coherent linearity of the drama of action, but gradual development also poses an obstacle to the absolute temporality of the vision. It is extremely irritating for a protagonist who is under the spell of a compelling idea to be confronted with a reality that only allows for gradual development. The temporality of her visionary reality requires immediate and complete fulfillment and makes her incapable of meeting another reality with incremental action (see Allemann 2005, 153). Allemann proposes that she only has two options: either to abstract from the socially shared and progressive reality and to trust absolutely in the reality of her vision (as Katie does), or to counteract the antagonistic reality with a frontal and intransigent assault (as Penthesilea does) (154). The latter conduct takes the shape of what Allemann calls "stationary rush [*stationärer Ansturm*]" (177). This formulation telescopes what Deleuze and Guattari (1987, 356) still observe as occurring in alternation when they describe "Kleist's personal formula [as] a succession of flights of madness and catatonic freezes." Penthesilea's flights of madness are catatonic. She takes by storm, but nothing comes of it; unteachable, she is again and again driven up the wall of rock, but the action of the play doesn't progress for it (cf. Reuß 1992).

The collision of action drama and stationary drama divides, breaks, or shatters the temporality of their overlap into anticipation, repetition, and insistence. Again, the valences that Allemann gives to the two temporalities couldn't be farther apart from those which queer theorists apply. While Allemann sees Katie and Penthesilea as stuck in utopia and unable to heed the reality principle, Edelman draws on Lacan to show that this so-called reality is based on fantasy, and that fantasy protects or prevents us from encountering the real.[5] Edelman argues that the very idea of continuous linear time is rooted in the narcissistic wish fulfilment fantasy of immortality: "Fantasy presumes a reality guaranteed, not threatened, by time, sustained by the certainty that a 'course of events' is bound to continue its course in due course long after we are gone" (Edelman 2004, 34). Presuming that the world will conform to our forms of intuition even when we are physically gone, we are fantastically able to voyeuristically witness what (will) take(s) place in our absence. Only this fantastic temporality can sustain the "hopeless optimism" (35) that impels us to save for the future what will save us. We construct ourselves as "the subject who clings to the nonsatisfaction that perpetuates desire" (86) and, with this very perpetuation, feed back into the coherence of time. While this fantasy structure sustains heterosexual succession, Edelman proposes the grafted term *sinthom*osexuality to designate another libidinal temporal economy. "*Sinthom*osexuality, on the other hand—denying the appeal of fantasy, refusing the promise of futurity that mends each tear, however mean, in reality's dress with threads of meaning . . .—offers us fantasy turned inside out, the seams of its costume exposing reality's seamlessness as mere seeming" (35), Edelman argues, performing the shifting repetitions characteristic of pulsating instantaneity in his work with the signifier that remains attentive to the insistence of the letter. "Impervious to analysis and beyond interpretation," he continues, "the sinthome . . . connects us to something Real beyond the 'discourse' of the symptom, connects us to the unsymbolizable Thing over which we constantly stumble" (38). Kleist could overcome his language skepticism or, rather, turn the linguistic crisis into the point of his writing only by radically reorganizing the syntax and the logic of ordinary language use and thereby opening language to the pulsations of an instantaneously yet also terrifyingly fulfilled drive.[6]

Shivers

Less concerned with dramaturgy than with rhetoric and verisimilitude, Campe (2012a) examines the production of stories and thoughts, especially in its technical aspect—of "fabricating my idea in the workshop of Reason," as Kleist describes it in his essay "On the Gradual Fabrication of Thoughts While Speaking" (Kleist 1982, 219). Campe explores the notion of practice or procedure (*Verfahren*), which he sees developing in the early nineteenth century, and defines it as "regularity without rule," as "courses of action that settle in, without jumping ahead to a method or falling back on a routine" (2012a, 3, my translation). He identifies Kleist as the first German writer who requires such a concept of practice (*Verfahren*) (6). The mechanical (neither rule-bound nor habitual) element of procedure constitutes an alterity to the subject—a not entirely calculable force that qualifies the subject's agency. Kleist develops practices and sets up experiments that roll back subjective influence and control, not in the name of scientific objectivity but in the interest of contingency (see Peters 2003, 66).

Campe also introduces the figure of *Erschütterung*, which I translate as "shivers" to bring out the material and the emotional, the intense and the gentle aspect of the unsettling event. *Erschüttern*, Campe reminds us, is the word Kleist uses in the letter he writes to his fiancée on March 22, 1801, which reports on the impact that reading Kant's first critique has on him. Because of it, critics tend to speak of Kleist's "Kant crisis"—a phrase that obscures the intricacies of the unsettlement. Campe notes the triangular dynamic of Kleist's letter to Wilhelmine about his reading of Kant: while Kleist describes his own shivers, he imagines Wilhelmine as unfazed. This brings to mind another triangular dynamic: the one Kleist sets up in his "On the Gradual Fabrication of Thoughts While Speaking" when he proposes that the best way to encourage ideas to emerge is to talk issues through in the presence of an uninvolved other. Kleist's example: as a student, trying to find the best approach to a legal or a mathematical problem, he finds it advantageous to monologize while his sister Ulrike sits in the room and pursues her own work. The friction of his intellectual agitation with Ulrike's calm disinterest—especially when raised to the imminent threat that she might turn away completely—sparks the crucial idea. Thoughts are not spontaneously created out of the interiority of the subject. Instead, the subject submits to an external quasi-experimental setup, which must involve another agency outside subjective control, and to a proceeding, which consists in speaking unauthoritatively—emitting speech not meant to communicate but to quasi-mechanically generate the friction energy, necessary for the fabrication of ideas, between the subject's own agitated concern and the other's indifferent calm. There is a Kleistian irony to the fact that Kant's twist on the Copernican Revolution, which moves the subject into the center of transcendental epistemology, causes the shivers that, as Kleist writes to his apparently unfazed fiancée, spark the notion of a procedure for the fabrication of ideas: Such procedure or practice—the modus operandi without established rule or method, without an idea understood in advance—limits the sovereignty of the subject.[7]

While Campe focuses on Kleist's prose—and analyzes the link between the fabrication of thoughts and of narratives—the figure of the spark (the decisive insight, the revolution of thought) draws our attention to the dramatic genre, where, since Aristotle's *Poetics*, the peripeteia is a standard requirement. Campe shows that, in Kleist, the insight doesn't necessarily mean progress, and the turn doesn't necessarily provide resolution. The peripeteia combines two opposed temporalities, according to his analysis: the *kairos*, *Augenblick*, or instant of change that is a point of rupture in time, and the course of time that allows for continuity.[8] Across the temporal point of radical change, before and after mirror one another. The linearity of discourse gets broken and jumbled, congealing for Campe into the rhetorical figure of the *hysteron proteron*—an inversion of normal word order where what chronologically comes later is put first. The *hysteron proteron*—which could be rendered in English as "preposterous," combing pre and post—figures the "paradoxical simultaneity of the one with the other" (10). It is a figure of thought as much as it is a figure of speech. In fact, both thought and speech are linked in Kleist's work by the *hysteron proteron* structure: before one even has an idea, one already starts to speak—and Kleist recommends such a preposterous proceeding.

Sequence is so radically unsettled in favor of simultaneity here that the last word comes without superior authority. The intertwining of old and new order and the overlap of continuance with profound change affect not only the new order but also the old.[9] With all the foregrounded attention he gives the *Augenblick*, the *kairos*, the crucial moment where things turn, Kleist also smears and spreads that punctuality with the structure of the *hysteron proteron*.

The doubled structure of Kleist's plays creates a specific emotionality. The more or less conventional drama of action operates with the pathos model (see Pahl 2012, 50–80). Characters position themselves with heart and soul; they act according to this emotional identification and suffer because of it—even if, as in the comedies, we don't take their suffering very seriously. In the stationary drama, Kleist plays up the logic of pathos to its extreme (see Allemann 2005, 21). The protagonist doesn't actively embrace a substantial cause but is suddenly and inexplicably struck, as if by lightning, by a vision that cannot easily be made intelligible and rationalized as a cause. It is the epiphanic form rather than the substance of pathos that enraptures. Allemann (2005, 34–35) clarifies that Kleist doesn't develop character motivation from the action but solely from this mysterious vision. That is to say, the protagonist of the drama of action is motivated by the pathos of the pathos formula: her cause (or pathos) is pathos. This raises dramatic emotion to a higher power (34; see also 151). In the doubling of drama, the form of dramatic emotion reflects on itself. But such exponentiation also empties out the pathos. The substance of pathos disappears in Kleist's double drama. There is no other content or substance to the pathos of the protagonists than the structure of pathos itself. Such dramatic self-commentary is not free of parody.

Empty pathos and the inexplicable power of its sheer form receive a virtual substance in the modern world. If modernity postulates individual autonomy, it also provides the specifically modern pathos structure or emotional plot to go with it: romantic love. Romantic love combines madness with grandeur in the passionate pursuit of a singular object, expressly without universal validity. Moderns invest in the notions of "love for no reason" and "love at first sight."[10] Incomprehensibility is considered essential to the modern idea of romantic love. Modern lovers cannot and should not explain their object choice, and the structure of this madness (this lack of rationale) is valued positively. The cause that moderns share, believe in, and live for thus consists in the inexplicable—because empty, yet exponential—structure of love itself. Moderns are in love with love. And Kleist's dramatic formula shows up this structure. Accordingly, most of the visions in Kleist's stationary dramas revolve around a beloved individual (for Ottokar it is Agnes, for Alcmene Amphitryon, for Eve Ruprecht dying in East India, for Penthesilea Achilles, Katie and Strahl see one another, and Homburg sees his own exalted image).[11] But we need to keep in mind that this is only half of the picture, since Kleist always superimposes the modern drama with a conflict provided by the old order. Even the stationary drama by itself is divided between old and new: if it has romantic love as its content, its form reflects the distinctly antiromantic pulsation of the drive.

Kleist only slightly exaggerates the inherent logic of fixation that the modern pathos of romantic love adds to the ancient pathos model when he presents his heroes as paralyzed by their pathos and unable to act or learn. The ancient pathos model involves an immediate passage to the act, as Hegel has demonstrated: the passionate hero acts before s/he thinks. Kleist's protagonists are struck by an image but cannot act. All of Kleist's marriage plots are stuck in paralysis; one lover's vision of the other ironically prevents their union (more often than not, the lover with the vision plays the female—if queered with strong masculine attributes—or feminine—if biologically male—part). As Allemann points out, this pathetic paralysis affects also the dramaturgy in that it pushes the couple into the background and allows a third person to take center stage—for example, Adam in *The Broken Jug*, Jupiter in *Amphitryon*, and a range of possible thirds in *Katie* (Allemann 2005, 115). The Kleistian formula thus makes a mockery both of traditional pathos and of romantic love.

In Hegel's analysis of Classical tragedies, reflection happens only after the fact. As the spectacle comes to an end—at the threshold of illusion—the pathos model of emotionality can be put into perspective and critiqued. The spectators reflect on the hero's suffering and see that it stems from his or her complete identification with his or her position. Kleist, however, integrates reflection and qualification into the "action" of the play by doubling the drama. Via his structural commentary on the logic of pathos, Kleist presents us with a different model of emotionality: when an excessive and structurally empty pathos pulsates into the developmental arc of a conventionally genuine pathos, their friction produces shivers (*Erschütterung*). Since Kleist superimposes the two dramas, we must jump to and fro or shiver back and forth between the two narrative arcs, the two temporalities, the two logics, the two takes on pathos.

What s/he sees in her vision is utterly real to the protagonist, even if one might qualify this reality as a singular, uncommon, or "divine" one. When s/he happens to notice the common, mundane, but socially validated reality, two worlds clash. And things break. When Katie sees in real life, and with an armor in need of repair, the man who appeared to her on the night of New Year's Eve glowing from the light of an accompanying cherub, she drops the tray of refreshments. As if shattering the dishes wasn't enough, she proceeds to jump out the window and breaks both her legs. This is dramatized *Erschütterung*: crisis. While Katie's scene strikes me as camp, as its drama easily tips over into the comical, these dramatic scenes and stories tend to monopolize our attention and obscure the slighter shivers that I find more interesting.[12] As readers or spectators, we are easily held hostage by the crisis. If we take a step back—or twist ourselves one turn further into the play—we notice how Kleist shows up as ludicrous both the crisis mode and the spectatorial investment in it.

The protagonists seem to be prone to drama and crisis—at least, if we follow convention and focus on the characters instead of on the specifically Kleistian structure of their impersonalizing and desubjectivizing doublings. When Penthesilea, for example, tells Achilles the story of how she first met him in person, she glosses over the fine emotional disturbances, which the misfit of two realities (or of "reality" and "dream," as Allemann conservatively puts it) might produce, with the shock and awe of Achilles's glorious appearance. Compared to the common Greek warrior, Achilles strikes her as

> PENTHESILEA: A day-star among pallid stars at night!
> I could not have felt otherwise if he
> Himself, the god of war, had of a sudden
> Come with his white horses thundering down
> From Mount Olympus to salute his bride!
> I stood there, dazzled by the apparition,
> After you had withdrawn—as, when at night
> Lightning falls before a wanderer,
> The rattling [*rasselnd*] portals of Elysium open
> With radiance for a soul and close again.
> (*P* 102/15.2207–16, translation altered)

Nothing but exclamation marks and hyperbole—thunder and lightning, epiphany and paradise, dazzle and (death) rattle. Kleist produces a campy exaggeration of the language of infatuation and makes a mockery of

Penthesilea's pathos. What Penthesilea buries under this grand retrospective version of their first encounter are the little doubts inspired by her current encounter with the real Achilles. She does notice for brief moments that he doesn't quite look like the Achilles of her vision: "You'd almost doubt, when he thus appears [*so erscheint*] / That it is he" (*P* 88/15.1792–93, translation altered).[13] Compared to the excessive splendor that characterizes her overexcited account of Achilles's first entry, mere appearance seems not good enough to vouch for truth. Contrary to the dislike of theatricality developed by the theater of the eighteenth century (see Wild 2003), only emphatic *Schein* (i.e., splendor) can guarantee *Sein* for Penthesilea.[14]

Kleist's dramatic practice, though, combines agitated involvement and calm disinterest. We have already seen that Kleist triangulates his intellectual disconcertment with his sister's or his fiancée's indifference and that the crucial spark or turn does not clearly provide relief or induce change. The *hysteron proteron* structure that Campe has expounded, which smears the point of the turn (peripeteia, revolution) and dilutes not only the new with the old but also the old with the new, wears down strong feelings. It compromises pathos and allays crisis.

In "On Thinking Things Over: A Paradox" ("Von der Überlegung") (Kleist 1982, 217)—another text in which Kleist discusses the idea of practice or procedure—"a glowing celebration of spontaneity is overlaid by a skeptical revisionism" (Campe 2012b, 7, my translation). Here Kleist seems to exalt pathos when he speaks of the "glorious feeling" that generates the energy and strength necessary for action. But Campe shows that feeling in this case actually functions as a synonym for procedure (7). Both terms refer to the same technique of mustering energy and enabling creativity. Granted, Kleist describes feeling as glorious and assumes practice to have been "faulty and frail," but feeling turns out to be just as faulty and frail as practice. Far from occurring spontaneously and naturally, feeling needs to be cultivated and trained. This takes a lot of effort—including the effort of retrospective critique, "namely, to make us aware of what was faulty or frail [*gebrechlich*] in the practice [*Verfahren*], so that we may adjust our feeling for similar cases in the future" (Kleist 1982, 217, translation altered). If practice or procedure are other names for feeling, the synonyms reveal the technical and experimental quality of feeling. And this, in turn, explains why Kleist also speaks of the "indecency" or, we might say, queerness of procedure.[15]

The practice-feeling that Kleist develops and experiments with in his writing and his life is thoroughly ambiguous.[16] It oscillates between the glorious and the indecent or frail, between the progressive and the reactionary. At the end of Kleist's plays, we never know whether the intrigue has been solved or whether the characters returned to the same old attitudes. We've seen action (in the dramaturgical, military, and psychological senses of the word), but it is unclear whether it led anywhere. The practice might allow for the unexpected to fall into place felicitously—because it welcomes foreignness and generates energy—but it also constantly points to its own unfoundedness, including the groundlessness of any success, and to the nonauthority of the subject who launches into the practice. In practice, "the opposition, between the pathos of the sudden rupture and the cynicism of a mere ability to connect, evaporates" (Campe 2012b, 18, my translation).

Such leveling of the hierarchies (between *Sein* and *Schein*, reality and probability [*Wahrheit* and *Wahrscheinlichkeit*], old and new, rupture and continuity, excitement and calm) does, at times, allow protagonists and spectators to distance themselves from the rush and the hyperbole and to feel the small dissonances that unsettle their world because their world is plural. Kleist's doubling of the drama produces a distance or a gap within both the sincerity and the violent excess of pathos and generates an emotional formation that neither completely identifies with nor completely annihilates feeling. Such shivering practice-feeling draws connections by way of jumps or leaps. The indecent procedure produces queer syntax.

"Improbable Realities" ("Unwahrscheinliche Wahrhaftigkeiten"), Kleist's anecdote published in the *Berliner Abendblätter* on January 10, 1811, furnishes the figure for the leap:[17] "Precisely at the moment when the vessels are floating down the river toward the bridge—a cadet, please note, is standing on the left bank of the Scheldt . . .—and it is now, please understand, now, that the explosion occurs: and the cadet, hide and hair, complete with standard and pack, and without the tiniest bit having happened to him on this journey [*ohne daß ihm das mindeste . . . zugestoßen*], is standing on the right bank!" (Kleist 1982, 292, translation altered). The story establishes continuity when it is noted that nothing "happened to him." The phrase can, moreover, be read emphatically, as meaning that nothing occurred on this journey, that everything stayed the same, or that everything that happened had already happened as it began to happen. "Precisely at the moment," the outcome is already complete. In a sense, no journey took place. Does this mean that it doesn't make any difference whether the cadet stands on the left bank of the river Scheldt with the standard or on the right bank?[18] How about the river Rhein? During Kleist's time, Napoleon had conquered the regions to the left of the Rhine, and from 1795 until 1814 the river functioned as the border between France and the German territories. In view of Kleist's infamous attempts to rouse the Germans against the French aggressor, Campe points out that Kleist always already speaks French before the French can consolidate into the enemy.[19] The leap has occurred. Peters describes the discontinuous repositioning of the cadet from one bank to the other as an incidental "action on behalf of (the cause of) the other" (2003, 123, my translation). While she implicitly coordinates this jump with translation, I would, especially in light of the uncertain or dispersed agency expressed in the formulation that this action "happens," draw the connection to an emotional transfer of empathizing or *sich (hinein) versetzen (in)*.[20] Kleist offers an exteriorized version of empathy, a *sich versetzen*. One is already transported to the other side of the border, working on behalf of the other's cause. A maddening displacement (*Verrückung*) of pathos. Once again, the prefix *ver-* plays its Kleistian tricks with its double meaning of departure from the path taken and continuation of this very path.[21]

The other can become familiar because it always already speaks through what one is conversant with, and a straightforward, immediate beginning is always already queered by retroactive reflection and thus by an unavoidable alterity (Campe 2012b, 10). The title of the essay—"On the Gradual Fabrication of Thoughts While Speaking"—exemplifies this logic of inconsequence: one does not lead to the other, but the other sends shivers through the one as soon as one begins.

The Broken Jug

I move now to a discussion of *The Broken Jug* and show how various ways of doubling the drama are combined in this comedy. As already indicated in the last chapter, it is immediately obvious that *The Broken Jug* superimposes two dramas: an analytic courtroom play with a metalegal action.[22] In the first, Eve's reputation is at stake; in the other, Adam's. These two human protagonists thus displace the artefactual title character, the jug.

According to Fichte's "Outline of Family Right" (an appendix to his 1796 *Foundations of Natural Right*), sexuality poses such a profound problem to a woman's dignity that her only chance for redress lies in submitting her life to the exalted notion of romantic love. For the bourgeois woman, then, her honor is a question of love. A man's dignity, in this paradigm of sex binarity and gender complementarity, is not threatened by his sexual activity.[23] Instead, his reputation might be severely compromised by professional misconduct. Kleist's comedy, then, on one level, reinforces the bourgeois segregation of the sexes into complementary positions that his historical cultural context had only recently developed. The modern, bourgeois woman faces the highest risks in the sphere of intimacy, hence the drama of Eve occurs in the bedroom (where she is supposed to be alone). Modern, bourgeois man's interests lie in the sphere of professional life, hence Adam's drama takes place in the courtroom (where he is supposed to reside as the judge). Kleist's use of the names of the first man and woman of the Abrahamic religions only underscores this sex/gender binary.

Yet, as usual, Kleist positions his play in a nonbourgeois context. Its characters are simple country folk living in a small village about two hundred years before Kleist's time, that is, at a historical and local distance from modern middle-class life. Kleist doubles the old with the new and has the play hover on the cusp between a feudal and a bourgeois culture. In this context, Eve plays the role of the modern, bourgeois woman and assumes the pathos of romantic love. To the charge of having sex, which is supposed to be socially devastating, she responds with an exaltation of love in the name of unconditional trust. When she insists that Ruprecht should have trusted her against all evidence (*J* 42/9.1164–74), she draws on the ideal of unconditional love to save her dignity as a person, in line with Fichte's argument. For moderns, dignity is a question of freedom (dignity of person), whereas before, it was a question of social class (honor). Fichte manages to argue that a sexual relationship endangers a woman's status as a person and that she therefore needs to use her inalienable freedom to give herself completely and out of love (i.e., freely) to one man. In the old world, sex does not endanger a woman's status; if anything, it has more potential to improve her rank than not. Moreover, a woman's orgasm is treated with much more respect in the old order than in the new. For the moderns, female sexual pleasure is suspicious (a sign that she might not be interested in her dignity as a person) (see also Gallas 2005, 123–58). In the old order, female (and male) sexual pleasure makes an important contribution to the economy of bodily fluids or humors. In *The Broken Jug*, the relatively asexual, even antisexual notion of romantic love is layered on top of an insistence on orgasmic pleasure.

While Eve's fiancé's incomprehension at her demand for absolute trust (*J* 42/9.1175f) and her mother's protofeminist savviness show that Eve defends a position that has not completely taken hold yet but is still emerging, Adam has a different kind of trouble with the new order. The legal meta-action becomes entangled with the primary action as the play suggests Adam's implication in the breaking of the jug. Thus, the question of Adam's dignity also involves his sexuality. The heteronormative notion of romantic love is thoroughly disturbed by this entanglement of the two supposedly separate dramas. Kleist not only inverts the original marriage plot of heterosexual love (Adam and Eve) by submitting it, at least on the surface, as a story of Adam's transgression and Eve's innocence, but he also slips in Steve.[24]

Not everybody—in fact, barely anybody—notices this somewhat silly figure for the homosexual in *The Broken Jug*—Steve, whose name and existence are so clearly derivative of those of the first woman. Klotz's (1996) suggestion that we consider the spectators and witnesses onstage as layering an internal drama of interpretation on top of the drama of action among the protagonists is intriguingly relevant for this play but needs to be extended to the readers and spectators offstage. The drama of interpretation (by theaters, audiences, readers, and critics) consists in the difficulty of making sense, but it also feeds back to the protagonist. One could speak of a secondary drama of interpretation: the difficulty that the readers' and spectators' interpretation poses for the one who is being read. That Adam has difficulties conforming to Kleist's time with its newly universalized rules of sex-gender alignment and the drastic increase in heteronormative pressure that these rules bring about, is barely ever acknowledged and such blindness compounds the awkwardness of his position. This lack of regard, which the comic ending redoubles, ironically reinforces the tragedy that imperceptibly doubles the comedy.

Allemann (2005) argues that *The Broken Jug* serves as a lesser example of the Kleistian dramaturgic formula he has elaborated. He sees most of the superdrama not as a layer on top but as a sort of supplement, tacked onto the end of the drama of action as published "variant." One of the reasons for his unfavorable judgment lies in the fact that he considers only the drama of Eve. In Allemann's eyes, Adam's drama does not count in its own right but only insofar as Adam usurps the stage that should belong to Eve and pushes her into the subordinate space of the supplement. Another reason consists in the fact that Allemann dismisses the mackled texture of the play as botched. He fails to take seriously the unique structure of *The Broken Jug*—its material doubling of a shorter with a longer drama, its irreducibility to one of the two versions, and its claim to be both complete (by virtue of its publication) and constitutively incomplete or supplementary.

Yet another hesitation on Allemann's part might stem from the particular flavor of Eve's vision in *The Broken Jug*. For Allemann, the visions that orient the stationary dramas are dreams, wishes, or ideals. Eve finds herself under the spell of the idea that her beloved Ruprecht will die of fever in Jakarta, which is difficult to describe as an ideal or wishful dream, unless one admits a death wish. While Allemann does not consider anything like this, the insistent repetitions of the same in the general structure of the stationary drama strongly suggest the workings of the death drive and it is helpful here to draw on Bersani's deconstruction of the binary of Eros and Thanatos.[25] In *The Freudian Body*, Bersani (1986) shows how sexual pleasure implicates the death drive, arguing that it "shatters" the self (in the increase of excitement beyond a level compatible with psychic organization) and sexual pleasure itself (in its teleological orientation toward discharge).[26] He equally argues that repetition compulsion, which Sigmund Freud forcefully, even "violently," relegates to the realm of a death drive opposed to the sexual instinct, can be mobilized in the service of pleasure and life (62).[27] In Eve's case, the manifest content of her vision concerns not the death of tension or of the self but of another. To wish another's death is usually regarded as an example of aggression. But the death of the beloved might also be conjured to intensify the feeling of love.

There Is a Double to Every Kind of Trouble

Previous scholarship has shown that this comedy does not exactly leave us with all problems solved.[28] The question of truth remains deeply troubled through the ending, including the issue of who is to be believed. One of the most comedic aspects of the play are the jumbled stories that Adam seems to make up on the fly as if to cement his innocence. Adam follows the procedure of fabricating thoughts while speaking. But he is not very successful and seems to get all tangled up in the net of his iridescent stories. The theater audience generally takes this to mean that Adam has lost his dignity from the beginning. From the outset, they pass judgment on Adam's stories. Is the fact that, as spectators or readers, we tend to side with Licht and look at Adam with suspicion a question of truth or a question of taste? Kleist seems to position his audience on the side of the Enlightenment, unable or unwilling to share Adam's predilection for extravagance.[29]

But some of the most outlandish details of Adam's stories are corroborated by other witness accounts (cf. Grugger 2010, 75). This doesn't give many readers pause, which only underscores the aforementioned difficulty Adam has with receiving recognition. Adam's stories are examples of improbable realities or of an unlikely truthfulness that everyone, if not quite tragically, dismisses.[30] So we might begin to wonder whether we weren't at fault not to trust him.

Failing to see that what is unintelligible now might someday make sense is a mark of stunted intelligence. We align ourselves with the dull-witted peasant type that Ruprecht represents if we refuse to give Adam the benefit of the doubt until the practice he is experimenting with has played itself out. This is not only a question of justice but also of taste, and not only an issue with truth but also with poetics: giving the benefit of the doubt overlaps here with suspending disbelief.[31] And as this suspension draws us further into the (modern) realm of literature, our distrust of Adam's person or ethos is fueled by modernity's suspicion of rhetoric (see Campe 2012a). Adam certainly has a way with words. And it is just as certain that his way is ludicrous at times. When his discourse pirouettes, it shows off the fact that it wants to convince us—it flashes its rhetoricity. Adam's brilliantly ready wit and flamboyance might make some suspicious. Yet, that something glitters doesn't mean that it is not gold. If we take Adam at his words—especially those that seem superfluous, excessive, or rhetorical—we will often realize that he does speak the truth.

We might want to push this method, of taking Adam at his words and trusting in their sense-to-come, beyond the puzzle of the whodunit—especially since the structure of the play strongly indicates that retrospective forensic etiology is not its only and perhaps not even its main point. The variant shows that the mystery has a life of its own, or that puzzling proves so enjoyable that one might want to continue after the issue has been solved. As the question of who broke the jug seems settled, the line of inquiry shifts, in the variant, to the question of whether or not the current conscripts (among them, Ruprecht) will be sent to the Dutch colonies in East India instead of serving at home. Walter's proof that they won't strikes one as dubious. Eve's acceptance of this proof remains equally ambiguous. Be this as it may: I will take Adam at his word when he says, "Yes, yes. There is a double to every kind of trouble [*Jedwedes Übel ist ein Zwilling*]," and assume that the statement is not exhausted in its initial enactment (yes, yes). Hence, I will argue that Eve is not the only casualty of this play.

Yes, Yes

But first to the trouble that Adam's expression gives before it informs us of its double occurrence. Yes (*ja*), in all its brevity, covers a rich array of meanings, especially when it is repeated. Eve says yes to Ruprecht, and there is no reason to doubt the singularly serious weight of her response to his marriage proposal (*J* 42/9.1166). But I will focus here on affirmations that call for reiteration: on "yes" as an articulation of consent to sexual intercourse, as an expression of pleasure, as an incitement, indeed as a cry of orgasm.

Bersani (1986, 38) calls attention to the ambiguity of sexual excitement: "The mystery of sexuality is that we seek not only to get rid of this shattering tension but also to repeat it, even to increase it. In sexuality, satisfaction is inherent in the painful need to find satisfaction." The same holds for the tension in plot development. While many conventional plays build an arc of suspense that consistently leads to the climax, we have seen, drawing on Allemann, that Kleist insistently uses a second, stationary drama to resist, interrupt, break apart this arc and thus to perpetuate both the increase and the decrease of excitement, both the intensification and the dispersion of satisfaction. All of Kleist's plays are dramas of sexuality in this sense. They enact this particular kind of libidinal economy.

I will read the shattering of the jug in *The Broken Jug* as orgasm. That is to say, I will read it if not quite "nonfiguratively" then certainly metaleptically as a poor metaphor—an example of bad taste (*J* 4/1.14).[32] As such, the figure does not stand in for the orgasm but the orgasm takes place in or as speech about the shattering jug—and this speech shatters the figurativeness of the jug. *The Broken Jug* is a play with multiple orgasms.

As noted earlier, it is a characteristic of the stationary drama that its peripeteia has already happened. In line with the genre conventions for analytic drama, *The Broken Jug* pretends to begin after the climax.[33] The morning after, we receive at least two narrative accounts of the orgasm. One from Ruprecht and then the authoritative though structurally marginalized one from Eve (in the variant). The fact that they both can give direct reports shows that Ruprecht and Eve are the primary participants in the sex act. But Adam also plays his role. We will later take a look at his, more indirect account. In our analysis of the three reports we will move in the opposite direction from the plot development. We will begin with Eve's report in the variant, which Kleist published as an addendum to his abbreviated version of the play, and then move backward to Ruprecht's account, before finally analyzing Adam's version of his own orgasm, which he gives in the play's first scene.

Here is Eve's account:

> EVE: That one falls [*Der stürzt*]; this one jumps [*er springt*]; and Ruprecht crashes through the door.
>
> . . . .
>
> I stagger senseless toward the bed.
>
> . . . .
>
> Gold-green, like flames, swims all about me,
> And I totter, and lean on the bed; then falls
> That one [*der*], crashing backward from the window;
> I . . .
> Bend over him and hold him in my arms,
> And say: "Ruprecht! Dear man! . . ."
>
> (*J* 84/Variant.2237–50, translation altered)

In the moment of climax everything around her simultaneously falls, jumps, and crashes. In her state of heightened sensitivity, she feels many things, not just Ruprecht who bursts in. There is no sequence to her feeling, no cause and effect; everything happens simultaneously in one line (2237); three articulated spasms, one eruption: "That one falls; this one jumps; and Ruprecht crashes through the door." While the other participants ("that one" and "this one") remain rather undetermined (since *springt* can mean jumps or cracks, she might be saying that Adam falls and the jug cracks or that the jug falls and Adam jumps), Eve in the end clearly identifies the scene as one of intimacy between her and Ruprecht. At the climax, she wraps her arms around Ruprecht, gathers the entire scene in his name, and expresses her love.

Yet Adam, in her account, provides the foreplay:

> EVE: "You," he says. "Be wise!"—and opens the window
>
> . . . .
>
> . . . And steps on the footstool,
> And on the chair, and mounts the windowsill,
> And examines, to see if he can leap,
> And turns, and reaches toward the shelf where he
> Had hung his wig, which he had forgot.
>
> (*J* 83–84/Variant.2226–33)

Busy with a smaller orifice of Eve's room (not the door, which Ruprecht will pierce), old Adam is more careful and deliberate than the tempestuous Ruprecht for whom this is, for all we know, the first time. Eve distinctly senses every lingering move Adam makes: "And steps on the footstool, / And on the chair, and mounts the windowsill, / And examines." The grammar of her report makes frequent use of the conjunction "and" as if to add one layer of sensation to the next without subordinating them to an intended outcome.

When Adam turns around and bends over to attend to something he passed over the first time, this fold accelerates her account, adds fervor, and then things come to a head very quickly:

> EVE: And grabs and pulls it from the jug, and pulls
> From off its shelf the jug, as well:
> That one falls; this one jumps; and Ruprecht crashes through the door.
> (*J* 84/Variant.2235–37, translation altered)

Instead of preventing or deferring the marriage of love, I see the guardian figure Adam effectively preparing and—we will have to come back to this—propelling the "wedding night" (*J* 35/7.955).[34] Far from staging a fundamental opposition between political institutions and private bliss, Kleist's play dramatizes how the state and his institutions spur the search for (not so) private fulfillment—in this case, sexual satisfaction. Let's take a look at the initial interference of the state in the life of the family-to-be:

> EVE: So we had just sat down, Mother, Father,
> Ruprecht, and I, around the hearth, to discuss [*halten Rat*]
> Whether Whitsun or Whitsun in one year
> To celebrate our marriage: when in steps,
> Suddenly, into the room, the recruiting
> Officer, and Ruprecht is called up,
> And with that blade-sharp dictum he decides
> The outcome of our happy quarrel, just when
> Whitsun seemed to be the choice, in favor of
> God only knows which Whitsun now?—
> (*J* 76/Variant.1972–80, translation altered)

Here it is the recruitment officer who bursts into the room, "suddenly." The parallel with Ruprecht's crashing through Eve's door is striking. And, indeed, the officer cuts, "with blade-sharp dictum," the first hole into the marriage. What Ruprecht refers to as "the marriage that has sprung a leak" (*J* 19/6.441)—in other words, the night of the broken jug—thus only repeats this intrusion. The originary crack materially appears in the text here as the dash after the question concerning the wedding date: "God only knows which Whitsun now?—." No pleasure is supposed to be gained from this suspension. The breach reveals a power dynamic between two forms of government—the family council (*Rat*), consisting of the two lovers and each of their single parents (Ruprecht's father and Eve's mother), which debates apparently not without joy ("in happy quarrel"), and the delegates of the state government who interrupt this debate with a fiat. Yet their order—that Ruprecht appear in Utrecht for military service—motivates the lovers to celebrate the marriage "not waiting for the parson" (*J* 35/7.957). The interruption, the crack, the deferral functions as a motivation, a spur, and even an anticipation. The premature wedding night then leads the family council to (this time more or less willingly) seek the intervention of another representative of the state, the judge. They ask him to decide their dispute, which, even if it is no longer so joyous for them, is certainly entertaining for the audience. It will turn out that this representative of the state has also been in bed with the lovers.

Another factor that hastens the nuptials can be found in Ruprecht's jealousy. Ruprecht is driven into Eve's chamber by his rage on noticing another man with her. In some tension with Eve's complaint about his inability to put absolute faith in her, his lack of trust actually contributes to their union, if perhaps not their love. This becomes clearer when we turn to Ruprecht's account (in scene 7).

Urged on by the questions of the judge and the assessor, Ruprecht's narrative very slowly unravels the events of the previous night. In this way, he catches up with the moment that was too sudden and too explosive for him to be alive to it at the time (cf. Klotz 1996, 115). Ruprecht gives his entire account of the event, including the hour or so leading up to it, in the historical present tense, but he counteracts the immediacy of the present tense with his painstaking use of the *inquit* formula (which greatly irritates his impatient interrogators). When he finally arrives at the description of the climax, he initiates it with a "now" that launches him into a quasi-reenactment of the moment. "Now" pulls us right in and has us gasping for air together with Ruprecht. The onslaught of presence is so overwhelming that even this retroactive report has to disperse the excitement by repeating the "now" three times and the call for air twice:

RUPRECHT: Now it wells, Your Honor Adam, it wells up
In me like a burst of blood. Air!
Off pops a button from my chest: Air now!
I rip my collar open. Air now, I say!
And run, and shove, and kick, and batter . . .
(*J* 35/7.963–67, translation altered)

The *inquit* in line 966 ("Air now, I say!") cannot provide much slowdown since the exclamation mark, positioned behind it, marks it as part of Ruprecht's direct speech. With the "I say" being part of his exclamation, Ruprecht, thus, adds emphasis to his order for air. He makes a fool of himself showing a lack of judgment on who or what can be ordered around (the air will certainly not heed even his repeated requests). On a more serious note, his desperate command reminds us of two of the major themes of this play: the limits of human control and the limits of communication.

We note the tremor between two temporalities in Ruprecht's account: on the one hand, the forward thrust of desire, which Ruprecht shares with the court authorities Adam and Walter; on the other, the retardations and digressions intercalated to enjoy (in) the moment again and again, which make him sound dumb. Ruprecht has experienced—even acted on behalf of—the cruelty of the libidinal economy that explodes all excitement. Now he retrospectively and discursively—one could even say aesthetically—struggles to find a different economy, a different way to engage the death drive. His delays and forms of indirectness are procedure.

> RUPRECHT: And run, and shove, and kick, and batter—because I find
> The slut's door locked—stand back a step,
> Then boot the door once more, hard, and in.
> ADAM: Ay! Blazes, boy!
> RUPRECHT: Now as it bangs wide open
> That jug topples from its shelf there into the room
> And—*whoosh*—out the window this figure leaps.
> I see those coattails flapping even now.
>
> (*J* 35–36/7.967–72)

Adam's metaleptic interference—"Ay! Blazes, boy!"—is rather interesting. He interjects into Ruprecht's report, surprisingly siding with him. It is hard to decide whether Adam is being ironic (so far, he has shown only derision for Ruprecht), or proud of Ruprecht's virility in an identificatory way (which would still preserve a distance between the events and their narration), or whether he is aroused by Ruprecht's sudden entry (which would transfer him into the narrated scene and thus constitute a metalepsis). In any case, the narrative mode of Ruprecht's version of the climax metaleptically coincides with the picture it paints and with the phrase illustrated by this picture: Ruprecht *fällt mit der Tür ins Haus*. The phrase means "coming straight to the point" or "blurting something out," literally: "falling with the door into the house." In his narrative as in his sexual behavior, Ruprecht proves clumsy, verging on violent.

Compared with Eve's account, Ruprecht's experience is less layered and more fleeting—"and—*whoosh*." Accordingly, it shows less simultaneity of events and sensations. Instead, the narrative mode suggests the subordination of the tightly linked events along the line of cause and effect: "Now as it bangs wide open / That jug topples from its shelf there." As if the air pressure from the thrust of the door swept the jug from the sill on the other side of the room. Except that the jug falls in the opposite direction—"into the room."

That the air from the flying door with which Ruprecht falls into Eve's chamber pushes the jug from the sill into the room would indeed be an improbable reality. It hardly accords with the laws of physics. But the text produces its own rules. At the beginning of the trial, it introduces a form of writing that functions as a symbol for the structure of this play about a broken jug: *Fraktur*. Adam claims to have written Ruprecht's name in *Fraktur* on the doctor's certificate that would release him from military service

(*J* 7.529). *Fraktur* is a calligraphic hand of broken lines. Unlike the Roman cursive, which is based on the continuous flow of the stroke, *Fraktur* involves frequent jumps—it demands disruptions and changes in direction. According to the practice of *Frakturschrift*, the flow of cause and effect moves from Ruprecht's kick into the door through the room to the windowsill, breaks there, and moves in the other direction, dragging the jug onto the floor of the room. In keeping with this procedure, state representatives break the flow of private developments but, by virtue of this interruption, continue and propel the development. The same applies to the structure of the drama: on the level of the organization of the play, Kleist applies the quill again and again.

As the jug falls into the room, Ruprecht's eyes are drawn in the direction of his momentum—out the window, where the flaps of an outer garment stir his attention: "I see those coattails flapping even now." Clearly, Ruprecht drops his interest in Eve. He declares, "I throw her over [*Die werf ich übern Haufen*]" (*J* 7.974, my translation) and means it both literally (that he knocks her over) and metaphorically (that he drops the idea of marrying her). Her room is only a transit space—in one side and out the other—to get to the guy: "Rushing to the window, [I] find him" (*J* 36/7.975). Eve stands between men, between Old Adam and Knecht Ruprecht—one as devilish as the other.[35] Or, rather, between them she collapses into something formless—a *Haufen* (a heap or pile). Ruprecht—who, comically, still has in his hand part of the door with which he fell into the room, now uses that piece—the handle, which, "a pound-weight," functions as a fantastically hefty version of a penis—to beat what, we can assume, is Adam's bald head:

> RUPRECHT: . . . The handle,
> It's in my hand from when I battered the door,
> So now I bring it down, a pound-weight, and thump his nob
> (*J* 36/7.978–80, translation altered)

After a brief tussle with the guy in the dark, Ruprecht experiences his version of orgasmic simultaneity:

> RUPRECHT: —And him and night and world and windowsill
> I'm standing on . . .
> Everything collapses into a sack [*fällt in einen Sack zusammen*]—
> (*J* 37/7.1004–6, translation altered)

The metaphor of the sack is a curious one. It alludes to the folklore figure Knecht Ruprecht, who carries a sack whose purpose—to contain badly behaved children—is only superficially masked by the sweets he produces out of it. The image of orgasmic release here thus conjures up several destructive aspects of the death drive: loss of world, (self-)punishment, and a general cruelty to children. Eve and Ruprecht are the children of the play and they certainly encounter no shortage of (verbal) abuse from their parents and from the officials of the paternalistic state.[36]

Ruprecht's orgasm is powerful: "As if a storm / Had swept me off a cliff ten fathoms high, / I fall . . . / And think I'll go right through the floor" (*J* 37/7.1010–13). When the attack is over it is as if it all had been a dream: "and I sit up and rub my eyes" (*J* 37/7.1017). Ruprecht was supposedly heading toward certain death in East India; now he, whom Eve will have brought into close proximity to Jesus, is resurrected: "As I now rise from the dead [*aufersteh*]" (*J* 37/7.1022, my translation).[37] It will take a while longer—the entire legal proceedings plus supplementary exchange with the assessor—until Eve recovers. But eventually she can also imagine a future again: "Our joy will blossom with that next spring" (*J* 89/Variant.2395).

In the end, the recruiting officer did not change much. The family was torn between holding the wedding this May or next. Now it will be next May. But it has also already, in some way, happened "this one January night as warm / As May" (*J* 33/7.872–73). So the nuptials will have been this year and next year. The state representative, who interrupted the family council, will indeed—as Martha suggested at the beginning of the trial—not have decided (*ent-schieden*).[38] As Campe argues, analyzing the *hysteron-proteron* structure of Kleist's narratives, the rupture in time (here figured as recruitment) that separates the old from the new functions also as a continuation of the old in the new and as a foreshadowing of the new in the old. The violent disruption by the authorities does not only expedite the climax, it also multiplies the nuptials. In fact, the "happy quarrel" continues (*J* 76/Variant.1978).

There Is a Double

We still need to analyze Adam's account of the nighttime climax. But before we do so, we will look at a different scene of intimacy—the one between Adam and Walter. It will serve as the lens through which to read the interactions between Adam and Eve.

The tenth scene gives the court proceedings and the legal action a break. The scribe Licht leaves to fetch a new witness and the court takes a recess until his return. Judge Adam asks the village people to take their break outside. He attempts to get rid of the intradiegetic spectators for a private tête-à-tête with Walter.[39] Kleist muddles the difference between the two stages—the court and the theater—when he has Adam use the vocabulary of stage directions ("Exit, people! [*Tretet ab*]," *J* 10.1420, my translation) and theater architecture ("to the foyer!," *J* 10.1421, my translation). This in turn troubles the difference between the spectators onstage and the audience of the floor (who could be asked here to take a break in the foyer of the theater).[40] In a sense, the break in the legal action also serves as a break in the performance. The scene between Adam and Walter falls somewhat outside the performance proper and can appear like a casual encounter not exactly meant for public consumption.

During this somewhat private break, some decisive information emerges—decisive both for the legal proceedings and for the interpretation of the play. Nevertheless, this information tends to remain largely without effect, that is to say, it fails to decide anything or divide anyone. During the break—as parts of the audience might stroll the foyer—Walter discovers Adam's queer feelings. It begins with a broad hint by Adam, referring to the delicacies he has just offered the assessor:

> ADAM: Such are the blessings
> We disreputable bachelors [*hagestolzen*] enjoy:
> What others scrape and scrounge to share with wife
> And child, we, with one good friend, may
> Fully savor when occasion suits.
> (*J* 52/10.1451–56, translation altered)

Historically, *Hagestolz* refers to a man who, due to his position in the family lineage and according to medieval laws of succession, is not in the legal position to marry. In modern times, the then-outdated term was used for older men (and sometimes women) who legally could but did not marry.[41] It served as a synonym, albeit with a pejorative connotation, of the expression "bachelor by conviction," a euphemism for gay men.[42] When E. T. A. Hoffmann has Antonio, in the novella *Signor Formica*, describe Signor Pasquale Capuzzi as "an old bachelor [*Hagestolz*], with every fault that belongs to that class of persons—avaricious, vain, anxious to appear young, amorous, foppish" (Hoffmann 1885, 90), he mobilizes stereotypes about men with same-sex desires.[43] The term *Hagestolz* doesn't explicitly reference homosexual conduct, and this vagueness both spurs and protects from prosecution—homosexual acts were criminalized under the sodomy laws that were in place in most of Europe, definitely in the Prussia of Kleist's time and in the Netherlands of his character Adam's time.[44] But Kleist furnishes heavy allusions.

Adam speaks of pleasures that are complete only when shared with a male friend: "with one good friend, may / Fully savor." In response, Walter touches (on) Adams wound: "a fearful gash [*Loch*], / Indeed, upon your forehead" (*J* 51/10.1458). Their intimacy thus moves quickly from the common enjoyment of delicacies—a glass of wine, a piece of cheese—to the particulars of Adam's body. Walter's comments imply that his interlocutor, namesake of the first man, shows a certain similarity with Eve in that he has two holes on opposite sides of the body: "You have two wounds—one front and one behind" (*J* 51/10.1467). And, if we abstract from the manifest meaning suggested by the immediate context, their conversation might as well serve to produce an agreement on which sexual position they might want to explore together:

WALTER: From behind [*von hinten*]?
ADAM: How's that? From behind?
WALTER: Or front?
. . . .
ADAM: Both fore *and* aft [*von vorn und hinten*].— . . .
WALTER: How?
ADAM: First so, then so.
(*J* 51–52/10.1466–69, translation altered)

The rest of the conversation is peppered with references to a culture that can be understood as gay. They function as a code that someone whose sexual practices are not sanctioned by the law might use to communicate with like-minded people.[45] When the civil servant Adam mentions his "silkworm twigs" (*J* 52/10.1479), such interest in silk, which in seventeenth-century Europe was reserved for the aristocracy, associates him with the emerging dandy culture. The two men signal recognition (of one another's preferences) via an apparently codified knowledge of delicacies. This is particularly obvious around the wine. Walter can taste that Adam serves Niersteiner and both proclaim a personal connection to the vineyard as if to a secret society.[46] Their knowing exchange about the cheese—that it is from Limburg—hints at the hateful stereotypes and persecutions of sexual deviants, which are also evoked in the references to Sodom and Gomorrah (*J* 53/10.1497) and to scapegoating ("How often did you pound the scapegoat, eh?" [*J* 54/10.1538]). Limburger cheese has a pungent odor akin to the stench of sweat. It thus participates in the metaphoric field this comedy employs around the devil, who effuses the smell of hell and figures deviant sexuality. The devil appears right in the next line:

WALTER: Limburg?
ADAM: Fresh from Limburg, ay, Your Grace.
WALTER: But, tell me, how the devil . . .
(*J* 52/10.1485–87)

While it might be exaggerating to speak of a full-fledged gay lifestyle or sexual culture as we know it today, we can assume that Kleist's contemporary audience would have at least heard of the phenomenon of vernacular codes and locations enabling gay sex, even if—or precisely because—their knowledge was not to be public, due to the penal laws in place in Prussia.[47] Kleist participates in the disavowal of gay sex that the penalization necessitates when he nowhere moves beyond allusion in this scene. On the other hand, he subjects normative heterosexuality to the same regime of equivocation and disavowal. He uses the figure of the jug to allude to the wedding and/or virginity of Eve, and he never provides explicit information about what (if anything) happened between Adam and Eve.

Walter's recognition of Adam's gay preferences (albeit impossible to prove, given that it is based in allusions) makes the desire for Eve, which most readers impute to the old Adam, a bit unlikely. If we nevertheless continue to assume this desire in Adam, we participate in a disciplinary technology—the theater—that (re)produces as normative the same desires it ostensibly penalizes on the level of the content (the trial).[48] The plot leads us to assume that the whole purpose of the legal and dramatic process lies in the expulsion and physical punishment (which will be meted out in the comical form of whippings by his own wig) of the dirty old man who uses his status to get the maiden against her will. I argue that underneath this layer of the play lies the drama of old Adam, who doesn't fit the new gender norms and the heterosexual compulsion they bring, and who is being prosecuted (in a circuitous way, since one cannot address any of this directly and explicitly), scapegoated, and driven out of town in order to secure and hasten the heterosexual marriage.

Only for a fleeting moment, at the end of the semiprivate interlude in scene 10, it is acknowledged that Adam is not attracted to Eve. Martha mentions that if she "could but set such wines before our friend / The justice, we could see more of him. / But, poor widow that I am, I've nothing / In my house to lure him" (J 56–57/10.1600–1665, translation altered). Apparently Martha can read the code; she understands that men with gay desires seem to be finding one another over fine wine. She doesn't have expensive wine, but, even more to the point, she doesn't have a man in the house—as a widow she lacks the husband who could be of interest to Adam.

I don't dispute that the play suggests that Adam sexually harassed Eve. Instead, I argue that Kleist overlays one case with another. As the Judge says, "We've got two cases here [*zwei Fälle gibts*]" (*J* 7.553, my translation). Adam proves doubly suspicious, "both fore *and* aft" (*J* 51/10.1467), both as a lecherous old straight man and in his unspeakable effeminacy desiring who knows what. Adam falls or fails twice; when he wants another man's bride and when he doesn't. The audience—as the history of the reception of *The Broken Jug* shows—generally prefers the first fall. But the doubled text also sustains and requires acknowledgment of the second. In fact, the failure to see Adam's lack of (hetero)sexual desire for Eve adds a tragic tone to the comedy. The incongruity between these two overlapping falls, two overlapping cases, two overlapping dramas, two overlapping audience expectations, and two overlapping affective valences needs to be acknowledged as evidence for the fundamentally queer character of Kleist's theater.

How do we acknowledge Adam's experience, his predicament, his needs? Despite his now apparent participation in gay culture, Adam is clearly interested in the physical presence of Eve. As he is chased out of her chamber, he urges her to visit him the next day (*J* 83/Variant.2227). But what exactly he wants from her, we are not told. We learn that, once in her room, he fixes his gaze on her:

EVE: He grasps me so, with both hands,
So, and looks at me.
MRS MARTHA: And looks . . . ?
RUPRECHT: And looks at you . . . ?
EVE: Two endless minutes staring at my face
MRS MARTHA: And says . . . ?
RUPRECHT: Says nothing ...?
EVE: You vile wretch, I say,
When he does speak. What do you take me for?
And push him back, so that he tumbles over . . .
(J 83/Variant.2215–20)

In the garden, he had assured Eve that what he wants will take only two minutes; so, presumably, he got his satisfaction.[49] It appears that he says something to Eve after the two minutes, but we only hear about her indignant reaction. The ellipsis in Eve's account not only serves as a sign of her modesty but also perpetuates the cruelty of withholding recognition. Nobody has words for Adam's desire.

The hole in Eve's account also serves Kleist as he plays with his audience. Omissions of this sort form an integral part of his strategy to force the audience to participate in the action via the drama of interpretation.[50] As Eve pushes Adam away, we begin to fill in the blank and produce a proper illusion or what counts for us as a "beautiful appearance [*Schein*]." In the absence of concrete evidence or reliable information, heterosexual stereotypes fill the void. They flesh out what Adam might have put in the empty space of the certificate (*Schein*): "And in the middle / I have left a space just as big as a puddle; this I fill in now" (*J* 82/Variant.2177–79, translation altered).[51] But this means that it will have been our dirty imagination that "brings to light" the crime from out of the muddy (forgiving and infectious) waters of the puddle. Here Kleist's mockery of the Enlightenment is subtle but unmistakable. What is more, the writer (Kleist) deflects the blame to the reader, critic, or judge (as scribe Licht does with Adam). Whether it is our dirty imagination or whether our imagination is not dirty (or deviant) enough, we become complicit in the sexualized violence that is committed against Eve and against Adam. The court setting makes us all want to invade Eve's private sphere, even as the lack or hole that draws our desire to know might rather be in Adam's court. Kleist turns us all into lecherous Adams. For the spectator, it can't go fast enough, as the fact that Kleist had to cut the play shows.[52] Kleist mirrors (or anticipates, or perhaps even produces) the critics' impatience when he has the intradiegetic critic figure—the assessor Walter—spur on the reports every time they get close to Eve's most intimate space.[53] Kleistian violence does not spare the audience members, who in turn scapegoat Adam for their own violence. Adam is punished for the audience's haste and the lecherous fantasies that Kleist almost forces on them.

Like Martha (when she specifies the prehistory of the jug) and Ruprecht (when he describes his path to Eve's garden), Eve insists that it takes time to do justice to the open space (be it the hole in the jug, the break in Ruprecht's nightly journey, or the maiden's genitals) and that it is no good just hastily filling it up: "But I: 'How, Your Honor, at this hour, / Beneath this pear tree, will you fill [*erfüllen*] that space?'—" (*J* 82/Variant.2181–82). She might be claiming that she will not find gratification, let alone fulfillment (*Erfüllung*), in a quickie under the pear tree but would care for a more thoroughgoing and sophisticated exploration of her private parts (this is obviously my dirty imagination, since—apart from the excessive *er-* in *erfüllen*—objective evidence has it that Eve refers here to the space in the certificate that still needs to receive Ruprecht's full name). But, in addition to Adam penetrating and (according to the new sex/gender system) completing Eve, and Adam usurping Ruprecht's place in the marriage certificate, we can read "this [place] I fill now" as Adam filling in for Eve.[54] *Schein*, then, in addition to "document" or "certificate" and theatrical "illusion" or "semblance" comes to mean gender performance or drag (in the widest sense of the term). Joachim Harst (2012, 181) notes that Adam mimics the broken jug with his visible wounds but doesn't quite draw the conclusion, which I propose here, that Adam imitates rather than complements Eve.[55] Adam, I suggest, wants to play the role Eve gets to play. He wants to take her place, in a bit of transgender self-expression. When Eve reports, "I introduced him (in)to my chamber," this can then be read as Eve teaching Adam the practices and secrets of feminine masquerade. In this case, it makes sense that Adam looks at her for two full minutes without saying or doing anything. He is not impatient to take her; rather, he needs the time to study her so as to better imitate her. Nothing in the text prevents us from imagining that he stares at her not because he wants to have her but because he wants to be her.

The scene, then, can also be taken as a campy riff on Lessing's bourgeois theater. For Lessing, the spectators are supposed to sympathize with the protagonist, which involves an identification with and, to a certain extent, imitation of what they see onstage.[56] Kleist takes a tag too seriously and thereby parodies this theater tenet when he installs Adam as a spectator who takes his seat ("he sits him down upon the chair" [*J* 83/Variant.2214]) and passively fixes his gaze in order to learn from what he sees. He does so not without aesthetic literacy, as his remark referencing the theater shows: "It's an illusion, according to the rules [*Ein Schein, nach allen Regeln*]" (*J* 82/Variant.2180, my translation). Adam here figures the critic who knows the rules and standards of creating an educational illusion and a beautiful semblance. To be sure, the standards that Adam employs are outdated at the time Kleist writes, but this only enhances the camp effect of this vignette.[57] When Adam, like the spectator in Lessing's Enlightenment theater, sits down to be educated by identifying with the protagonist, he imperceptibly slips into the role of the actor who wants to learn Eve's performance of femininity. Now we see Adam as if in his dressing room at his makeup table taking off his wig and unbuttoning his costume in order to study for a new role. Adam divests himself of the wig—this insignium of his authority, at least as overdetermined as the jug—and readies himself to put on a different masquerade. In this light, the wig contracts the sense of drag paraphernalia. When it is later found in or near Eve's chamber, the wig incriminates Adam as a sign both that he abused his authority and that he played with mom's accessories or put on his wife's clothes, as it were.

Eve is not amused. Adam's performance doesn't fly. She responds with disgust and abuse: "'You vile wretch,' I say . . . And push him back, so that he tumbles over" (*J* 83/Variant.2218–20) and Ruprecht bangs at the door. Adam feels "betrayed" (*J* 83/Variant.2224) and quickly recovers the appearance of heterosexual gender conformity—"resorting to semblance [*den Schein ergreifend*]" (*J* Variant.2224, my translation)—which he had cast off in the form of the wig a few minutes before. Eve remains so horrified by the revelation and apparently so traumatized by somehow having become associated with it, that she would rather suffer accusations of promiscuity than speak about Adam's transgender inclination.

Eve's initial fear/wish that Ruprecht will catch a deadly fever abroad finds reiteration in a somewhat different form here: "Then falls / That one [*der*], crashing backward from the window; / I think: in this life he [*er*]'ll not rise again" (*J* 84/Variant.2245–47). The sentence suggests a causal link between Ruprecht's fall and his inability to get up again.[58] But the phrases also remain disjointed—and not only syntactically so—since the use of slightly different pronouns (*der* and *er*) leaves uncertain whether they refer to the same person, especially as, a few lines earlier, these pronouns were used to distinguish between referents (even though it could not be conclusively determined which one refers to the jug).[59] The blurriness of the picture, as to who is the subject of the fall and the (impossible) resurrection, results from the superimposition of at least two death wishes. Eve wishes Ruprecht dead (possibly as a punishment for his pending departure) and Adam dead (possibly as a punishment for his gender performance) and perhaps she wishes her virginity (the jug) broken. She gets her wishes and is able to resolve all these conflicting tendencies in the apotheosis of Ruprecht. She emits a cry and cracks (*springt*), and leaps (*springt*) into a tableau vivant of the pietà in which she plays the role of the sorrowing Mother of God and Ruprecht serves as the Crucified:

> EVE: I cry: "Oh, Savior of the World!" and jump [*spring*],
> Bend over him and hold him in my arms,
> And say: "Ruprecht! Dear man! [*Lieber Mensch!*]"
> (*J* 84/Variant.2247–50, translation altered)[60]

She can thus be sure of Ruprecht's resurrection and gets to enjoy the crack while also fitting perfectly into the new gender norm of affectionate and suffering mother. Every illicit pleasure can be retained in this glorifying

Aufhebung of the properly heterosexual couple, except for Adam's. He has dropped out of the picture.

Three Falls, Three Peaks

In light of what we developed in the previous section, we can now analyze Adam's account of the nocturnal climax. It is offered in the play's opening scene, as part of an exchange between Adam and Licht, who wants to know how Adam got the wounds to his head.

> ADAM: Battle! What!—With that blasted goat buck
> Jutting from the stove I strove to battle,
> If you would have it so. It comes back now [*jetzt*].
> I lose my balance, yes, and, at the same time,
> Reach out, arms flailing like a drowning man,
> Clutch at my trousers which, last night, I'd hung
> All wet to dry upon the rack, now [*nun*] I clutch hold
> Of them, you see, believing, like a fool,
> That they will hold me up, and now [*nun*]—*rip*—my waistband
> Tears; waistband now [*jetzt*] and trousers and me, all three
> We fall, and there, smack on the corner
> Of that stove, where the goat buck sticks out his nose,
> I come hurtling headfirst down.
>
> (*J* 5/1.50–61, translation altered)

Like the other two we analyzed, this account establishes an overwhelming presence, here achieved by the adverb "now" (*nun*, *jetzt*) that marks the beat and quickens it at times against the slowing effect of repetitions and unnecessary explanations. The extraneous phrases, as well as the possibly elongated pronunciation of "now" when the German features *nun* instead of *jetzt*, suggest that Adam uses the practice recommended in "On the Gradual Fabrication of Thoughts While Speaking" and plays for time until the crucial idea arrives.[61] But since the point of his story has been clear from the beginning—he fell—the playing for time can only concern the particulars of this twist of the ever-insisting drive. And so the account performs what it conveys—a delicious delay right before the climax.

Again, the incident comprises the orgiastic coincidence of three falls: "waistband now and trousers and me, all three / We fall." The ménage à trois with the pants and the waistband mirrors his threesome with Eve and Ruprecht. But these are not exactly three separate things, let alone persons—as a piece of clothing, the trousers are part of Adam's appearance, and the waistband is part of the trousers. The account exuberantly or painfully produces a threesome out of a rather lonely affair. Whether it comes to tripping or getting off,

Adam does it by himself—he "bears, within himself, his own stumbling block for impulse [*Stein zum Anstoß*]" (*J* 3/1.6, translation altered). This brings us back to Fichte, who underscores, in his *Wissenschaftslehre,* that the I posits not only itself but also the non-I as a check (*Anstoß*) to the I, which thus turns into endless striving. In what seems more masturbation than sexual encounter, Adam makes do with props because his desire is either unintelligible or unacceptable to other people. (Un)like the waistband and the trousers, Eve and Ruprecht can't give Adam the required support. They don't see him and can't tell what he wants—his only witness is the nosy goat buck who cranes toward him from the edge of the oven. Or else they take offense (*nehmen Anstoß*)—like Eve when he eventually tells her what he wants. But then the bone of contention (*Stein des Anstoßes*) renders her mute as a block or as the goat-shaped ornament on the oven.

Adam insists that his orgasmic fall took place in the morning—"now, the instant I climb out of bed" (*J* 3/1.16, translation altered). If we take him seriously—and I think that we need to, because we have no criterion to decide which parts of his story are made up on the spot and which are true—this indicates that the somewhat botched intercourse at night radiates into the morning. The next day Adam is still drunk or in dire need, "like a drowning man [*ertrunken*]." During the night in question he seems to have enjoyed somewhat of a release when he emptied his bowels on the way home (see *J* 62/11.1771–75). This incident leaves its mark, as it were, on his account of the next morning: we can assume that his pants had been wet and needed to be hung on the oven because of the runs the night before. Even though, or indeed because, Adam receives no recognition for his desire, he enjoys three climaxes: the leap through Eve's window, the explosive bowel movement, and the masturbation the morning after. The drive pulsates through Adam. He fully savors, one could say, what others must share.

To conclude, let us return to the drama of interpretation. The audience's participation in injustice takes not only the forms of a dirty imagination (and thus possibly unfounded accusations) or of the Enlightenment compulsion to bring things to light (and thereby not only uncover but also, ironically, produce secrets), it also manifests as ignorance and lack of understanding. Readers and spectators offend the Adams of this world by pressing them into a story of normative desire—postulating that they covet the young woman. As Adam's gay desire and transgender wishes are being ignored and suppressed, he is nevertheless subterraneously despised and ostracized for them. The entire play builds up to presenting Adam as the devil—"You mean you think the Devil / Lives here, in this courthouse?" asks Walter toward the end (*J* 62/11.1784–85). Adam acknowledges the experience of social deprecation when he refers to "[us] disreputable bachelors [*uns verrufnen hagestolzen Leuten*]" (*J* 52/10.1452). Meanwhile, the representatives of bourgeois enlightenment, Licht and Walter, benevolently reintegrate Adam or, rather, disavow their own violence when they insist on the humanity of the one whom village superstition identifies as the devil (*J* 90/Variant.2415–22 and J 61/11.1740). But such reintegration is based on an even further repression of Adam's queer sexuality and genderqueerness. It corroborates Edelman's analysis of gay antisociality in *No Future* (2004) that Adam is demonized for his excessive jouissance, for wanting to destroy a marriage-to-be and thus the possibility of future generations, and for spreading the pulsations of the death drive like a disease—infecting Eve with the fixed idea that Ruprecht might die. His reintegration is possible once the happy ending has been secured for the couple and his infernal character has been trivialized. But that also means that Adam's queerness has been lost. Kleist's comedy illustrates the dangers, which Edelman points out, of a gay politics intent on disidentifying with the villain.

Chapter 3

✦

Mammalogic and Analgrammar

We can recognize the possibility of multiple (queer) symbolic orders. Instead of one phallic symbolic order, consider a triad of symbolic orders. They might—perhaps almost inevitably—be mapped onto the Lacanian registers of the symbolic, the imaginary, and the real—with the phallocentric still claiming isolated singularity in the symbolic, a mammatangential getting easily miscategorized as imaginary, and the analgrammatic having a strong relation to the real. We can also map them onto the major literary genres—with the phallus sustaining narrative, the breast catching the eye and producing drama, spectacle, theater, and the anus tearing speech from behind into verse. Perhaps we can even map them onto the three kingdoms of nature (animal, plant, and mineral). Then Kunigunde could serve as a personification allegory for Kleist's multiplication of the symbolic.[1] But I will beware of such taxonomy and suggest that we take the proposed distinctions and affinities with a grain of salt.

First, we will explore a symbolic order that privileges the breast as the organizing signifier. However, I don't mean to suggest that Kleist replaces the phallocentric symbolic order with a mammacentric one. For one thing, he also develops a symbolic order in which the organizing signifier is the anus. Kleist thus seems to be interested in multiplying logics rather than recentering the symbolic around a different signifier. Furthermore, Kleist's mammalogic proves to be a far cry from the ideas of plenitude, immediacy, full presence, and perfection that often characterize attempts to move the breast into the center of our cultural imaginary. One could perhaps say that Kleist develops a mammatangential logic instead of a mammacentric one. This term captures both the way in which Kleist goes off on a tangent with his text breasts and other metalepses (that would be corny if they weren't so campy), and the fact that he cuts through the oedipal idealization of the breast as (only) full. Put differently, the breast, while it also plays a visual role in Kleist's text, does not constitute an order that is only imaginary. Kleist indeed develops a symbolic in the Lacanian sense—in other words, a language that is based on the circulation of differences—from the breast.[2] If Lacan situates the imaginary in the undifferentiated dyad of mother and child and calls on the father as the third term to break up the dyad and introduce the symbolic law, then the symbolic from the breast presumes the ability of the dyad to differentiate itself.[3] This ability or propensity for self-differentiation, I will address in the following as cleavage.

While the idea of several (successive or simultaneous) symbolic orders does not seem entirely incompatible with Lacanian psychoanalytic theory, Lacan never introduced a different master signifier that would restructure the signifying relations. In response to the problem that Lacan's privileged signifier is strongly associated with masculinity, feminists have alternately invested in the idea of equal (non)access—stressing that "the phallus is what no one can have but everyone wants" (Luepnitz 2003, 226)—and challenged the supremacy of the symbolic in favor of a different register—either that of the imaginary or that of (feminine) jouissance.[4] From queer theory came the impetus to explore the possibilities of multiplying the symbolic order.[5] In protoqueer fashion, Kleist engages in the phallic gesture of employing a master signifier to devise an alternative symbolic but chooses a supposedly female signifier (the breast) while queering its gender connotation (there are aggressive female breast_s and male lactating breast_s in Kleist).[6]

Kleist's texts do not escape or disregard the phallic symbolic system but retain it (somewhat anachronistically, since the symbolic order took a thorough beating in the eighteenth century in favor of the imaginary) by overlaying it with the mammatangential and with what I will call the analexpansive symbolic order. Such a pastiche of old and new has the tendency to dissolve the importance of being earnest in favor of a pleasure and a humor that we will explore further, in the next chapter, under the heading of camp. Kleist's experiments with (dis)organizing the symbolic from the vantage point of the anus function as a supplement to phallocentrism and the mammatangential. They come after or from behind. While the phallus, the breast, and the anus motivate different textual and bodily practices—penetrating, overflowing/emptying out, and opening/tearing—this multiplication of textual gestures produces a mess that bedevils attempts to correlate Kleist's texts coherently to one symbolic order. The layering of different symbolic orders creates a vague or blurry image. This is not to say that each order doesn't strive for supremacy over the others and that within each symbolic order, the privileged signifier doesn't affect mastery, but they each also, in their own way, counteract the fantasy of mastery and intrude on the other orders, partially thwarting them.

Just as Kleist reworks the breast, which modern Western culture idealizes as a figure of (imaginary) plenitude and perfection, into a queer signifier, his version of the anal has little to do with the prevailing Freudian notion of the anally retentive disposition. Kleist's analgrammar does not invest in building more sphincter muscle but rather extends the hole (in being, in the symbolic, in satisfaction), relaxing or tearing the anus. To express this quality, I call it the analexpansive symbolic order. Here anality does not imply obsessive cleanliness, pedantry, parsimony, and ill humor, but rather a tolerance for mess and for the lacerating grammar of coming "from behind." While it does have its moments of aspiring after mastery, control, order, and organization, the Kleistian analexpansive symbolic mostly embraces laxness, confusion, and lapses.

The phallocentric symbolic, which organizes Western modernity, sexualizes language in a particular way. Against all assurances to the contrary, its signs are not strictly arbitrary but are invested with the promise of the one, the right one—the signified that pins down the shifting signifiers, the formulation that establishes transparent communication (see Halle 2004, 15–18; Mieszkowski 2014a). Words produce and respond to this desire—which is, at its base, sexual and sexually normalizing—but no formulation lastingly satisfies it.[7] The medium is indifferent to human heterosexualizing efforts. The phallic order demands binding ties and pledges secure and stable connections by coupling supposedly fixed terms. This is to say, the phallus privileges the statement, claims universality, and appears syntactically as copula. At the same time, it poses a double bind by prohibiting absolute attachment and thus creating the lack that keeps the circulation of signifiers going. Exchange is based on lack. It requires (and thus produces) differences (see Waltz 1993, 98). Sexual difference claims a privileged status as originary difference, in the phallic order. The phallus seizes our bodies and demands identification. Under its regime, you either have a piece of flesh that can rise to the position of the privileged signifier or you don't.[8] The body that doesn't have a penis (the only body part given a temporary visa to the realm of the phallus) is the other of man, the other sex. Members of this sex become objects of exchange rather than its subjects: the traffic in women between men is the result (see Rubin 1975; Sedgwick 1985).

Mammalogic offers a logic of ambivalence that is based on the overlap of incompatible valences—of one and two, of cleaving and cleaving to, of the visual (imaginary) and the linguistic (symbolic), of good and bad, and so on. This logic generates its own syntax—it creates "another chain" of signifiers, which Kleist's characters describe as nourishing, strengthened by emotionality, and as both lighter and stronger than the phallocentric one (*P* 89/15.1832).[9] A strong force of attachment distinguishes this chain: it is made of the emotional, need-based, and desirous attraction to touch the breast, to keep the eyes glued on the breast, to suck and give succor, as well as of the material links that drive the associative logic of metonymic substitution.[10] Breasts cleave to one another across the cleavage of the breast and build rather elaborate and dense textual phenomena (or textual breasts). With the weakening of the symbolic order in the Enlightenment and the French Revolution, the breast is caught by the imaginary (see Yalom 1997, 117: "The iconography of the French Revolution quickly became peopled with bare-breasted women. . . . Countless paintings, engravings, medals, reliefs, and statues transformed the breast into a national icon") and by the new bourgeois system of complementary genders ("with eighteenth-century politics favoring maternal breast-feeding and an exclusively domestic role for women" [ibid., 109]). This makes the use of breast_s as a privileged signifier very difficult and politically fraught because the breast is easily trapped in the complementing role and then phallic ideas about the breast—that is, what the breast means in the phallic order—intrude. Hence the importance of genderqueering breast_s.

The anus is not gendered; it doesn't produce or even register sexual difference. Instead, it calls forth a sexuality that differs from the heteronormative sex that the orders of phallus and breast (to the extent that the breast is trapped by the phallic and thus considered female) underwrite.[11] The symbolic order that the anus arranges ignores the phallic insistence on sexual difference but supports the queering of breast_s in Kleist. While the mammatangential symbolic traverses phallocentrism on the question of gender, analgrammar structures sexual pleasure differently. Analgrammatic sex does not stand in the service of procreation but is seized by a death-driven jouissance. The anus "fucks with the copula"—if I may riff on Edelman's witticism.[12] Doing so, it tears. That is to say, it "tears the fabric of Symbolic reality" by "exposing the latent impropriety informing the structures of the proper, [and by] embedding grammatical violation in the very logic of grammar itself" (Edelman 2004, 25, 133). Rather than binding and fixing, analgrammar dissolves ties and identities—sometimes more playfully than violently. Its mode of the exchange of signifiers does not produce the narrative cohesion of a story line (as in phallocentrism), but rather the jumble of swapping identities, confusion, and contamination.[13] Here exchange cannot be measured and credited to individual accounts, but instead produces a dirty mess that sometimes overlaps with a quasi- or postvirginal (if such a temporality is possible) innocence.[14]

As might already be suggested by the link between jouissance and analgrammar, which I have established using Edelman's quotes, and by the attributes I employed earlier—such as "extending the hole," "relaxation," "tolerance for mess"—the symbolic that is organized around the anus opens onto the real. Given that one of the functions of the symbolic is to protect us from the real, it may be problematic to claim that the anal symbolic order entertains such a strong relation to the real.[15] But Kleist does in fact attempt something more radical than pitching the real against the symbolic and thus reinscribing a binary difference. He creates a symbolic (dis)order that accommodates the real.

The last part of this chapter analyzes Kleist's analgrammar, exploring syntactic and thematic instances of the hole which extends playfully or violently but, in any case, pleasurably. There, we will encounter "coming from behind" and "finding a loophole" as gestures that (dis)organize the symbolic. The first part of this chapter addresses the cleavage of the breast. The signifier is multiply cleaved—as visual and verbal, full and empty, good and bad, as well as open and closed. Sandwiched between those two is a middle part that continues to play with the ambivalence cultivated by mammalogic (between the good and the bad, as well as the open and the closed) while also attending to the overlaps of the three different symbolic orders.

I. Cleavage

The signifier of the breast cleaves human being without drawing clean distinctions. A breast is both one of two (breasts) and one combining two (chest, bosom). Grammatically female in German (*die Brust*), it can refer to male or female anatomy (mammary glands, thorax, pectorals), to any curving shape that presents a front, and to the seat of emotion and thought. Throughout this chapter, "breast" will refer to male or female or indeterminate anatomy in the sense of both bosom and breasts.[16] The breast is one or two: one of two or two in one. To render this slippage between the plural and the singular, I will use, where appropriate, an underscore between the singular and the plural ending, following the custom of the "gender gap" that makes room for undefined genders (AG Feministisch Sprachhandeln der Humboldt-Universität zu Berlin 2014/15, 23–25). Breast_s are differentiated and continuous, certainly contiguous. The breast divides and splits and the breasts in the plural stick to one another and keep the subjects, produced by this symbolic order, attached to breast_s. The breast cleaves (us) and (we) cleave_s to breast_s.

In this first part of the chapter, we will first consider the breast imaginary and the breast symbolic, that is to say, the breast as visual and as verbal signifier. This is followed by an analysis of full speech, which Kleist parodies and thereby, to a certain extent, empties out in his metaleptic scenarios of word become flesh. The middle part will draw on Melanie Klein's theory of the fantasies of the good breast and the bad breast and her psychoanalytic work on aggression and repair.[17] It will also explore the motif of the breast as musical instrument and critically interrogate the ideal of the open breast (or of spontaneous communication) in response to the figure of the glorious and armored breast that the first section of the first part introduces. As my discussion of mammalogic thus comes full circle, it overlaps with the analysis of analgrammar and never neglects to attend to the various ways in which Kleist finds fullness lacking.

Breast Image and Breast Language: Glorious and Overflowing

The breast features in Kleist's works as a privileged, attention-catching, shining image. In this visual function, the breast comes across not so much as erotic or maternal, but as glorious and proud. We find one of the most stunning examples of the glorious breast in *Penthesilea*, when Achilles makes his first appearance—not quite in person yet, but via a vivid description. After the Greeks received reports of his capture by the Amazons and thus feared losing the Trojan War,[18] Achilles (re)appears on the battlefield, and his entrance is drawn out by the lusciously lingering tempo of the description:

> A MYRMIDON (*looking out over the countryside*)
> Look! Rising up above that mountain ridge,
> Is that a head I see, an armored head?
> A helmet, overshadowed [*überschattet*] by plumes?
> The neck that bears the head, the powerful neck?
> The arms, the shoulders dressed in flashing steel?
> The whole shape of the breast, don't you see it, friends,
> Down to the golden belt around his waist?
> (*P* 18/3.356–62, translation altered)

From top to belt, the slowly forming "whole shape of the breast [*das ganze Brustgebild*]" glows with a powerful radiance that stems primarily from Achilles's armor and amplifies his exceptionally strong physique. The glorious breast image here consists in the strong and shining armored breast.

Another image of the proud and glorious breast, which does not rely on metal for its shine, can be found in one of the later scenes of *Katie of Heilbronn*. All eyes are called onto Katie's chest: "Just look at her! Asparkle and agleam! / Like some fair swan with swelling bosom rising, / Fresh from the crystal waters of a lake!" (*K* 240/4.6.2210–12, translation altered). The shining whiteness of the swan symbolizes an immaculate character and the puffed-up chest, with which the swan breasts the waves, signals pride and physical strength.

In both examples the breast is likened to a rising star: the swan Katie twinkles and shines (*funkelt*, *glänzet*) rising (*steigt*) above the horizon of water and Achilles rises above the horizon marked by the ridge—"Just like the sun [in the case of the swan, perhaps the moon] / Rising in splendor on a clear spring day!" (*P* 18/3.368–69). Interestingly, the description of Katie as glorious swan breast comes at a moment when Katie feels decidedly less strong than usual. She emerges from the grotto, where she has been taking a bath, trembling and calling for support: "KATIE (*trembling*): Leonora!" (*K* 240/4.6.2208). In a similar vein, the insistent question marks at the end of almost every line in the description of the rise of Achilles's breast counteract the glory that the image conveys. The breast image gives the appearance of strength, glory, and pride, but this appearance is also shot through with frailty, anxiety, and uncertainty. The darkness from which it emerges remains as a more or less powerful trace on the radiant breast. Such detraction comes not from the outside but is inherent to what constitutes glory to begin with: the plumes, with which Achilles appears, both contribute to and also "overshadow" his luster.

In tandem with these articulations of the fragility of glory, the Kleistian text nevertheless insists (on making believe) that the image of the proud breast can never be sullied. The highest authority—Jupiter himself—declares the image of the radiant breast immune to all assaults:

> JUPITER: Suppose it was a devil last night appeared to you [*dir erschienen*]
> And from the depth of hell he cast over you [*über dich geworfen*],
> Laced with spittle, all the mire of sin,
> With not one spot could he soil the lustre of
> The bosom of my spouse.
>
> (*A* 102/2.5.1282–86, translation altered)

It is as if brilliance itself—even without the metal support—works as an armor that repels all sorts of attacks.

Jupiter's description of Alcmene's abiding luster implicitly presents her breast as a mirror. A mirror remains unaffected by the images that are projected onto it (*über dich geworfen*) or that appear in it (*dir erschienen*). Similarly, Penthesilea refers to the armored breast image as a surface that reflects the glory (or the shortcomings) of the self, when she asks, "Is this the conquering Queen, the fearsome one, / Who's mirrored back . . . / By the steel harness covering his breast?" (*P* 31/5.642–44). The mirror relation sustained by the glorious breast is fraught not so much with illusion and misrecognition as with the structural impossibility of establishing an emotional connection. While Penthesilea and Achilles experience this difficulty to connect, it is perhaps most explicitly thematized in the drama of Jupiter and Alcmene. Jupiter yearns for love: "Ah Alcmene! / Even Olympus is a desert without love" (*A* 108/2.5.1518–19, translation altered), but Alcmene's shining innocence completes her and repels Jupiter. Her breast is whole, and this "whole shape of the breast," which Alcmene presents like Achilles, comes in a perfection that makes everything and everyone else—even Jupiter—bounce off.

This is to say that lack (in the form of the lack of emotional connection) is inscribed in wholeness. Or, to put it in the terms that will guide us through the next section, the breast is not only full and giving but also repellant and therefore lacking. So far we have seen that Kleist's breast imagery can be mapped onto the Lacanian imaginary, in that it produces the ideal of self-sufficiency, purity, and grandeur, but that such perfection is less figured as an illusion than as a liability and a weakness. It is also notable that Kleist's breast image is not marked as female, nor is it gendered in a different way. It remains to be analyzed what constitutes the symbolic from the breast and how it functions.

The beginning of *Katie of Heilbronn* introduces a paradigmatic link between language, the law, and the breast. The first act presents a session of the secret tribunal, or *Vehmgericht*, taking place in a cave. Friedrich Wetter Count vom Strahl appears as defendant, Katie's father Theobald Friedeborn as plaintiff, and Katie as witness. It rather quickly becomes evident that this cave court does not exactly establish a regime of clear-cut distinctions. The participants shift their roles in bewildering ways: the witness barely speaks and moves gradually into the position of the accused, while the defendant, Count vom Strahl, assumes the roles of prosecutor and judge. In the first lines of the play the cave is linked to the chest cavity and we find out that the mission of the *Vehmgericht* is to look for amphibious or ambiguous crime in the breast:

(*An underground cavern, . . . decorated with the insignia of the Vehmgericht . . .*)

COUNT OTTO (*stands up*): We, judges of this high and secret court—God's sentinels on earth . . . whose mission is to uncover crime, wherever it lurks, beyond the reach of worldly justice—like a salamander in the cave of the chest [*in der Höhle der Brust*] . . .

(*K* 163/1.1.1–6, translation altered)

There is a logic to moving the investigation into the interior of the breast, so as to find criminal or sinful ideas that are harbored in the bosom and are not quite existent in exterior, "earthly" reality. But can these ideas be found by way of verbal argumentation? Can words reach them before they have come to light? Is there language in the breast? If Katie's mutism seems to respond in the negative to these questions, this would be in line with postoedipal language skepticism and the idealization of the breast as a prelinguistic space.

With the beginning of the second act, Strahl is released from the chest cavity into the woods. Even if there is something odd about the analogy, his emergence from the cave of the law reads like a birth. The cave as chest cavity overlaps with the cave as womb. Again, clear differences are not maintained and the language of the breast operates with confounding correlations. The newborn Count seems to feel like lingering a bit in the forest of pubic hair rather than going straight into his life:

(*Forest in front of the cavern where the secret court was in session.*)

(*Enter VOM STRAHL, blindfolded, led by two orderlies who remove his blindfold and retire at once into the cavern. VOM STRAHL throws himself on the ground and weeps.*)

VOM STRAHL: Here let me lie down like a shepherd and lament. The sun's ruddy glow still shines through the trunks on which the forest treetops rest. If I get up again after a brief quarter of an hour, soon as the sun has sunk behind the hill . . . , I should be able to reach Castle Strahl before lights out. I want to imagine that my horses down below, where the spring trickles, are sheep and goats, climbing among the rocks and tearing at tufts of grass and bitter shrubs; myself covered in a light linen garment with red sash, while playful breezes flutter about me,

> carrying straight up to the ears of the gods the sighs that well from my grief-laden breast. Really and truly! I shall comb through all my mother tongue [*Muttersprache*] and so thoroughly plunder that whole rich chapter headed "Emotion" that no rhyme-smith of the future will be able to find a new way of expressing his melancholy.
>
> (184/2.1.660–76, translation altered)

The Count sees the light of day ("*led by two orderlies who remove his blindfold*") and covers it right away with a veil of tears. Is this a case of the baby blues? If so, the law of the breast confused the mother's and the infant's feelings. He throws himself on the ground and into the pose of the infant. For a rather precisely measured amount of time ("a brief quarter of an hour"), he allows himself to linger—resting perhaps on the mother's pubic hair like the treetops rest on the tree trunks—with what might be the sight of the vagina (the "ruddy glow still shines through the trunks"), until it closes and disappears behind the mons pubis ("sunk behind the hill"). During this brief quarter of an hour, he imagines himself in paradise, in the pastoral setting of Arcadia: "Here let me lie down like a shepherd." Breast metonymies abound: there is a trickling stream as well as sheep and goats, which are milk-giving animals and which themselves here draw nourishment from boulders that might come in the shape of breasts. Language is explicitly linked to the mother ("mother tongue"), and, rather than being described as a structure of differences, it is imagined here as a collection of positive entities—a physical, book-shaped lexicon that can be opened, leafed through, and plundered. The mother tongue does not just come from the breast, it actually *is* the breast—a treasure chest that the Count wants to "plunder" or "scoop out," as Melanie Klein puts it (1986, 116).[19] Yet the oedipal idealization of the maternal as the land of harmony and plenty is queered not only by the less than nourishing characteristics of "bitter shrubs," which the goats must violently "tear" from the boulder breast, and the not exactly paradisiacal connotations of "lament," "grief," and "plunder," but also by the fact that in the middle of it all lies a lactating man.

Strahl nurses the world with his elegiac poetry: "Playful breezes flutter about me, carrying straight up to the ears of the gods the sighs that well from my grief-laden breast [*die Seufzer, die meiner, von Gram sehr gepreßten, Brust entquillen*]." Sighs belong to the pneumatic order, but *entquillen* (well up) clearly suggests a liquid discharge. We have here another instance of overlapping differences. The Count's lactating breast finds straight access to the gods' ears. The language that comes from the breast thus seems more direct than the language of the phallus, which must rely on representation. His exclamation, "really and truly!," might underscore the direct physical truth of speech from the breast. *Ex negativo*, this point is supported by Alcmene in *Amphitryon* when she implies that what comes from the breast should ring true: "O curse the breast / that gives forth such false tones!" (*A* 131/3.11.2253–54, translation altered).[20] But let's not forget that everything in this pastoral scene plays out in the subjunctive and under the sign of the imagination: "I want to imagine that my horses down below . . . are [*wären*] sheep and goats." Kleist's choice of the word rhyme-smith (*Reimschmied*), to describe his lactating poet, introduces an element of violent cultivation and mechanical blunting into this supposedly effortless harmony with nature. And the fact that the Count can produce scarcely more than the infantile rhyme *Käthchen, Mädchen, Käthchen!* ("Katie, girl—Katie!"), twice repeated (once in the even more inane form "*Käthchen, Käthchen, Käthchen*!"), turns this scene into parody (*K* 184/2.1.687, 185/2.1.690).

The overlap of fullness and loss, which we already registered in the elegiac mode of the newborn, characterizes this breast scene also in the sense that the count serves as a figure of the overfull breast that cannot contain its abundance any longer—the engorged breast that needs relief. The gods are good not because they have the good breast that nourishes, but because they have the good orifice (mouth or ear) willing to receive and to relieve the one who has too much. When Nietzsche later insists that exuberance and overabundance contribute to the will to power and that the wish, even the need to spend wealth distinguishes the Übermensch, this is received as a novel and counterintuitive thought. But Nietzsche's thought relies on a historically well-established hydraulics of the body as a system that depends on keeping all its elements in flux. Within an economy that demands uninterrupted flow, congestion—for example the accumulation of milk in the breast and the swelling of the breast—registers as injurious and painful. It makes for, as *Penthesilea* has it, "a woman hampered by full breasts" (*P* 94/15.1981).

Several scholars have shown that the economy of uninterrupted flow was in the eighteenth century relegated to the female sex.[21] Premodern medicine relied on an economy of fluidity for all bodies and recommended regular purging of fluids, notably in the form of bloodletting, so as to keep the bodily economy liquid. Beginning in the eighteenth century, the male body (as distinct from the female body) is thought of in terms of an economy of containment (where bodily fluids, especially the most precious semen, must be accumulated rather than wasted) (see Laqueur 2003, 194–97). For better or worse, women are largely exempt from this capitalist medical and moral regime. A new gender and sex asymmetry is introduced, where only women are seen as weak—weak when too full and weak when generous (according to the newly ruling economy of self-interest)—while men are perceived as strong and solid and as growing stronger the less they expend, the more smartly they invest, and the more they accumulate.

Kleist gives us many images of the overfull, the engorged, and the bursting breast. Characters with these breasts are usually addressed with the equally pervasive demand to contain or compose themselves: *fasse dich* (for example, *P* 14.1585 or *PH* 3.5.1006). Kleist's bursting breasts are usually male and thus present a queer twist on what the eighteenth century defined as a female problem.[22] In the scene we just analyzed, Strahl daydreams of being clad in light linens only, whereas normally he has to walk around in heavy armor. While the armor offers material support for male containment, it makes relieving the engorged maternal breast excruciatingly difficult. Thus, at the core of the count's dream that his breast discharge is whisked straight away (*gradaus*) might lie the wish for relief rather than the fantasy of direct communication. The need for relief is not to be taken lightly, especially since, as we have heard in the first act, the maternal breast can build up enough force to destroy the armored breast: it literally burst the Count's armor and the armorer, Katie's father Theobald, had to repair his breastplate.

Theobald misinterprets the burst breastplate as a sign of the Count's ability to protect the borders of the county as an agent of containment and completion: "'Well,' says I, 'if your breast bursts your armor like that, the Count Palatine will leave our walls intact!' " (*K* 166/1.1147–48, translation altered). Theobald feels that this outburst will ward off a burst-in. He doesn't realize that a different version of the abundant breast is at work here—not the glorious strength that characterizes the breast imaginary but the incontrollable overflow that (dis)organizes the mother tongue or maternal breast symbolic. The maternal breast destroys the knightly armor (and might not stop in front of the ramparts). Such destruction happens in this particular moment most likely because of the Count's unwitting proximity to his portended beloved. Katie calls forth the maternal breast in Strahl. In her vicinity, the glorious picture of a breast, the radiance (*Strahl*) of the Count, turns into a squirt (*Strahl*) of milk forcefully escaping his engorged breasts. Despite Theobald's physical and ideological labor to reinforce containment, the armored knight subtly changes into the nursing mother even in Theobald's own account:

> THEOBALD: "There we are, Master Knight!" says I. "Now you're fit to meet the Count Palatine. Plates all safely back. Next time your heart won't blow them apart!" The Count stands up, looks thoughtfully at the girl—who reaches scarce higher than his chest cavity [*Brusthöhle*]—up and down from top to toe, bows, kisses her on the forehead and says: "God bless and keep you and His peace be upon you, amen!"
>
> (*K* 167/1.1.174–80, translation altered)

Strahl's gesture of bending over the child whose head is close to his breast echoes his mother's gesture when he is critically ill: "The Countess bent over him and raised his head to her breast" (*K* 201/2.9.1204–5) (see Cavarero 2013). Count Wetter vom Strahl's blessing of Katie returns us to the pastoral version of the maternal.

Interestingly, Kleist omits the line "May the Lord make his face to shine upon you" from the traditional blessing.[23] His queer dyad does without the gaze of the third, the transcendental father. And the Count's chest cavity harbors the salamander (*Molch*), that is to say, his breast serves as a signifier that amphibiously, ambiguously oscillates from one version of the breast to another. Admittedly, nobody would characterize the Count as particularly caring. His fits of anger—during which he hits and kicks Katie and lashes out with a whip—strongly contradict the image of a maternal *Strahl*. But our analysis has shown that the Count has a tendency to move into the maternal position. Then a struggle ensues between the mother tongue and the armored breast image. This struggle produces explosions, bursts, and outbursts. The Count's moodiness, the atmospheric vicissitudes that are inscribed in his name (*Wetter* means "weather") and that make him fulminate (*wettern*), the ambiguous connotations of the *Strahl* in his title (shine and fluid), come with the fact that he must somehow manage to be two—"I am double! [*Ich bin doppelt!*]" (*K* 237/4.2.2144, translation altered). He is both the maternal breast and the glorious breast, the breast language and the breast image, the ever-changing breast (that swells, explodes, bends, and droops) and the perfectly round solid breast.[24] The Count doesn't integrate these two versions of the breast. He has a temper because he struggles to respond to two very different regimes. His nonidentity comes across as emotionality. The breast organizes a structure of amphibious-ambiguous differences and an imaginary without the judgment of the transcendental gaze. Both the imaginary and the symbolic drawn from the breast constitute orders that differ from those organized by the phallus.

Full Breast Speech Emptied

We have begun to see in the previous section that Kleist explores the possibilities of a symbolic drawn from the breast. While this mammalogic operates with abundance instead of rigor, overlaps instead of distinctions, and presence instead of deferral, we have also already noticed that Kleistian fullness includes lack, loss, and emptiness. I have proposed the notion that Kleist launches a mamma-tangential symbolic order—a logic that cuts through the idealization of the breast as a symbol for fullness. In this section, I will build on my discussion of metalepsis in chapter 1. As I elaborated there, the minor and rather disreputable rhetorical figure of metalepsis involves the ontological merging of the figurative and the literal. Metalepsis plays an important role in Kleist's language from the breast, which is characterized by excessive and deviant literality. Completing the analysis begun in chapter 1 with the discussion of prosopopeic literalization, I will analyze two further modes of parodic fullness or metalepsis found in Kleist's text (a): hypotypotic text swell and (b) metapenetrative speech.

Hypotypotic Text Swell

There are pockets of hypotypotic speech that function like breasts in Kleist's text. Kleist frequently uses narrative hypotyposis—description that creates a vivid scene with words—in his plays and often they are powerful enough to fix the inner gaze at the expense of the action in front of the eyes. Hypotyposis derives from the breast its power to attract the gaze. As Simon Richter demonstrates, the maternal and erotic breast absorbs our attention with unquestionable force. As soon as it appears, we are transfixed. We cleave to the full breast with our eyes and—if at all permissible—with our touch. Evoking this apodictic presence, Kleist builds textual breasts and quasi-haptic opportunities by thickening the materiality of language.[25]

Let us consider two examples from different plays. In both cases, the textual breasts present a distraction, a detour—one could even say, a debauch—from a particularly rapid plot development and great intradiegetic urgency of action. Both passages mimic the breast textually while also referring to a breast; they thus mix linguistic modes and redouble the appearance of breast_s to the point of almost overdoing it. The first comes at the beginning of the ninth scene of *Penthesilea*, after Achilles has crashed with his lance into Penthesilea's breast and then torn his armor from his own breast, allowing Prothoë to snatch the severely wounded Queen from his arms:

> PROTHOË: My love! We all implore you—
> MEROË: Listen, please!
> PROTHOË: He's close upon your heels, the Peleid;
> If your life's dear to you at all, then flee!
> PENTHESILEA: This bosom, Prothoë, how could he strike it,
> So shattering a blow?—As if I were
> To smash a lyre because the night wind stirred it
> My name to whisper softly to itself.
> I'd nestle between the great bear's paws,
> And stroke the panther's fur, that came to me
> With such emotion as I brought to him.
> MEROË: You won't escape, then?
> PROTHOË: You refuse to flee?
> (*P* 54/9.1174–84)

The situation calls for flight; its extreme urgency is palpable in the hemistichomythies between Meroë and Prothoë. But Penthesilea lingers in description. She paints an orphic scene where wild animals are tamed with music from the breast.[26] Her elaborate comparisons and convoluted syntax make curls and folds, creating a rounded breast that counteracts the forward press of time suggested by her sisters. Enveloping Penthesilea's speech with their chiasmatic hemistichomythies, even Prothoë and Meroë contribute to the creation of the breast swell and give the impression that each of them wants to hug the breast. Penthesilea's speech compels both visually (captivating the imagination) and haptically (with its texture). Her sisters model the irresistible urge to touch the breast. With what Richter (2014, 111) calls its "sheer apodictic and all-consuming presence," the breast holds our attention and distracts from the issue at hand (namely that Achilles is approaching). We cleave to the breast.

Homburg calls on the powerful presence of the (textual) breast in the conversion scene at the beginning of the third act of *Prince Frederick of Homburg*. In this scene, we are witnessing the slow process of the Prince's turn from trust (in the Elector's clemency) to despair (in the face of his severe punishment). When he is finally willing to hear from his friend Hohenzollern that the Elector is about to sign his death sentence, he still keeps full realization in suspension and plays for time while looking at and embracing the breast he creates for himself with hypotypotic speech:

> Could he—no!—turn [*wälzen*] such atrocious
> Resolutions in his breast [*Busen*]?
> For a flaw upon the diamond just received,
> A flaw that's barely visible with spectacles,
> To have the donor trampled in the dust?
> A deed that purges white the Algerian Dey,
> Adorns Sardanapalus with shining silver wings,
> All cherub-like, and, as if innocent,
> Cradles in God's right hand all Roman tyrants
> Like babes who've perished at their mother's breasts [*Mutterbusen*]?
> (*PH* 307/3.1.897–907, translation altered)

The Prince's flowery language forms a textual breast rounding out in the triple hyperbole of the Algerian Dey, Sardanapalus, and the Roman tyrants. The image of the glorious breast is also evoked three times—by the brilliance of the diamond, and by the signifiers "white" (*weiß*) and "shining silver" (*silberglänzig*). The Prince seems to be trying to call into being a nurturing and protective breast to ward off the despair into which he feels himself plunging. The signifier *Busen* (breast) appears twice, the second time explicitly as maternal (*Mutterbusen*) and the first time implicitly and figuratively—as a bosom that nurses resolutions. The doubled signifiers hug the textual breast that the hypotyposis causes to swell, but they also slightly cut into its tissue by their placement in its second and second-to-last line—a first hint of violence.

Homburg is unable to protect the breast, which he needs to protect him, from becoming a harbinger of death. The diamond shows a blemish, even if it is minuscule. Inadvertently, the Prince builds the breast by accumulating figures that stand for extreme violence—the Dey, a military dictator; Sardanapel, the Assyrian king of the seventh century BCE, known for his brutal politics of oppression; the Roman tyrants, infamous for their cruelty. All of them would look innocent compared to the Elector, if the Elector really executed the "atrocious [*ungeheure*] resolutions" he pores over in his breast, rolls with, and wallows in (*wälzen* has strong physical connotations that afford opportunities for extensive touch). The image of the children who die at their mother's breast serves as an allegory for innocence—until one begins to wonder whether it is the breast that kills them. The thought of the deadly mama trickles in.

This thought doesn't quite reach Homburg. Now in despair, he runs straight to mom—the wife of the Elector, who scolds him for his lack of composure. His approach and address claims her as a mother, in fact, generates her as such—at least for the audience, who only now finds out that she has promised his dying birth mother that she would care for him as for a son. The Prince continues to linguistically create a nurturing breast—with waning strength, it seems, as this one is smaller:

> O my mother!
> . . . .
> O let me clasp your knees, mother!
> . . . .
> O my mother . . .
> . . . .
> You appear [*scheinst*] with heavenly powers, to save,
> You to me, the Princess, your ladies, endowed,
> To me the whole world around you, the menial in your baggage train
>   I could,
> The lowest, who tends your horses,
> Hung about the neck implore: save me!
> (*PH* 309–10/3.5.965–66; 971; 973–77; my translation)

The capital letter O appears by itself three times in rapid succession to paint the round breast. The lips, pursed to make the sound *o*, are ready to receive the nipple. Alliteration affords aural pleasure, and the repeated alliteration on *m*—"my mother [*meine Mutter*]"—also expresses oral satisfaction (in German, as in English, the *m* sound works like "yum"). With the overdetermined phrase *du scheinst* ("you appear," which means "you seem" but can also mean "you shine") the Prince launches into hypotyposis. What follows makes the mother appear; it produces a shining image of the mother in words. In addition to offering rich, vivid, picturesque language, the sentence syntactically forms a breast. Each insertion—and there are many in this one sentence—curves the syntax and contributes to the fullness and density of the breast. The repeated evocations of female and maternal figures ("mother," "Princess," "ladies") and of gestures of maternal intimacy ("tends" and "hung about the neck") paint a scene of physical proximity to the breast and build the texture of the linguistic breast. The kernel of intimacy—"you to me [*Du mir*]"—can be found somewhere in the middle. It is charged by the glorification of the "you"—"you shine with heavenly powers"—and intensified by a first syntactic curlicue in the form of an insertion—"to save." This tight roundness opens when the depiction and scope of the motherly is extended to the Princess, to the Electress's female entourage, to the whole world around the Electress (*Alles rings umher*), to her baggage train, to the lowest of her servants, and to the horses. With the menial of the baggage train (*Troßknecht*) the image of the mother takes a queer turn. It blends the female with the male (*Knecht* refers to a male servant), the maternal with the military (*Troß* is used only in the military context), and the most exalted ("heavenly powers") with "the lowest."[27] Everything gets syntactically squeezed and visually focused into the image of a child hanging around the mother's neck—until the sentence-breast squirts: "Save me!" With his speech, the Prince has produced a little jet of saving milk.

Instead of expressing the Prince's psychological state, the sentence affects its speaker. Not quite on purpose but with the awareness of a sleepwalker, he puts before his eyes and in his mouth an object that gives comfort.[28] The act of creating this hypotypotic text swell is reparative in Klein's sense of repairing in fantasy what aggressive fantasies have destroyed. Sedgwick (1997, 150) points to the mutual effect of repair when she clarifies in her seminal essay "Paranoid Reading and Reparative Reading" that the "reparative impulse . . . is additive and accretive. . . . It wants to assemble and confer plenitude on an object that will then have resources to offer to an inchoate self." The breast sentence saves the Prince.[29] Beyond plenitude, the breast provides him with a much needed detour. The swelling of the sentence into a breast (curling in phrase-lump after phrase-lump) offers relief from all-too-straightforward subjective purpose. The syntactic object and the hypotypotic scene cover again the abyss that opened when the Prince, on the way to the Electress, stared into his own grave. It disperses the speaker's attention, which would otherwise be fixed directly on death. With their roundness, roundaboutness and density, hypotypotic text breasts escape urgency even in the most urgent situations.

Yet attention to the incongruence of the textual material saves readers from facile or ideological notions about the fullness of speech. The O is full and empty at the same time. Death resonates even where language seems closest to the breast. Clinging to the world in all its richness, somebody—the "me," the Prince, or the menial—is already executed: "hung" by the neck. Fullness overlaps with emptiness and death with life in the emotional, overdetermined, dense tissue of this linguistic breast.

Metapenetrative Speech

Alongside the hypotypotic text swell analyzed in the previous section and the prosopopeic literalization discussed in the section on metalepsis in chapter 1, Kleist makes use of one further metaleptic figure of parodic fullness: metapenetrative speech. By penetrative speech, I mean a speech act that is felicitous in that it hits the mark and moves the interlocutor—an instance of words changing minds. Its effect makes it an example of full speech. Kleist undermines such fullness by doubling the performative with its description. He usually has his characters describe penetrative speech as cutting into the breast, thus highlighting the wounding aspect of such felicitous speech while also ironizing the authenticating role of the breast. The Kleistian use of the figure is metaleptic because the description renders literal the topos of penetrative speech (*treffende Rede*). One could also say that it inverts the usual procedure of metalepsis in that Kleist, instead of collapsing ontological levels, has an additional level of commentary grow out of his character's speech. Thus adding the metaperspective to the performance, Kleist introduces an element of parody right from the start. For example, on their way to the Ursuline cloister, Katie says to her father Theobald:

> (*Likewise lying down in front of him*) Oh, God in the highest! You're destroying me! Your words cut into my breast like knives! I don't want to enter the convent anymore! I'll go home to Heilbronn with you, forget the Count and marry anyone you like—even if my bridal bed be a grave eight feet deep! (*K* 210–11/3.1.1488–94)

Katie describes Theobald's words as knifes that cut into her breast and destroy her. According to her, his speech kills. But, unlike Penthesilea's suicidal speech act that fully crosses over into the literal, Katie remains in the realm of the figurative with the simile she employs: "like knives [*wie Messer*]."[30] The lethal effect she describes is trivialized by her inflationary use of this assessment. Everything that comes from her father seems to "kill" Katie: going back to Heilbronn with him and following his orders also promises to land her in the grave. Katie here comes across as an exaggerating, rebellious, but not exactly serious teenager. She feels the pain of a cross-shaped cut in her breast and is moved to abandon her plan to join the Ursulines. Thus renouncing the saint who was martyred for refusing an arranged marriage, she resigns herself to marry whomever her father wants her to.[31] But is she moved by Theobald's words? Her response is rather incongruous with the proposal he just made that she should personally plead with the Count to allow her to live in his vicinity. Theobald's speech cannot really serve as an example of penetrative speech, even though Katie describes it as such. With the incongruous, hyperbolic, and inflationary commentary by one of his characters, Kleist gives the twist of parody to his language skepticism, which in his early letters he had still expressed in the melodramatic mode.[32]

The scene also involves physical comedy: in his effort to lend credence to his proposal, Theobald enacts his plea to the Count by prostrating himself before Katie—"I'll lie down in front of him, as I now do before you, and I'll say: 'My noble lord . . .'" (*K* 210/3.1.1480–81). As if embarrassed by this gesture, she prostrates herself before him (as the stage directions indicate, *K* 210/3.1.1488). Now they both lie flat. The drama of her sudden conversion and the physical effect words can have is parodied by the silly choreography of two speaking bodies belly-down on the stage floor.

There are other descriptions of speech as penetrative that seem more serious. In *Prince Frederick of Homburg*, for example, Hohenzollern attempts to change the Elector's mind and ends his argument with, "I'm convinced / My words have fallen heavy into your breast [*in deine Brust*]!" (*PH* 335/5.5.1721–22, translation altered). Rather than describing penetrative speech, Hohenzollern here attempts to declare his speech penetrative. He thus engages in a speech act of the second order—a speech act that calls a speech act into existence. Whether the Elector is indeed moved by this redoubled effort is hard to say but remains doubtful considering that he holds all the strings in this marionette theater.

In an earlier scene, Homburg uses the same image of the weight that falls into the breast. On learning that the Elector has fallen, the Prince and the Princess console one another and almost inadvertently slip into a lyrical scene with mutual declaration of love. When their tête-à-tête is interrupted by the update that the Elector remains in fact alive, Homburg warns the messenger, "Like gold, your word falls heavy into my breast [*in meine Brust*]!" (*PH* 297/2.8.638, translation altered). In this case it seems certain that the words hit the mark, but whether they produce joy or disappointment is hard to tell, despite the positive connotations of gold. Kleist's descriptions and metaperformative declarations of penetrative speech acts retain an air of ambiguity, uncertainty, and comedy.

II. Mackled Symbolics

Good and Bad: Pierced Breasts

We will now shift from the rhetorical account of penetrative speech to a more psychoanalytic account of breast penetration and breast laceration. The gestures of penetrating and tearing belong to the orders established by the phallus and the anus, respectively. While none of the symbolic orders Kleist experiments with ever apply in their pure, unadulterated form, the following two sections will require us to pay even more attention to the overlap of symbolic orders and the intrusion of one into another. In particular, we will see that mammalogic defends itself against the false image that the phallic order has of the breast by employing the gestures typical of the analexpansive order: opening and tearing.

Aggression that targets the breast, the pleasure that this aggression affords, as well as anxiety about such pleasure are feelings Melanie Klein explored in her reorientation of psychoanalysis around the breast_s. Klein recognized sadistic trends in the earliest stages of infancy.[33] According to her, the suckling infant's aggressive fantasies don't wait for the teeth to come.[34] Before biting the breast becomes possible, "the oral impulse to suck dry, bite up, scoop out and rob the mother's body of its good contents" are alive and strong (Klein 1986, 183).

Kleist offers such a fantasy, launched in rage at Jupiter by an adult but existentially threatened Amphitryon:

> And, like a wasp, I press the sting
> Into his breast, sucking empty, so that the wind
> Will play with his dry bones to my contentment.
> (*A* 122/3.5.1952–55, my translation)

The phrase "sucking empty" (*aussaugend*) is placed right in the middle of this textual and hypotypotic breast—applied at its nipple, as it were. It is offset from the rest by two commas and endowed with intensified presence by the continuous tense. The sucking is clearly pleasurable and could go on forever, were it not for the asymmetric power relation between the mortal Amphitryon and the god Jupiter. This asymmetry echoes the one between infant and mother. The infant presumably feels at the whim of the breast whose appearance or disappearance lies beyond its control. At random intervals Jupiter challenges Amphitryon's social status and existence. As the only available recourse in these situations of powerlessness, fantasy offers delusions of grandeur: Amphitryon will turn the Father of Gods and Men into meager bits of matter exposed to the whim of the elements; the infant will suck the breast completely dry.

Stung by the desire for revenge, Amphitryon grows a fantasy sting that penetrates the breast and sucks it empty. This most explicit example of the fantasy of sucking dry targets a male breast. Kleist knows no gender difference when it comes to the attribution of breast and phallus—women routinely wield the phallus in his plays (not only in *Penthesilea*), while men commonly lactate.

Klein observes that, in the first few months of its life, the infant experiences uncoordinated feelings of satisfaction and frustration stirred by unrelated appearances of what Klein terms "the good breast" and "the bad breast." Later, this uncoordinated commotion begins to coagulate into a more consistent feeling of self and an understanding of the object as "a whole"—that is, as a person who cannot always gratify the infant's wishes. With this new apprehension of the caregiver as a person and not just a (dis)appearing breast, the infant develops love, but at the same time the infant's hate and sadism reach their peak (Klein 1986, 141). The coincidence might be arbitrary: in other words, there may not be a causal connection between the development of a more unified sense of self and other, and the intensity of hate and fantasized attacks on the object world, but the infant certainly tortures itself with blame, regret, and fear. It is shattered by terrible internal conflicts at the same time that it begins to form a coherent self and a coherent sense of the other (124). Subject formation and dissolution co-occur, and love encompasses its own opposite, including anxiety, guilt, and sadness.[35] Klein's take on the constitution of subject and object via shattering begins with the infant's relation to the breast, and Kleist dramatizes this struggle with psychic ambivalence in many of his characters.

Let's turn to the second scene in the first act of *The Battle of Herrmann*, where Thusnelda, Herrmann's wife, introduces the Roman deputy Ventidius to the Germanic chieftains. For political reasons, Thusnelda and Ventidius want to flatter each other. They give one another credit for the killing of a wild aurochs, each attributing the phallus to the other. But the terms in which this flattery is produced hark back to the level of oral-sadistic relations to the maternal breast. First, his privy scribe Scäpio manages to devise a compliment that doubles as a scene of revenge and allows Ventidius to work out his hatred, fear, and guilt ("you" refers here to Thusnelda):

> SCÄPIO: You must have a heart as hard as Parian marble,
> For I felt that the black knight of death had descended
> When the beast bowed its head, and bent on vengeance,
> With its horns set on the breast,
> Came charging towards you.
> But you remained motionless, not even flinching.
> What can I say? Worry [*Sorg*] did not for one instant
> Cloud the fair firmament of your countenance!
> (*BH* 8/1.2.96–103)

During a hunting expedition gone awry, the human and the wild animal literally switched places—as they do so often in Kleist—and the wounded aurochs charged toward Thusnelda. The hyperbolic tone of Scäpio's description does not seem to be fully accounted for by flattery. Instead, the scene appears charged with an enigmatic excess of meaning. The signifier "breast," located in an exposed position at the end of the line (*mit auf die Brust / Gesetzten Hörnern*), and the anthropomorphic attribution of vengeance to the animal reveal this scene as an oral-sadistic fantasy. While the Romans are the invaders on the level of the plot, they apparently feel in the inverse position on the level of fantasy: a powerless infant at the whim of the mother's breast. Such helplessness warrants revenge—at least according to the rationale that protects the ego from (and simultaneously involves it in) the hatred of the id.[36]

With his artful composition, the scribe allows the Romans to indulge in the fantasy of revenge via the incidence with the aurochs while he exculpates them by projecting the aggression onto "the beast [*Untier*]." In a feat even more salutary to the Roman psyche, Scäpio paints an image of an indestructible breast.[37] No matter how violent the infant's sadistic fits, the mother will not withdraw her love; she will not even worry about the fits—"Worry [*Sorg*] did not for one instant / Cloud the fair firmament of your countenance!" The beast may rage, but the wife of the Cheruscan chief by no means behaves like the hunted animal or the victim. She doesn't yield and doesn't waver but remains present—good mother and good breast.

After this "experience"—the exculpatory and reparative effect of which is topped off by Thusnelda professing that Ventidius saved her from rather than attacked her as the aurochs[38]—Ventidius is ready again to receive the good breast: he can ask for a token of love:

> VENTIDIUS: give my breast
> A token, it doesn't matter what,
> Of the feeling that I inflamed in you!
> . . . .
> Let it be the posy that adorns your breast,
> Or this ribbon, or this lock of golden hair.
> Yes, Your Highness, let it be the lock of hair!
> (*BH* 26/2.5.559–65, translation altered)

The sign (*Zeichen*) is arbitrary—it could be anything: posy, ribbon, lock of hair, "it doesn't matter"—but only as long as it comes from the metonymic realm of the breast.[39] The posy is explicitly attached to Thusnelda's bosom, and ribbon and lock are found nearby. What is more, Ventidius asks not for a symbol that will help his mind to remember or refer to her but for a token he can press against his breast: "Give my breast a token [*meiner Brust ein Zeichen*]." He wants a sign that comes from her breast and goes to his breast. The good breast can speak a good language: a nourishing breast language that transfers material signs directly from one breast to another.

We have encountered this direct language in the guise of penetrative speech in the previous section. And indeed, beyond the desire to hug and squeeze the sign (for the feeling of love), Ventidius expresses the wish for a love that penetrates the breast. While he here assumes that he "inflamed [*entflammt*]" a feeling in Thusnelda, he described his own breast a moment earlier as streamed through by a ray of delight:

> VENTIDIUS: My queen, I count myself blessed
> To have elicited this emotion from you!
> An almost unbearable ray [*Strahl*] of ecstasy
> Streams through me, paralyzing all my limbs
> And piercing my enraptured breast[.]
> (*BH* 26/2.5.547–51, translation altered)

Strahl refers to liquid and to light or fire. The ambiguity of the word takes the edge off the breach, but some fiery sting must have penetrated Ventidius's breast, and his description of its effect as "unbearable" and "paralyzing" does suggest cruelty. Thusnelda's milk or the feeling that he was able to draw from her breast, which now streams through his body, is poisonous. He is numbed, and at the same time his blood is stirred by a ray of light from the flames he imagines burning in Thusnelda: a scene of mutual penetration. The rhetorical register of penetrative speech is here twisted together with the psychical register of the need to invert the sadistic attacks on the breast. Via anxiety, remorse, and responsibility, the earlier sadistic attacks generate a desire to be pierced in the breast.

In the end, Ventidius quite literally gets what he wants. He becomes the target of Thusnelda's cruelty. Via the she-bear, Thusnelda pierces Ventidius's breast—"She is sinking her claws into my soft chest" (*BH* 111/5.18.2413). From wounded aurochs to famished bear, the circle of projective fantasies (with existential consequences) closes between them. The aurochs doubles the bear as the anus (that tears) doubles the breast (that gloriously withstands all paranoid attacks). Ventidius asked for a physical sign that communicates directly with his heart and he receives claws in his breast. Did he mean "give my breast a sign" in such a crude physical sense? Perhaps. In any case, Kleist's literalization, quite counterintuitively, counteracts the integrity of the breast.

There are many attacks on the breast in Kleist's text. Done by various means and with all sorts of weapons, they usually play out between parent and child (even if the parent-child relation is hidden behind the façade of an erotic love relation),[40] but the parent involved does not have to be the mother. Kleist gives us many examples of lactating male breasts and frustrated attacks against the bad paternal breast as well as inverted attacks that pierce the child's breast. For example, Kleist's first play, *The Schroffenstein Family*, ends in a curious constellation: two lovers dead (Agnes and Ottokar) with breasts pierced not by their own or one another's hand but by their own fathers, each of whom mistook his child for the child of the feud. The structure of the foursome queers the heterosexual couple. According to Ottokar, the cross-dressing of Agnes and Ottokar "succeeded"—they pass (*S* 569/5.2.2558). Their gender identities are exchanged and confounded in the (deadly) mediation of their intimacy by their fathers, which queers the role of the father, in turn. Instead of the law of exogamous heterosexuality, the father's phallus—his sword—establishes (and immobilizes in death) the gender-swapping in this near-incestuous relationship.[41] And below the oedipal level, we find the sadomasochistic relation to the breast—queer again—as a relation to the father's breast. As between Amphitryon and Jupiter or Homburg and the Elector, the sadomasochistic fantasy of the pierced breast plays itself out between father figure and child.[42] The foursome allows for but muddles the distribution of ambivalent feelings, of hate and love. Rupert loves his son Ottokar and pushes his sword into Ottokar's breast aiming at Agnes (or, rather, her father). Sylvester loves his daughter Agnes and pushes Ottokar's sword into her breast while aiming at Ottokar (whom he takes to be her killer).

We must assume that such incidences of the father (inadvertently) stabbing his child presuppose the child's attack (in fantasy) on the father's breast, and serve as more or less realized fantasies of revenge or punishment, and as (perhaps misguided) attempts to repair the paternal breast.[43] Unresolved infantile sadism abounds in the Schroffenstein family, made evident from the beginning by the fact that the plot is driven by extreme paranoia—most notably in the house of Rossitz, where every incident is interpreted as persecution.[44] The tragic ending of *The Schroffenstein Family* constitutes, in Kleinian terms, an advance from the more basic paranoid position to the more developed depressive position (which involves the ability to love but faces the difficulty of ambivalence). In queer terms, it constitutes the closure of and a departure from the morbid model of the heteronormative family: the two families of the clan have killed their entire offspring.[45]

Indeed, the tragic ending involves an insight or anagnorisis and thus progress. But the anagnorisis is also multiplied and mackled by the queer structure of repetition compulsion and the pleasurable insistence of the (death) drive that informs what we still have to elaborate under the heading of analgrammar. The fourfold constellation of the double murder based on mistaken identities replicates the scenes of recognition:

> AGNES: Where art thou, Ottokar?—A sword—in the breast—my God!
> Redeemer of the world! My Ottokar!
> (*She falls upon him.*)
> OTTOKAR: It—
> Succeeded.—Agnes, flee!! (*Dies.*)
> (*S* 569/5.1.2556–58, translation altered)

> SYLVIUS (*touching the body*): A sword—in the breast—of a corpse.
> (*S* 572/5.1.2644, translation altered)
> RUPERT (*looks again at the body and tears his hair*): I myself! I myself!
> Twice driven through the breast! Twice the breast.
> (*S* 578/5.1.2678f, translation altered)

Anagnorisis again and again. The moment of acute and painful discovery—the change of heart—is replicated, the breast torn into several such moments or several changes of breast. The first two quotes syntactically render the tearing of breasts and thus textually proliferate breasts: "A sword—in the breast—my God!" and "A sword—in the breast—of a corpse.—" Two times we have here the queer cleavage of three breasts, marked by dashes. Such amplifying erosion of the conventionally singular turning point of recognition brings to excess the oscillation between singleness and doubleness that is characteristic of breast_s. We have termed "cleavage" this propensity toward self-differentiation that distinguishes mammalogic, and we find it syntactically performed in the third quotation by the doubling of the reference to the singular "I" ("I myself! I myself!"), as well as in the doubling of the phrase "twice the breast" (*Zweimal die Brust durchbohrt! Zweimal die Brust*), which raises the power of duplication to a particularly eerie degree.

When Sylvius, the father of Sylvester, repeats Agnes's line and changes her apostrophe (of the Redeemer, with implied resurrection) to a diagnosis (of a dead body), he seals Ottokar's failure to transform through sacrifice into a savior. Ottokar's death does not save Agnes, nor is he resurrected. Nevertheless, his verdict "It— / Succeeded [*Es ist— / Gelungen*]"—which echoes Jesus's words on the cross—holds true with regard to the couple's transgender performance.[46] Because of Ottokar's failure, Agnes does not remain fixed in the feminine role of the passively saved but can fail on her own.

When a fifth party, the grandfather, is added to the foursome, the element of touch is introduced. It reduces the field of mediations (via gazes, clothes, and swords) to an immediacy—a touch of the breast—that brings out the truth and eventually reconciles.[47] But it wouldn't be Kleist if the healing power of the breast weren't parodied once again by the overly tangible presence of a little body part. A boy's finger literally gets thrown into the mix: "URSULA: Here *is* the finger of the child! (*Throws the finger into the middle of the stage and disappears.*) / ALL: What's that we saw?" (*S* 574/5.1.2680f). In the end, a little quasi-penis heals the family feud. But it does so not as symbol or privileged signifier. The little finger does not stand for intellectual prowess, discovery, or recognition. It does not stand for anything—its sheer presence is enough ("is" is italicized in the original). To exercise its healing powers, it has to be physically included in the stew of evidence, just as Ursula would have added it to her witches' brew (*S* 551/4.3.2190–94). Kleist queers the father and the phallus by way of regress to the physical condition of the infant and parodies at the same time the idea of undifferentiated presence that is traditionally, within the phallic order, associated with the psychic condition of the mother-infant dyad governed by the maternal breast.

Open Breasts Closed

By way of violently pierced breasts and the ideal of direct communication, we have arrived now at the notion of a breast that is open: open to the other, open to the elements, and also—and this reintroduces ambiguity—open to being played, both as a musical instrument (or a communication device) and in the sense of "being taken advantage of." In this section, I will discuss how Kleist resists and troubles the phallocentric ideal of direct breast communication, of an understanding that comes from the heart, of a symbiosis between mother and nursling and a maternal sensibility for the beloved's needs and wishes. As usual, we will see that for Kleist what I just called maternal doesn't coincide with the female.

Let's begin with an inoffensive take on the open breast, one that leaves its physical constitution intact but furnishes the signifier that interests us here.

The Prince of Homburg is introduced via the stage directions to the first scene of the eponymous play as sitting with "open breast [*offner Brust*], half-awake, half-asleep, . . . under an oak tree, weaving himself a wreath" (*PH* 271/1.1). More than an unbuttoned shirt, this means that the Prince experiences an altered state, which, with him, is in fact a character trait: he remains unusually receptive throughout the play even as his eyes are closed to much important information (most notably the plan of action for the battle against the Swedes, and the reason for his detention). The Prince hovers between sleep and wakefulness and hangs poised between chestiness (the Prince indulges in self-idealizations and weaves a wreath or crown for himself) and vulnerability (as the ensuing scene shows, the Prince is easily played).[48] The drama shows Homburg as fatally open and responsive to every sign of love or recognition he receives (or anticipates) from his father figure, the Elector, and the Elector's proxies, his wife, who serves as a mother figure for the Prince, and his niece Natalie, whom the Prince wishes to marry.

The Prince's open breast mirrors the open grave that affects him so strongly. The two open bodies communicate: via a direct connection from open breast to open breast. Or, since the grave is meant for the Prince, we might say that his breast communicates with itself and becomes terrified by its own openness. Thus, he revolves around himself after all. This becomes further evident when he remains unable even to register the extraordinary courage and active support of Princess Natalie, who not only disregards the Elector's order (as the Prince did) but also fabricates an order from the Elector to move her regiment on site to support a possible insurrection against the Elector and in favor of the Prince (act 4, scene 2; see Allemann 2005, 251–56).

Cleavage (as I have conceptualized it so far) does not require sexual difference to establish sexual relations. Nevertheless, we see here that the symbolic order drawn from the breast_s has the same tendency as the phallic to preclude sexual relations. Lacan articulates the circulation of the signifier, which sustains the symbolic order, in terms of male/female sexual relations and suggests that "there's no such thing as a sexual relationship" in the phallosymbolic, because, as the phallus penetrates to the signified or copulates as subject with a predicate, it enjoys itself and in doing so fails to reach the other.[49] The signifier is barred from access to the signified (and the subject is barred from predication) by its own (phallic) jouissance (see Lundberg 2012, 98–123). Similarly, as the breast feels itself radically open, it nevertheless feels itself—enjoys and fears for itself—and ignores the other (who does not need to be of an other sex). So mammalogic does not necessarily produce less narcissistic subjects than phallocentrism. But the cleavage of breast_s can accommodate ambivalence—including an ambivalent position between open and closed as well as self and other.

Only when the plural is severed from the singular (the breasts distinguished from the chest)—as is the case in phallogocentrism—does the breast lose its capacity for ambivalence and contributes to the establishment of sexual difference. This is why it is so crucial to note Kleist's queering parody: in the scenario at hand, he mocks the phallic symbolic and its disparaging of the maternal dyad as ostensibly incapable of differentiation. If the conventional symbolic order introduces "the father" to split "the mother-infant dyad," Kleist here paints the picture of a man child stuck in a dyad with his adopted father—a dyad that Natalie—with all her authority, even when she raises her power to the military level—remains unable to break. Female masculinity here challenges in vain the jouissance of the adoptive son.

We find another version of the open breast closed to the other in *Penthesilea*. Achilles, whom we have already encountered as the epitomic image of the glorious breast and whom, in any case, we know from Homer for his rage and for his shield and shining armor, comes in Kleist to a point where he abandons all of these attributes:

> ACHILLES: Well, maidens, who's the target for these arrows?
> I trust it's not this unprotected breast?
> Shall I tear off for you this silken shirt [*den seid'nen Latz*]
> To show the harmless beating of my heart?
>
> (*P* 66/11.1406–9)

He has discarded arms and armor and claims that his heart beats innocently and without rage. I would like to think that Achilles's contact with the genderqueer Amazons liberates his own gender fluidity and allows him to relive his girlish youth.[50] But in fact Kleist exposes (or reinscribes) here in unusually sharp and explicit terms the story—a well-known story within the phallic symbolic order—of male violence within an intimate relationship. Less than ten lines after this proclamation of the Greek leader that he comes with love, the first Amazons are being murdered by Greeks. Achilles's professed openheartedness is a lie. While he engages in sweet talk, Amazons drop dead onstage left and right.

The analysis of this second example has shown that Kleist presents openness as something that can be feigned and thus urges us to take the open heart/breast with a grain of salt. At the same time, Achilles evokes the heart not as a symbol but as an organ. He proposes (mockingly) to tear off his skin (*den seid'nen Latz*) so that the Amazons can see his heart. How such direct visual access to the organ should reveal his true feelings remains unclear, but Achilles's provocation adds a literal or physical dimension to the "open breast" that haunts all its occurrences in the Kleistian text.

Other examples of literally open breasts come in the form of breasts that function as wind chimes. The ability to feign openness and the terrifying vulnerability to being played has here metaleptically turned into the capacity to serve as a musical instrument. These breasts are open to the elements and the wind generates music with them. We find a first example in *The Schroffenstein Family*—still harmless and without the typically Kleistian breach of the figurative:

> OTTOKAR: O, sway me, hope, as in a swing and as if
> Hovering with closed eyes [*geschloßnen Auges schwebend*]
> A breeze were playing on my breast [*offne Brust*: bare or, literally, open breast]
> Let my inmost soul turn with joy.
> (*S* 551/4.3.2173–77, translation altered)

An almost perfectly naturalistic image of delight: a light breeze on the bare chest; the wall between inside and outside is still intact. But the unclear attribution of "hovering with closed eyes" is disquieting. Who is hovering here? Common sense suggests that it is the first person speaker, Ottokar—hovering, like the Prince of Homburg, with closed eyes on the edge of sleep. But the phrase is placed before its referent, which, if it is indeed the speaker, is somewhat hidden in the inflected pronoun (*mir* or "my" in the translation). The unusual syntax prompts one to ascribe the phrase to the breeze, which intensifies the personification of the wind. While the description of the wind as an agent playing with human bodies remains conventional, the possibility that the breeze may be wafting with closed eyes renders the scene somewhat ominous—possibly erotic, possibly dangerous. When Kleist's syntax becomes disjointed, body parts are never far from being torn from the organic whole.

Penthesilea also compares her breast with a lyre played by the wind, but here the wall between inside and outside is breached—Achilles has broken her chest (*P* 54/9.1177–80). While she renders this physical violence as a wanton destruction of the lyre, her image already implies a physically open heart that allows the wind to pluck her heartstrings, that is to say, quite literally, to pick the nerves or the tendons that brace her heart. *Amphitryon* provides a similar image:

> JUPITER: Who else could cheat the instantaneous
> Gold-scales of your feelings
> And circumvent the multifariously articulated [*vielgliedrig*]
> Outreaching touches of your woman's soul
> And yet not cause to sound, although the softest
> Breath will do it, your breast's fine chimes of bells?
> (*A* 105/2.5.1395–1400, translation altered)

Again wind or breath enters the breast. But the inside also reaches out ("outreaching . . . soul") by growing extra limbs (*vielgliedrig*). Alcmene is described as having a complex sensitivity, capable of multifarious articulation. The wind chime that is her breast responds to the slightest breath of air. It echoes, in the realm of love, what Amphitryon fantasizes when his rage turns against the rival: "I press the sting / Into his breast, sucking empty, so that the wind / Shall play for me with his dry bones" (*A* 3.5.1952–54). Dead dryness and sensitive richness overlap in Kleist's image of the breast chime.

Like the Prince of Homburg, whose open breast seems tuned to the sound of only one name—the Elector's, which is his own: Frederick—and so bounces back and forth within its own echo chamber, Alcmene only ever perceives Amphitryon in everyone who relates to her with desire. There is a curious meagerness to the richness of her feeling. Similarly, the intensity of Amphitryon's hatred closes in on the one individual who is his rival and his double, and whom he elects as significant other beyond death when he fantasizes that his bones will continue to vibrate "for" him.

Despite the radical potential to (be) open(ed) to the elements (mainly the wind), in these examples, the breast remains enclosed in a dyadic relationship that largely functions as a reverberation chamber of the self. The self is reduced to the dream of an absolute symbiosis—yearning to be open to or opened by one trusted human being. Kleist shows that this trust is unjustified: the Elector plays with the Prince, Achilles and Penthesilea never really let their guard down, and Amphitryon is certainly not as interested in Alcmene as she is in him. The radical potential of the literally open breast, in Kleist's work, thus lies not in enabling an ideal communication, but in (albeit violently) liberating from the oppression that undergirds the fantasy of symbiosis.

III. From Behind

In this section, I will discuss the motif of the "back door" and the gesture of "coming from behind," analyzing a scene of *The Battle of Herrmann*, which is set in the Teutoburg Forest behind Herrmann's tent. While the back door is a recurrent motif in Kleist's work, it is also connected to a linguistic gesture, namely the syntactic inversions and insertions, which undo or reorganize in preposterous fashion the forward press of Kleist's sentences, tearing these sentences apart (see also Heimböckel 2003, 301).

This cluster of gestures—"leaving a back door open," "coming from behind," and "tearing apart a supposedly organic whole"—are all part and parcel of Kleist's use of the anus as a privileged signifier. The anus (in)forms the law of language with a sexuality that revolves around opening, closing, relaxing, evading (the law), swapping, sandwiching, and tearing. We will find the anus evidenced thematically (as rape, laceration, loophole, and back door to paradise), syntactically (in interpolations, inversions, and disarticulations), and metatheatrically (in Kleist's camp treatment of voyeurism and theater reviews). Kleist's analgrammar tears apart what seems organic in both the bodies of sentences and the bodies of his protagonists. It restructures body parts and the parts of a sentence (*Körperteile* and *Satzteile*) by redoubling and sandwiching them in a way that produces overlaps, allows for contamination, and creates confusion.

The scene in question takes place somewhere sandwiched between Herrmann's tent and a curious park in the back: "Teutoburg. A garden behind the royal tent. In the background an iron gate that leads to a deserted oak wood enclosed by cliffs" (*BH* 105/5.15). It begins with a splintered sentence, spoken by the Roman legate Ventidius, who has been courting Herrmann's wife Thusnelda not without politically motivated encouragement from Herrmann:

> Here is the silent park, ringed in by mountains,
> Which, in reply to the lisped question: Where?
> Came to my intoxicated mind yesterday! [*Mir gestern in die trunknen Sinne fiel!*, or, literally, "Fell into my intoxicated senses yesterday!"]
> (*BH* 108/5.17.2354–56, translation altered)

The first line already features insertion and syntactical disruption—"the silent park, ringed in [*eingeschlossen*, i.e., enclosed] by mountains." It is an example of performative language use in the sense that the syntax does what the phrase says. The participial phrase is locked between the main clause and the relative clause, and separated from the rest of the sentence by a comma on each side. This syntactical arrangement reinforces the scene of enclosure. Ventidius anticipates paradise in the arms of Thusnelda under the mild light of the moon in the silent park. But paradise is locked. The word "paradise" is of Old Iranian origin and means "enclosure" or "enclosed park"; it is related to the Greek *peri* (around) and *teichos* (wall). Here mountains rim the park and an iron gate separates it from Ventidius. We know that Ventidius will be let into paradise. We also know that he won't make it out in one piece.

The phrase "in reply to the lisped question: Where?" comes from behind. Usually, we read sentences linearly—from left to right; and each sentence, presumably, drives home a certain meaning. Kleist interrupts the forward movement of syntax and meaning with interpolations that seem to insert themselves behind the back of the manifest meaning and the principal syntactical arrangement. The straight version of the sentence would read: "Here is the silent park, which came to my intoxicated mind yesterday." The interpolation "in reply to the lisped question: Where?" breaks the flow of the sentence and gives additional trouble with its colon and question mark. Stretching over almost the entire line, it slows down the tempo of the verse. Indeed, we realize that time is already reversed. The sentence moves not from past to present to future, as the graph representing linear time does, but begins in the present tense ("here is") and ends in the past tense ("came to . . . yesterday"). Chronologically, the sentence moves backward, inviting us to read it backward and to reverse the order of its segments, which in turn produces a sense of recurrence: the Fall already happened (yesterday) and now we stand again before paradise—"Here is the silent park."[51]

In Kleist's essayistic story "On the Theater of Marionettes," Mr. C not only observes that "paradise is bolted and shut and the cherub is on our tail [*hinter uns*]," but also suggests a possible solution or, rather, a way around the problem: "We are obliged to circle the globe and go around to the other side to see if there is perhaps a back way in" (Kleist 2009, 269). This sketch of redemptive history differs from the one provided by Kleist's contemporaries, the German Idealists and Weimar Classicists. They would agree that the paradise of naive harmony lies behind us and that we cannot—indeed, that we do not want to—return to it. We want to move forward and pass through the rifts and divisions that come with reflection toward a higher unity, so goes their progressive notion of history. But Mr. C suggests something quite different: not a higher unity that reconciles innocence and reflection but a movement—perhaps jokingly performed ("I laughed," adds the narrator [269])—that turns to the behind of what lies behind us.

With the cherub behind them—his sword raised for penetration—the naked bodies of Adam and Eve make their way around the world. One of their descendants, Count F, preempted by a gatekeeper (a version of said cherub) from taking the front entrance to the estate of the Marquise of O, walks around the garden and finds his way to her arbor "through a back gate that [he] found open." Apparently, he follows Mr. C's suggestion. "I believed I might count on your forgiveness, and I entered," he adds (Kleist 2004, 300)—a bad joke that repeats the initial rape (even though this time she fends him off). We find the motif of the back door in a lighter register—echoing the laughter of the narrator of "On the Theater of Marionettes"—in Kleist's dialogic poem "A Fright in the Bath" ("Der Schrecken im Bade"), which the subtitle identifies as an idyll:

> But clever, sly and cunning, is Greta.
> . . . "Mommy," she says
> . . . .
> "Leave the gate, the one in the back, open for me;
> Because on the pasture one of my lambs fell ill,
> . . . ."
> And, whoosh! Rather than to the pasture, the traitress,
> She sneaks down to the shore of the lake.—
>
> (Kleist 2005, 60, my translation)

Paradise multiplies here. There is the comfort of shelter—at home with Mom, there is the pastoral garden of innocence—the pasture, and then there is the garden of delights—down there where the lake is. The lake is not so much an idyllic space of innocence as a place for unconventional desires, gender bending, and the pleasurable fright of being watched.[52] And yet Kleist's genre designation rings true because nobody is expelled from paradise in earnest—we know that Mom left Greta a loophole. On this night before her wedding, when everything points toward normative heterosexuality, there is room to escape for an evening of gender bending and active female sexuality. And after their playful adventures with trying out different positions in the scene of voyeuristic desire, Greta and Joan will be allowed to return home. The jest and lightness of the entire episode relies on an ethics of play—on the fact that the back door, passable in both directions, prevents desire and confrontation from being brought to a head.

Evidently, Kleist frequently avails himself of the motif of the back door to paradise. The very fact that there is a back door or a loophole in the law (which otherwise guards and bars us from paradise) compromises the innocence and purity of paradise. The symbolic that is organized by the anus does not invest in purity; instead it generates a logic or counterlogic of contamination, overlap (in particular, gender overlap), and disintegration.

Returning to the first sentence of the scene of *The Battle of Herrmann* we have been analyzing, I would like to begin to address the implication of the theater, of theatricality, in the anal logic of coming through the back door. The phrase that is inserted from behind into the sentence that turns around, moving backward in time—the phrase "in reply to the lisped question: Where?"—contains a microtheatrical scene, a tiny bit of play within the play: Ventidius renders in direct speech what Gertrud said to him yesterday: "Where?" The direct speech and the physical quality of its lisping pronunciation produces presence. Together with the already-noted deceleration of the meter, it gives an afterlife to the "here and now" that, as we have observed, has already turned (in)to the past with the beginning of the relative clause. The inserted phrase, "in reply to the lisped question: Where?" extends paradise.

And yet the question "Where?" was also the gate through which Ventidius was expelled from paradise. Yesterday, he was "intoxicated" with delight. The anticipation of the rendezvous with Thusnelda inebriated him—he was already in paradise. To have to identify a place for the actual realization of his pleasure ruins the pleasure that anticipation provides.

"The silent park . . . which, / Came to my intoxicated mind yesterday!" then reads rather like an aggression and a frustration: the thought of the park invades (*einfiel*) his amorous intoxication and interrupts the pleasant play of the imagination.[53] Locating paradise is tantamount to the fall from paradise or, rather, it means the falling of paradise: "The silent park . . . fell [*der stille Park . . . fiel*]." And indeed, the stage directions describe the park as "deserted" or barren (*öde*). As soon as paradise is identified, it seems lacking. A feeling of shortcoming and dereliction creeps in—shouldn't this park have been cultivated? Must one not prosper and multiply? That would require a straight or head-on approach. Suddenly the back door seems like a waste. The *Lispelfrage*—with the pronunciation that fails to distinguish between *s* and *z*—introduces an ambiguity into the garden of innocence. Paradise is contaminated.

Ventidius cannot be entirely unaware of being sandwiched in between two instances of ambiguous paradise—between the park before him and his past intoxication, between Thusnelda and Gertrud, and between the bear and

Thusnelda. Ventidius asks Thusnelda, thinking that she is Gertrud, "—With whom were you speaking just now?" (*BH* 109/5.17.2377). Thusnelda, playing Gertrud, answers, "With my lady, Thusnelda" (*BH* 109/5.17.2378). She continues the verse his speech began as if she was completing his line of thought. Perhaps this quick corroboration lulls him into abandoning doubt and suspicion, but the answer should make clear that Thusnelda cannot quite be in the park if she was just here speaking with Gertrud. Nevertheless, Thusnelda/Gertrud assures him, "She's in the park, in accordance with your wishes, / And, breast filled with burning passion, awaits you there!" (*BH* 109/5.17.2380, translation altered). With this conflicting information, Ventidius vaguely registers Thusnelda's redoubling and feels her both behind him and before him. Just like Ventidius finds himself between the Thusnelda in the park and the Thusnelda who locks the gate behind him, the adverbial phrase "in accordance with your wishes" is sandwiched in between the two main clauses that are joined here with the conjunction "and."

The untoward positioning of the conjugation "and" at the beginning of the line exemplifies another characteristic of analgrammatic syntax. The line opens by adding. Or it adds by opening. Analgrammar loosens the order, relaxes the rules, opens the loopholes, and keeps extending without aim or direction from behind, sandwiching (word) bodies and multiplying contact zones, even if this means that the rim tears and the sentence falls apart. While the phallus conjoins by establishing an order and a hierarchy—primarily a hierarchy between presence and absence—the anus tenders the reverse, loosens and tears, and thus invites the metaphysics of presence, which undergirds the functioning of the phallus, to disintegrate. By the same token, the anus multiplies, extends, and agitatedly cumulates, producing a bleary confusion. Analgrammatic syntax is not articulative but cumulative without accumulating meaning or value. If "word for word," one of Kleist's often-used expressions, means gapless consistency in the symbolic order of the phallus—as when Amphitryon asks Sosias to give an account of himself: "Answer me point by point and word for word [*pünktlich, Wort für Wort*]" (*A* 84/2.1.619, translation altered)—the same expression, "word for word," refers to a loose sequence of swappable repetitions or bits of incomplete sentences in the anal symbolic order.[54] Here the sequential order of the word-by-word disintegrates into repetitions of the same point or into an accumulation of mere points or bits that lose all punctuality in the process and, instead, launch the text into what Bersani (1986, 67) calls a "designifying mobility."

Exploring the possibilities of analgrammar, Kleist sometimes sets words next to one another without conjunction—for example, when Astolf, one of Herrmann's captains, comments on Ventidius's death and Thusnelda's collapse with the words "Anyway! Anyway! [*Gleichviel! Gleichviel!*]" (*BH* 112/5.19.2435, my translation). One word stands next to another that is the same word. Their syntactic arrangement enacts what they mean: equivalence (literally, *gleichviel* means "same amount"). This equivalence is not the product of a deduction; no logical consequence governs the relation of these words. Instead, one word comes to stand in for the same word—"Anyway! Anyway!": same difference.

Like words or phrases, the bodies onstage replicate, stand in for, and get confused with one another in analgrammatic (dis)order: Thusnelda gets mixed up with Gertrud, the bear fills in for Thusnelda, and so on, and the scene of Thusnelda trapping the legate stands in for Herrmann fighting in the battle against the Romans. Bodies stand and fall with, next to, and for one another. In the end Thusnelda falls for Ventidius—which also means, she falls in his stead. The audience sees her collapse in the moment Ventidius is killed offstage—Thusnelda, Ventidius: *Gleichviel! Gleichviel!*

Beginning with the first sentence, the scene folds theater into the play. There is the micro play-within-the-play of the question "Where?," there is Thusnelda playing Gertrud and Ventidius willingly suspending disbelief, and then there is the bear: a favorite performer in some of the lower forms of theater—the circus and the fairground. "The shaggy black she-bear of Cheruscia / Is standing beside me, paws drawn [*Steht, mit gezückten Tatzen, neben mir*]," exclaims Ventidius as soon as he has passed the gate (*BH* 110/5.18.2388–89, translation altered). Grammatically speaking, the adverbial phrase *mit gezückten Tatzen* need not be separated with commas from the rest of the sentence. "Steht mit gezückten Tatzen neben mir" is an example of perfectly regular word order. Yet Kleist adds commas to set the phrase off as a pseudo-interpolation. Indeed, a foreign body has been inserted: the adjective *gezückt*. It turns the paws into weapons—into swords that are drawn. Thus, the bear towers next to Ventidius like a crude and clumsily exaggerated version of the cherub who chases Adam and Eve out of paradise: with not one but two raised swords. At the same time, a certain delight (*Entzücken*) resonates in Ventidius's unusual choice of *gezückt* as a qualifier for ursine paws.

The literal tearing to pieces of human bodies in Kleist's plays also functions as a shocking and over-the-top figure (a theatrical metalepsis) for the figural tearing to pieces that theater critics engage in with the judgment they pass on dramatic texts and performances—"*zerreißen, verreißen*: it rhymes," one could say, borrowing Penthesilea's excuse for mauling Achilles.[55] Interestingly, Ventidius here offers the first round of sharp critique. He is locked into the scene, in the gated back of the stage, but he also transcends the scene as its critic, speaking from an outside or offstage position.[56] In what I would call a teichoscopy of feeling, he articulates how appalled he is by the "shaggy black" "hellish monster" that presents itself instead of the expected beauty of Thusnelda (*BH* 110/5.18.2388; 109/5.18.2386).[57] While Ventidius might want to separate those two appearances, Thusnelda, still playing Gertrud, teaches mammalogic and gives a lesson in ambivalence as she reminds him that they need to be held together: "The bear of Cheruscia? . . . Why no, it's just Thusnelda, of course" (*BH* 110/5.18.2392–93). Thusnelda thus functions as a mouthpiece for Kleist's aesthetic—an aesthetics in which beauty and terror, innocence and fallenness overlap. Ventidius, on the other hand, employs a notion of beauty that is aligned with the dominant models of bourgeois theater around 1800, that is, with the viewpoint that tears Kleist's plays to pieces during his lifetime. This puts Ventidius radically outside Kleist's theater—a foreign body on Kleist's stage. At the same time, the scene creates compassion for him, mediated through the characters of Gertrud and Childerich. But the two attendants can't quite find the key to this play. They don't have access to its pleasure. Gertrud and Childerich feel compassion and fear, but these sentiments, belonging to Lessing's theory of bourgeois tragedy, are—together with its gender policing—out of place in Kleist's theater where all bourgeois moderation has been abandoned.[58]

In Kleist's scene, the key is not in the lock: "Where is the key . . . ? . . . The key, . . . is it not in the lock?" (*BH* 111/5.18.2414–15). The phallic order has been disabled, and immediately masculinity is presumed to be in a sorry state—"it must be on the ground" (*BH* 111/5.18.2416; *am Boden liegen* means "to be devastated"). But, instead of simply subduing and dismissing the masculine signifier, Thusnelda holds it in her hand. Such illicit use of the phallus, which exposes the phallus as a contraption, i.e., as dildo, appalls Gertrud at least as much as Thusnelda's deployment of the bear does.[59] It prompts her to exclaim: "The monster! She has it in her hand" (*BH* 111/5.18.2417). Who or what is the monster now—the bear, the dildo, or Thusnelda? The blurring of reference shows that Gertrud is already under the sway of the anus. Gertrud and Childerich are so outraged that they feel the need to sever the key from Thusnelda: "Rip [*Reiß*] the instrument from her! . . . Rip the instrument, Childerich, from her!" (*BH* 111/5.18.2418–20, translation altered). But the signifier *reißen*—the root of the verbs *zerreißen* (rip up, maul) and *verreißen* (rip, disparage)—contributes to the symbolic of the anus and its tearing of the organic body. Gertrud's use of the verb *reißen*, which indicates the severing of an organic bond (and thus suggests that the key naturally belongs in Thusnelda's hand) undermines the very distinction between tool and organ that she seeks to establish.

Thusnelda's drag performance offers a witty critique of bourgeois gender and theater norms in their mutual entanglement. Even in its extreme violence, the scene behind Herrmann's tent, structured, as it is, by the signifier of the anus, leaves some wiggle room or a loophole for reading and playing it as camp.[60] By camp, I mean a sensibility or an aesthetics that, as Christopher Isherwood put it, "make[s] fun out of . . . what's basically serious to you (Isherwood 2013, 110). Camp performs performance and thus reflects on performance. It tends to combine, in excessive amplification, different modes of illusion or show. Its parodistic style relies on exaggeration and on the flashing of elements that undercut the illusion. It foregrounds lowbrow forms of culture, frequently in incongruous conjunction with high-art elements, and often exposes and comments on gender performance and heteronormative violence by using frivolity and shocking excess.

Thusnelda's comment "Is she bristling at your advances [*Sie sträubt sich dir*]?" alludes to the hairy issue that motivates her cruel revenge against Ventidius (*BH* 111/5.18.2419, translation altered).[61] Ventidius stole a curl of Thusnelda's hair after she declined to give him one. Herrmann amplifies the note of rape and dismemberment in the legate's behavior when he interprets it as colonial exploitation. He maintains that the Romans extract Germanic women's teeth and hair for the embellishment of their ladies. This revelation comes right after Ventidius shows Thusnelda how Roman women dress and do their hair (see act 3, scene 3; MS 45). Thusnelda receives an introduction into feminine masquerade, and at the same time, her belief in honest love is ruined, intertwining cultivated looks and staged feelings. This hair-raising initiation is mirrored, in the fifth act, by the phallic bristles of the she-bear: "O, how these stiff black bristles, dearest, / Will suit your empress Livia" (*BH* 110/5.18.2406–7).

Thusnelda turns into an outrageously overdetermined character in this drag scene. While she sends the she-bear as a stand-in to the rendezvous with Ventidius, she plays Saint Peter, who holds the keys to heaven with his judgment (only that she locks Ventidius in, not out). In Christian iconography and papal heraldry, the teeth of the Key of Heaven (in German, *der Bart*: the beard of the key) sometimes form an *S* and an *R* for *solve et retine*—the power of loosing and binding that the symbolic of the phallus purports to impart (she separates Gertrud and Childerich from the Roman legate).[62] She also plays Samson. Both Milton's *Samson Agonistes* and Kleist's *The Battle of Herrmann* are stories of partisan war. Like Samson, Thusnelda was castrated by the removal of hair and the perfidious discourse of a lover (in her case, the knowledge of the power of hair was not revealed to the enemy but, ironically, to her—with the same castrating effect). As Samson, she takes revenge against the colonizing enemy by giving an excessive show of force (using a famished bear as proxy) that leaves her, if not quite buried under the rubble, at least mentally destroyed. On top of all that, she plays the erotic lure that Herrmann needs to trap Ventidius, but her impersonation of the naive and willing blonde flashes black bristles to undercut the illusion.

Conclusion

We have seen that breast_s do not function as a signifier of plenitude in Kleist. His breast_s combine lack with excess and are both full and hollowed. Kleist's experiments with a mamma-tangential symbolic order produce the breast as both that which gives language and that which is struck by language. The language that comes from the breast does not preserve the breast as an imagined origin intact before language. Instead, breast_s always already self-differentiate into a (self-)cleaving signifier.

When this (self-)cleaving takes the shape of a violent piercing and tearing of the breast, it does so not always only in the (dis)service of integration (of good and bad breast or of love and hate) but often also as a reaction to the false images that the phallocentric symbolic order paints of the breast. The crude opening, piercing, or crushing of the breast provides relief and even liberation from false ideals.[63] Penthesilea comments on the act of piercing through her own breast with satisfaction—"Now it is good [*nun ists gut*]" (*P* 148/24,3034, my translation). In *The Battle of Herrmann*, the last words of Ventidius, as his breast is being lacerated, are "O Thusnelda!" (*BH* 111/5.18.2421, translation altered). The O gives both the roundness and the emptiness of the breast and must be read in its oscillation between pain and pleasure. That such tearing is experienced with pleasure, because it liberates the subject from the constraints of the law and the image, shows that the mammalogic overlaps with the analexpansive order, which engages sexual pleasure as pulsed through by the (death) drive, and with analgrammar, which cultivates pleasure in tearing and jumbling.

While certainly different from a phallocentric symbolic, Kleist's mammalogic is not the other or better half of phallocentrism. It does not provide simple truth, nor does it enable nonviolent communication. In fact, the yearning of the Kleistian breast to come undone is bound up with a desire to escape the opposition between breast and phallus, to multiply the sex changes, or to leave the binary sex-gender system in favor of a nongendered sexuality underwritten by the anus. The Amazons shoot arrows out of their right breast. Thusnelda replaces the soft blond locks that curl around her breast with the stiff black bristles of a bear. Both serve as examples of phallic or, within the sex/gender binary, male breasts. Penthesilea changes Achilles to female, within the sex/gender binary, when she makes him two breasts (a right one and a left one) in the moment that she tears up both: "Oxus and Sphinx chewing into his right breast, / And she into his left" (*P* 128/23.2672f). And the breast of Ventidius develops more fatty tissue as Thusnelda, via the she-bear, "is sinking her claws into [his] soft chest" (*BH* 111/5.18.2413). Hally escapes the sex/gender binary altogether even though such liberation is the result of a horrific defilement:

> CROWD: O the poor, shame-covered creature!
> Kicked about, dirt-smeared,
> Head and chest all smashed.
> SOME VOICES: Who is it? A man? A woman?
> A CHERUSCAN (*accompanying the figure*): Good people don't ask!
> (*BH* 70/4.4.1545–48)

The person cannot be recognized as Hally because the face is disfigured and the person's gender cannot be identified because the breast is shattered. In the end, compulsive sex assignment is abandoned and it is recommended to refrain from inquiring into sexual identity. The breast_s of Kleist's breast language are neither clearly female nor clearly maternal—neither an object of erotic desire in the conventional sense, nor only a symbol for nourishment and plenitude. Breast_s have phallic aspects and masochistic tendencies. They desire and bring about their own destruction because the round, whole, intact breast has been historically caught in the bourgeois gender complementarity where it was relegated to the status of the object of the male erotic gaze and/or of the symbol for maternal nourishment and sacrifice. Kleist features strong female characters and female characters with an active sexuality, but (or, precisely for that reason), where the ambivalence of cleavage is reduced in favor of an idealized image of the breast that serves phallocentrism, Kleist produces images of breast_s that get torn, amputated, pierced, breasts that burst or otherwise break and thereby respond to the analexpansive symbolic (dis)order that shatters sexual difference.

Chapter 4

✦

Camp (Drummer Boys)

Comedy has become a major venue for feminist and antiracist interventions, even if it "has issues" (Berlant and Ngai 2017). In "women's comedy . . . feminism speaks, talks back, and is contested" (Mizejewski 2014, 6). Characters from *I Love Lucy* to *I Love Dick* perform femininity, affective labor, and female desire in a comical key, making "disruptive spectacle(s)" of themselves (Karlyn 1995, 31) to test the subversive force of feminist and other forms of subaltern humor. Theorists find lenses to think with and against the stereotype of the "feminist killjoy" (Ahmed 2010) such as "fem(me) science" (a spoof on Friedrich Nietzsche's *Gay Science* by Lisa Duggan and Kathleen McHugh 1996), zaniness (which Sianne Ngai 2012, 174–222, has established as the comic category of post-Fordist capitalism) or feminist cringe comedy, insisting that "the joke is on you (dear Dick)" (Marso 2018) while also calling attention to the politically ambiguous character of this kind of humor and noting that it oscillates disturbingly between the funny and the unfunny.

Kleist's jokes are similarly queer or cringy, unfunny, uncomfortable, and politically ambiguous. Perhaps for that reason, his humor has usually been overlooked.[1] Many scenes in Kleist's plays—often the most gruesome and the most enigmatic ones—have a comical undertone. Heinrich Zschokke, a fellow writer, reported that Kleist frequently had to interrupt a reading of the final act of his first tragedy, *The Schroffenstein Family*, because he and the small circle of friends in attendance laughed so hard (see Sembdner 1996, 63). That a tragedy (and especially its tragic ending—in this case, the double mistaken infanticide) gives rise to laughter might seem strange, but it is consistent with Kleist's dramatic practice. I read the hilarity that Kleist allows to erupt in tragic contexts and desperate situations as camp.

Camp saw its last heyday (before its current [post]feminist and possibly postcamp turn) in the fight against AIDS of the 1980s and '90s (see Christiansen and Hanson 1996). Known before mostly as an aestheticizing attitude, its deconstructing and denaturalizing capacities were honed into a political strategy by ACT UP. Later, Eve Kosofsky Sedgwick shed light on the "reparative" aspect of camp, which played an important part also in the irreverent camp of AIDS activism (Sedgwick 1997, 149). In this chapter, I will draw on

Sedgwick's notion of camp as a reparative practice, while trying not to lose camp's comic energy. Humor itself, we will see, can help with recovery and integration without losing its disintegrating and critical function.[2]

Kleist's camp leans retro, reviving obsolescent aristocratic values in a time of transition to the hegemony of bourgeois culture. Still, he is less an aesthete than a fan of the lowbrow. His camp humor is over the top and shocking, but it also provides comfort in the violent and dark times he encountered (the Napoleonic Wars and the new defamation of same-sex desire).

In a biting epigram titled "Comedy Bill [*Komödienzettel*]," Kleist classifies his second tragedy, *Penthesilea*, the one that is sure to shock with its Dionysian violence, as a comedy—specifically, a "dog comedy [*Hundekomödie*]" (Kleist 2005, 47, my translation). Does the human tragedy look like a comedy from the canine vantage point? Did Kleist write a comedy for hounds? If so, it would indeed be important to find out what dogs find funny (see Rinck 2015, 13). Not all dogs have the same sense of humor, to be sure. Presumably this epigram targets the critics of *Penthesilea*, because they are the kind of dogs who don't get Kleist's sense of humor—bird dogs, I would say, specifically "chicken dogs [*Hühnerhunde*]," as featured in Kleist's fable "The Dogs and the Bird," also published in *Phöbus*. Kleist's chicken dogs share the proverbial simplemindedness of chickens as they are left dumbfounded and gawk when the esprit takes off like a bird[3]—when it shakes its wings and flies (or "flees") like the "safe gender" that Kleist wishes his "amphibian" sister Ulrike for the turn of the century.[4]

Kleist's sense of humor is missed by the wise dogs among his readers—these hounds who ironically figure as "sages" in his fable.[5] Scholars have repeatedly pointed out that he blends the comic with the tragic register, but they are apparently more at ease noticing the tragic aspects of his comedies than the comical traits in his serious themes and violent scenes.[6] Why this is so, one can only surmise. Kleist's humor might be threatening because it knows no boundaries; it is too pervasive, too corrosive, too dark, and too uncontrollable to be easily indulged. Today's audience might be blinded to the silly aspects of Kleist's works by their respect for one of the great German authors. Kleist's queer camp humor might be difficult to recognize because there is no record established yet of camp being a cultural practice during his time. And even today, queer camp—like the amphibian that flies—remains largely unintelligible to mainstream sensibility.[7]

Camp is a style, a sensibility, and a "system of humor" that is cultivated in gay, lesbian, and queer circles and used mainly in performances (not necessarily onstage) that favor incongruity and involve verbal wit and elaborate costumes (often but not exclusively devoted to cross-dressing) (Newton 1979, 109).[8] It responds to stigmatization by theatrically exaggerating and thereby making light of stigmatic markers and stereotypes.[9] The term "camp" derives from the French *se camper* (to posture or to flaunt). The underlying mood of camp, the structure of feeling out of which camp emerges, derives from the existential experience of ignorance, isolation, hate and brutality, to which gay and lesbian, bisexual and transgender people are frequently exposed, especially during times of self-discovery.[10] Out of this mire rises the wit, the caustic criticism, the care and attention to detail, as well as the infectious (and community-generating) exuberance and warmth that characterize camp performances. But camp never disavows the crap that queers are forced to take; it refuses to refuse the stigma and the stereotype.[11] The shit and the slime, the pain and the loss, the violence and the shame are not purged but embraced, flaunted, and wallowed in to increase the pleasure.

Camp consistently combines abjection and amusement, gloom and glamour, seriousness and frivolity. As a mode of critique, camp never sets things straight but mobilizes irony, reclaiming the tools used to suppress queers and employing them not to dismantle the bourgeois house but to move in and put all its structural and decorative elements in quotation marks. Such "transgressive reinscription" remains controversial in that it cannot guarantee (or even retrospectively prove) success—largely because it has abandoned one of the principles of politics as we know it, namely identifiable positions.[12]

The objects of camp critique vary depending on the historical, geographical, and local situation, but in general camp targets bourgeois values, in particular the heteronormative order. Needling mainstream fantasies and challenging such valued tenets of bourgeois society as seriousness, simplicity, and sincerity, camp serves as a denaturalizing technique. Especially when it flaunts bad taste, it exposes the (otherwise repudiated) effort that is required to produce so-called natural beauty and harmony and to naturalize sexual and gender roles.[13]

In his article "Queer Comedy," Ken Feil (2005, 478) identifies four elements of camp: pastiche, trash, masquerade, and displeasure. We consistently find these four elements in Kleist's works. His plays are pastiches of different styles, genres, foundational myths, and canonical scenes from the history of the theater, which Kleist remakes and defamiliarizes to great humoristic effect (Genesis, *Iliad*, Greek myths and their Ancient, French, and German theatrical versions, Gospels, Shakespeare, Spanish theater of the Siglo de Oro, Lessing, Goethe, Schiller, etc.—the list is long).[14] He is not afraid of integrating low forms of theater into this pastiche—nonliterary theater like commedia dell'arte (Mercury's slapstick),[15] pantomime (Penthesilea after mauling Achilles), marionette theater, mystery plays (the cherub in *Katie of Heilbronn*), fairy plays (the fairy-tale structure of *Katie*), as well as other kinds of spectacles like the Roman *ludi* (the hunting scenes in *Penthesilea* and *The Battle of Herrmann*), fairground shows (the bear in *Herrmann*), executions (Hally being cut into pieces and Septimus being clubbed to pulp in *Herrmann*), and tilts (the jousting scene between Penthesilea and Achilles), for example. Indeed he seems to revel in such "trash" and to invite identification with "trash subjects."[16] We will encounter in this chapter one such trash subject in particular: a military drummer. But even Kleist's treatment of heroes and rulers marks these subject positions as on the verge of obsolescence—as history's waste.[17] Kleist's staging of nonnormative gender, sexuality, and kinship structures as well as his frequent use of drag—the gender drag in *The Schroffenstein Family*, Katie's appearance as knave, Natalie taking on the mantle of a military leader, the excessive thematization of amputated breasts in *Penthesilea*, Kunigunde, Guiscard's physician dressed as knight, Adam's wig, and the animal drags of Thusnelda (bear), Penthesilea (hound), and Achilles (deer)—are examples of Kleist's ironic use of masquerade. His flagging of the theatricality of the theater with various, often ludicrously self-undermining, forms of play within the play (the sleepwalking in *Prince Frederick of Homburg* and sleeptalking in *Katie*, which reference Schiller's notion of acting as a kind of sleepwalking (see Schiller 2005b, 235)—and the idyllic interlude in *Penthesilea*, where Prothoë and Achilles pretend that she subdued Achilles) and his dissection of the theater into its elements, which he then has play one another's roles (gazes speak, words show, text gestures, etc.) make Kleist the early nineteenth-century master of masquerade. And finally, his combination of the comic register with excessive violence (gruesome scenes of war and dismemberment) produces such displeasure while his penchant for incongruous and hyperbolic—or should I say "outrageous" and "over-the-top"—gestures (the repetitive fainting, the military leader Homburg clasping his mother's knees in fear of death, Penthesilea killing herself with an imaginary dagger, Katie throwing herself out the window, etc.) is in such bad taste that it smells of camp.[18]

As these examples demonstrate, the two main themes of Kleist's camp humor are gender, sexuality, and kinship, on the one hand, and war and martial law, on the other. They are both amplified and ironized by self-reflexive references to the theater. Kleist, so I argue, reacts to the momentous change in the sex-gender system of the West, which was partially prepared by the Protestant reformation in the late sixteenth century, brought about by Enlightenment thought in the eighteenth century and then compacted into a complementary and oppositional binary by the less-than-universal distribution of civil rights and liberties in the wake of the bourgeois revolution of 1789.[19] The experience of war—religious wars, revolutionary wars, Napoleonic Wars—thus accompanies what I call the historical sex change. This might be enough of a reason for war to serve as a prominent subject in Kleist's queer camp. In addition, Kleist's own life is steeped in martial culture and existence: his family—ancient Pomeranian nobility—included many high-ranking military leaders, he grew up in a garrison town, Kleist himself served in the military from age fourteen to twenty-one (participating in the Rhineland campaign against revolutionary France and in the siege of the only German republic founded in the spirit of the revolution, Mainz), and a number of his erotic male friendships stem from this military context (in particular, Ernst von Pfuel). The military lives of his immediate relatives include devastating experiences. His father, Joachim Friedrich von Kleist, received a profound blow with prolonged effects (on his status and economic situation) when, for reasons which are not entirely clear, King Frederick II, also known as Frederick the Great, refused to promote him and then ignored his brash request for discharge so that Kleist's father ended up as the officer longest-serving at the rank of major of the entire Prussian army (see Schede 2008, 9–10). Kleist's brother, Leopold Friedrich von Kleist, fought in the Battle of Auerstedt, which, together with the Battle of Jena, resulted in the decisive defeat of Prussia by Napoleon.[20] The work of substitutions is striking: Kleist struggles with the same short temper and sense of entitlement or honor that his father manifests in his conflict with Frederick II, and his younger brother begins his military service in the same infantry regiment as Kleist in the very year Kleist resigns, and he retires to a civilian post in the year Kleist commits suicide. Therefore, I wonder whether Kleist might not, with his campy humor, work through vicarious experiences of loss of martial status (be it the militaristic reputation of Prussia or the military rank of his father) and whether these might not be subjectively (if problematically) related to the threats to honor and recognition that stem from the social stigma against same-sex leanings and transgender tendencies. This would then provide another reason why sexual and gender stigmatization and loss of military honor are dealt with as entangled in his camp approach. Given that fifty-eight men in the Kleist family served in the wars of Frederick the Great, that his father's fate was so profoundly impacted by an apparent whim of the king, and that the Prussian king combined in his very personage the themes of homosexuality and militarism, it is also possible that Kleist grappled with the ambiguously charged example of Frederick the Great in his queer martial camp.[21] Finally, heteronormative notions solidify and social discrimination against sexual minorities—the experience of which I have identified as the underlying mood of camp—increases dramatically when the Prussians are defeated by Napoleon in 1806. With the Holy Roman Empire vanquished and Prussia threatened with complete irrelevance on the European power stage, bourgeois ideology (including that of two complimentary genders and that of romantic love) compensates for these setbacks, mobilizing everyone and leaving no room for tolerance, much less for equality or the plurality of values. After 1806, treason and homosexuality are discursively linked.[22]

Thus, for Kleist and in Kleist's time, homosexuality and militarism were interconnected in a variety of ways: be it that militarism compensated for homosexuality, furthered it, or increased its stigmatization, be it that war accompanied the emergence of a heteronormative complementary gender binary, or that sexual norms and militarism provided analogous occasions for the withdrawal of reputation.

I have called up these examples because Kleist has at times been seen as a warmongering nationalist producing anti-Napoleonic propaganda.[23] In fact, these aspects of his work are a vital component of his camp performance: Kleist sends up and theatricalizes anti-Napoleonic patriotism not (or not only) to compensate for what his personality might be lacking in the field of gender and sexual normativity, but (also) to ridicule what underpins the new stigmatization of homosexuals.[24]

Many critics have sensed a will to total destruction in Kleist's work.[25] I disagree with this evaluation and will here resume the argument, which I began to develop in chapter 2, that Kleist's aesthetics indeed counteracts annihilation. While in the earlier chapter I drew on the queer psychoanalytic theorists Bersani and Dutoit (with their aesthetics of inaccurate replication to prevent violence from taking hold) and Edelman (with his notion of the sinthome), here the feminist psychoanalyst Joan Copjec will help us understand the necessarily partial and beneficially temporary satisfaction of the (death) drive. To be sure, Kleist does attack the bourgeois symbolic and imaginary orders, but the fear of some of his readers that, if successful, such an attack will lead to complete chaos and utter annihilation instead of enabling a new and alternative order, is exaggerated, verging on the paranoid and, unwittingly or not, reactionary.

My discussion will be centered on an anecdote—which, as we will see, functions like a very small piece of theater—about a military drummer captured by the enemy. It will branch out to two scenes of heroism softened by physical comedy: Herrmann's melodramatic gesture of leaning against a tree when he listens to the song of the bards, in the war drama *The Battle of Herrmann*, and a scene that smacks of slapstick, in the unfinished tragedy *Robert Guiscard, Duke of the Normans*, with the weak, possibly plague-ridden body of the eponymous hero on the verge of fainting and then safely coming to sit on a kettledrum as if on a throne.

Shoot for the Moon

On October 20, 1810, Kleist published the following anecdote in his daily evening paper, *Berliner Abendblätter*:

anecdote from the recent war

> The most tremendous joke perhaps ever to pass human lips, as long as the earth has been standing, was made in the course of the recent war by a drummer; the drummer, I believe, of what was then the Puttkamer regiment; a man of whom, as we shall now hear, neither Greek nor Roman history can show the equal. This fellow, after the rout of the Prussians at Jena, managed somehow to scare up a musket, and with it carried on the war single-handed; with the result that, having struck down and fleeced everything French that let itself be seen within range on the road, he was searched out and captured by a troop of gendarmes, taken to the city, and, as he deserved it,

> sentenced to be shot. Arriving at the square where the execution was to take place, and probably seeing that all efforts in his own defense were in vain, he requested a mercy [*eine Gnade*] of the colonel in command of the detachment; and when the colonel, his officers collecting about him in suspense, asked the man: what he wished? he stripped his trousers and spoke: that they may shoot him in the . . . , so as not to tear a h . . . in his s . . . . And one must note the Shakespearean propriety of the drummer, who in making his joke did not exceed his sphere as one who gives hidings to drums. (Kleist 1982, 268, translation altered)

This anecdote forms a couplet together with the "Anecdote from the Last Prussian War," published on October 6, 1810. Each features a lone German warrior in the wake of the Battle of Jena, who belatedly defies the French by way of vulgar humor. Here a Prussian drummer moons a group of French officers and their colonel. In the "Anecdote from the Last Prussian War," a single Prussian cavalier beats a group of three French chasseurs while yelling blasphemous vulgarities at them.[26] Kleist publishes both anecdotes during the month of the fourth anniversary of the battles of Jena and Auerstedt. The "Anecdote from the Last Prussian War" appears roughly one week before the date of the German defeat—October 14, 1806—and the "Anecdote from the Recent War" roughly one week after. Kleist theatrically orchestrates the publication dates, building a commemorative sandwich. The first anecdote meets the victors head-on, and the second presents the German behind, in terms of both the date of their appearance and the gestures they describe.[27]

In both war anecdotes, the Germans have already been defeated and are in the minority, isolated and scattered across a landscape that has been taken over by the French army. The feeble and yet awe-inspiring power retained by the scattered warriors lies in the curses and jokes they hurl against their enemies and, even more so, against their own desperate situation. In Kleist's time, drummers figured as the proverbial lowest species of the military community.[28] The second anecdote thus gives center stage to a low or "trash" subject. Since it focuses on the experience of marginalization and isolation, while also producing sexual innuendo (of an unusual kind), I read this anecdote as an example of the desperate humor of camp. In my view, the images and narratives of German supremacy are tied together with nonnormative gender, sexuality, and kinship structures.[29] These anecdotes target anti-Napoleonic patriotism because it produces nonnormative gender and sexual identities and ostracizes them.

Kleist creates and ruins, destroys and protects, in one gesture. As he launches a pervasive and erosive attack on the dominant order, he also acts out that order and invites the reader and spectator to identify with it. Kleist's guerrilla camp thus emotionally manipulates the audience to embrace a position (and be destroyed with it), and at the same time to become a partisan against that very position.[30] While he uses this technique in all of his plays, the anecdotes—with their small size, relative marginality, and fast pace—are particularly apt fighters in Kleist's literary camp guerrilla war.[31]

Kleist begins the second anecdote by announcing "the most tremendous joke [*der ungeheuerste Witz*] perhaps ever to pass human lips." The phrase combines the register of comedy with that of tragedy. Since the first stasimon of Sophocles's *Antigone*—which declares, "There are many tremendous things, but nothing more tremendous than man"—we know to regard humanity with admiration for its civilizational achievements while also trembling before its tendency toward impudence.[32] Never has humanity dared to jest like this. The joke—if it doesn't freeze on human lips but passes them—shakes the earth that Kleist here so curiously describes as "standing."[33]

Yet the anecdote is narrated in the past tense. The joke has passed the lips and the ground has already shaken. The Holy Roman Empire is not standing anymore. The defeat at Jena not only insulted Prussia's military self-image but also resulted in the Kingdom of Prussia being subjugated to the French Empire.[34] The Battle of Jena thus dealt a severe blow to Prussian pride. It also foregrounded, once again, the most fundamental narcissistic insult known to man: death. The chorus of *Antigone* warns that man, this most tremendous thing, "lacks resources for nothing the future can bring, / Only from death can he devise no escape" (Sophocles 2003, l. 334–35). Goethe offers a particularly striking expression of this insult that is death in his 1771 speech "Zum Shakespeares-Tag." The speech constitutes another intertext of Kleist's anecdote, since his reference to Shakespeare here is certainly mediated by Goethe's admiration for Shakespeare during his *Sturm und Drang* period.

> This life, gentlemen, is much too short for our soul, . . .—because, even if somebody is lucky for a rather long time on his path, eventually he will fall nevertheless—and often within eyeshot of the goal he hoped to attain—into a ditch, which God knows who has dug for him—and count for nothing.
>
> Count for nothing! Me! Who is everything for me, since I know everything only through me! Thus everyone exclaims who feels himself . . . (Goethe 1981, 224, my translation)

Kleist's drummer finds himself in that ditch, his death up close. That one's own life counts for nothing in the grand scheme of things—or, more precisely, that one's aspirations count only from one's own perspective, and as soon as this perspective has ceased to exist, these aspirations are irrelevant—is an insult to everyone's sense of self-importance.

Kleist's warriors' impudent jokes in the face of death and defeat are as desperate as they are lighthearted, as accepting as they are defiant. They are acknowledgments of human insignificance in an indifferent universe, at the edge of what Lacan calls the order of the real. The real ignores human delusion (the realm of what Lacan calls the imaginary order) and human structure (the symbolic order). Humans cannot dwell in it but they experience the real at its edge or limit.[35]

Particularly riotous—funny in a terrifying kind of way—is that, at the edge of the real (when he experiences the godforsakenness of the universe), Kleist's drummer asks for one last favor (*eine Gnade*—the religious overtones are clear in the German) only to defiantly reject all mercy. The drummer derides the reduction of absolute, divine mercy to a ritualized and insignificant element of the legal process (from mercy to "a mercy"). In a world that tyrannically demands cooperating (even with hypocritical rituals) but could care less about a subject marked as outrageous and criminal—the granting of a last wish must fly in the face of the convict like mockery. Kleist's drummer retrenches—like Antigone—into isolation.[36] Only by way of rejecting divine grace and all human association can the drummer and Antigone preserve their antisocial and perverse integrity.[37] Yet their antisociality remains social in that it is performed for an audience. By disrupting the disciplinary regime of mercy from within and exposing it to a campy and ironizing spectacle of his bare skin, the drummer forges a connection, even a physical one, with his audience.

The most tremendous joke, even though it is announced in the first line as a verbal one ("to pass human lips"), relies heavily on physical comedy. Kleist expertly stages the scene, which is his revision of a story he found in the weekly paper *Beobachter an der Spree*. He adds several elements that dramatize the narration and conjure up the action before our eyes. He creates a stage—the execution square, presumably prominently located in the town to which he has the gendarmes bring the drummer. The scene that is given on this stage has intradiegetic spectators—a circle of French officers. Kleist creates suspense by interrupting the narration of what unfolds center stage to describe the movement of these spectators—out of curiosity, they move closer to the center of the action, where the Prussian drummer asks the French colonel to grant him one last wish. By now, we, the readers, have identified with the French spectators—like them, we move a bit closer to hear the drummer's answer to the colonel's question about "what he wished"—and, abruptly, a naked butt is shoved right under our noses. The gesture literalizes camp's in-your-face attitude. And the crudeness of the physical comedy strikes us doubly, as it is utterly incongruous with the gravity of the situation.

In the modern Western world, exposing one's bare buttocks—or "flashing a browneye"—has an apotropaic function similar to that of displaying the phallus in ancient Greece.[38] The lone Prussian warrior has reached an impasse: the French are clearly in the majority, he stands no physical chance, and rational arguments won't help him either ("all efforts in his own defense were in vain"). So he resorts to magic. This anecdote contributes to Kleist's experiments with alternative symbolic orders by staging a bold exhibitionism of the buttocks, a defiant demand for a rim job, and a campy (profoundly committed and highly absurd) request for anal penetration that all fly in the face of reason—that is, of the phallogocentric order that developed from the phallic apotropaic magic of the ancient Greeks.[39] The anecdote celebrates such in-your-face attitude as genuinely Germanic or, in the terminology of Herder's Shakespeare enthusiasm, as truly "Nordic" ("neither Greek nor Roman history can show the equal"), but also as an affront to German humanism, which finds in Greek and Roman antiquity the pillars of a humanistic education and in the self-contained harmony of Greek sculpture a supreme model for beauty.[40] Kleist's drummer counters the sculpted human bodies and well-proportioned, self-contained human faces of Johann Winckelmann and Weimar Classicism with the open orifice of his derriere and, as we will see, with skinned flesh and a love for that which is beside the human.[41]

The drummer's act of mooning to ward off his enemies echoes Goethe's *Sturm und Drang* drama *Götz von Berlichingen* (Goethe 1991), which also resonates here in the reference to Shakespeare.[42] The aesthetic of Goethe's play presents an assault on the rule-governed poetics of French Classical drama. In this sense, Götz—like Kleist's drummer—serves as a figure for Germanic anti-Romance nationalism.[43] In Goethe's drama, the good old German characters are frank and at one with themselves. Goethe conveys this authenticity primarily through their way of speaking. They each speak their own vernacular, while the personages who belong to the abstract and deceitful new world speak a phony and stylized educated High German. With their idiom, no character in Goethe's *Sturm und Drang* play "exceed[s] his sphere," as Kleist describes "Shakespearean propriety" in the "Anecdote from the Recent War." But when it comes to his own work, we cannot take Kleist's Shakespeare comment at face value. Far from extolling character consistency, his anecdote, as we will see, makes a rather ironic case for bodily and character integrity.

In Goethe's drama, the free Imperial Knight Götz tells the spokesman of the imperial column besieging his castle that he will not renounce his right to self-defense: "Surrender? . . . Whom are you talking to! . . . Tell your Captain this: Before Imperial Majesty I have, as always, all due respect. But as for him, tell him he can kiss my arse [*er kann mich im Arsche lecken*]!" (Goethe 1991, 84).[44] Like Götz, who, from the beginning of the play, fights his last stand (as the free knights belong to the old world that is already palpably obsolete), Kleist's drummer is on a hiding to nothing. And, like Götz, the drummer defies abstract, institutional power with concrete vulgarity. Götz refuses to accept a deputy. In other words, he dismisses not only the fact that, with modernity, the center of power has been emptied out but also that sovereign power should at all be based on a hierarchical system of vicarious authority.[45] He rejects the rule of law in the form of state justice (the imperial army was sent as a corrective measure of the state against Götz, who was judged the offender in the quarrel with the bishop of Bamberg). Instead, he defends his rights only person to person and body to body and relates to the emperor only directly and personally.

It is this bodily contact that Kleist's drummer reintroduces into the formalized situation of the execution by drawing the bodies of the officers close and sticking his bare butt in their faces. This physical joke is followed by a verbal joke: the drummer asks to be shot in the rectum to save his hide. This joke is deeply puzzling; it perplexes and intrigues in the way of an "enigmatic signifier," as elaborated by Jean Laplanche.[46] There seems to be something implicitly sexual about it (a sexual fantasy that speaks un-revealed through this joke) but we have difficulty grasping its pleasure. We may understand it as an invitation to a homosexual sex act, but what would be the fun of being penetrated from behind by French soldiers when the penetrating object is a bullet that kills you right away? The desire the joke articulates—to save the skin—strikes us with its paradox. As he does frequently, Kleist here seems to be using an idiomatic expression as the backdrop for the scene. *Seine Haut retten* or *mit heiler Haut davonkommen* means "to escape danger," "to emerge from a difficult situation unharmed or from trouble unpunished." But despite the vitality and defiance of his physical comedy, this drummer knows that he won't get away with it, and his verbal joke shows this knowledge. He is aware of his imminent end, he feels isolated in a world seized by the enemy, and he knows that nobody cares—not even his creator, the narrator, who underwrites the death sentence with the moralizing comment that "he deserved it."[47] The drummer must feel completely forsaken. He responds to this experience of the indifference of the universe (the experience of the real) with care: the drummer cares for his drum. Kleist modifies the anecdote he found, insinuating the word *Fell* by the letter *F—damit das F . . . kein L . . . bekäme* ("so as not to tear a h . . . in his s . . .")—which echoes *Trommelfell* (drumhead).[48] The drummer refuses to give his heart to the bullet because his heart beats for the drum. What is more, with an attention to the material details of that which is beside the self (as in "beside the point"), the drummer takes care not to hurt the drum while being executed. By extending his anal orifice, he tries to make sure that his skin doesn't get pierced when he is shot, so that his skin can serve as a drumhead when he is no more.

This returns us to camp culture and to the idea that it combines critical (what Sedgwick also calls paranoid) with reparative valences (Sedgwick 1997). Drawing on Klein's notion of "reparation" and on her analysis of the nurture and the support that objects can offer the self (Klein and Riviere 1964, 57–119), Sedgwick (1997, 149–50) describes camp as deriving its affective involvement largely from the care that is given to old, unwanted, broken, and discarded things—from the voice lent to objects and the body lent to voices, and from the communal character of these practices. Campy attention to material detail can be experienced as solacing and nourishing a self that feels broken and unwanted. In this sense, camp builds a world in which emotional attachment and mutual repair shape the relationships between things and psyches, materials and histories.

As much as the drummer punctures the solemnity of the scene of execution and scoffs at the gravity of his situation, he also provides himself with comfort and repair. He does so by creating a scene of character integrity (remaining true to himself, he boldly faces overwhelming adversity and utter abandonment) and an image of physical inviolability (saving his hide past his execution). In doing so, he might seek to recover a self that was damaged and lost in the hostile environment.

Stentor

Some scholars argue that Kleist not only put his own literary work in the service of armed patriotism, thus becoming a drum major in the German war against Napoleon, but was also instrumental in the development of the propagandistic function of German national literature in general.[49] Critics of this assessment, who propose, relying on the idea of the autonomy of art, that Kleist's texts expose the necessary failure of the propagandistic project of literature, still leave unquestioned the presumption that Kleist aims at propaganda.[50] Their differences notwithstanding, all of these readings ignore the humor of Kleist's texts. In my view, Kleist uses camp humor both to satisfy and to ward off the call of the death drive as well as to pervert anti-Napoleonic sentiment because this new nationalism is codified as heteronormative. Rather than agreeing to serve as Stentor—a thundering voice for war—Kleist defuses the thunderstorm with his campy—sometimes melodramatic, sometimes slapstick—interludes. Relying on the logic of the mackle (which I have presented in chapter 1), Kleist disperses and thus attenuates the passion for violent exuberance as he plays at fueling it. I don't think we can understand Kleist—and the overlap of fueling and dispersing or satisfying and deterring in his work—if we don't move, at least temporarily, beyond the logical-libidinal system that became dominant in his time (and still remains so today) to a different logic, a different symbolic order, and a different way to engage the drive.

Bernhard Greiner describes what I call metalepsis—Kleist's manneristically literal language use, which simultaneously interrogates and authenticates signs—as metonymical displacement of ideas into bodies.[51] These displacements (*Verrückungen*), far from grounding the subject in a materially anchored means of communication, lead to an obsessive queerness or madness (*Verrücktheit*) that takes the specific form, according to Greiner, of a mad need to annihilate the human shape, a rage to kill and to destroy even the corpse, a death-driven desire for the amorphous:

> What is seemingly unequivocal, the sign taken as material, has displaced [*ver-rückt*] the idea to which it was supposed to lead. . . . The

> bridging from the field of determination . . . to the field of the idea, which is being explored in this drama [*The Battle of Herrmann*] through the practice of anchoring the sign in its materiality, is being shown as on the one hand failing, and on the other hand nevertheless succeeding, albeit in a displaced and maddening [*ver-rückend*] manner. . . . The idea, onto which the metonymically shifted sign opens, . . . manifests, . . . as the liberation of animalistic frenzy or, to reference Hölderlin, as the unleashing of a tendency toward the amorphous [*Aorgische*]. (Greiner 2000, 119, my translation)

In Greiner's view, Kleist's linguistic style drives the reader mad with displacements and transforms logos into uncontrolled passion. However, after his relatively perceptive analysis of the smudging and mackling effects of Kleist's linguistic practice, Greiner succumbs to the pervasive fear that messing with the phallocentric symbolic order (which demands arbitrary signs), will end in madness, chaos, and destruction—in fact, in sheer nothingness—and charges Kleist with advocating for unbound passion and rallying for a total war of complete annihilation: "So it is clear what kind of struggle for freedom this play [*Herrmann*] promotes: as later also in *Prince Frederick of Homburg* evidently the war of annihilation" (117, my translation).

In his seminal analysis, *Die Geburt des Partisanen aus dem Geist der Poesie* (*The Birth of the Partisan out of the Spirit of Poetry*), Wolf Kittler zeroes in on Kleist's use of the bards in *The Battle of Herrmann* as a poetological reflection on the role of poetry to bring about total mobilization for the war against Napoleon (and possibly beyond):

> The cheering harangues of hatred that the chorus of the bards delivers thus have the function to liberate, according to the spirit of philanthropic pedagogy, the self-directed autonomy of the partisans.
>
> In the night of the guerilla war, the German poets thus take a key position. . . . So, German national literature, which emerged as a concept in the second half of the eighteenth century, advances to the rank of a decisive element in the strategy of guerilla warfare. (Kittler 1987, 250–51, my translation)

While the Spaniards are engaging in what will turn out to be a successful guerrilla war against Napoleon, Kleist pursues via literature, Kittler argues, what some of the most advanced military strategists of the time—Gneisenau, Scharnhorst, and Clausewitz—advise the Prussian king to do, namely to incite the populace to a guerrilla war against French troops. Kittler points out the paradoxical and antidemocratic nature of this idea of centrally, and by royal decree, mobilizing a decentralized insurrection (224). The very German notion of *Bildung* or pedagogy plays an important role in this endeavor, with its contradictory and problematic effort to move people to act out of their own free will (or desire) in accordance with the goals of the society, the nation, the culture. Literature offers an important field for theorizing and practicing *Bildung* and this gives the German poets—and the Teutonic bards who figure them, according to Kittler—a chance to claim a central role.

But Kleist's humor mocks such writerly self-importance. Robert Guiscard, Duke of the Normans, for example, is supposed to be a Stentor. The text on which Kleist drew for the subject matter—Ferdinand von Funck's *Robert Guiskard: Herzog von Apulien und Calabrien*—stresses that he had a strong voice that could be heard above the turmoil of the battle (see Kleist 2000, 41). Like the bards, Guiscard thus functions as a figure for the war-rallying poet whose voice incites the fighters. But Kleist ridicules him wherever he can. Beginning with the excess of masculine signifiers in his title *Robert Guiskard, Herzog der Normänner*—the unusual *Normänner* instead of *Normannen* unduly foregrounds a virility that is echoed, but not exactly authenticated, in the *Herr* (lord, sir) that sounds in *Herzog* (duke). We find the same campy doubling of signifiers of masculinity in the unusual spelling of the Teuton leader, Herrmann. The fact that Kleist's Guiscard assures his audience that he in no way falls behind the historical image of the strong leader whose voice counts—"who stands in front of you possessed of all his life and vigor . . . / whose pure [*reine*] voice peals freely from his breast / and fills, like steeple bells, the air around" (*G* 370/10.439–42, translation altered)—does not exactly help against the erosion of manliness prompted by the rumor that he is severely ill and confirmed by the fact that shortly after this boast he swoons and lands on a kettledrum, presumably giving off a sound distinctly less "pure" than the peal of bells.

The historical Guiscard was a man of tremendous ambitions—strong, clever, and lucky enough to realize most of them. He achieved an impressive expansion of territory and power. As his last and most ambitious goal, and the one he failed to reach, he pursued the Crown of the Byzantine Empire. Kleist situates his Guiscard at the threshold to this final goal, just outside Constantinople—that is to say, on the threshold of failure. Guiscard used to know how to draw (out) an army of icy men (*er zog das Heer*, he was a *Herzog* of the *Normänner*, men of the North). They still love him. Only because of their loyalty was he able to consolidate his reign after serving as the representative of his nephew, the heir of the throne by birthright. But at this point, just outside of Constantinople, his men don't heed his call anymore. They are tired, they are sick with the plague, and they want to go home.

As a matter of fact, Guiscard's men are less icy than their name would suggest. The play begins with the people "praying fervently [*Mit heißem Segenswunsch*]" (*G* 355/1.1), in a heat that is both physical and emotional. It stems from the fever, a symptom of the plague, and from the fear that they are "mad with [*angstempört*]" (*G* 355/1.5). The Normen prove to be less than steely warriors as their feelings run high and their plague-ridden bodies decay while still alive. The organic decomposition and mental breakdown of the characters onstage is communicated to the audience in an immediate, sensuous, and contagious way by the "strongly smelling herbs" that Kleist's stage directions demand to be burned.[52] They are sure to conjure up the smell of rotten flesh that they are supposed to mask.

In this uncontainable atmosphere of turmoil, an elder is appointed to bring order and to address the Duke in the name of the people. The people want their elder to amplify their concern to the thundering voice of Stentor:

> But if he will not listen,
> The unrelenting man, then like a trumpet
> Of loud brass set the misery of all
> Our people to your lips and thunder what his duty
> Is into his ear!
>
> (*G* 356/2.49–53)[53]

Kleist has here radically subverted the figure of Stentor's voice. Rather than as a call to war, it serves as a demand to retreat. Instead of a single voice that cuts through the noise of the battle, a chaotic multitude of voices—"the misery of all our people"—is channeled into a single ear. Rather than leading to action by instigating the passions, it insists on duties and strictures in order to soothe the passion. Kleist subverts and undoes all the figures for aggressive strength he presents in this fragment—Guiscard, the Normen, and Stentor.

Partial

Like Stentor, the drummer of Kleist's anecdote would be an obvious candidate for inciting—or drumming up support for—violence. But the overlap of the drummer's art with the experience of the battlefield and the immediate involvement of the drummer's body both in the war and in his art (to the point that his body provides the material for his instrument) create a lack of distance that corrodes the instrumental function of drumming as well as the identity and integrity of the drummer.

The drumbeats are supposed to rouse the warriors to action and orient the dispersed partisans toward the common goal. As such, they would function like the song of the bards in Kittler's discussion. But unlike the song of the bards, with its combination of words and melody, the percussion of the drummers has an immediate connection to war: it doubles and merges with the noise of the battle—boots and hooves hitting the ground, bodies crashing into other bodies, weapons clashing, shots. The signifying function of drumming as a call to war is thus muddled by the immediate continuity (to play on Greiner's terms) of war and drumbeats or idea (of war) and sensuous signifier. The same continuity exists, in this message, between sender, instrument, and receiver. The sound waves of war beat on the tympanic membrane, on the eardrums of warrior and drummer.

But these metonymic contiguities do not, as Greiner fears, form a slippery slope toward total annihilation. Rather, they generate a feeling of care.[54] The battle creates a soundscape that presents an immediate reciprocity between the aggressive and the receptive position, between the warrior drummer as one who deals out a hiding and as a hide being beaten by sonic waves. The sound of gunshots, in particular, threatens to split the warrior's eardrum. Thus, when the drummer of Kleist's anecdote is sentenced to be shot and when he asks to be shot in the rectum so as not to tear a hole in his hide (*Fell*), he might be referring to the membrane in his ear (*Trommelfell*). He might be saying something along the lines of: I know how loud a gunshot is, please shoot me in the other end of my body, as far away from my ears as possible. The drummer is drum even before he articulates his desire to save his skin and become drum. He is eardrum being beaten during battle as he beats the drum. His desire to become drum thus overlaps with his desire to remain drum. Whether he refers to the skin of his body or the membrane in his ear, we find no frenzy of destruction, no rage toward the amorphous, no drumming for a war of annihilation here but, rather, a drummer's care for the integrity of his drumskin, his need to preserve and to become.

Kleist's camp humor thus does not only consist in mockery and critique. It also includes a pervasive generosity and deep sympathy with the characters it exposes as less than all that.[55] As Mark Booth (1983, 18) puts it, "To be camp is to present oneself as being committed to the marginal with a commitment greater than the marginal merits."

I don't mean to suggest that there is no death drive at work on the drummer. Kleist's characters clearly enjoy coming unglued, lacerating themselves and others, and being torn apart or otherwise rendered shapeless in very literal ways, and the drummer is no different in this respect. But I do want to challenge the position that equates these pleasures with a "yearning for pure annihilation" (Stephens 1983, 215). Manfred Schneider (2001), also presuming such a yearning, argues that it cannot be realized and shown onstage because the stage is bound by the forms of perception—place and time—and the rules of language, which all would be destroyed were "pure annihilation" carried out. He therefore maintains that "Kleist's war theater is always only the foreplay" (104)—foreplay of the death drive, prelude to its climaxing, which would consist, according to Schneider, in "turning all limits of nature, of religion, of the law, even the structure of space and time into a biological and epistemic desert, into a non-place" (114). In my view, such fears are baseless. There is no need to fear the climaxing of the death drive because, as Copjec (2002) shows, the death drive curbs itself and sublimation is part of the drive, not an external force applied to it. I see Kleist's drummer as a figure for this pleasurable self-inhibition of the death drive.

Copjec (2002, 20) clarifies that "the death drive achieves its satisfaction by not achieving its aim." The quandary that a dead body can hardly experience satisfaction is felicitously met by the fact that annihilation is never complete because the real, or being itself, is not one, that is to say, it is neither full, nor all, nor whole. By virtue of this incompleteness of being, the drive to merge with "the thing" or to return to unindividuated being (i.e., the death drive) itself exists only in partial form.[56] There are holes in being, and each subject experiences this situation in its own unique way as jouissance—a jouissance elicited by a small piece of being—an *objet a*, in Lacan's terminology—which absorbs and satisfies the death drive without ending in full annihilation (which would correlate with full being) or full satiation.[57] There is always a remainder. The holes that render being piecemeal resist the pathos of the Hole (the honorable, sublime gap in being), which, in my view, still corresponds to the pathos of the whole.

Kleist's drummer desires skin. Here skin serves as the partial object that keeps his desire alive.[58] Tautened skin's tendency to vibrate when it is beaten gives him jouissance. In a kind of perverse version of Kleinian "reparation," he responds to the holes in being with a riotous and certainly pleasurable humor that wells up from a profound acknowledgment of the abyss of the real but that also, in a way, stretches a skin over a hole, thus fabricating a drum. He cares for and protects the integrity of his drums even beyond his own biological death.[59] He thus ends up with a Sedgwickian reparative version of camp that "confers plenitude on an object" in the midst of the inchoate world of war and the terrible reality of generalized hostility (see Sedgwick 1997, 149). While war, aggression, and annihilation clearly factor into his desire and are perhaps even its aim—care, nurture, and solace feed his desire, getting in the way of this aim.

The same is true for the poet who might feel called on to serve as a drum major for war. The care and attention he gives his "pieces" of theater—composing them, attending to certain scenes and motives (including those that splatter and mangle organic bodies and elegant phrases), adding layers of variations—necessarily obstructs the passage to war and destruction.[60] Kleist fails to reach the complete annihilation of form. He must fail. But, ironically, or rather, campily—since camp finds success in passionate failures and fails when it is too successful—such failure is a mode of satisfying his desire for the amorphous.

The death drive attenuates itself across the work of the poet. The drummer's skin absorbs the war god's powerful voice. The desire for the amorphous, the desire to annihilate and dissolve, fades into the desire to repair, solace, and nurture. It does so naturally, as it were. That is to say, culture and the superego need not subdue nature and its ostensibly terrible passions. Instead, nature itself uses cultural work—the transformation of nature—to better forget the aim of its deadly desire.

Slapstick

Kleist uses physical comedy to diffuse pathos and to counteract the force of narrative coherence and logical consequence—the tragic power of fate. Eve, in *The Broken Jug*, knows that it is not so much the drumbeat by itself but the logic of inferences and the compelling order of story lines that, if consequently followed, colonize everything and reach their conclusion only in death and destruction:

> Let him follow the drum:
> The drum follows the sergeant, he the captain,
> Captain follows the major, he follows
> The general, and he in turn follows the government
> And the government—hang it!–
> It's rambling on and cooking up schemes all over the globe [*die ziehen in Gedanken weit herum*].
> They'll drum and drum til the drumskins split!
> (*J* 77–78/Variant.2035–41, translation altered)

While one link in the hierarchy tightly follows the other, this gapless syntax not only leads to but is also anchored in nothing. The highest authority (here the government of the United Netherlands) betrays its aimlessness by roving around in thought and letting their imagination run riot—until the drumskins split.

What will be the course of Kleist's unfinished tragedy, what the (con) sequence of Guiscard's ambition? We know from history, and particularly from Funck's account, that Guiscard, after having been lucky for a rather long time, will fall into a ditch, as Goethe has it in his speech "Zum Shakespeares-Tag," within eyeshot of the goal he hoped to attain: the Crown. Given the morale of his troops, we might expect that Guiscard's army will drown in its own fear after the death of its leader (see Samuel 1981, 344–45). But before any of these deaths happen—or, rather, instead of any of these deaths happening (since we only have this fragment of the tragedy)—Kleist gives us the pleasure of the death drive with the hilarious image of Guiscard's fall cushioned by a kettledrum.

Guiscard is as deaf as a rock. He is insensitive to the disease and to the fears that have befallen his people.[61] In this situation, the people feel that Guiscard is in need of tremors, of vibrations, of trembling and so they send an elder "to shake the rock [*den Felsen zu erschüttern*]" (*G* 355/1.4). But the Duke uses his authority to demand quiet and imposes a regime of silence. He needs rest. At that point, he seems fragile, overstimulated, autistic even: the chaotic ocean noise of the people, who "seethe and boil / just like the open sea," irritates him, and it doesn't help that the name of the delegate elder—Armin—forms an anagram of "marine" (*marin*; *G* 356/2.37–39). The Duke's son relays his orders when he asks Armin to disappear without a sound: "So when I order you to leave this place at once, . . . do it instantly, without a murmur [*lautlos*], now!" (*G* 362/6.218–20). And when his nephew, Abälard, mingles with the people, adding to their noise, the Duke orders him back into the silent fold of the family: "Stay right there—and not a word [*lautlos*]" (*G* 369/10.412; see also Reuß, Staengle, and Baumann 2000). No talking back, no seething back! Guiscard needs quiet.

At the same time, Kleist's text orchestrates the roar of two competing Stentor calls. There is the Duke's call to war—a call forward, a call to expand and to win the imperial crown: "I'll come to stop in Stambul, not before!" (*G* 370/10.448).[62] And there is Armin's call back, back home, back to the father, back to the lost paradise: "Lead us back home, back to the fatherland! [*zurück, zurück, ins Vaterland*]" (*G* 373/10.524, my translation).[63] In an atmosphere saturated with the competing smells of frankincense and decaying flesh,[64] in the midst of the tension between two thundering voices calling in opposite directions and a nervous attempt by the ruling family to impose silence, Kleist cracks a joke:

GUISCARD: Why have you come here? Go on and speak! And be brief.
I've matters waiting for me in the tent.
OLD MAN (*after a short pause*):
You know it, sir, you feel it just as much as we—
On whom does our distress weigh heavier than you?
At the decisive moment, as already—
(*Guiscard looks around him and the Old Man stops.*)
DUCHESS (*in a low voice*):
Is there something
That you want—?
ROBERT: Would like—?
ABELARD: You need—?
DUCHESS: God in heaven!
ABELARD: What's the matter?
ROBERT: What is it?
DUCHESS: Speak, Guiscard, do!
(*The Empress pushes a large drum behind him.*)
GUISCARD (*easing himself down on the drum, under his breath*):
Dear child!–
Now tell me what is on your mind, Armin?
Say what you have to say and let off
Freely the words, I don't like nervous stuttering!
(*The Old Man, thinking, stares down at the ground.*)
A VOICE OUT OF THE CROWD:
Why does he delay?
ANOTHER VOICE: Old granddad, speak!

OLD MAN (*recollecting himself*):
You know
Why we are here—and who should know better
Than yourself on whom the hand of fate
Rests heaviest? Just as, great bridegroom
Of the goddess Victory, you went to fling yourself
Into the bed of your bride, bosom all
Afire, your arms already reaching out
To consummate the nuptials—directly in your way
The horrid pestilence stepped!
(G 371–72/10.484–99, translation altered)

Guiscard wants to seize Constantinople, but "at the decisive moment" he falls into a kettledrum. It's Chaplinesque. What is more, he pretends nothing happened. Now, sitting on the drum as if it were a throne, he almost blames Armin for the holdup—asking him with impatience to finally make his speech. The phrase "let off [*laß es frei*]" carries an unfortunate undertone of flatulence. This tone is perhaps only audible because it follows a scene of physical comedy and thus is amplified by its echo. Guiscard, according to the stage directions, "gently eas[es] himself down": that is to say, in his distress, he labors to control his falling body so as to muffle the thud with which his butt will land on the drumhead. It is an effort to keep from embarrassing himself too much—just like the contortions one sometimes engages in to prevent or conceal the noise when passing gas in company. "Under his breath," he says something to his daughter to cover the breath of the kettledrum. All in all, Guiscard comes across more as a Zanni than as a Capitano.[65]

"Do Not Confuse My Feeling!"

Kleist's particular version of the self-curbing of the death drive—the way he gets to enjoy his desire for the amorphous—lies in doubling, mixing, and confounding the visual and its shapes with the acoustic and its power to entrance. Kittler (1987) categorically separates vision from hearing. For him, the visual paradigm belongs to the Enlightenment, to rationality, and to conventional warfare with its formations, its banners, its plans of action, and its orders. He places Kleist in the realm of the acoustic, which, for him, characterizes Romanticism, affect, German national poetry (as founded by Klopstock), and guerrilla warfare with its various tactics to prevent the enemy from gaining an overview of the situation.[66] Our analysis, conducted throughout this book, of Kleist's insistent mackling of the senses shows that Kittler's identification of Kleist with the acoustic cannot be maintained. Instead, Kittler's separation and ensuing taxonomy seems steeped in an anti-emotional ideology.[67]

Greiner's (2000) account of feeling is more sophisticated. He points to affect as the decisive motivator in undecidable situations (111–13). He then, as I already mentioned, warns of its destructive power (114–18). And, most interestingly, he shows that it requires a special effort to keep a feeling strong, focused, and clear (so that it can motivate a decision). Greiner points out that "the song of the bards seems to have aroused an 'unequivocal feeling' in Herrmann; since, when his captain asks him about the plan of action, the song of the bards having just faded, Herrmann barks at him: 'Do not confuse my feeling!' " (Greiner 2000, 119, my translation; *BH* 105/5.14.2285). Because feeling is not only easily but indeed inherently confused, the unambiguous feeling needs to be specially constructed and purified. This requires the labor of isolation and focus. Herrmann forcefully screens out the demands of the moment and the concerns of his army chiefs to be able to concentrate solely on that one feeling of hatred for the enemy that the song of the bards labors to produce. He purifies his hatred by rejecting the conciliatory notes that other emotional subjects mix in and by pointing the feeling exclusively at one target.[68] He refuses to dilute his hatred for the Romans with the punishment of Germanic traitors: "Forgive! Forget! Reconcile, embrace and love one another! / . . . Varus and the cohorts, I tell you: / This is the enemy that enflames my heart!" (*BH* 104–5/5.14.2282–87).

Greiner (2000, 119) seems to disparage feeling for needing to be shored up, when he mockingly comments that "the aroused unequivocal feeling seems quite uncertain if it cannot bear questioning." I find it rather felicitous that the painstakingly constructed unambiguous feeling proves rather precarious while affect left to its own devices inhibits and sublimates itself like the death drive in Copjec's reading of Lacan. The opposition between reason, measure, form, and the visual, on the one hand, and unmeasured affect, the amorphous, and the acoustic, on the other, doesn't hold. Affect has its own rationality, with which it analyzes, partializes, and moderates itself.

Meanwhile, those who attempt, more or less willfully, to harbor, nourish, and protect an unconfused feeling are left in a deranged state by the very process of isolating and purifying their emotions. Having joined the bards in their labor of love for the feeling of hatred, Herrmann is effectively lost to the battle. First he is too busy listening to the bards to give orders; one of his captains has to lay out the plan of action in his stead (*BH* 103/5.14.2245–47). Then Herrmann and his men miss the decisive battle against the Roman army. Delayed by his efforts to concentrate on his hatred, he arrives on the scene only after another Germanic prince has already led the Teutons to victory (*BH* 113/5.20.2459–62). Finally, he cedes the opportunity to kill the Roman leader Varus in a duel to yet another Germanic prince (*BH* 116/5.22.2515–16). We see that the subject who takes it upon himself to purify feeling (and thus to render it more logical in the traditional sense) can do so only by becoming absorbed (paralyzed and rendered absent (*entrückt*) verging on the insane (*verrückt*) in the process.

Kleist's staging of Herrmann being distracted from war by his focus on the bards, whose stated task is to lead the warriors into battle, indulges an irony that is comical rather than tragic. It is as if Herrmann has found a loophole to escape the very battle that carries his name. Kleist's title for his most nationalist play refers to a dropout. Herrmann got too excited by the call to follow the call. He found his jouissance even before he missed his goal. With his ironic—if not exactly pacifist—example, Herrmann could show the way to a society where nobody will come when a war is declared (see Sandburg 1936). The historic battle in the Teutoburg Forest did take place, but since Kleist has it fought and won in Herrmann's absence, the title of his play refers perhaps rather to Herrmann's battle with his feeling.

Appropriately enough, given the gendering of feeling around 1800, Kleist adds elements of gender drag to this comedy of evasion. Structurally speaking, Herrmann appears in drag as his wife Thusnelda right after he asks not to be disturbed in his feeling and, not coincidentally, mentions the swelling of his breast.[69] Greiner has called our attention to the fact that, in the composition of the play, the scenes that show Thusnelda luring the Roman legate Ventidius to a rendezvous with a famished bear replace the expected battle of Herrmann against Varus (Greiner 2000, 117). Dramaturgically, the laceration of Ventidius is substituted for the battle in the Teutoburg Forest. Thusnelda thus stands in for Herrmann as she is doubled by the bear. In this play of displacements and derangements, her fit of madness provides an over-the-top version of Herrmann's disabling absorption in his passion.

Thusnelda's show of savage brutality and her mocking usurpation of the phallus is paralleled in quasi-complementary fashion by Herrmann's performance of melodramatic femininity.[70] With the melodramatic gesture of "*leaning against the trunk of an oak tree, propped on his hand before him*" while listening to the bards, as the stage directions not only specify but repeat—"*deeply moved, he sinks back against the oak trunk again*" (*BH* 103/5.14)—Kleist offers comical relief to parody the seriousness of emotional labor and to highlight its inherent contradiction. His campy staging exposes the (usually repudiated) effort it takes to keep a feeling strong, focused, simple, and clear. When absorbed in the labor of purifying feeling, the towering leader is unable to stand on his own. His excessive masculinity—marked by the double masculine signifier of his name (*Herr Mann*)—falters. The shrewd manipulator needs the support of the next-best—but, of course, properly Germanic—tree trunk.[71] Putting on the masquerade of what is conventionally described as womanliness he throws his arm out as if to say, "Oh, I am so weak. Oh, I cannot fight!" (see Riviere 2015).

Unlike the low, ignoble drummer whose immediate involvement in the field of destruction turns into care, the sovereign leader Herrmann is able to extract himself from the action by carving out a space for his absorption in art. Herrmann only comes to, as it were, in the very last scene of the play. And he does so to mete out the death sentence to one of his own, the Germanic prince Aristan, leader of the Ubii. The separation of hate from love, in which one is aimed exclusively at the Romans and the other at all Teutons, has clearly worn off. The effect of art is neutralized on reentry into life-as-usual. This segregation of life into an aesthetic existence and a social existence is bound up with the demand for purified feeling—a demand that cannot be lastingly satisfied. As it turns out (with the admittedly significant exception of Septimus), all direct objects of Herrmann's cruelty (Hally, Thusnelda, Aristan) are Teuton rather than Roman:[72] ample evidence for the confusedness of his feeling.

While exposing the paralyzing absorption in affective purification and the impossibility of escape from confusion in the figure of Herrmann, Kleist gives us, with the "Anecdote from the Recent War," a figure of affective integrity that overlaps with disintegration and doesn't screen out its intrinsic confusion but, rather, plays with it and draws comical and sexual pleasure from it. On the structural level of his texts, Kleist presents feeling as, in an enabling way, confused and displaced (to bring back Greiner's wordplay on *ver-rückt*). His analgrammar orders by way of nonorder or structures by way of tearing the structure. Rather than as a frenzy of annihilation, confusion by displacement (*Verrückung*) plays itself out in Kleist via the self-partializing and self-moderating tendency toward the amorphic as a dispersion and blurring of form and image in repetition—which I have described as mackle.[73]

Good Gracious

We have already discussed how the drummer in the "Anecdote from the Recent War" ridicules the regime of mercy and "exposes" its "insufferableness."[74] Kleist also packs a more serious tone of critique into the kettledrum scene of slapstick and flatulence humor in *Robert Guiscard*. The scene assaults some notions that keep close company with mercy (*Gnade*), namely favor (*Gunst*) and grace (*Grazie*, *Anmut*). Guiscard enjoys the favor of his people and is graced by nature with exceptional gifts. The themes of favor and grace refer us to Schiller's argument in *On Grace and Dignity* that "grace is a favor granted to the sensuous by the ethical" (Schiller 2005a, 145).

In Greiner's (2000, 140) view, Kleist aspires to Schiller's reconciliation of ethics and aesthetics but fails somewhat similarly to his protagonist Guiscard, who is thwarted, Greiner claims, by the plague and its powerful "No!" I don't think that the plague speaks as intentionally and clearly as Greiner suggests or that we should read the plague as a sign of Guiscard's guilt and I don't think that Kleist emulates Schiller here. I take the references to Schiller in *Guiscard* instead as parodistic.[75] Guiscard is not only being mocked by Kleist for his lack of dignity and grace: Kleist's camp also exposes the insufferableness of Schiller's ethical values and subverts them. This is corroborated by his later creation, the drummer, who doesn't want anything to do with ethics—especially not in the starkly gendered version that Schiller promotes.[76]

According to the dancer in Kleist's own essay on grace, "On the Theater of Marionettes," grace consists in antigravity (Kleist 2009, 269). While such light-hearted antiseriousness is something for marionettes, male virgins, and bears (as the three examples discussed in the essay suggest), to those who cannot quite live up to these ideals of carefreeness, finding a back door to the behind of paradise is recommended.[77] This basically means falling/failing again (and again). Kleist fails well, when, instead of completing the tragedy (of Guiscard), he gets sidetracked by a humoristic interlude, finds satisfaction there, and abandons the aim of the death drive: the desire to eclipse all of his fellow poets. He discovers that "the gaping hole," which Wieland saw in the literary accomplishments of the time, does not need to be filled, that bare skin stretched over holes can vibrate and hold our attention, and that pieces can satisfy again and again.[78] Tragedy doesn't carry through because the death drive curbs itself.

Related to these concerns about grace and gravity, Kleist presents a counterdogmatic version of the sublime (*Erhabene*). He insists on the inseparability of the fallen from the elevated. Instead of the a priori (i.e., timeless) superiority of reason over sense perception or the glowing shine of the moral through the sensual, Kleist distills from Kant's and Schiller's notions of the sublime the campy image of the character who rises from the dead because his death has been declared by mistake.[79] Kleist exploits this hardly ennobling intertwinement of pathos and bathos to comical and dramatic effect. Take, for example, the rapid turn in *Prince Frederick of Homburg* when the protagonists discover that the elector is alive after they just received eyewitness reports of his fall in battle.[80] These scenes cause serious confusion and emotional turmoil for the protagonists but they never turn uncanny or religious because it is always clarified that the character in question did not actually die.[81] Kleist thus shifts the stain of appearance and error from the sensuous to reason, shows up as nonserious spectacle the self-ennobling move of reason that characterizes the sublime, and lets his joke soar to supreme heights by reminding us that Kant himself endorsed antiseriousness when he considered the actual death (of the person encountering the sublime) a detriment to sublime experience.[82]

In addition to deriding the idea of the sublime (and other dignified aesthetic categories like tragedy and epic), Kleist's scenarios, which insist that elevation is always *re*-erection, corrode the pathos of both the outdated aristocracy and the modern political uprisings.[83] And he gives the sense, with his scenes of—faux—revenants and resurrections, that tyranny cannot be overcome in a serious fashion.

His *Guiscard* suggests that failure has the last word in this correspondence of rising and falling: that resurrection is bound to fail/fall. Guiscard might be a darling of fortune but he is no Jesus. Armin makes it very clear that if Guiscard said to a leper "Be clean!" or to Lazarus "Rise and walk!," no miracle would happen. The old man insists that any plague-ridden Norman falls "unable to stand up again [*auferstehungslos*]," which is to say that he falls without resurrection ("and where he sinks, there is his grave [*und wo er hinsank, sank er in sein Grab*]" [*G* 372/10.505 and 506]). If his fate (*Los*) is to rise again (*Auferstehungslos*), it's only to fall again: "Again he tries . . . and back again he sinks [*und wieder . . . und wieder nieder*]" (*G* 372/10.507–10).

Guiscard seems anything but graceful when it comes to managing and securing his power and preventing exaltations and uprisings (*Erhebungen*) by his army or the people. His blunt coercion becomes particularly palpable in the repressive and censoring quality of his demand for silence. Kleist turns this demand against Guiscard by reclaiming (thus using a foundational queer tactic avant la lettre) silence for an interlude of pantomime. He displays and plays along with the imposition of silence only to defuse its disciplinary spirit by having Guiscard speak in half-silence with his butt.[84]

Armin's speech draws the link (that Kleist never tires of exposing) between antagonism and genital heterosexuality. But Kleist's campy staging, through layers of interruption, provides a positive alternative. Armin just began to narrate how Guiscard was interrupted by the outbreak of the plague "at the decisive moment," and we will find out after Guiscard's episode that this is the moment when he wanted to "consummate the nuptials" with the goddess of victory (*G* 370/10.489, translation altered; *G* 371/10.497).[85] The story of the coitus interruptus is also interrupted by the plague—or by Guiscard's dizzy spell, which is likely a symptom of the plague. The dizzy spell not only figures impotence, thus softening, as it were, the restrictive and disciplinary character of coitus interruptus, but also transgresses the boundary of figuration by transitively blurring both the narrative levels and the oppositions and antagonisms in play here. The interruption "at the decisive moment" has a metaleptic effect: it mingles what is told with the act of telling onstage. Armin's story about failure and interruption is interrupted by Guiscard's performance of a fall. This performance takes the edge off the serious either-or of thundering voice (in whatever direction) or complete silence. It offers instead the muffled sound, "under the breath" of pantomimic camp (*G* 372/10.490). And instead of the face-off in which two leaders penetrate each other with thundering Stentor calls, we get Guiscard's intimacy with the kettledrum—his butt propped on its head, the drumhead, in a posture that, because it is so comical, cannot be read as domineering.

Decomposition

In camp, serious dedication overlaps with an explosive antiseriousness. Susan Sontag oscillates between describing camp as the sensibility that embraces artifice, and prescribing naive, passionate, and serious involvement in camp.[86]

Christopher Nealon (2004, 581) elaborates on this awkward and incongruous naïveté when he suggests that camp "invites us to take up a polemical affection for what's obsolete, misguided, or trivial, and to risk the embarrassment of trying it out." We find this overlap of the serious and the antiserious also in the irony with which Kleist makes his case for bodily and character integrity. While I stand by my reading of the drummer's wish to keep his skin whole as a sincere endeavor to become drum and an earnest love for the musical instrument, I want to hold with it the observation that the solace the drummer takes in the idea of turning his skin into a drum head is so obviously misguided that its antiserious artificiality cannot be missed. The character integrity of the drummer combines propriety (staying within his bounds as a drummer) with an egregious assault on propriety (figured as dropping his pants in front of the judge). This combination makes his sphere shake like the earth, what Kleist's peer, the great master of the pun—Shakespeare—would have endorsed with the signature Shakesphere.[87] The drummer's self-mockery overlaps with his integrity; he is earnest and antiearnest at the same time.

Kleist marks his antiseriousness about integrity with the composition of this anecdote. He lets the authenticity of the artifice and its aesthetic precision disintegrate. Kleist's text stutters—the joke doesn't so easily pass human lips, after all. At first the narration strives for realism, identifying the specific military affiliation of the drummer ("of what was then the Puttkamer regiment") with authenticating uncertainty: "I believe." But with the reference to Shakespeare, the effort to ground this story in the real world is abandoned and the world of theater is established as the frame of reference. Yet even as an aesthetic artifice, the story falls apart. At first take, the anecdote impresses with its tight composition. In Wilhelm Grimm's judgment, for example, "the anecdotes of Kleist are very well told and very pleasant; but the drummer, who preferred not to present his heart as a target, hit his mark" (Sembdner 1996, 366, my translation). On a closer look, which I will provide now by way of a conclusion of my reading of this anecdote, its composition shows so many incongruous layers that it dissolves in a perhaps disconcerting manner, involving a pleasure very different from the one Grimm expressed. While the drummer asks for an execution that saves his hide, Kleist mackles the execution of his joke and thus refuses to sublate the terrible story in a higher, aesthetic unity. At all levels, this anecdote undoes its own seriousness when it comes to the commitment to integrity.

The composition of the joke has a physical, visual, or performative side and a verbal, oral, or narrative side, and the two are improperly overlaid. We have already encountered the vivid, i.e., hypotypotic, and dramatic setup of the joke, which creates suspense and demands participation through identification. Like the setup, the punchline also combines theatricality with narration. In the punchline of the joke, Kleist mackles presence with representation, the verbal with the physical, enactment with narration, and textuality with orality: "and when the colonel [. . .] asked the man: what he wished? he stripped his trousers and spoke: that they may shoot him in the . . . , so as not to tear a h . . . in his s . . . ." As we have already discussed, the physical comedy consists in the drummer puncturing the execution ritual of the last wish by showing his bare behind, thus accomplishing a surprising turn from the solemn to the vulgar, from speech to body, from the accepting anticipation of death to a defiantly lively presence, and from supplicant to disinterested giver (the drummer tenders his rear and shows that he gives a shit). Then there is the second, more enigmatic joke that lies in the articulation of the last wish and the reasoning for it. The drummer wants to be shot in the rectum so as not to tear his skin, because, as a drummer, he prefers nonpierced (ear)drums. In addition, there is a textual aspect to the joke. The two colons and the question mark function as gestures, as little instances of textual theater. They motion toward direct speech. But, since that direct speech fails to appear (the narration continues in indirect speech), the listener is not able to notice the colons and question mark when the punchline is read out loud. These punctuation marks are gestures of the text in that they need to be seen but cannot be heard. Secretly making a mockery of the demand for economy essential to esprit, they slightly disturb the textual version of a narration that flows smoothly when delivered orally.[88]

The smooth oral delivery of the punchline is arguably one of the most important requirements for the effectiveness of any joke. Here its clean execution (the guillotine certainly belongs to the point) is gravely inhibited by another set of visual stagings: the three ellipses that Kleist inserts. If the sphere of the drummer remains unbreached by his joke, the joke itself—the line that serves the punch—is riddled with bullet holes. In its incompleteness, the joke desires a reader. It asks to be mended, filled-in, fulfilled. Each reader has to decide whether and how to (not) do so.[89] A faithful oral rendition of the text will turn out a clumsy telling of the joke; an effective delivery of the punchline will mean that the reciter exceeds her sphere and begins to ad-lib.

And then there is the add-on of the narrator's final comment. On its own, the verbal joke "they may shoot him in the . . . , so as not to tear a h . . . in his s . . ." is funny just because it is absurd. Only the narrator's commentary provides a deeper layer to the humor by connecting the drummer's last wish to his professional identity and to his desires and pleasures as one who gives a hide a hiding. This supplement is truly original and thus supplies an additional punchline. The last sentence gives a hint, which turns the joke into a riddle. It produces another joke, which is neither told nor performed but consists in the beginning of an interpretation. The exegetic bit nevertheless belongs to and constitutes the joke itself (even if only because we need it to fill in the ellipses). It is a piece that is outside and inside the joke at the same time; it traverses the boundaries of its own sphere—the sphere of the joke—and shows again that the integrity of this tight anecdote is riddled, after all. Across the different layers—of performance, narration, and commentary, of body and character, of the oral and the textual—the most tremendous joke is torn, replicated, and mackled.

As it shreds itself, Kleist's camp humor partializes violence and aggression and disperses the stigma. Thus, Kleist's camp practice supports the suggestion made by Ann Pellegrini (2007, 179) that "perhaps, then, camp does not so much 'neutralize the sting' [Newton 1979] of social disapproval as multiply and extend it."

Chapter 5

✦

Offstage Onstage, or How to Crack an Emotion

"A major virtue of the visual arts is their capacity to make the invisible visible"—with this bold statement Leo Bersani and Ulysse Dutoit (2004, 1) open *Forms of Being*, their book on cinema, aesthetics, and subjectivity. From a different perspective, Annamarie Jagose questions the virtue of visibility and the struggle for it. Her book *Inconsequence*, on lesbian representation and the logic of sexual sequence, analyzes how the incoherences of the modern sex/gender system produce the lesbian as a figure for the limit conditions of cultural visibility (2002, 12–13). Noting that the status of the lesbian within the hierarchy of gender and sexuality is doubly secondary and therefore mostly disregarded, she argues that we are able to question identity categories in general by exploring the invisibility of the lesbian. Inspired by these competing yet connected approaches to the visual, this chapter will discuss Kleist's unusual strategies to create a stage for the visibility—or the visible invisibility—of what the emerging paradigm of expression has in the eighteenth century begun to relegate to interiority, namely feeling or soul. In the next chapter, we will build on this discussion and explore Kleist's chimeric lesbians.

Creating a stage for the visibility of the invisibility of feeling is different from rendering feelings visible onstage. The latter phrasing presumes that there is something invisibly existing in the interior that could subsequently be expressed and made visible. This sequential logic has consequences, as Jagose demonstrates. She considers "sequence as a regulatory technology" (Jagose 2002, xiv), where the hierarchically organized terms of first and second, before and after, or origin and derivation normalize "hierarchical relations between categories of sexual identity" (xv)—so that the first sex can present itself as superior to the second, heterosexuality claim precedence over homosexuality, and male homosexuality seem more relevant than female homosexuality. Emotionality and sexuality are mutually implicated not only in the bourgeois love plot but also in the project of *Bildung* (formation and education) in general, including its cultivation of sensibility. Jagose situates what she calls "sexual sensibility" (the cultural shaping and channeling of sexual pleasure in the eighteenth century) within the bourgeois politics of the refinement or *Bildung* of sensibility and taste, and elucidates the hetero-sexualizing regime of sequence (Jagose 2007). The eighteenth century develops a culture of sensibility by establishing expression as the only proper way to communicate feeling. Yet the outward thrust of expression is commonly defined as derivative and thus presupposes the existence of an inside original.[1] In an unacknowledged reversal of primacy and derivation that is as paradoxical as it is characteristic of the logic at work here, the paradigm of "expression" thus constitutes and naturalizes interiority. The sequential logic of *Bildung* annexes the body as expression of interiority and naturalizes feeling and desire in an intensely gendered regime of emotional expressionism.[2]

Bersani and Dutoit offer a theory of vision that provides an alternative to the mode of seeing that reads the visual as the expression of a prior interiority. They develop an aesthetics of doublings and inaccurate replications through discussions of visual artworks as historically distant from one another as Caravaggio's paintings and the films of the twentieth century. I argue that Kleist, using a similar aesthetic, extends the doublings and replications across the line that distinguishes the visual from the textual components of theater.

Kleist resists the naturalizing, gendering, and heterosexualizing effect of sentimental *Bildung* by developing unusual and rather queer strategies to present feelings as spatiotemporal shapes. He does not favor the expressive capacities of theater—its theatrical gestures, for example—to make emotion visible. Nor does he use the four walls of the theater to create an allegory for the interior space of the soul—a new technique that the Weimar Classicists develop. Instead, Kleist doubles the embodied action onstage with narrative pre-, re-, and postpresentations and intertwines textual and performative strategies by bringing textuality onto the stage and drawing the stage into the text. The mackles that erode genre distinctions form a theatrical aesthetics that counteracts the bourgeois models of expression and allegory.

The expressional paradigm so powerfully organizes the field of vision that it appears to be the only one possible. Thus, those concerned with developing a different mode of seeing must at first appear as defenders of invisibility. Or, as Bersani and Dutoit (2004, 2) put it, they find themselves "under an obligation, at once ethical and ontological, to paint a call to invisibility at the heart of the visible world." In Kleist's theater, this call to invisibility emerges from his heavy reliance upon narrative elements, such as messenger reports, teichoscopies, and hypotypotic speech. While Jagose explains how the teleological force of narrative retrospectively consolidates and naturalizes identity, Kleist's excessive use of narrative within the theater has the opposite effect.[3] In combination with but insubordinate to dramatic mimesis, narrative creates here what Bersani and Dutoit describe as the aesthetic dispersal of identity. When Kleist doubles the performative elements of theater—letting us hear, letting us see, and letting us feel—with one another rather than organizing them hierarchically (as when speech expresses the character, for example, or gestures convey the message of the text), this creates disorder—especially because each element affects the other and so the structure of the play as a whole affects and troubles itself.

In this chapter, we will analyze how Kleist's scenes oscillate between the visual and the verbal and layer slightly different accounts of a feeling into what I have proposed to describe as a multiple impression or mackle (see chapter 1). Such layering blurs the contours of feeling. While feelings, in Kleist, can, with some effort, be seen, they are not clear and distinct. They never quite come into focus. I don't view this as an epistemological deficiency.[4] Instead, Kleist's aesthetics of layered emotionality and dispersed feeling suggests a new emotional ontology.[5] It brings into view that emotions are constructed (simultaneously with their being experienced and by way of reiterations) and that, as Sara Ahmed (2004, 15) has argued, they "open bodies to others." Kleist shows us a soul without contoured identity and feelings that are not singular but layered. They are created through inconsequential (to echo Jagose), that is, both nonsequential and negligible repetitions. Again and again, Kleist models not-quite-event-like, theatrical yet undramatic, imperceptible emotionality. Despite his flashiness, Kleist gives us minute differences and disperses the event.

Teichoscopies of Feeling

The Greek term *teichoscopy* can be translated as "viewing from the walls." It is a dramatic device that places a character on a lookout to offer a synchronous description of events that take place outside of the other characters' and the audience's field of vision. Especially when the eyewitness is literally positioned on the town wall, teichoscopy underpins the separation between the cultural space of the city (including the theater) and the uncultured, chaotic, dreadful events that happen outside—between things that can be shown onstage and those that need to be kept at a distance.

It has been noted that Kleist makes ample use of teichoscopy while also exceeding and ruining its traditional function. Klotz points out that in *Penthesilea* Kleist has so radically subverted the theatrical space—in the sense that the setting does not offer a familiar, organized, civilized space but only savage terrain—that teichoscopy cannot function anymore as a modulating gate to the horrific outside (cf. Klotz 1996, 90). The outside is already inside, there are no walls and there seem to be no boundaries. Gabriele Brandstetter (1997, 89) argues that Kleist's teichoscopies, together with other narrative elements (she mentions messenger reports; one would have to add the epic quality of some passages of dialogue), open the material, theatrical space onto a virtual stage and thus constitute a transgression of the theater in the Classical Aristotelian sense. Kleist's theater mobilizes another scene—the scene of the unconscious—not as other to, opposed to or outside of but as next to, overlapping with and intruding upon the conscious, the cultured, and the political. The obscene sets the scene.

If the outside is already inside, then teichoscopy functions differently than usual; it effects a different relation between the virtual and the material. Rather than distancing physical reality by transforming it into speech, Kleist's teichoscopies actualize the virtual through speech. They construct concrete scenes in the overall indistinguishable chaos (which can be reassuring or liberating, fascinating or horrifying). This generative element of Kleist's teichoscopies is particularly relevant when it comes to teichoscopies of feeling. By "teichoscopy of feeling," I mean a scene where a character offers a synchronous description of a feeling as it is being constructed, taking shape and coming into view by that very description. Teichoscopy constitutes the feeling's entrance onto the stage, so to speak.

At the end of *Penthesilea*, for example, the Amazon Queen stands at the figural edge of the scene and describes in real time what her sisters cannot see, that is, how she manages to revive a buried feeling by forging it with words into a thing. Her teichoscopic speech relays what is conventionally relegated to the realm of interiority as if it were happening in exterior reality, and her feeling actually does take shape as a dagger.

Similarly, the plot of *Katie of Heilbronn* turns on narratives of Count vom Strahl's out-of-body experience. While the journey of his soul on New Year's Eve is quite astounding, it is even more remarkable that Katie can see Strahl's traveling soul. She relates the spatiotemporal existence of the soul and of the feeling of love, which the spectators on and in front of the stage are at first unable to perceive.

With his teichoscopies of feeling, Kleist gives us a model for the construction of feeling and, what is more, exposes the (unacknowledged) constructedness of emotion in general, thus counteracting the naturalizing move of the eighteenth-century culture of sensibility (which continues to this day).[6] The assumption that emotions exist or arise first inside and can subsequently be expressed or refined to presentability is undone by the simultaneity of construction and experience, verbal creation and description that characterizes the teichoscopy of feeling. The notion that feelings are natural and universal, rather than an effect of ideas, interests, and power relations, is challenged as Kleist's teichoscopy theatrically unmasks the constructedness of feeling.

In traditional teichoscopies, an eyewitness reports what is actually and visibly taking place outside our field of vision. Kleist draws on this situation of privileged vision or selective visibility when he uses the teichoscopy of feeling to present the virtual as actual. Most don't see the feeling, but that doesn't mean that it doesn't exist. As F. László Földényi remarks, in Kleist "the dreamer doesn't retreat and confine himself to a corner but universalizes his condition" (1999, 420, my translation).[7] Kleist thus critically mirrors the Enlightenment strategy of claiming the universality of so-called natural feelings, which in one fell swoop erased all sense of their historicity and cultural relativity.[8] Instead, he insists that reality and dream, the actual and the virtual (or what has been categorized as such), are not only equally relevant but even indistinguishable.

His invention, the teichoscopy of feeling, can be used as a tool for the political struggle and didactic autonomy of the outcast and those who, for some reason, have cast themselves out of their societies (like Katie, who refuses to stay in her proper place and literally throws herself away [cf. Butler and Athanasiou 2013, 21], and Penthesilea, who mocks the rules of her nation with her grotesque desire). These teichoscopies open a window to another scene; they adumbrate another world—not merely a world to come, but one which is, in a radical sense, already here.[9] While they help us "learn to see and build here" the "responsibility for an imagined elsewhere" (Haraway 1991, 295), they also refuse to distinguish clearly between the present and the absent. Kleist draws the "then" into the "now" and the "there" into the "here" (cf. Klotz 1996, 105). He thus expands the sense of what we have identified as the crucial and distinguishing characteristic of teichoscopy, namely its synchronicity. Such blurring of literary devices (of teichoscopy and prophecy or anticipation, in this case) metaleptically shapes the ontology and the effect of his texts.

Interiority

Katie—who will occupy us in the second half of this chapter—is as much of a visionary or dreamer as the Prince of Homburg, who has been read as notoriously unable to distinguish reality from dream. From the ambiguous response to the Prince's final question, "No, tell me! Is it a dream?"—"A dream, what else?," back to the opening scene of the play where the Prince appears as a somnambulist, the characters onstage join the audiences and critics in playing, ridiculing and chastising Homburg for disregarding reality and following his dream (*PH* 341/5.11.1856). And yet, as we have seen in our discussion of Kleist's mammalogic, Homburg lives in an alternate symbolic order, according to which the distinction between dream and reality or virtuality and actuality makes little sense.[10] His "open breast [*offene[] Brust*]" knows no interiority, his soul is "dispersed [*zerstreut*]" across spatiotemporal reality and his body is receptive and open to others (*PH* 1.1.stage directions and 5.5.1678, my translations).

There is no need to view Homburg's mode of emotional existence and relationality as deficient. The problem—for Kleist, too—lies rather with the distinction between interiority/privacy and exteriority/public life that the bourgeois order creates and cements. In *Penthesilea*, Kleist gives a humorous account of the tragedy that is the (historically, politically, and with regard to public and personal health) fateful production of interiority. Rather early in the play (in the seventh and eighth of twenty-four scenes), he literalizes the genre requirement (or what Hegel identified as the characteristic of Greek tragedy), namely the tragic collision (a conflict of ethical causes represented by characters), by having his protagonists, Penthesilea and Achilles, physically crash into one another:[11]

> COLONEL: Achilles and the Queen with lances poised,
> Meet on the field with a resounding crash,
> Two thunderbolts colliding in mid-heaven;
> Their lances, weaker than their breasts, are split;
> He, the Peleid, stands; Penthesilea
> Sinks down, unhorsed, death's shadow close upon her.
> And now that she's laid bare to his revenge,
> Writhing in the dust before him, everyone thinks
> He'll send her flying all the way to Orcus;
> But pale he stands, incomprehensible,
> Himself a shade of death. Oh gods! he cries,
> How she did strike me with that dying look!
>
> (*P* 51–52/8.1122–33, translation altered)

In the next chapter, I will analyze how this campily (or metaleptically) literalized tragic collision shocks the queer protagonists of *Penthesilea* into becoming straight. Here I focus on the implications of the same scene for the theory of emotion. Achilles's first reaction to the traumatic encounter with Penthesilea creates in the moment a new and unexpected emotion in him. Instead of revengefulness, he produces love. The novelty and perceived incongruity of his emotion highlights the fact that emotions generally are made on the spot—only that, usually, such productions rely on socially or experientially available patterns and thus appear natural rather than constructed (cf. Barrett 2017, 25–41). In this case the socially required emotion would be the thirst for revenge ("revenge . . . everyone thinks"). But Achilles creates something unexpected and thereby initiates a new social order (or figures a change of historical proportions). In the Ancient order, where gender does not follow anatomy but the cosmological position of a person, Penthesilea (the Amazon queen whom Mars pronounced warrior) is an appropriate rival for Achilles. According to premodern emotional culture and its honor code, any chance or weakness of the rival must be used to subdue or kill such antagonist. Achilles here perceives a weakness but produces a different reaction—he spontaneously creates what will subsequently be codified as romantic love. We see the first indications of this codification in the fact that the Amazon Colonel reproduces and thus authorizes with her account Achilles's unusual, perhaps initially somewhat haphazard reaction.

The emotion Achilles experiences is not only unusual and created in the moment but also predicated on a perception that is equally fabricated: Achilles perceives Penthesilea looking into his eyes as she is supposedly dying and feels struck by her "dying look." Whether or not Penthesilea indeed looks at him is open to debate; the fact that the Colonel's report also describes her as rolling in the dust (*sich . . . wälzt*) would suggest that her gaze falls on many other things besides her adversary. That Achilles finds the gaze that meets his particularly salient might be understandable, but it means that he creates the contours of this one perception by screening out others. Equally questionable seems the impression that Penthesilea is dying, since, again according to the Colonel's own report, her chest is as unharmed as that of Achilles. When she says that "their lances, weaker than their breasts are split," this suggests that, in the fictional reality of the play, both breasts withstand the impact.

We will consider in more detail in the next chapter how this perception of the dying look reorganizes gender positions and determines who will be taken seriously and who will get tangled up in the figurative and be played down. Of interest to us here is that the fabrication of the "dying look" also produces another newly conventional idea, namely that of the inwardness of emotional life. According to the Colonel's report, not just Penthesilea's weapons (as we will discuss in the next chapter) but also the impenetrability of her chest, are to be taken metaphorically from now on. "Bosom" no longer denotes a part of the body, but now refers to the seat of one's feelings. Its impenetrability no longer signifies physical strength but means that the feelings harbored in the bosom have become inaccessible. While Penthesilea's physical chest is perceived (i.e., in the moment produced) by Achilles as torn and then repeatedly confirmed as such by him and other characters (including Penthesilea), her metaphorical bosom closes and is now understood as a receptacle for the intractable enigma of feelings. These feelings are later explicitly characterized as feminine: "How many a thing moves in a woman's breast that was not fashioned for the light of day" (*P* 75/13.1507–8).[12] The alleged one-sided penetration produces a gendered interiority and, somewhat counterintuitively or ironically, cements the boundaries of subjectivity.

The inwardness produced on the spot is reinforced discursively in the next scene by Prothoë's defense of Penthesilea:

> HIGH PRIESTESS: . . . nothing holds her from outside, no fate,
> Only her foolish heart—
> PROTHOË: That is her fate!
> To you, steel fetters seem unbreakable,
> Is it not so? Yet she might break them, see,
> But not this feeling you hold up to scorn.
> What force compels her, only she can know,
> And every breast that feels is an enigma.
>
> (*P* 59/9.1280–86)

Feelings are here posited as intangible: beyond the grasp of our hands and our reason. Steel fetters, in their concrete reality, can be broken if one only uses enough force, but the feelings that are shut in the impenetrable metaphorical bosom cannot be argued with: they are either dismissed as irrational ("her foolish heart") or extolled as mystic authority ("that is her fate! . . . an enigma"). With the new paradigm of interiority, feelings thus become ideological in the sense that they are not to be critically analyzed. Since no one is supposed to be able to know what somebody else feels inside ("what force compels her, only she can know"), feelings have become the inalienable property of the individual. Penthesilea must now own "her" feeling of romantic love for Achilles, even though, as I have just shown, Achilles fabricates this feeling, the Amazons discursively prepare and authorize this fabrication, and, as we will discuss in the next chapter, her desire for Achilles is largely an effect of her mother's wishes. The idea that our feelings are our own is part of the ideology of emotion.

For good measure, interiority also generates suspicion. Can we be sure that the Colonel accurately or objectively reports what Achilles perceived and felt? Clearly not. For one thing, eyewitness testimonies are notoriously unreliable—our legal system has an inbuilt awareness of this. I don't mean to treat this literary text like a legal case study; obviously there is no direct real-life referent to the reports and accounts of this drama. My point is, rather, that Kleist's play demonstrates and parodies the creation of interiority that comes hand in hand with the construction of the second sex.[13] Once interiority is established—and, to be sure, the next time Achilles speaks after the collision, he gives witness to interiority's existence: "I've been wounded deep inside [*im Innersten*], I feel it"—we cannot know anymore what goes on in Achilles's bosom (*P* 67/11.1416). Such is the effect of interiority. Yet, Kleist's parodic stance invites us to take a step back.

If we do so, we find that the discourse of romantic love already emerged in the preceding scene and then colors the Colonel's account of Achilles's reaction. Not Penthesilea herself takes "her stand upon a single name," as the high priestess charges (*P* 47/7.1046), but all the Amazons, especially those who are here tellingly called "girls," seem in a tizzy about the supreme warrior (see *P* 46/7.1033–43). In typically Kleistian doubling, we receive a first account of Penthesilea and Achilles's momentous physical collision one scene earlier—here in the form of a teichoscopy:[14]

> FIRST GIRL (*on the hill*):
> Ha, they're meeting now!
> Dear gods, please hold your Earth and keep it firm—
> Now, at this moment, as I speak, they're flying
> Into each other, crashing, like two stars!
>
> (*P* 49/7.1077–80)

But nobody pays attention to this sublime spectacle; everybody in the scene just chatters about Cupid's arrows.[15] When Achilles and Penthesilea retroactively confirm that they have been wounded in their innermost being, they cannot mean that they were struck by the lance of their adversary (the lances split); they were struck, rather, by the looks, words, and metaphors (Cupid's arrows) that are abundantly furnished by those who surround them. Whether or not the Colonel accurately represents Achilles's feeling and perception, Achilles is already primed by the discourse of the Amazons as he fabricates both in the wake of the clash. After such priming, both heroes start to mouth their parts in the new tragedy of interiority, romantic love, and the "battle of the sexes."

Dagger, the Feeling Thing

Penthesilea kills herself with a nonexistent dagger. This final scene of the tragedy teeters on the edge of slapstick. Only the linguistic force and profoundly gripping texture of Penthesilea's final monologue saves it from embarrassment—unless we read the scene as camp.

Carol Jacobs has argued that language itself is the weapon here. But while Jacobs, contending that "here there is nothing to tell *about*" (1989, 114), emphasizes the immediate self-realization of language in and as death, I would like to attend to the almost imperceptible mediation through hetero-reference or, rather, homo-exchange that takes place within this self-realization. Penthesilea's words do not so much kill as produce a feeling.

It has to be noted that Penthesilea's speech not only acts but also describes. With her final speech act, Penthesilea continues the teichoscopic mode of most of the play with a teichoscopy of feeling. She reports what remains invisible to her audience on and before the stage, namely, that she is forging a hot, sharp, and poisonous weapon from a cold feeling buried in her chest:

> PENTHESILEA: For now I descend into my breast,
> Like a shaft, and quarry out the cold
> Ore [*Erz*] of a feeling that annihilates.
> This ore I purify in fire of lament
> To hardest steel; in poison then, of bitter,
> Burning remorse, I soak [*tränk*] it through and through;
> Now carry it toward Hope's eternal anvil,
> And grind and sharpen it into a dagger;
> And to this dagger now I give my breast:
> So! So! So! So! Again!—Now it is done.
> (*She falls and dies.*)
>
> (*P* 148/24.3025–34, translation altered)

The feeling that she finds inside her bosom is cold as ore. The bosom, like a mining shaft (*gleich* einem Schacht) hides a corpse (*Leich*). Only dead feelings are buried in the interior of the heart. What Penthesilea conjures up out of the depths of her bosom is at this point more annihilated than annihilating; it is nothing. Penthesilea's heart is empty.

Prothoë diagnoses this emptiness after the tremendous collision of the two heroic bodies, the allegedly one-sided penetration, and the creation of (gendered) inwardness. While Penthesilea slowly regains consciousness, Prothoë admonishes:

> PROTHOË: Penthesilea! Where have you been, oh dreamer!
> In what far fields of radiance does your spirit
> Still soar and sweep, with restless beating wings,
> As if displeased with its own home,
> The while your happy fate, like a young prince,
> Seeks lodging in your bosom and, surprised
> To find such lovely habitation empty,
> Turns round again . . .
> Will you not bind [*fesseln*] this guest, my foolish friend?–
> Come, raise yourself to my breast [*hebe dich an meine Brust*].
> (*P* 77/14.1538–48, translation altered)

The personification of happiness as a young prince has a terrible ring to it, given that a literal prince is said to have pushed through her chest. Figured as a harbinger of happiness, Achilles supposedly penetrates her, realizes that he didn't crack a riddle together with her chest—that her core (*Herz*) does not hide a treasure of ore (*Erz*)—and turns around, leaving her behind with a broken heart.[16] This familiar heterosexual story has been told a thousand times. The ideology of inwardness not only creates fascinating mysteries and "ghastly riddles"; it also, and most often, produces emptiness and boredom (*P* 125/22.2600).

Prothoë adds insult to injury by presenting the attack on Penthesilea's breast as something that should make her happy. Inverting cause and effect, she suggests that Penthesilea's emptiness can be filled by Achilles. Posing Penthesilea's absence from herself as a matter of choice ("as if displeased with its own home") and insinuating self-identity and satisfaction with one's identity as a normative ideal allows her to blame Penthesilea for not taking the opportunity to correct her emptiness by embracing Achilles, the prince of "happy fate." She almost chastises Penthesilea for not "bind[ing] this guest," Achilles, to her. We can be sure that Prothoë, whose entire speech moves in the realm of the figurative, does not mean the binding literally—in the way the Amazons use iron chains to shackle their captives—but means to suggest that Penthesilea captivate Achilles with her charm.[17] With the last line of her speech ("come, raise yourself to my breast"), Prothoë installs herself as the nursing mother who feeds Penthesilea these ideas of post-1800 female void, bourgeois gender complementarity, and heteronormativity. Penthesilea has a hard time escaping the various mother figures who push her toward Achilles.

Often the existence of interiority is thought of as a sign that the subject is alive, but in Kleist's text interiority appears as a harbinger of death. It threatens the factual life of the individual. Since the establishment of interiority, Penthesilea has been dying. And the high priestess specifies that "when she falls, the enemy that fells her will be the one she meets within her breast" (*P* 50/7.1108). The fabrication of a dying look, which we have discussed in the previous section, is deadly. What is more, interiority also kills feelings. The bosom forms a grave for feelings. Interiority constricts and threatens to suffocate the public life of women—their affectivity and effectivity. Before the founding of the Amazon state, "a woman hampered by full breasts" while posing as a warrior was the "laughingstock of men" (*P* 94/15.1981, 1977). The Amazon state almost failed in its incipience because of the women's overfull bosoms, crammed with emotions that were banished inside—feelings mass-produced by the genocide and the rape of the Scythian women. But Tanaïs saved the formation of the state by tearing off one of her breasts and thus tearing down the ideology of interiority. She literally and symbolically opens her bosom and breaks though the barriers of individuality and gender.

Now Penthesilea tries to revive and reinflame the "c[-]old (*k*[-]*alt*)" inside. Against common interpretations that regard Penthesilea's "suicide" as a defection from, even as the abolition of, the Amazon state, I would like to point out that with this act Penthesilea repeats, and thus subscribes to, Tanaïs's founding gesture of tearing open her chest. In order to escape the interiority that was (re)introduced earlier in the play, Penthesilea has to open her closed bosom. Its metaphorical impenetrability has become so real that only a literal cut will do. In our discussion of mammalogic (chapter 3), we have already seen why such gruesome mutilations feel necessary and liberating within a phallocentric order. The pressure that the ideology of interiority exerts is so strong that it requires such drastic physical action. But as I elaborated in the last chapter, there is also something antiserious (and thus not quite literal) about these scenes in Kleist. We are now in a position to analyze how the teichoscopy of feeling mackles literality with metaphoricity, the imaginary with the material, and ideology with an antiserious seriousness.

The teichoscopic mode of Penthesilea's final monologue—precisely because, by definition, teichoscopy describes what happens offstage—interlaces the outside world beyond the scene and the inside world of the bosom. Hence, before Penthesilea opens her bosom with repeated stabs of the dagger, she has already ruptured the established barrier between interiority and exteriority with her unusual use of teichoscopy. As a result, the buried feeling comes alive, but it does so decidedly not in the mode of expression (which presupposes and reinforces the distinction between inside and outside). Instead, by cracking the wall that separates the inside from the outside, the teichoscopy of feeling undoes the paradigm of interiority that buried Penthesilea's feelings.

Against the pretense that feelings are natural and thus unquestionable—a force of nature that must be controlled by rational means, Kleist's teichoscopic mode makes explicit that feelings are (and need to be) made and that such fabrication involves rational, cognitive, and linguistic powers from the very start. Penthesilea's tools and secondary material are feelings and words—feelings that are words and words that are feelings: lament, remorse, and hope. It seems a bit circular to forge a feeling with and out of feelings. But the "feeling that annihilates" is different from "lament," "remorse," and "hope." The first is found inside as an abstract concept ("a feeling that annihilates") and a crude material ("this ore"), while the others take shape outside and circulate as concrete names that have a cultural life. Grief, remorse, and hope carry the traces of heterogeneous situations and contexts. Lament (*Jammer*) recalls Aristotle's theory of tragedy, "Hope's eternal anvil" evokes Pandora's box and Prometheus's fire, and the "poison of remorse" awakens images of the Erinyes. Each name encapsulates and transports several elaborately moving stories and refers to the history of the theater. These outward feelings are therefore livelier and hotter, more "burning," than the inward one, and Penthesilea can "purify," harden, "grind," and "sharpen" the annihilated feeling by firing it up and "soak(ing)" or feeding it with these stories and references (*tränken* means not only "to soak," but also "to water").

The fabrication of a feeling, even if it happens in the moment, draws on a history of archived feelings and their cultivation over time. Penthesilea knows that feelings need to be formed layer by layer or link within link. Already in the interlude of relative intimacy with Achilles, she insists that the fabrication of a feeling takes time. The love or commitment she intends to produce there has a temporality very different from the love at first sight—or first dying look—that is part of the notion of romantic love we encountered earlier:

> For there's another chain I still intend
> To wrap around your core [*Herz*] and bind you with,
> As light as flowers, more durable than ore [*Erz*].
> But till it has been forged, link within link,
> In ardent feelings and glowing tenderness
> . . . .
> You shall return to me, as duty bids you,
> (*P* 89/15.1832–38, translation altered)

Here again, Penthesilea uses the image of a feeling that has to be forged in the fire of feelings. But is this really an image? Are the metaphors not precisely in the process of turning literal? Her task here is to intertwine the loose lines of flowery speech to the point where they are more durable than an iron chain. The words that are feelings or feelings that are words—the feeling words—then become tangible and powerful things: like the dagger, which she can apply to her breast.

Penthesilea's final monologue intertwines or mackles embodied performance, descriptive narrative, and performative speech. When she eventually offers her breast to the dagger, this is not an original act committed by an individual but one iteration in a series of deindividualizing repetitions. The last two verses of her monologue—"And to this dagger now I give my breast: So! So! So! So! Again!"—describe actions that physically repeat, five times, what the teichoscopy has already carried out. Beginning with "For now I descend into my breast," the teichoscopic approach pierces the border between interiority and exteriority.

Yet even the mimetic reenactments of this piercing (the jabs with the dagger) do not bring the series of repetitions to a definite end. To be sure, the stage directions, "*She falls and dies*," retroactively confirm the descriptive character of the preceding verses and seem to bring closure to the scene. But Kleist's peculiar word choice creates an extravagant imagery in excess of literal description. The phrase "and to this dagger now I give my breast" does not exactly produce the image of a suicide by stabbing. When Penthesilea says that she "gives her breast," one rather imagines a scene of breastfeeding, that is to say, of a nurturing and life-giving practice. In a stage production, Penthesilea could, alongside every "so!," mimetically act out and thereby clarify or make visible the meaning of her words. Whether this be a repeated stabbing or a repeated breastfeeding remains open for the actress's interpretation. Either way, these mimeses of an act already mackled by narration are doubled once more by further speech acts. Prothoë repeats the stage directions with her verdict "She's dying!" (*P* 148/24.3035). And Penthesilea, in addition to her physical gestures and her literal and figural descriptions, performs a speech act that actualizes—forges, to be precise—in the very utterance of words what the conventions of the teichoscopic mode cast as the unpresentable beyond: a feeling. Penthesilea thus doubles and couples the concrete reality of the presentation onstage with the imagined realities both offstage and inside her bosom.

Seeing Ecstasy

We find a similar twining together of performative and descriptive, theatrical and narrative, mimetic and textual modes of presentation in *Katie of Heilbronn*. Here the vision is explicitly mutual: Strahl has a vision of Katie and Katie has a vision of Strahl (cf. Allemann 2005, 202). In their intense fixation on one another, Katie and Strahl turn their backs on the world and become unavailable to the people around them. For this reason one might describe their dyadic relationship, in Lacanian terms, as imaginary. But they also throw each other into ecstasies; that is to say, they undo each other's identity. Their relationality thus differs from Lacan's imaginary as a mirroring that establishes, even if only as an illusion, wholeness and integrity. In fact, we will see that the visions repeat themselves and that other characters at times stand in for the subject or the object of the vision. The repetition undoes self-identity, and the implication of other characters reveals this play to be much less about the couple at its center than often thought.

The primal scene of Katie's and Strahl's mutual vision takes place on New Year's Eve, less than two years before the time of the play. I call it "the primal scene," evoking Freud's notion of *Urszene*, because it remains inaccessible (the play offers only indirect accounts or inadvertent repetitions) and because its status as fantasy or reality remains unclear.[18] On the New Year's Eve in question, Katie and Strahl don't yet know one another. Strahl had fallen critically ill and has withdrawn completely from the life of the world. In this situation, an angel announces to him the future love of a woman, and Strahl asks to see her. At the same time, Katie receives the prophecy that she will marry a knight. She prays to God that the knight appear to her in a dream. Led by the angel, Strahl enters Katie's bedroom, Katie rises out of bed and kneels down before Strahl. The scene is lit by the radiance of the angel and lasts for what cannot be longer than a couple of minutes.

We get—this comes as no surprise by now—a double account of this primal scene: one from Strahl's perspective and one from Katie's perspective, one a narrated teichoscopy and the other an unconsciously performed dialogic quasi-teichoscopy. Toward the end of act 2, Brigitte, an old maid of the knight, tells the story from Strahl's perspective to Kunigunde, the rival of Katie. At the beginning of act 4, under the elder bush, Strahl makes Katie talk in her sleep about what she sees and saw back then, during New Year's Eve. Both accounts superimpose description and performance, offering both voice and spectacle, as well as mimesis and textuality.

The visions multiply beyond these two accounts. Scholars usually focus on Brigitte's tale and Katie's somnambulant performance under the elder bush because they both explicitly refer back to the primal scene of the mutual vision. But the ecstatic vision is repeatedly reenacted throughout the play. This happens without explicit reference to the primal scene, and the characters get involved in the replication inadvertently or unconsciously, sometimes in more magical or dreamlike, at other times in more mundane ways. While Allemann observes that the static intrigue that underlies the developmental intrigue in Kleist's plays consists in repeated instances of the same behavior motivated by one dreamlike vision, in *Katie* it is the vision itself that is reiterated and reenacted again and again.[19] And in each of these iterations, Kleist differently combines word and image, narrative and theater.

We hear of Strahl's vision of Katie first through Brigitte's story. In Strahl's absence, she tells of his illness of two years ago and half-enacts in direct speech his teichoscopy of his nocturnal vision from back then. Thus familiarized with his vision, we are then privy to a spectacular reenactment: in act 3, scene 14, Katie emerges from the flames that engulf Kunigunde's castle, through a portal left standing, the angel behind her. Thus the audience is treated to a direct version, unmediated by narration, of Strahl's vision of Katie. Nevertheless, even though she is the object of this vision, the details of her appearance are very similar to how she sees him (led by a cherub through a doorway, radiant, and in solemn silence). One vision seems contaminated with the other. Eventually, when Strahl manipulates Katie into sleep-talking and into telling him the story of how she knows him, he begins to remember his vision of her and the two visions, or two perspectives, begin to intertwine and match (though not without confusing disagreements).[20] As if as a result, a noble (Strahl's cousin Eleonore) finally recognizes Katie's splendor (*K* 240/4.6.2210). This recognition by the aristocracy doubles the rather different vision that her father Theobald has of the bourgeois Katie, the vision through which Katie is in fact introduced. At the end of our analysis we will understand that Katie emerges as radiant whenever she had contact with Kunigunde, whereas she remains overlooked even in her most intense interactions with Strahl.

It is from Katie's father Theobald that we first learn of Katie's vision of Strahl, when he describes her enigmatic behavior on encountering Strahl in her father's shop. Only retrospectively (once we hear Brigitte's story and Katie's somnambulous account) can we identify this narrated scene as a repeat of Katie's vision of New Year's Eve: she sees the knight in her house and falls to the ground. The scene under the elder bush includes a somniloquatious teichoscopy of the Count on a white horse. Finally, we receive a report, mostly in the historical present tense, of the negative double of her vision. Katie sees Kunigunde bathing but is so horrified that she cannot complete her report. She begins with, "My eye catches sight—," and interrupts herself (*K* 241/4.7.2240, translation altered). As is the case when she sees the knight, the vision of the other woman reduces her to silence.

Strahl is not quite present for his own vision of Katie—largely not at home, so to speak. He doesn't quite see or, at least, doesn't remember Katie. It seems that what allowed him to push through the crisis of his depression was an unassimilable experience. Perhaps this is why the vision is repeated in various forms throughout the play. In Katie's proximity, Strahl consistently acts out in odd and inexplicable ways—his armor bursts, he throws himself to the ground and abandons himself to a ridiculous effusion of desire, and out of panic and disgust he threatens her with a whip (cf. Grugger 2010, 171–73). Somewhere he kept a dark and vague memory of the impact of his vision.

Katie remains unseen. She gives the play its name but is consistently overlooked. Before the time of the play, she was known by everyone—if we believe her father Theobald.[21] The whole city of Heilbronn saw her, had respect for her, and considered her family.[22] But she throws away this well-established social life when she throws herself out the window to follow the Count. Does she do so because she wants to marry up?[23] Or because she somehow knows that she doesn't deserve the recognition of the city because she is not of pure bourgeois birth but is really the Emperor's daughter? Or is her behavior an act of refusal, resisting social norms?

As if to find the answer to these questions, Katie (who remembers her vision of Strahl) is subjected to a series of trials. It begins with the secret court session of the first act and culminates oddly in the missed spectacle of Katie's trial by fire in act 3, scene 14, which is also featured in the play's alternative title (*Trial by Fire*). This scene treats the audience of most stage productions to a showy use of special stage effects but goes almost unnoticed by the characters onstage—nobody but Katie's rival Kunigunde witnesses Katie emerge from the flames. After the high pitch of the trial by fire, Strahl subjects her to another unseen test.[24] He approaches the sleeping Katie and provokes her to sleep-talk in order to get at the truth of her obsession. Eventually, Katie's status as the Emperor's daughter is confirmed, once more without any intradiegetic witnesses.[25] The trials she passes do not earn Katie any respect or visibility. In the next chapter, we will consider whether Katie actually wants visibility. There, we will also explore what does let her shine, namely, her intimate encounters with Kunigunde.

Out of Mutual Alignment

From Brigitte's account we learn that, about two years prior, a suicidal melancholy befell the Count. At the crisis point of this illness, on New Year's Eve, Strahl is bedridden with a life-threatening fever, and in his feverish delirium he offers what I call a teichoscopy of feeling. The Count sits on the figural wall between two realities and describes what his caregivers cannot see, namely how his soul is moved. His teichoscopic speech relays what is conventionally relegated to the realm of interiority as though it was happening in exterior reality, and indeed his soul begins to travel: it moves through exterior space. "Everything that had been kept locked up in his heart" is driven out by the heat of the fever and churned into things or word-things that were "now . . . on the tip of his tongue" (*K* 2.9.1159, my translation).[26] He speaks of his desire for love, his despair, and his conversion to trust. He talks of the grave and the cradle, and reports seeing an angel whom he asks to show him the woman who is able to love him.

During this teichoscopy of feeling, his mother sits by his bedside and acts as a kind of director. She spurs on his performance by asking questions like "Will you be seeing her?," "When?," and "Where?" (*K* 200/2.9.1170–71). At the same time, she is also a somewhat ignorant spectator who doesn't quite know what to ask because the field of reference is so utterly foreign and invisible to her. The angel then indeed leads Strahl to the chamber of a young woman. The details of this adventure are omitted in his teichoscopy as the Count falls silent after saying goodbye to his mother. While his soul travels, his body lies dead in his bedroom. To the probing caregivers who, among other tests to determine whether he has passed, try to listen to his heartbeat, his chest is "quiet as an empty room" (*K* 200/2.9.1191–92). Strahl is outside himself. Eventually he reports back with a last bit of teichoscopy: "Ah! Now they're bringing in the lights! Now I can't see her anymore!" (*K* 201/2.9.1202–3, translation altered).

Even though the crucial part might be deemed lacking, this is a teichoscopy of feeling. What the Count doesn't synchronously report, he enacts—his body lets the intradiegetic audience see, feel, and hear (not through speech but with the absence of his heartbeat) that his soul is elsewhere. The narrative character of teichoscopy is doubled with this performative element. Both are largely inadvertent. Strahl does not consciously communicate what he sees. Much like Katie, who will later talk in her sleep, he speaks in a feverish delirium, and it is unclear whether his words are actually addressed to anyone. Nevertheless, his teichoscopy is performative also in the sense that it produces a new feeling. Strahl's ecstatic transport changes his outlook from the initial suicidal melancholy to a joyous affirmation of life. When his mother asks where he has been, he answers, "joyfully: 'With her . . . who loves me! With the bride that heaven means me to wed! . . . Now I wish to live'" (*K* 201/2.9.1207–10). And now he can't stop talking about how the angel led him to the bedroom of the girl, how the girl lay there scantily dressed, how she got up and knelt down before him and called him her high lord, how the angel told him that she was a daughter of the Emperor and showed him a reddish mark on her neck, how he was just about to draw her face to him—when they were interrupted by her friend, Marianna, and the entire scene vanished.

I should note again that we don't witness Strahl's teichoscopy of feeling onstage like Penthesilea's. Instead it takes place roughly two years before the action of the play and we hear about it from the servant Brigitte, who tells the story to Kunigunde. It is a retrospectively narrated teichoscopy, even though Brigitte is carried away by her own story and partially transported back to the time of the event. At times she verbally enacts in direct speech the scene she reports, but this metaleptic transport is also hindered by her diligent use of the *inquit*. This mixture of immediacy and mediation is further highlighted by the fact that Kleist puts quotation marks around the Count's utterances but not his mother's, even though Brigitte quotes both directly:

> When the Countess asked him whether he hadn't felt strengthened by his heavenly appeal? He replied: "Strengthened? No!"—and added with a sigh: "Yes! yes, mother, when I see her again!"—The Countess asks: and will you be seeing her? "Certainly" he replies. When? She asks. Where?—"On New Year's Eve, . . . he'll lead me to her." Who? She asks, dear; to whom? "The angel," he replies "to my girl"—turns over and falls asleep. (*K* 200/2.9.1166–75, translation altered)

The first line offers the mother's question still in indirect speech, but Kleist nevertheless marks it as direct speech in the end. The ungrammatical question mark troubles the intonation as the sentence moves from indirect to direct speech in the middle of its articulation. If we saw this scene on stage, we wouldn't know where Kleist did or did not put quotation and punctuation marks. Kleist thus introduces a textual element—a difference that can only be seen in the dramatic text but remains unnoticed in the stage production. The spectacle that Kleist stages with quotation marks in the text remains invisible onstage.

It is striking that Strahl, even though he explicitly asks to see the girl and is indeed granted an opportunity to do so, does not remember what she looks like. Apart from the circumstance that she wears barely any clothes, Strahl focuses more on the linguistic messages—the information about her status as daughter of the Emperor, and the birthmark on her neck, which functions as a sign or grapheme (*K* 201/2.9.1231). It is not her character or her face that draws him; rather, his desire (he notices her beautiful body under the thin dress) is fueled by symbolic status (she is identified as a member of the most powerful family in the country). His vision—though seemingly not of this world and replete with fairy-tale topoi (the Emperor's daughter, a body mark as identification)—very much confirms a structured world. It is the structure of the old order, based on lineage and the exchange of women.

At the next opportunity, when Katie is again presented as a quasi-supernatural vision, Strahl still fails to see her. At the end of act 3, she appears surrounded by flames and led by an angel through a large freestanding portal onto the scene.[27] But the Count doesn't look at her. Thinking that Katie succumbed in the flames when the burning castle collapsed, he turns his back to the scene and holds his hands over his eyes in a gesture of grief and despair. Kleist couldn't render more pronounced the disregard that Katie suffers. Even her most spectacular entrance doesn't draw any attention. In fact, there are a large number of characters onstage (about ten speaking characters plus supernumeraries) who all turn their backs on Katie. Only the theater audience is privy to this dramatic vision; Katie's entrance here is our vision. But the staging of this scene poses technical as well as aesthetic challenges. Having a girl surrounded by flames and led by a blond male angel complete with wings and palm leaf (as the stage directions specify) enter through a portal that is the only thing standing among the burning rubble almost inevitably turns cheesy. Kleist puts the audience here in the position to see and perhaps experience ecstasy, but he gives us a campy version of ecstasy, which many will not be able to bear to look at.

Narrative is conspicuously absent from this particular scene. The crucial vision remains largely mute. During the entire scene—which enacts the trial by fire announced in the alternative title of the play and therefore enjoys central importance, one would assume—only two short sentences are spoken.[28] Given that Kleist usually doubles theater with narrative, we acutely feel the presence of this absence. Even more irritating is the fact that nobody in the light can see what we, in the audience, are seeing from our immobile position in the dark. For both reasons, we are itching to speak, to call and awaken the introverted characters onstage. It is as if this canonical piece of German theater had turned into a participatory performance for children. We are tempted to turn the tables and to perform a teichoscopy that tells the characters onstage what we see and how our souls are moved. If we remain in the proper bourgeois adult position, we are left without a mediating figure on the other side, without a character who speaks for us. If we are ready to give our own teichoscopy of feeling—instructed by Kleist's theater and encouraged by Strahl's example—we will still lack a director/spectator figure who formulates the necessary if always slightly inadequate questions that would allow us to report the unseen we see.

Kunigunde is the first of the characters to come out of the stupor that befell them—but only to spoil the vision. She sees and exclaims, "Now, by the living God! I must be dreaming! . . . Look here!" (*K* 226/3.15.1888). We cannot take her exclamation as an expression of awe or exultation. By then the cherub has disappeared, and the sight of Katie alone would not send Kunigunde into ecstasies. She has sinister motives and would rather see Katie dead. So her cry has to be heard more like a curse that escapes her when she realizes that sending Katie into the flames didn't yield the half-intended result. Then Kunigunde proceeds to pierce the pathos with bathos. She points out the kitsch factor of the scene by cracking a joke about the insincere theatricality of Katie's act: "A lot of grey-beard oafs! The girl they think / Was burnt to ashes in the conflagration / Is lying there before them, safe and sound, / Sniggering in her apron at them all!" (*K* 227/3.15.1897–1900).

Only in the elder bush episode do we finally encounter a loquacious Katie and hear her account of her vision. Katie is asleep under an elder bush near Strahl's castle and the Count approaches her to carry out an experiment or to perform a draft (*einen Entwurf mit ihr auszuführen*), as he calls it (*K* 4.2.2029).[29] The stage directions specify that he kneels in front of the sleeping Katie and embraces her softly.[30] Then he begins to ask her questions and Katie replies in her sleep. Strahl asks her to describe what she sees and plays along, assuming the role she gives him in the scene that she describes. Like Penthesilea and Strahl in their teichoscopies of feeling, Katie does not literally view from the walls but sits on the figurative fence between two modes of being and reports what she sees in that realm that is invisible to the others. Besides a white horse that carries Strahl, and a meadow filled with flowers, she sees that Strahl is in love with her "like a beetle [*wie ein Käfer*]" (*K* 234/4.2.2075, my translation). For all we know, it is not Strahl but Katie herself who is attached to the Count like a lovebug.[31] But Katie's somniloquy will effect a change in Strahl's feeling and behavior. Her teichoscopy will teach him to see things differently.

While Penthesilea's teichoscopy intertwines literal and figurative, referential and performative modes of speaking, Katie exhibits such intertwinement in her modes of seeing. What Katie sees is neither quite reality in the conventional sense (after all, she is sleeping), nor is it just a representation, an anticipation or another kind of stand-in for reality. Her seeing is largely performative—it brings about what she sees. Like Penthesilea, Katie creates feelings with and as word-things, only that her word-things are images while Penthesilea's are names (lament, remorse, and hope). These feeling images (a white horse, violets, a bug) have a powerful sensuous presence and also (like the feeling names for Penthesilea) transport an array of references and situations that have been cultivated over time. The white horse is a status symbol; it conveys nobility, purity, and strength. Katie's assertion that the horse will not run off shows her absolute trust in the reality of the feeling she sees. The violets that she sees in the meadow serve as a symbol for love, specifically, for a love that wants to remain secret. Her vision thus moves from the proud showiness of the white horse to the modesty of a softly speaking violet. The simile of the beetle has sexual undertones. It also continues the trajectory of the images from the tall (white horse) to the small (violets), approaching the realm of the imperceptible and the unintelligible.[32] The ecstasy that Katie fabricates with these diverse images thus moves through different ideas about love—from the old order of status to the bourgeois order of privacy to something that is not quite intelligible yet. Love is not simple for Katie; it is a dynamic concept that changes significantly over the course of her teichoscopy, from one image to the next toward an undetermined end.

One could thus say that her soul, like Strahl's, travels—that it moves through the different available notions of love in order to liberate her from these conventions and to arrive at a new notion that is still not quite discernible. We will come back to this in the next chapter; in the context of this chapter, Katie's vision presents itself as in the service of the Count's ecstasy. But just as love is not simple for Katie, it is not simply true that Strahl loves Katie or that the two are meant for each other. The truth does not lie "locked up in his heart [*in seinem Herzen verschlossen*]" (*K* 2.9.1158). Brigitte's search for a higher truth in mad speech and divine signs is as narrow-minded as Gottschalk's common sense that dismisses accounts of other modes of being, adjacent to empirical reality, as mere ghost stories. The Count's servant, who otherwise shows a lot of sympathy for Katie, belittles her by saying, "Dear child, you're seeing empty phantoms!" (*K* 218/3.6.1700, translation altered). Both this enclosing of truth in transcendental interiority and this prioritizing of empirical reality is undone by the teichoscopy of feeling. Instead of revealing true love, the porous relationality between bodies, visions, and words that produces real feelings is open to manipulation and deception. Strahl's love is partially generated by his own provoking and participating in Katie's somniloquy. As his mother did when she sat at his bedside on New Year's Eve, Strahl leans over the sleeping Katie and spurs on her performance. He thus directs the scene that Katie creates. But he also acts in it: he embraces Katie and calls her sweetheart, he makes noise with his armor pretending to get off his horse, and so on. Such playacting eventually turns into conviction: he will end up marrying Katie.[33]

Unsettled by Katie's teichoscopy of his feeling, Strahl asks her to tell him the story of their first encounter. As soon as she mentions the angel, he begins to remember the scene:

> KATIE: A cherub, my noble lord, was at your side,
> With wings as white as snow upon his shoulders;
> And light—O lord! That sparkled and gleamed!—
> He led you by the hand to where I lay.
> VOM STRAHL (*staring at her*):
> True as I hope for heaven, I believe,
> You're right!
> KATIE: Yes, my honored lord!
> VOM STRAHL (*in a strained voice*):
> You lay there, on a hair-filled pillow,
> The bedsheets white; the woolen blanket red?
> KATIE: That's right! Just so!
> VOM STRAHL: You only wore a flimsy little shirt?
> KATIE: A little shirt?—No.
> VOM STRAHL: What! Not so?
> KATIE: A flimsy little shirt?
> VOM STRAHL: Marianna, you called?
> KATIE: Marianna, I called!
> Come quick! You girls! Come right to me, Christina!
> VOM STRAHL: You looked at me with great black eyes?
> KATIE: Yes, since I thought it was a dream.
> VOM STRAHL: Then, slowly,
> Trembling in every limb, climbed out of bed,
> And sank at my feet—?
> KATIE: And whispered—
> VOM STRAHL (*interrupts her*):
> And whispered, my highly honored lord!
> KATIE (*smiling*):
> Now! Don't you see?—The angel showed you—
> VOM STRAHL: The birthmark! Protect me, ye heavenly! You have it?
> KATIE: Of course!
> VOM STRAHL (*tearing off Katie's neckerchief*):
> Where? On the neck?
> KATIE (*stirring in her sleep*):
> Please, please.
> VOM STRAHL: O you eternal ones!—And as I then
> Lifted your chin, to look into your face?
> KATIE: Yes, then came that superfluous Marianna
> With light—and everything was gone;
> (*K* 236–37/4.2.2118–41, translation altered)

In line with Allemann's observations (2005, 22), Katie emphasizes the radiance of her vision: "And light—O lord! That sparkled and gleamed!—." Her little room turns into a stage when it is suddenly powerfully illuminated by the light-filled aura of the angel—and here Strahl enters. This scene feels exaggerated and over-the-top (not unlike the scene of Katie's entrance from out of the fire), especially since we, unlike Katie on New Year's Eve, know the Count's name: *Strahl* means "ray of light." The doubling of the visual with the verbal signifier has the effect of hollowing out his glory to the point that he comes across as silly. We get an increasing sense that Kleist pokes fun at the pathos and all-too-neat reciprocity of this couple's romantic ecstasy when he stages the mutuality of their vision all too literally by having them both open their eyes wide in response to the overwhelming experience. On New Year's Eve, Katie stares at the Count with large black eyes, and with a time lag of about two years, the Count stares at her (as the stage directions specify) under the elder bush.

Kleist runs through different variations of this mutuality to arrive, via power reversals that enact the idea of the complementarity of the sexes, at a queer doubling and blurring of roles. While there is obviously an element of abuse in the way the Count pins Katie down with his embrace and makes her divulge things she never talks about when awake, Katie also manipulates him. Because he approaches her only with a "draft [*Entwurf*]," the stage director Strahl, who directs Katie to speak lines beyond her conscious control, exposes himself to contingencies. He allows his actress to play without a finalized script: that is, he abandons control over what is said. He feeds her lines, but in the end she authorizes what is said. Katie instructs the Count in his vision—"Now! Don't you see?"—while he slowly tests his memory. The power relation is reversed. Like a pupil, he tries out sentences and waits for the confirmation of his teacher. She answers with encouragement: "That's right!" Then they both grow bolder. She begins to talk and he interrupts: "KATIE: And whispered—/ STRAHL (*Interrupts her.*): And whispered, my highly honored lord!" Even though this apparently successful completion of her sentence earns him a somewhat ambiguous praise, one can hardly say that Strahl proves his memory here. It is easy to "remember" these words of hers, because she says them every time she sees Strahl. Does Kleist parody the Count's capacity to learn or Katie's pedagogical skills? Do the two flirt here? Or is something else going on? Perhaps Strahl feels threatened and needs to interrupt Katie because she is giving him a taste of what happens when she improvises. We will come back to this in the next chapter. In any case, the scene that Strahl began to stage has turned into a duet of two voices that take turns leading, confirming, and irritating one another. Neither of them is completely in charge, but each complements and, what is more, manipulates the other.

So far, so conventional. But Kleist also subtly unsettles this for his time-newly conventional duet. The Count and Katie repeat each other's lines;

together, they speak doubly: "Marianna, you called?—Marianna, I called!" Saying the same thing twice over easily turns into doublespeak. One time, Katie doesn't authorize his line but repeats the same question: "STRAHL: You only wore a flimsy little shirt? / KATIE: A little shirt?—No. STRAHL: What! Not so? KATIE: A flimsy little shirt?" As a result, the truth value and even the significance of his proposal and her response become unclear. Is she getting angry? If so, why?—what did he say? Her repetitions hollow out the meaning of his words. In the end, the doublespeak changes into a double take: Strahl sees double: "Now support me, ye gods: I am double!" (*K* 237/4.2.2144, translation altered). Count Strahl has learned to squint. Katie has taught him to see (himself) double. And in the process, he himself has doubled.

We see (Strahl) double before he does. I don't mean his nightly travels to her chamber, since we don't see those onstage. Rather, I am referring to the fact that Katie's stalking provokes, or manages to re-create, the original out-of-body experience that is the source of Strahl's desire—except that instead of being ecstatic with passion, he is beside himself with rage. More than once, Strahl experiences a choleric attack and uses verbal and physical violence against Katie (he kicks her and threatens to whip her). He doesn't recognize himself in these attacks and usually snaps out of them as quickly as he fell into them. But we witness the gentle Strahl right next to the violent Strahl in one and the same scene.

When he finally acknowledges his duplication, it empties out his sense of self and makes him vulnerable: he needs to call on the protection of the gods. His prayer—"Now support me, ye gods: I am double!"—echoes Katie's cry when she emerges from the flames: "Guard me, ye heavenly! What's happening to me?" (*K* 226/3.14.1888, translation altered). And right after Strahl understands that he is doubled, Katie wakes up and wonders, "God, Lord of my Life! What's happening to me!" (*K* 237/4.2.2146, translation altered). So, we have:

> KATIE: Guard me, ye heavenly! What's happening to me?
>
> . . . .
>
> STRAHL: Now support me, ye gods: I am double!
>
> . . . .
>
> KATIE: God, Lord of my Life! What's happening to me!

They repeat each other's sentences with a difference. They speak beside themselves. To be double means to be beside oneself with ecstasy. One's heart beats outside oneself and in another. This experience is frightening, too, because one is open to the influence of the other. So one wishes a god would anchor and stabilize the situation. But the Christian god—usually distinguished from the capricious Ancient gods by the marked singular—has also doubled. Katie's surprised exclamation gives him twice—as "God" and as "Lord of my life." There is no grounding, no anchor, no big other whose law counts, no one Father who lends his name to organize the realm of the visible and who decides with authority what may be proper to see and what may be seen properly.

The feeling that is created in seeing ecstasy by way of a teichoscopy of feeling turns out blurred. Is it love? Whose? What kind? For whom? And what did he want with the whip? Everything Katie sees is what it is and also something else.

Toward a New Ontology of Feeling

With his theater Kleist offers a new take on the ontology of feeling. He mocks the idea that feelings are a natural force that overcomes us (like a thunderstorm) and needs to be controlled rationally (no matter the chances for success). He reveals the obscured constructedness of emotions, of the paradigm of interiority and of gendered sensibility. And he shows how feelings can be constructed differently. His teichoscopies of feeling model the iterative, shared, ideational-material, and dispersive construction of feeling. Iterative means here that feelings are created in the moment (or simultaneous with their communication) while relying on and expanding a history of convention and experience. The fabrication of feeling happens between people and is thus shared—we have seen that the teichoscopies are regularly encouraged by questions and that these questions furnish material ideas that influence the production of a feeling. The material and the ideational aspects of the production of feeling cannot be separated. Ideas have real effects and physical actions also have a metaphorical or antiliteral valence. Kleistian teichoscopies of feeling cut across the boundaries commonly drawn between the interior and the exterior or the virtual and the actual. One could say that these feelings form a language. Every feeling is a sign, an image, a word, or a communication that is culturally produced, transported, and shared without the possibility of being owned or controlled by one individual. Feeling and language also have in common that their formal and their material sides or their intellectual and their physical functions cannot be separated. Finally, the teichoscopic mode of producing feelings disperses feeling across time, across individuals, across genders, across inside and outside, across ideas and bodies and things, across modes of being. These feelings disperse the gendered interiority of the culture of sensibility.

That feelings are produced means that they are amenable to manipulation and susceptible to convention and stereotypes. Therefore it must be permitted to critique feelings. Nevertheless, it makes no sense and would be unfair to target the individual, who seems most closely associated with the feeling, with such critique. No individual is solely responsible for a feeling. It is a distortion of facts to speak of "his" or "her feeling" as if feelings could be owned or controlled. In *Katie of Heilbronn*, for example, Katie seems most closely associated with love. We have seen however, that the Count is more interested than she is in the articulation of the feeling that therefore binds them together. We have also noted that Strahl manipulates Katie the way his mother manipulated him. It thus appears that the desire of a mother for the happiness of her son (i.e., his heterosexual marriage) lies at the origin of it all. Still, it would be wrong to blame her, because the fabrication of feelings relies on convention, and it is therefore quite difficult to fabricate a nonnormative kind of love. Teichoscopies of feeling, however, have a greater potential to make visible what the family cannot see.

Chapter 6

✦

Obscene Lesbians and Lost Queers

How does it happen that an array of differences settles into a tragic conflict? I will address this question via a discussion of Kleist's *Penthesilea* and propose that a link exists between tragedy, conventional heterosexuality, and gendered interiority. Kleist's play dramatizes how the hazards of interiority emerge with tragic inevitability when queer haphazardness turns into straight decisiveness.

Torn between her dying mother's wish that she pursue Achilles and the Amazon law that prohibits heterosexual romance and demands that the partners for procreative sexuality be arbitrary, the Amazon queen Penthesilea ends up tearing Achilles's body apart and taking her own life afterward. Many readers have cast this plot as an example of the classical tragic conflict between state law and individual passion. But they usually omit Penthesilea's commitment to her mother's dying wish, pretending that Penthesilea's interest in Achilles is self-generated. The elision allows them to simplify the play, construing it as a critique of the uncritically deemed anti-individualistic laws of the Amazon state and as an endorsement of Penthesilea's supposedly nonconformist desire for Achilles. A grave misreading of the entanglement of forces that Penthesilea has to contend with, this interpretation notably obscures the significance of Penthesilea's intense relationships with some of the women she is surrounded by. It straightens out Kleist's text, as it were, and stages the piece as a tragedy in "the battle of the sexes," as if there were no other sexes than the two opposing and complementary ones—in *Penthesilea* of all plays.[1]

I will instead trace the various modes of (self-)embrace among the female protagonists. Since the Amazon state knows neither nuclear family nor incest taboo, Penthesilea's mother, Otrerë, can become the object of Penthesilea's extra-oedipal homosexual desire. The play also offers an alternative to heterosexually coded interiority in the physical, emotional, and linguistic exchange between Penthesilea and her comrade in arms Prothoë. With its detailed explanations of the Amazon laws and its examples of concrete relationships among women, *Penthesilea* presents a nonpatriarchal, nonoedipal, and nonmarital organization of sexuality, procreation, and kinship. Kleist thus responds, as it were, in the realm of fiction, to Judith Butler's challenge in *Antigone's Claim* to "accommodate change within kinship relations" (2000, 18).

Yet, as if to complicate the matter, the lesbian relationships dramatized in the play are as susceptible to heterosexual and oedipal modes of intersubjectivity as the cross-gender attractions of the play are modeled on homosexuality. Prothoë at times reinforces gendered interiority, and Otrerë's haphazard dropping of a male name gives rise to oedipal tension. Meanwhile, Penthesilea's desire for Achilles is fueled by her desire for Otrerë, just as her behavior toward him at times reproduces the mingling of identities she practices with Prothoë. This lack of strict adherence to either order—Greek or Amazonian, male or female, homosexual or heterosexual—makes these relationships queer.

We will also attend to Penthesilea's double: Katie. Kleist explains that Katie and Penthesilea "belong together as the + and – of algebra, and are one and the same nature, but imagined under opposite circumstances."[2] In our reading of *Katie*, we will again shift the focus from the heterosexual romance to the contact between women (that is, between figures who are mostly read as such). With regard to their relations to their female doubles, Katie and Penthesilea are indeed opposite poles: Penthesilea can rely on the support and absolute loyalty of her sister in arms, Prothoë, while Katie receives only spite from her rival Kunigunde. Prothoë allows Penthesilea to play the active part and be the (if at times tragically failing) hero, while Katie submits to Kunigunde's every whim.[3]

We noted in the previous chapter that Katie, although she is the title character, remains consistently overlooked. She may serve as a figure for what Terry Castle (1993) has termed the "apparitional lesbian." We have also seen that Kleist uses teichoscopy to disrupt the interior/exterior distinction. This distinction, now in the form of incest (sexual relations inside the family) versus exogamy, or private life (inside the home) versus public life, is also indispensable for the functioning of patronymic lineage and the emergence of the nuclear family. And it is thus this distinction, I argue, that makes it impossible for female to female sexual relations to count under the regime of the patronym or to come into focus for the "eyes" of the nuclear family.

Castle (1993, 2) and other scholars of critical lesbian studies attempt to "bring the lesbian back into focus, as it were" and "to secure for lesbianism a clarity, an outline that might give it some representational heft of its own" (Jagose 2002, 2). But, as Jagose points out, they inadvertently continue to discursively produce the lesbian as invisible.[4] We might thus be better advised to reduce (or try to escape) the grip that singularity and distinction, visibility and recognition have on us and instead to embrace and cultivate the out-of-focus. Here I will consider whether Kleist, who produces and multiplies images that are out of focus, may provide support for a kind of politics that critiques the paradigm of visibility and representation and instead places its bets on finding escape routes and becoming imperceptible. In keeping with

Jagose's analysis and with the tactics of "imperceptible politics," our goal will be not to bring into focus but nevertheless to attract notice to unclear, blurry, and inexplicit lesbian relations.[5] In this chapter, we will encounter Katie as an unclear lesbian and Penthesilea as an ignored queer.

Name

In the fifteenth scene, Penthesilea recounts the official narrative of the founding of the Amazon state and relates its laws and customs. The Amazon state was founded by the female survivors of the genocide and the mass rape of the Scythian people after their successful revolt against their Ethiopian oppressors. Every year, the Amazon queen convenes the Feast of Maids in Bloom, preparing to send an army of women warriors out to attack a foreign people determined by the high priestess in ritual communication with Mars, the god of war. Whoever the Amazon warriors beat in battle, they bring back for a ritual orgy called the Feast of Roses. The heterosexual liaisons of the Feast of Roses do not lead to marriage or to the building of nuclear families. Rather, the conquered and kidnapped men are sent home after they have been presented with gifts as part of the Feast of the Ripe Mothers.

In inverse analogy to patriarchal societies that practice an exchange of women, which Lacan and Claude Lévi-Strauss describe as a trade with signs fostering a symbolic male bond, the Amazons treat men as signs. The individual man in his singularity is just an arbitrary signifier that disappears behind his significance as a sperm donor and substitute for Mars. A large part of the Amazon rituals are designed to safeguard the arbitrary character of signs—that is, of male sex partners. Lasting love relations between the sexes are thereby avoided.

Such lasting love relations develop independently of biological procreation. They are forged among the Amazons. The bond that is sanctioned by the state and cultivated by the customs of the Amazons is that of the women who wage war together, engage in orgiastic sex acts together, are pregnant together, and so on. Kleist figures the homopolitical desire for female autonomy in an inverted analogy to the fraternity slogan of the French Revolution as sisterly love. In the Amazon society, all women are sisters. Among the women of the same age, such kinship is produced and regulated by the jointly celebrated ritual festivities (the Feast of Maids in Bloom, the Feast of Roses, and the Feast of the Ripe Mothers). Intergenerational relations are also experienced as sisterly love because the generational difference is leveled by the orientation toward the one symbolic mother (the founding mother, Tanaïs) and the one father, Mars.[6]

There is no reason to assume that the Amazon sisters cannot have sex with each other. The symbolic order of the Amazon state does not need the incest taboo because it does not know the oedipalized nuclear family. It also does not naturalize heterosexuality but, as we have just seen, ritualizes it to a high degree. Therefore, it does not need to condemn homosexuality as unnatural. In addition, the politics of reproduction in the Amazon state does anything but foster monogamy. The Amazon law thus requires neither incest taboo (regarding incest among Amazons) nor monogamy nor the prohibition of homosexuality.[7] *Penthesilea* presents us with literary evidence that a nonpatriarchal, nonoedipal, and nonmarital organization of sexuality, procreation, and kinship is possible.

Kleist exposes the universalizing effect of the heterosexual, oedipal organization of kinship when he has Achilles assume that his own (i.e., the Greek) order is self-evident and everything else unnatural:

> What place, what time could issue such a law,
> Unfeminine, forgive me, unnatural,
> So foreign to the remaining sex of humans [*dem übrigen Geschlecht der Menschen*]?
>
> (*P* 92/15.1902–4, translation altered)[8]

When Penthesilea suggests in response that gender and kinship norms are culturally determined—"The word of our first mothers did decree it, / And it commands our silence, son of Thetis, / As your first fathers' word commands your own"—she brings into view that, despite each culture's religious respect for their norms, in the larger picture these norms are subject to change (*P* 92/15.1909–11). Such cultural relativism corresponds to Kleist's own experiments in designing alternative symbolic orders and structuring his texts according to them.

The effect of the Amazon regulations of kinship and desire can be observed in the relationship between Penthesilea and Otrerë. The symbolic order of the Amazons links the search for a male sexual partner to armed capture. That much Achilles understands correctly, when he says to his comrades, "What the divine maid wants of *me*, I know it; / She sends me bride wooers enough / On feathered wing, they speak her wishes / With deathly whispers in my ear" (*P* 29/4.595–98). What he does not quite grasp is that Penthesilea's "bride wooers" are not so much meant for him as for Otrerë. Penthesilea enters combat "less to please the great god who had sent [her] there than to please Otrerë's shade" (*P* 101/15.2167–69, translation altered).[9] Her desire for Otrerë sends her into battle. For the "brides of Mars" Achilles is but one of many substitutes for the god of war (*P* 97/15.2056). If the "great god" himself pales even next to Otrerë's shadow, let alone her actual self, then the god's surrogate Achilles would be virtually irrelevant were he not inadvertently endowed with significance by Otrerë.

Penthesilea's desire is frustrated when Otrerë passes on before Penthesilea has a chance to "please" her, which I take the liberty to read also as "to pleasure her." In this already frustrating situation, Otrerë whispers some other name into Penthesilea's ear. Although the fact that Otrerë introduces a third into their tête-à-tête could count as betrayal, Penthesilea construes this gesture as a sign of trust. It is the last trace of their intimacy that Penthesilea can hold on to.

> PROTHOË: And so she named him to you, Queen Otrerë?
> PENTHESILEA: She named him, Prothoë, as well a mother
> May take her child into her confidence [*Vertraun*].
> (*P* 100/15.2141–43).

In the intimacy of the sisters who are also mother and daughter, a signifier is exchanged or, rather, the exchange of the signifier creates this last moment of intimacy. The sign thus loses its arbitrary character. Since sexual intercourse with Otrerë is impossible at this point, the sign stands in for such intercourse and reminds Penthesilea of it. As often as possible, Penthesilea conjures up (and circles around) her intimacy with Otrerë by using said signifier: "Oh son of Peleus! / My one unending thought when I was waking, / my endless dream, was you!" (*P* 101/15.2186–88). The Greek hero thus functions as a metaphor for the late Amazon queen; his name covers over hers, but—for those who are attentive—also lets it shine through.[10]

Again and again, Penthesilea tortures herself with the name that reminds her of the impossibility of any real intimacy with Otrerë: "And into my heart . . . / I branded each of [the Peleid's deeds] with flaming colors" (*P* 102/15.2192–93.). The name begins to suffocate her. Not only does she seem to barely remember her fellow Amazons, even her thoughts of Achilles—whose heroic deeds are supposedly so numerous that one can be "woven into" each "mesh" of the world's large "patterned web"—have reduced to one infinite loop: Achilles's defiling of Hector's corpse (see *P* 101–2/15.2188–98). It remains undecidable whether Penthesilea's obsession with this violation is nurtured by her identification with Achilles or with Hector. It is thus unclear whether it encodes aggression or self-aggression and, if aggression, then whether she wants to violate Achilles or Otrerë. In any case, the symbolic order of the Amazons aims at preventing precisely such obsessions. This is why the high priestess admonishes Penthesilea: "Does is behoove a child of Mars, a queen, / To take her stand upon a single name?" (*P* 47/7.1045–46).

The tragedy of Penthesilea's and Otrerë's relationship is not predetermined by conflicting laws or ethical orders, but develops incidentally in the hour of death, when time is short and both improvise. The dying Otrerë reaches for the first name carried through her window from the voices of the "marketplace" below, to make up for Penthesilea's impending loss (see *P* 99–100/15.2110–41). Initially, Penthesilea has only "half an ear" for this name and instead her eyes are glued to Otrerë's face (*P* 99/15.2128). Only after the fact does this moment of improvisation congeal into an oedipal relation and thus turn against the symbolic order of the Amazons.

Penthesilea is asked to identify with the mother rather than desire Otrerë. "Become a mother, proud and glad, as I am," suggests Otrerë, thus cementing the oedipal structure (*P* 100/15.2139). But Penthesilea can find no pride or happiness in this lifestyle. Instead, the unrequited love and impossible hatred for Otrerë show through the cover of identification in the form of self-aggression and yearning for death. The melancholy identification with the mother is brought to an extreme in the final scene of the play when Penthesilea nurses not a baby but a weapon.[11] Self-aggression here is inseparable from aggression against the lost and melancholically incorporated love object. Penthesilea's suicide is aimed at Otrerë. At the same time, it provides a way for Penthesilea to rejoin Otrerë. That Penthesilea claims to follow Achilles into death ("Yes, I will tell you, Prothoë. / . . . I shall follow him, this youth" [*P* 146/24.3011–13]), as Meroë perhaps a bit too eagerly corroborates ("She follows him indeed!" [*P* 148/24.3035]), serves as a cover for the deeper homosexual desire.

Regard

When Otrerë lies on her deathbed, Penthesilea cannot keep her eyes off her face. But Otrerë doesn't return the gaze:

> "Let me stay for you [*mich dir bleiben*], I cried, my mother,
> Your regard [*Dein Ansehn*], use it [*brauch es*] today for one last time,
> And bid these women go."
> But in her dignity, the Queen, who long
> Had wished to see me on the battlefield—
> For she would leave no heirs, and there were kin
> Ambitious to succeed her on the throne—
> She said: "Go, my sweet child! Ares is calling!
> Your garland shall adorn the Peleid's brow:
> Become a mother, proud and glad, as I am—"
> And gently pressed my hand and passed away.
> (*P* 100/15.2130–40, translation altered)

On the surface, Penthesilea asks Otrerë to use her standing or her "royal privilege," as Agee translates Ansehn, to send away the delegates who bring the call to arms that threatens to separate the two women. Penthesilea wants to be left alone with Otrerë. If the two made common cause, one could imagine a loving scene of irreverent disregard for the rules of the state. But this is not the case. Instead of collusion, there is hierarchy. Even as Otrerë is dying she holds the power in this relationship that has somehow turned oedipal. Penthesilea doesn't feel that she can send the delegates away herself. Instead of freely enjoying sisterly love (the promise of the nation of women), Penthesilea submits to the figure of "my mother [*meine Mutter*]," which is accentuated by the alliteration and the syntactically isolated position at the end of the verse. Even more emphasis is placed on the phrase at the beginning of the next line: "Your regard [*Dein Ansehn*, which can mean both "standing" and "gaze"]." Penthesilea is engrossed in the drama of the gaze. She is impressed by her mother's reputation but also wants her mother's attention. Most of all, she longs for an intense communion of gazes (note the syntactical intimacy and semantic interchangeability of "me" and "you" and of "I" and "mother" in line 2130). In the imperative mode of *Dein Ansehn, brauch es* (Use your standing!) thus resonates an expression of want: I "need your gaze" (*Dein Ansehn*, [*ich*] *brauch es*).

Otrerë, apparently concerned with succession, castrates her daughter by withdrawing her regard. She does so in the sense of both turning away (closing her eyes forever) and withholding recognition from Penthesilea. Otrerë responds to Penthesilea's request with a no (*non*) that simultaneously introduces a name (*nom*). She thus introduces heteronymity into the Amazon context. On her deathbed, Otrerë writes her will. When she chooses the Peleid for her daughter instead of looking at her with validation and love, she actually disinherits Penthesilea, choosing the son she never had *over* her daughter. At this point, Penthesilea has already lost against Achilles. Her defeat will only be repeated on the battlefield and thus confirmed.

Nevertheless, when Penthesilea and Achilles first meet on the battlefield, there is a ludic element to their chase.[12] Their haphazard alignments with different systems of gender, sexuality, procreation, and kinship negotiate differences without establishing them as tragic conflict. The Amazon queen Penthesilea does not easily fit the heterosexual patriarchal gender binary, which in this tragedy is figured as Greek.[13] The Greeks of the play figure the bourgeois gender norms of Kleist's day, whereas the Amazons present a possible alternative to that culture. The play traces the insidious victory of heteronormativity and the tragic collapse of the possible models for a different organization of desire, gender, kinship, and procreation: the Amazons and Achilles.[14] Penthesilea's relation to Achilles cannot be described as straightforwardly heterosexual, since it is charged with the homosexual desire for Otrerë and the collective cathexis with Tanaïs. Achilles likewise wavers between genders and sexualities. Even when he boasts of his virility: "Go then, and fight like eunuchs, if you want; myself I feel a man, and to these women I'll stand my ground"—he seems comfortable assuming the role of the bride when he notes that Penthesilea sends him "bride wooers" (*P* 29/4.587–89; 29/4.598). Hederich's lexicon of Greco-Roman mythology notes that Achilles began wearing women's clothes when he was nine years old and that his mother, the nymph Thetis, started to call him by the female name Pyrrha. Thetis provided this unconventional upbringing in order to keep him away from the Trojan War, which produces and reproduces the war of the sexes.[15] Her education shows some success when Achilles, even though he never becomes a conscientious objector, as it were, falls in love with Patroclus and engages in various love relations with women that disregard both the front lines of war and the boundaries of gender.[16] Vacillating thus between the sexes, Achilles presents an impossibility for the binary logic of the Greeks and their modern heirs.[17] Odysseus promptly excludes him from the game: "Seize him, remove Achilles from the field!" (*P* 11/1.212).[18] The umpire in the arena of opposites cannot but send Achilles off.

The tragedy is that Odysseus's worldview tends to obscure others. The play fight between Penthesilea and Achilles becomes a head-on collision even though, initially, there is nothing tragic about this collision. Instead, in its literalizing of a genre requirement it seems a bit silly, eccentric, or campy. There is no physical victory, either. And yet, the collision serves as an enactment of Penthesilea's defeat, which is thus solely a matter of interpretation. Discursive acts onstage and hermeneutic acts by the spectators and readers retroactively presuppose and thereby establish conventional heterosexuality where, just a moment ago, we could note nothing but queer cross-identifications. The queer relationship between Penthesilea and Achilles is tragically straightened out into a heterosexual opposition. Two queer characters crash into one another and, as if confused by the concussion, begin to assume conventional heterosexual roles. Their world shifts cataclysmically. A gendered discourse of interiority sets in and suffocates Penthesilea. An amnesia about queerness shapes the combined efforts of protagonists, observers onstage, and observers in front of the stage to rationalize an arbitrary occurrence. Most readers of *Penthesilea* forget the queer quality of the relation between Penthesilea and Achilles, presume heterosexuality, and spin undecidability to a tragic conflict. Even literary critics thus contribute to the production of a tragedy they claim to simply observe[19]—until Penthesilea again shatters conventional heterosexuality by tearing Achilles apart while giving him female breasts and again ruins interiority by opening her bosom with a thing-like feeling.[20]

In chapter 5 we already began to see how the report that informs us about Penthesilea's and Achilles's collision immediately establishes as firmly rooted reality what could have been a passing moment of confusion:

> COLONEL: Achilles and the Queen with lances poised,
> Meet on the field with a resounding crash,
> Two thunderbolts colliding in mid-heaven;
> Their lances, weaker than their breasts, are split;
> He, the Peleid, stands; Penthesilea
> Sinks down . . . death's shadow close upon her.
> . . . pale he stands . . .
> Himself a shade of death.
>
> (*P* 51–52/8.1122–32, translation altered)

Penthesilea and Achilles meet as equals: two thunderbolts that collide in mutual penetration. Both have artificially extended members: poised lances. Both lances split. After this climax, both heroes are as if dead ("death's shadow close upon her" and he "a shade of death"). Mutually satisfying homosexual sex, one could say, with "homosexual" here meaning that they are both of the same rank and thus of the same sex or, to put it differently, that they are sexual equals. Verse 1126—"He, the Peleid, stands; Penthesilea [*Er, der Pelide, steht, Penthesilea*]"—brings both names together literally in one line, abreast both physically (in the same verse) and phonetically (in the alliteration on *p*). There is just one slight difference: he stands and she then sinks. But why should it matter in what position the bodies end up after their encounter?

Starting with this unimportant difference, the entire scene will be rearranged in retroactive interpretation. Achilles gets first chance to comment and the Colonel renders his reaction in direct speech, thus privileging and adopting his perspective. Or, one might say if wary of the influence of the messenger on the message, the Colonel employs the rhetorical tool of direct speech to lend more weight to the view expressed. In any case, the account is outrageous if—or, rather, because—it is utterly conventional. According to the Colonel, Achilles exclaims: "How she did strike me with that dying look!" (*P* 52/8.1133, translation altered). Just a moment ago Penthesilea and Achilles attacked each other with their lances, but now he feels struck merely by her look. The queer encounter has been turned into a conventionally gendered and sexualized scene (based on the conventions of the two-sex model established in the eighteenth century or of what in Kleist's tragedy is figured as Greek). If there is talk of a woman's lance, then one is apparently supposed to understand it purely metaphorically. A woman is supposed to wield not steel or wood weapons but eye-daggers. What is more, Achilles perceives hers as a glance on the verge of nonseeing: a dying look, rendered passive by the loss of aim and purpose as it fades. Convention demands that he penetrate her with his lance. The dying, passive glance provokes the charge of his lance like a reflex, and the aggressive penetration in turn is supposed to precipitate her fall. While an instant ago both their chests withstood the impact of the lances and yet both were as if dead afterward, the established reality now is that only Penthesilea is dying, and not just metaphorically.

Even though there is no inherent significance to the accidental configuration of their bodies, Achilles makes sense of the haphazard incident that she sinks while he stands via the fabrication of a dying look that in turn interpellates him as the virile lover of the dying woman.[21] His retrospective misinterpretation of the clash as a one-sided penetration confuses the literal and the figurative register—and confuses us along with it: are we supposed to take his penetration as a literal pushing through her chest, or is it meant as a playful and pleasurable sex act, after all? Yet confusion and distinction of these registers is distributed and controlled across the new gender line: while he can oscillate between the literal and the metaphorical, there is no doubt now that her weapons are metaphorical and her death literal.

We have seen how the physical collision of two queer bodies (reported in scenes 7 and 8) triggered the sudden contraction of the tapestry of homo-relations toward an empty center with a tremendous identificatory pull. This force produced an amnesia about queerness. But, as everything is moving toward the tragic, there is also a counterforce that makes dissemination, spreading, and jumbling possible again. Alongside the concerted effort by the spectators on and offstage (including Achilles and Penthesilea as spectators and interpreters of their own actions) to establish as normative the production of two complementary sexes, Kleist's play also features the struggle of the protagonists to escape this new paradigm and perhaps find a new kind of recognition for their queerness. Repetition proves both harmful and beneficial to this endeavor. One could, for example, read Achilles's construction of a dying look as a repetition of what Penthesilea perceives as she sits at Otrerë's death bed: the dying look of Otrerë. Such repetition compulsion, as we have seen, consolidates the new norm, but it also includes the potential for change in that, via this repetition, Achilles identifies with Penthesilea as he unknowingly restages the scenario that traumatized her (he feels the same anguish at the disappearance of Penthesilea's gaze that Penthesilea feels when Otrerë withdraws her regard: "Moaning with grief, he woos her back to life!" (*P* 52/8.1142).

At the end of the next scene, Penthesilea restages the sinking movement that proved so fatal in her encounter with Achilles. She lets herself sink into a river and toward the image, she sees there, of Helios, whom she had initially attempted to pull down from the sky. Again, such repetition compulsion might reinforce gendered stereotypes (in chapter 1, I highlighted the embarrassment the Amazons feel at Penthesilea's passive behavior—her sinking down while asking to be taken), but it might also open some wiggle room for queer resignification.

Penthesilea's desire to sink into the river has an additional mythic source overdetermining the image. The prime mother of the Amazons, Tanaïs, shares her name with a river that plays an important role in another origin story of the Amazons.[22] Hederich lists Tanaïs as a male youth who gave the river its name: "Others consider him a son of Berossus and the Amazon Leucippe. He was an enemy of the female sex and despised marriage. But Venus, as a punishment, made him fall in love with his own mother. For a long time he resisted this passion. At last, since he could not completely overcome it, he drowned himself in the river Amazonius, which then received his name" (Hederich 1996, 2281, my translation). The young, not-exactly-heterosexual man with the incestuous desire drowns himself in a river called by an epithet that belongs to his mother—Amazonian—and thereby overwrites this name with his own name, Tanaïs. Penthesilea also shows a strong, quasi-incestuous desire (but we have seen that the Amazon state needs no incest law) to stay with her (dying) mother as she is called into battle to fight without passion.

Echoing one story in the other, Kleist liberally exchanges and renders mobile gender as well as subject and object positions. Achilles serves as a replacement for Penthesilea's first object choice, her mother. And when she wants to die by drowning, asking Helios, who might serve as a replacement for Achilles, to take her (*P* 64/9.1388), the Tanaïs myth suggests that she might want to escape her passion for her mother Otrerë. Or she might want to unite with another mother, the founding mother, Tanaïs, whose gender is not that straightforward, and not only because she carries a male name. This last desire points beyond the personal trauma and repair to a collective one—the trauma of the Scythian people and the building of a new world, the Amazonian world, to recover a life worth living.

Finally, Penthesilea repeats, with subject and object exchanged, the alleged penetration of her breast by Achilles. She does to him what he supposedly did to her. One could call this revenge, but I would like to suggest a different reading. Penthesilea and Achilles's final encounter dissipates the tragic agon of the sexes initiated by their clash. It undoes the gender dichotomy that was produced by or in the wake of the literalized tragic collision.

When Penthesilea emerges from the mauling scene, she has blood on her throat and chest where she wounded Achilles. She is also unable to speak after her last and lethal attack on Achilles, as if it were she who had the arrow that she shot through his neck stuck in her throat. Indeed, her women discover a wound in her neck (*P* 137/24.2820–21).[23] The boundaries of the bodies of Achilles and Penthesilea have dissolved.[24] This must qualify our first impression of the scene as a unilaterally savage encounter. Instead, the identities and the bodies of Penthesilea and Achilles become confused in a way that calls to mind E. A. Grosz's (1995, 200) description of the sexual act or, in her terminology, "the carnal caress" as the experience of "being thrown into an interchange with an other whose surface intersects with one's own."[25] In the confounding confusion of contours and body parts, the sexual act has something shattering about it. It finally allows Penthesilea and the Peleid to queer each other again.

Abreast

From Penthesilea and the Peleid, let's turn to another couple that shares the same initial, *P*—Penthesilea and Prothoë. When Penthesilea appears onstage for the first time she is looking for her breast: "Where is the seat, which didn't become bosom . . . ?" (*P* 32/5.651, my translation). Prothoë answers: "If you would only stay, my precious [*teure*] Queen, / and rest your head upon this faithful [*treuen*] bosom" (*P* 32/5.657–68). Prothoë offers her breast in lieu of Penthesilea's missing one. The Amazon body, marked by the excision of the right breast, does not form an organic whole, so Amazons don't have to worry about integrity and individual identity. Instead, one body can supplement another body. Prothoë exchanges breasts with Penthesilea.

Identities get similarly confused in the ninth scene when Penthesilea dissolves in tears. Prothoë urges Penthesilea to save herself from the Peleid's next attack, but Penthesilea collapses:

> PROTHOË: Sister! My dearest heart! My life!
> So you won't flee? Won't leave?
> (PENTHESILEA *bursts into tears and leans against a tree.*)
> PROTHOË (*suddenly moved, sitting down beside her*): Do as you will.
> (*P* 58/9.1269–70)

Penthesilea's ejaculation of tears conjoins the bodies of the two women. Often the eye keeps at a distance what it perceives and thus introduces a gap between inner life and outside world as it makes out individual shapes. Here the eye functions as an orifice, undoing any distance and distinction. The tears rush (*stürzen*) out of Penthesilea's eyes like a waterfall, uncontrollably. The sudden force of this fall creates a ripple effect. Penthesilea also sinks down right away, and then Prothoë's spirit slumps and her body sits down. Seen through tears, the world blurs and Penthesilea loses orientation. She needs to lean against something—a tree. Then the "easy-moving" tears begin to move Prothoë as well (*P* 134/24.2787, translation altered). "Suddenly" she too loses the will to save herself—to preserve her identity intact and separate from all others. She takes on the role of the tree and nestles her body against Penthesilea's body. Disrobing of their separate individualities, they exchange their breasts and play each other's part. Instead of confronting Penthesilea, Prothoë doubles her. They both sit down.

The urgency of action is suspended. Instead of fleeing from Achilles, who is fast approaching, Penthesilea breaks down, follows her tears, and draws Prothoë with her. Her collapse opens an interval in space and time, in which Prothoë and Penthesilea embrace one another. It creates a threshold on which the women sit down for a while. When Penthesilea bursts into tears, she tears Prothoë's line apart (*P* 58/9.1270). Not without theatricality does Penthesilea's ejaculation onstage interrupt both the course of time and the flow of meter and syntax. In lieu of temporal, syntactic, and prosodic succession, the "sex [*Geschlecht*], the easy-moving," of tears establishes a side-by-side, a doubling coexistence (*P* 134/24.2787, translation altered). Two bodies sit abreast on the threshold. Their identities and properties blur in the flow of tears.

Such tearing of regular speech does not mean that tears don't communicate. Tears produce language but this language follows a different logic.[26] It communicates feelings and thoughts, but not as distinct properties of the individualized person. The sisters touch one another also with words, and feelings are fabricated gradually during the verbal exchange and physical mingling of two bodies sitting side by side on the threshold. In the last chapter, we discussed the fabrication of feeling through teichoscopy (on the threshold between inside and outside); here, we have the confounding of inside and outside as doubling.

In his essay "On the Gradual Fabrication of Thoughts While Speaking," Kleist proposes that "it is not *we* who 'know'; it is rather a certain condition—in which we happen to be—that 'knows'" (Kleist 1982, 222). With the crying scene in *Penthesilea*, he also shows that it is not *we* who feel, but that it is rather a certain condition—in which we happen to be—that feels. The tears are thus not to be understood as an expression of a feeling already had. Such an expression of something already felt would again relegate feelings into the interiority of the bosom, just as with the "mere expression" of finished thoughts spirit, so the essay argues, is left trapped inside.[27] In both cases, the external signifier would only be a metaphor—or a catachresis, to be precise—for an authentic inside that never appears as such. Kleist offers an alternative: the simultaneity, adjacency, overlap of words and thoughts or feelings. During the gradual fabrication of thoughts while speaking, "the lines of thought and articulation move abreast, and both mental processes are congruent to each other. Speech is not a fetter then, like a drag chain on the wheel of the mind, but a second wheel running parallel to it on the same axle" (Kleist 1982, 221). Words and thoughts run parallel, they move abreast—but they also get exchanged and confused in this messy, metaleptic logic. With *Penthesilea*, Kleist opens the binary of speaking and thinking to the jumble of feelings, thoughts, words, and bodies that forge and dissolve one another in a dynamic fabrication and disintegration of feeling while speaking.

"Beloved, speak!" so Prothoë encourages Penthesilea (*P* 61/9.1341). And Penthesilea sets one wordbody next to the other on the threshold: "pain, pain"; "nothing, nothing, nothing"; "too high, I know, too high"; "well, well" (*P* 59–61/9.1291, 1292, 1341, 1344). Like the bodies of the two sisters, Penthesilea's words double each other in this language of tears. Like two wheels running parallel to each other, the signifiers support and energize one another but also drop and drag each other down. Kleist articulates here not pain that comes before and remains beyond words, leaving each and every word empty and without a direct connection to pain, but "pain, pain": a repeated feeling-body-thing-word.

Even within a single word, regular succession becomes inconsequential: the letters sit abreast of one another and get mixed up. In the interval of tears, they blur, come loose and move around. Letters begin to communicate with one another and affect one another across the space that opens within the word itself. This auto-affection of words announces itself already in Prothoë's first address to Penthesilea: "If you would only stay my precious [*teure*] Queen, and rest your head upon this faithful [*treuen*] bosom" (*P* 32/5.657–58). At that point, their breasts are not yet intermingled and the words *teure* and *treue* still behave well and keep off each other. Or do they?

Language and feeling are often seen as being in conflict or at war with one another. According to this topos, words kill feelings and emotionality destroys eloquence. Their fight is related to the battle of the sexes that occupies so much of the surface of Kleist's *Penthesilea.* But Kleist offers a different, a same-sex model for the relation between words and feelings. Against the heterocoital imperative that commonly governs sign and referent, or language and feeling, Kleist presents their tribadic adjacency, allowing for a slippage between the realms. After he has Odysseus proclaim in the first scene that, in general, nature knows "no third," Kleist proposes an alternative to the oppositional logic of hetero- versus auto-reference, an alternative that one could call homo-exchange (*P* 8/1.126). Like Penthesilea and Prothoë—who move abreast while confusing their identities—feelings, bodies, words, and thoughts run alongside one another, doubling, confounding and forging one another.

(Radical) Trust

When Count vom Strahl was afflicted with suicidal depression, an angel asked him to trust. The call came in an excessively repeated form: "Trust [*Vertraue*], trust, trust!" (*K* 200/2.9.1166, my translation). Strahl doesn't quite trust but wants to see (the girl). When he is shown the girl, he doesn't quite see her. Clearly, his trust cannot be called radical, even though his health improves dramatically after the vision. In the elder bush scene, the Count finally professes his faith: "True as I hope for heaven, I believe" (*K* 236/4.2.2122). At the end of the duet under the elder bush, both have awoken—Katie literally and Strahl in the sense that he now understands (that he is double) and believes (in a different reality). This understanding doesn't bring an increase in liveliness. On the contrary, he now feels a "spirit [*ein Geist bin ich*]" (*K* 237/4.2.2145). But he needn't worry because, as mentioned before, Katie can see ghosts (*K* 218/3.6.1700). She has a different kind of sensibility.

Katie participates, avant la lettre, in what thinkers in the wake of Deleuze and Guattari have theorized as "imperceptible politics." Trust in the reality of ghosts—in the reality of what escapes representation and therefore cannot quite be seen—plays an important role in the counterintuitive politics of becoming imperceptible. As if inspired by its practice of "cultivating trust in speculative figurations of a radically different future in the present," Katie perceives things that others around her cannot quite see (Papadopoulos, Stephenson, and Tsianos 2008, 81). She follows her desire without explaining what she does and why she does it. When people question her, she answers, "I don't know" (*K* 176/1.2.467).[28] This should be taken not as ignorance but as a mode of escape from the constant pressure of representational policing. It is an act of resistance, albeit an unusual one: "Desire. Trust. Escape! This is the only understanding of resistance which is relevant for imperceptible politics" (Papadopoulos, Stephenson, and Tsianos 2008, 80). Katie does not answer the normative demand for evidence and explanation. She "is driven by a firm belief in the importance and truthfulness of ('her') actions, without seeking any evidence for, or conducting any investigation into ('her') practices" (ibid., 76–77). At the beginning of the play, she states clearly that she will not answer the tribunal because she does not recognize its authority, and that she will only respond to the superior authority that she sees embodied in Count vom Strahl (*K* 174/1.2.395–401, 175/1.2.438–40). Katie unconditionally believes in her desire and follows it on a sure footing. But, to anticipate what I will explain in more detail below, Strahl is not the true object of her desire.

For sure, when Katie responds to Strahl's probing questions, as he himself reports, with the words "You know very well why," she shows her unconditional trust in his superior sensibility, against all evidence (*K* 233/4.2.2041). She firmly believes that he shares her vision. It's a waste of trust. But it insures that her true desire remains imperceptible.

When Katie throws herself out the window and leaves her father's house, she forgoes the beauty, the riches, and the respect that she could claim as a public person—a daughter of the city of Heilbronn. She becomes imperceptible. Why would she renounce all that? What is she rebelling against? I think that she wants to become invisible because of the way her father Theobald looks at her. The first image of Katie that the play offers, comes from Theobald (*K* 164–65/1.1.63–98). His speech strangely oscillates between apotheosis and reification. On the one hand, he deifies Katie, portrays her with visual and verbal allusions as a divine or mythic figure. On the other, he treats her like a thing—a precious gem that was stolen. He finds himself without his daughter and accuses Strahl instead of her—as if she had no agency and can therefore not be blamed. According to Theobald, Katie thus has everything—all the beauty, all the riches, all the virtue, all the spiritual power, and all the respect of the world—except for her own will. His encomium includes erotic overtones. These are most obvious when he uses a passage from the Song of Songs to describe Katie as "a child . . . that went up from the desert . . . like a column of smoke of myrrh and juniper" (*K* 164/1.1.67–69).[29] He is strangely jubilant when Katie agrees to marry a young farmer even though, if one believes his own praise of her, she could have made a much better catch (*K* 165/1.1.93–105). Theobald and this young farmer, Gottfried, carry the same last name—Friedeborn—and Gottfried lands surround Katie's estate, which she has inherited from her grandfather. Both facts indicate kinship relations between Theobald and Gottfried. Perhaps Theobald wants to consolidate with this marriage his precarious kinship with Katie (he will turn out to be her cuckolded father), or perhaps he sees in Gottfried a younger version of himself. In any case, Theobald has a passionately charged vision of and for Katie, complete with the luster that Allemann has analyzed as indispensable for the visions that absorb Kleist's protagonists. Since Theobald is no legitimate protagonist, the luster of his vision is comically reduced: Katie appears to her father bathed in the radiance of "her straw hat gleaming yellow" (*K* 165/1.1.74).

When Katie leaves her father's house, she escapes his vision of and for her. When she throws herself out the window, she wastes herself—her body and her status—in the service of her "own" vision (the German phrase *etwas zum Fenster hinaus werfen*—literally, "to throw something out the window"—means "to waste something"). She leaves the comfort of home, escaping economic common sense. She pushes her body through a boundary regardless of the cost, breaking both her legs as a result of the fall. In fact, this must be taken not only as a loss (of bodily integrity) but also as an active desire for a different body, as realizing "the embodied and unrepresentable desire which people follow as they cross borders despite the regime of control which tries to close them off or to constrain and control them" (Papadopoulos, Stephenson, and Tsianos 2008, 79).[30]

Katie's (supposedly) mutual vision with Strahl helps her to escape the (eroticized) paternal vision. But, since the extradiegetic (reading and theatergoing) public is primed by Theobald's portrait of her in the first scene of the play, the heroine must try to escape the audience as much as the confines of her father's expectations. This is why her leave from home extends to a wish or even a politics of becoming imperceptible.

Katie follows her ghost. But how radical is this love story of Katie and Strahl? Isn't this fairy-tale romance, as it is represented in the play by various characters, the most commonplace ideological story? Can trust then be co-opted by the system in place to counteract radical politics? It can, and her politics of becoming imperceptible mostly get lost in the fact that Katie's fixation on Strahl tends to keep her captive in rather traditional notions of romance and gender roles (the audience's vision for Katie).

But Kleist doesn't present the issue of trust all that straightforwardly here. As already noted, the angel utters the word "trust" in its imperative verb form three times. The three iterations of the feeling word or word feeling sit abreast and rub against one another in homo-exchange, bringing to the fore slight differences. The angel uses the word *vertraue*. As common and here correctly applied as it is, the particle *ver-* spells trouble. As we saw in chapter 1, *ver-* can be used in the sense of completion and also in the sense of perversion. Here it modifies the verb *trauen*, which can mean "to dare," "to trust," and "to wed." As the angel exhorts the Count to dare more and to trust completely, he also, I think, includes a call to mess up the wedding.

The fairy-tale ending of the wedding between emperor's daughter and knight in shining armor is obviously disturbed by Katie responding to the question of whether she wants to marry Strahl—posed by him and her two fathers (the Emperor, her biological father, and Theobald, who raised her)—by crying, "May God and all his saints protect me!" (*K* 259/5.14.2678). Then she faints. Her cry falls on deaf ears. The highest political authority of the land, the Emperor, seems to take it as an expression of consent or else regard it as irrelevant. He proceeds to marry the unconscious Katie off and to encourage Strahl with the words "Then take her, Count vom Strahl . . . !"

(*K* 259/5.14.2679). Given this blatant disregard, perhaps we can lend her our ears.

Why does Katie respond with such horror, with a refusal so vehement that she needs to withdraw from the situation by fainting? Does Katie not want Strahl, after all? Did she not follow him in the sure expectation that he would marry her? Earlier we noted that Strahl, in his role as theater director, lets his actress go off script. In fact, each time he feeds her a line he puts a question mark behind it, as if to give her room to improvise. Improvise she does, if only once—with the line "Come quick! You girls! Come right to me, Christina!" (*K* 236/4.2.2129, translation altered). This line shifts the report about their encounter on New Year's Eve, which, as we have analyzed, is produced in a rather tentative fashion between the two of them, to a free enactment that collapses the temporal difference between the current dialogue and the narrated situation. Because the line suddenly breaks out of the established form, it seems particularly close to her experience. And the urgency and exuberance conveyed by the three exclamation marks adds to this impression. Is this desire for female company in the plural, which emerges here without precedent or succession (nowhere else does Kleist's text mention a Christina or other girls in Katie's house) to be taken as Katie's true desire?

Katie is a bit of a tomboy. She sleeps in the stable or in the open. In a scene that recalls Goethe's *Götz von Berlichingen*, she plays the squire to Strahl (*K* 221/3.9; cf. Goethe 1991, 8/1.2). Later she rushes into the flames to save Kunigunde's favorite possession. When the knights ride into battle, though, she refuses to gather up her clothes even a little bit to cross a river (*K* 232/4.1.2001–7). Is this refusal really driven by feminine modesty, as Gottschalk seems to suggest? Or is a different discomfort with her body involved here? She might want to pass as a boy in this martial context and for this reason be hesitant to expose her feminine legs. Or—and this seems even more the case—she might not be prepared to show the world her modified body. Her legs are a sensitive issue. She broke both of them right above the knee to follow her desire (*K* 167/1.1.181–87). I read this as a displaced DIY gender-reassignment surgery.

Katie has no interest whatsoever in her fiancé, and this complete lack of interest already points to Katie's nonnormative desire. Is she like Schiller's tomboy Joan of Arc, who can escape the bond that is prepared for her by her father only by going to the extreme of conjuring up a divine vision and being deemed insane for it (or, worse, in a pact with the devil)?[31] Joan follows the Virgin Mary and fights to save the king of France, feeling enflamed by the courage of the cherubs (cf. Schiller1959, Prologue.4.428)—only to be thoroughly roped into heteronormativity in the end. Katie follows the radiance of the cherub and of Strahl; she is able to save her knight and his fiancée from an impending attack, goes into the flames for her and supports him as a squire—only to get kicked in the butt.

The options for independent young women who don't fit bourgeois gender roles and matching sexuality seem narrow and all wrong. The one line that Katie improvises to speak of women is thoroughly covered over by the fairy-tale script of predestined heterosexual love that miraculously enhances the station of both lovers.

Her articulation of a desire for the knight in shining armor and the trust that he will marry her is force-fed by the combined powers of bourgeois ideology and fairy-tale conventions. As noted, Katie resorts to silence as a weapon or mode of resistance, but this strategy also works to her disadvantage. Schiller's Joan, who likewise cannot or does not want to speak when accused, even though everyone of status in the French camp is eager to excuse her, might have served as a model in this respect as well (Schiller 1959, 4.11.2985–4.12.3041). Schiller's often-critiqued use of thunder as a sign of divine judgment has made its way in a campy fashion into Kleist's name for the second protagonist, Count Wetter vom Strahl.[32] While Schiller allows his glorious Joan to be fatally trapped by bourgeois gender roles and sexual norms in the end, Kleist makes a subtle mockery of heteronormativity. In fairy tales, it is usually the wife of some easygoing guy who, through her curiosity, chases away the good spirits by asking too many questions or literally shedding too much light on them. Here Marianna ruins the magic, which, according to fairy-tale structure, puts Katie in the position of Marianna's husband. That the little light Marianna carries can even be noticed in the tremendous radiance of the angel, let alone be so disturbing that the angel must vanish with the Count, seems rather hilarious and calls into question the power of the fairy-tale allure and its misogynistic operations.

In fact, Katie experiences strong bonds and intense physical encounters with women, even though these are generally passed over by both the play's plot and its reception. It has to be noted, for example, that Katie saves not only Strahl but also his fiancée Kunigunde from the attack by Kunigunde's enemies. The first noble to recognize her emphatically, after Strahl finally figures out that she is the object of his vision, is his cousin Leonora. Katie reacts with conspicuous intensity when she sees Kunigunde naked. And, in the end, when she faints on being asked to marry the Count, she falls into the arms of the Countess Helena, Strahl's mother.[33] Katie has female company in the plural.

The Theater of Swan and Salamander

When Katie wakes up under the elder bush, the Count does not tell her that they had a conversation in her sleep and that he now understands who she is. Even after he received confirmation of her status from the Emperor, he still does not tell her that he plans to marry her. Strahl thus continues to stage his act with an ignorant Katie. Their power relation is not lastingly altered.

Meanwhile, Strahl's female double, his cousin Leonora, stages another kind of theater. She designs a glorifying scene with Katie at its center: "Just look at her! Asparkle and agleam! / Like some fair swan with swelling bosom rising, / Fresh from the crystal waters of a lake!" (*K* 240/4.6.2210–12, translation altered).[34] At last, Katie is perceived as radiant. Strahl's double supplements the mutuality of their vision.[35] But Leonora's words don't align with Katie's physical appearance onstage. In the fictional reality of the play, Katie comes across in this moment as rather puny. She trembles and calls on Leonora for help. Leonora's enamored, somewhat eroticized response strikes one as utterly incongruent.[36] Katie's recognition by the aristocracy comes at an inopportune time. Right now—even more than usually—Katie would rather disappear. She urges Leonora to leave the scene with her: "Leonora! Come away" (*K* 240/4.6.2214, translation altered). Leonora's visual celebration of Katie—her act of conferring onto Katie a radiance and representative noblesse—is out of place. Katie would rather remain imperceptible.

Since Kleist dug burrows between his texts that allow the reader to crawl from one to the other, let us follow his invitation and consider a passage from *The Marquise of O*. It features a vision of another Katie that is similar to the one Leonora paints:

> Thereupon [Count F.] recounted several little things made interesting by his passion for the Marquise: how throughout his sickness she had sat at his bedside; how in the fever brought on by his wound he had constantly confused his image of her with the image of a swan that he had seen, as a boy, on his uncle's estates; that one memory had moved him especially, of how once he had thrown dirt at this swan, which had then gone silently under water and had risen again pure white; that she had swum to and fro without end on a fiery flood and he had called out Thinka, which was the name of the swan, but that he had never been able to lure her towards him for all her delight had been in paddling and in breasting the waves; declared suddenly, crimson in the face, that he loved her exceedingly: looked down at his plate and was silent. (Kleist 2004, 290)

Leonora's comparison of Katie to a swan emerging luminous and "with swelling bosom"—an image of the glorious breast—from the water, seems to be taken directly from *The Marquise of O*.[37] The swan there is called Thinka—short for Kathinka, a Slavic version of Katherine, of which Katie is a diminutive. Katie of Heilbronn, the swan of Count F's childhood, and the Marquise of O belong to the same family by virtue of their names and the confusion of the Counts. There are echoes between the plots of the two texts that also support the textual rapprochement. Count F lies sick in bed and has visions, like Strahl on New Year's Eve. Katie survives a trial by fire, like both the Marquise, who escapes the flames of her family's home set on fire during a military attack, and Thinka, who swims on fiery water in F's fever dreams. Both Counts desire absolution from an offense they have committed. While Count F is, presumably, referring to his rape of the Marquise when he offers the metaphor of throwing dirt at the white swan, Count vom Strahl regrets having attacked Katie with a whip (*K* 233/4.2.2045–46).

Count F admits that "he had never been able to lure her towards him for all her delight had been in paddling and in breasting the waves." Thinka, the swan—a noble animal—enjoys using and displaying her physical strength and doesn't heed the call that tries to lure her. This image communicates pride, prowess, and independence. In the particular context of the grotto scene, one might immediately connect the swan Thinka with Kunigunde, rather than with Katie. Kunigunde is powerful and knows what she is worth, and, as William C. Reeve (1991, 119) points out, she does not give herself to any of her suitors. But Leonora is right—Katie too leads an independent life and enjoys the strength of her body. She walks long distances and rests either among the horses or under the elder bush with its finches (*K* 181/1.2.593–96). Katie also has many suitors, as Theobald underscores, but doesn't accept any of them.

Katie oscillates between this pride and an indifferent submission to her father's wishes. She doesn't care which man her father has chosen for her because her desire moves elsewhere, to women. Each man is as useless as any other to her. The choice is insignificant and arbitrary. Yet, she latches onto Strahl: he is compelling, even unavoidable, because of his luster, but, at bottom, he is also an arbitrary signifier in the sense that he cannot fulfil Katie's actual desire.[38] Pursuing Strahl has the advantage of providing her with two things—the negative freedom from the regime of her father, and the masculinity of the stalker position. And it does so while placating heteronormativity.

Like Count F, Katie sneaks through the back door into paradise: she gets to the lady by way of the knight.[39] Likewise, she slips into the revitalizing body of water by way of a smaller, darker one. While Leonora turns around at the gates of paradise (the gate to the grotto in the garden) to fetch something to cover up their naked bodies, Katie ventures inside alone but doesn't dare to straightforwardly enter the main grotto (*K* 240/4.5.2204–6). She enjoys herself first in the small one. Emboldened by the pleasure she finds there, she moves into the central grotto (*K* 241/4.7.2233–37).

To her surprise and horror, however, paradise turns out to be a theater. The grotto is brightly illuminated, like a stage. Whereas at first Katie found some shelter "in one of the side chambers which are dark and hidden," she has now moved into the limelight (*K* 239–40/4.5.2203–4, translation altered). Suddenly she bathes in attention. Her naked body is on display. And, what is even more horrifying, she sees behind the scenes. To enter the stage means to move from the position of the enchanted spectator to the position of the actor who is aware of, or one could say, subjected to the sight of the theatrical machinations. Katie sees Kunigunde "naked," which is to say, she sees the mask, the theatrical apparatus, all the work that goes into creating the beautiful semblance.

Up to this point she moved in a fairy-tale world, dreaming of becoming a princess by way of marrying a knight. So far she has wanted to *watch* the glamour of the aristocracy and the beauty of bourgeois love rolled into one: on New Year's Eve, she asked to see the knight, and her wish was granted (*K* 235/4.2.2098–2104). Now her vision is contaminated by contact; the sight is entangled with touch.[40] When Katie catches—or, we might say, is caught by—a glimpse of Kunigunde, she has already slipped into the water, she is irrevocably part of the scene: "But just as I was entering the basin, / My eye caught sight—" (*K* 241/4.7.2239–40). Katie has transgressed the fourth wall, the boundary that the bourgeois theater imposes. She bathes in the same element as Kunigunde.[41] And her reaction is physical. Naked, she encounters a naked body and begins to tremble. While readers and audiences generally assume that Katie is shocked by Kunigunde's ugliness or by the artifice necessary for her to look beautiful, I read her in this scene as feeling a transgressive attraction interwoven with trepidation. As if not quite sure what to do when wet with another woman—another woman whose body, it turns out, doesn't quite fit the category—she'd rather retreat. The result of her rompishness is *eleos* and *phobos*, or wailing and gnashing of teeth, as one would say in a more disparaging way. The grotto episode offers a reflection on the aesthetics of the effects of the theater doubled with a portrayal of a Katie not quite ready for transgression. The play projects the negative aspects of Strahl onto Kunigunde, so Katie's vision of Kunigunde serves as the negative double of her vision of Strahl (*K* 249/5.3.2446–52). While Strahl is not judged for his composite character (he is a mosaic of at least two pieces), Kunigunde becomes the object of horror, disgust, and contempt the moment it is discovered that she is not a harmonious whole. Even Katie must fear being torn to pieces. The punishment for observing a powerful woman taking her bath is death, usually by dismemberment (a lesson taught by the Actaeon myth, to which Kleist alludes in various contexts).[42] Katie's namesake, Saint Catherine, was also supposed to be torn apart, by four wheels moving in opposite directions. After an angel destroyed the instrument of torture, they ended up cutting off her head—the typical punishment for overly intelligent and articulate women.[43]

But what exactly happens in the grotto? As Katie is reduced to silence, the spectators or readers are forced to fill in the blanks of her account with their imagination. Does she tremble only from fear or also from a different, more pleasurable excitement? Katie feels that she would gravely disappoint Count vom Strahl were he to find out "everything [*von der ganzen Sach*]" (*K* 241/4.7.2242). Perhaps the "horror [*Greuel*]," which she wants to suppress and divulge at the same time, consists not only in what Kunigunde is but also in what Kunigunde and Katie did (*K* 241/4.7.2246). Or do we want to separate desire from act and concede only that there is something that Kunigunde and Katie may have wanted to do? Such separation between interiority and exteriority breaks down in the climate that is established in the first scene of the play by the judges of the secret court declaring that their "mission is to uncover wickedness, wherever it lurks, beyond the reach of human justice—like a salamander [*Molche*] in the cave of the breast [*in der Höhle der Brust*]" (*K* 163/1.1.3–6, translation altered).[44] And the water into which both women slipped has already mediated the touch of the two naked bodies. Katie is involved in "the whole thing," and she expresses her deep dismay about her contribution to the Count's disappointment (*K* 241/4.7.2251: *durch mich enttäuscht*). What torments her more?—that she cheated on him, or that she stole his girlfriend?

Katie and Kunigunde form a couple—a couple that is based on homoness in Bersani's sense (1996, 10, 41, 128). Katie refers to Kunigunde with the pronoun "it"—"It's coming! [*Es kommt!*]" (*K* 242/4.7.2253, translation altered)—while her own grammatical gender is also neuter (*das Käthchen*). In addition, the two share the same initial: K and K. And neither of them forms an organic whole—while Kunigunde is revealed as a mosaic, Katie's body has been shaken and broken.[45]

Across Kleist's texts, fire serves as an index for sexual passion. When Kunigunde, who uses her male suitors to increase her material wealth but leaves them all unsatisfied, sees her castle in flames, she gives Katie the key to her writing desk and prevents Strahl and his men from entering the virginal staircase: "What is't you fear? . . . She won't perish [*verderben*] on this journey. The stairway still remained untouched [*unberührt*] by fire [*Strahl*]" (*K* 224/3.13.1844–46, translation altered). I read the last sentence and especially the unusual choice of the word *Strahl* (ray) for fire, instead of *Feuer*, as attesting that Kunigunde has not yet experienced sexual passion (this stairway was not yet on fire) and, specifically, that Strahl has not taken (her on) these steps yet. Kunigunde clarifies that she does not consider it a sin for Katie to venture on this way (it will not spoil [*verderben*] her character). A struggle for Kunigunde's sexual satisfaction ensues. Katie is still a bit clumsy, so Kunigunde gives directions. She leads her more to the right and points to her wet clitoris, the "pivot [*Stift*] . . . set so shiny [*glänzend*] above my toilet-table" (*K* 224/3.13.1858, translation altered). But Strahl interrupts and insists on his superior experience: "Let go, I say! / Toilet-table and mirror and pivot too / Are quite unknown to her but not to me" (*K* 225/3.13.1874–76). Promising to satisfy her ("to suit your heart's desire" [*K* 225/3.13.1878]), Strahl and his men decide to apply a ladder to the opening in the back, but must realize that their instrument is too large (*K* 225/3.13.1878–81). They push through—"knock out the crossbar! That's the way to do it! / The ladder's steady now" (*K* 226/3.13.1882–83). But before he can enter, the house collapses: Katie was able to open the right drawer, which caused the flames in Kunigunde's castle to flare up and the accumulated excitement to suddenly discharge.[46]

Katie reacts to this adventure with a severe attack of homo-panic the second time around. Ashamed of the pleasure that drove her to frolic "light-heartedly" across the boundary "to try the centre (grotto)" (*K* 241/4.7.2237),[47] she projects all evil onto Kunigunde. The naked Kunigunde presumably strikes her as so horrifying and repelling that she only wants to flee. The incident bars her from putting the horror into words, but her silence also keeps her involved in her liaison with Kunigunde. It has the effect that K and K divide the main elements of the theater between them (see Klotz 1996, 79–80). Katie is seen while Kunigunde is heard. Katie emerges from the grotto, beautiful—like the proud, male-connoted swan and the foam-arisen Aphrodite rolled into one. Kunigunde remains hidden, but we hear her voice calling from the grotto—demanding and luring. One refers to the other and remains contiguous with the other.

Since Katie does not respond to interrogations (this time by Leonora), no verbal image of Kunigunde is presented. Kunigunde remains in the cave like the salamander in Katie's breast. Whether this salamander gets decried as a lecher (*Lustmolch*, literally "lust newt") or as "wickedness," it is, in any case, an amphibian—a creature of two kinds (*K* 163/1.1.3). In the version of the play that Kleist published in his journal *Phoebus*, Kunigunde appears as a siren—another kind of composite creature that belongs to the water. Katie, for her part, walks through fire like a salamander. K and K are both amphibians, and together they share Thinka's oxymoronic "fiery flood" (Kleist 2004, 190).

Conclusion

The paradisiac theater of the grotto—a cave-like structure—doubles the secret tribunal of the first act, with notable differences. The *Vehme* trial also takes place in a cave, that is to say, it also consists in a theater closed to the public's view. Strahl is led there blindfolded and the members of the jury are masked. But this enclosure, secrecy, and anonymity holds only for the intradiegetic public. The court proceedings provide the spectacle of the first act and the readers of Kleist's play know even the names of the jury members.[48] While the quasi-parodos (the introductory speech by the chair of the court, Count Otto von der Flühe) establishes an analogy between psychic interiority and the enclosed space of the scene by announcing that the present court searches for the crime "in the cave of the breast," the theatrical disavowal of the presence of the audience (which the new, bourgeois theater encourages by way of the fourth wall and the darkened auditorium) creates the impression that the theater audience directly witnesses the crimes as they unfold in the interiority of the soul (*K* 163/1.1.4, translation altered). We find this analogy and disavowal, in different variations, throughout bourgeois theater as the mechanism that facilitates the theater's participation in the production of modern (culpable) interiority. Kleist mobilizes this mechanism (not without irony) in the first act and also in the fifth act when the Emperor confides his secret "to these four walls," thus drawing the rather inconclusive trial of the first act to a satisfying close (*K* 248/5.3.2432).

What takes place in the grotto between Katie and Kunigunde is not performed on this stage. This means that it does not participate in the bourgeois or modern paradigm of interiority and (confessional) representation. With the amphibious couple, the fraught figuration of interiority as a material, external space, which Kleist ridicules with the image of the transcendental newt, has always already come undone.[49] Similarly, the ambiguous doublings of K (Katie and Kunigunde) or P (Penthesilea and Prothoë or the queer couple of Penthesilea and the Peleid) point to a route of escape from the tragedy of the modern sex/gender binary. The lost queers of *Penthesilea* mackle the hetero norm of domestic tragedy. And if, as Chris Cullens and Dorothea von Mücke (1989) argue, *Katie* participates in the discursive production of modern sexuality as something to be considered perverse, it also presents lesbian sexual relations as out in the open (i.e., not constrained by the logics of representation and recognition)—for those who have eyes to see it. By using the teichoscopy of feeling in the heteronormative would-be center of the plot, Kleist trains his audience, without giving in to compulsory visibility, to notice what, in all logical rigor and without the deluding theatrics of the modern theater, cannot be seen. Such is the entanglement of deviant sexual relations, new forms of feeling, and untimely theater practices in Kleist's theater.

NOTES

Introduction

1. The terms "homosexual" and "heterosexual" were invented by Karl Maria Kertbeny and used for the first time publicly in 1869 in two pamphlets against Prussian antihomosexual laws. See Katz 1995, 52–53. Tobin's (2015) *Peripheral Desires: The German Discovery of Sex* analyses scientific, literary, and political texts from 1830 to the early twentieth century to chart the origins of modern categories of sexuality in nineteenth- and early twentieth-century German-speaking central Europe.

2. The forensic psychiatrist Krafft-Ebing drew heavily on literary articulations of sexuality, including—most famously—the writings of Marquis de Sade and Leopold von Sacher-Masoch, but also of Kleist (whose *Penthesilea* served him as an example of female sadism).

3. Without uniformly applying it, Krafft-Ebing's *Psychopathia Sexualis* establishes the term "homosexual," among other freshly developed sexual terminology (like "sadism" and "masochism"). The pioneer of the gay rights movement, Karl Heinrich Ulrichs, had earlier proposed *Urning/Urninde*, which was in circulation for a while. Magnus Hirschfeld still uses various terms, including *Urning* and "third sex"; in 1910, he invents the term "transvestite."

4. For the German context, see Mayer 1982; Derks 1990; Kuzniar 1996; Tobin 2000; Gustafson 2002. See also the scholarship on gender queerness, such as MacLeod 1998; Krimmer 2004; Horst 2003.

5. "The discourse of sentimental friendship is therefore of special interest, because it is here, in this fertile ground, that the fixed images of masculinity are disrupted and a gay sensibility can manifest itself linguistically, without being forced to define itself as such" (Pfeiffer 1996, 218).

6. Krimmer (2004, 13, 36) argues that economic reasons (the belatedly emerging capitalist structures) too explain why the philosophy of the gender binary gained such force in Germany. Of interest in this respect is also the work of Eva Illouz (1997), who analyzes the capitalist structures (for example, the economy of choice) of heterosexual romance.

7. For a more detailed description of this turn in the discourse on homosexuals, see Derks 1990, 295–369. Patricia Anne Simpson (2006, 19, 24) also shows that with the wars of liberation against Napoleon, the discourse on war and related nationalism put normative pressure on heterosexuality and naturalized complementary gender roles.

8. I mean "naive" here in the sense that Friedrich Schiller develops in "On Naïve and Sentimental Poetry."

9. The nighttime experiments of Nathanael's father in E. T. A. Hoffmann's "The Sandman" are a good example of this tendency. Richard Sha (2008, 16) sees

the literature and science of Romanticism as acknowledging "the perverseness of human sexuality," by which he means "its resistance to reproductive telos and discipline," and argues that this has liberating, democratic, and even revolutionary effects. This might be true for British Romanticism (the object of Sha's study); I am less sanguine about the German context.

10. On the concept of revolution as a linguistic product of modernity as well as its change, inflation, and continued rhetorical power from the eighteenth century to the present, see Koselleck 2004.

11. Matthias Waltz (2001, 124) makes the case for a postmodern ethics of the real.

12. Same-sex sexual passion does not exist for Gallas because she presumes that only sexual difference can produce sexual desire. See, for example, Gallas 2007, 284.

13. Honegger (1991) traces the naturalizion of gender difference and the development of a separate anthropology of the female from the late eighteenth century to the middle of the nineteenth century. Laqueur (1990) provides historical evidence that not only gender but also the biological sex is culturally constructed. See also Schiebinger (1986, 51), who refers to late eighteenth-century anatomy, particularly publications by Pierre Roussel and Jakob Ackermann, as crucial evidence for the shift in the definition of sex differences. Koschorke (1999) discusses the transition from the humor-based notion of the human body (fluid, porous, and leaking) to the neural body (closed, prim, and accumulating or, rather, sublimating energy) in connection with the newly pervasive culture of writing used to fashion and regulate emotional life. For pathbreaking scholarship on the polarization of gender roles, see Duden 1977 and Bloch 1978.

14. See Honegger's (1991) critique of the *Sonderanthropologie* of the early nineteenth century.

15. See Hull 1996. Looking at eighteenth-century Germany, Isabel Hull analyzes in detail how "the great transformation from absolutism to the earliest form of the modern state redrafted the 'sexual system' " (1) and shows that "the legacy of Enlightened-absolutist reform law proved to be a stronger guarantor of freedom of sexual expression (particularly regarding gender equality) than the consensus forming in the new civil society" (3).

16. This is the basic argument of Comay 2001.

17. See also Gailus (2006, 1–13, 107–49).

18. Christian Wolff, *Deutsche Ethik*, paragraph 167.

19. Waltz (1993, 220–21) shows the prevalence of this ascetic yet sentimental withdrawal from life at the example of a passage in Rousseau's *Julie* that describes the unexpected arrival of Claire. While the women and children act out their intense emotions, Wolmar, the figure for the autonomous subject, sits in a chair and covetously watches the spectacle of Julie fainting, Claire swooning, the child crying, and Saint-Preux falling into convulsive movements. Theater has invaded real life.

20. See Schiebinger 1986, 63–66, on women being classified with children and "primitive" peoples.

21. Women, however, according to Rousseau, cannot and should not liberate themselves from the gaze of others. See Rousseau's *Emile* (1979, 365): "Opinion is the grave of virtue among men and its throne among woman."

22. Kant (2000, 125) points out that the sight of the dynamically sublime "is the more attractive, the more fearful it is, provided only that we are in security," i.e. not physically exposed to its force.

23. For the child, everything is real (including the play); the bourgeois spectator behaves as if everything were just play (including reality).

24. "This birth of reason out of the spirit of the sublime not only proves traumatic as, perhaps, any birth must, but also comes at a steep price. For what is surrendered in exchange for the subject's defensive affirmation of its supersensible, rational destiny is nothing less than the integrity of 'feeling' itself. . . . The 'feeling' of the sublime . . . throws into relief the strictly 'virtual' character of all feeling" (Pfau 2005, 42).

25. "The 'primal anxiety' of the homosexual is falling out of all identity-creating societal referents—the anxiety of groundlessness outside all norms and practices" (Pfeiffer 1996, 223). Also: "Already in an early letter, from November 12, 1799, Kleist complains to his sister not only about the difficulties of intersubjective understanding but also about the foundational traumatic experience of finding *no place* in society—the experience of a far-reaching alienation and homelessness" (223).

26. I thus reject the minoritizing gesture in Pfeiffer's (1996) identification of the trauma as personal. My claim about Kleist's uniqueness is only valid for literature that made it into the canon. There are a number of women writers with fascinating responses to the historical shift in gender and sexuality who have been excluded from the canon. See Krimmer 2004.

27. "Sexual difference is political difference; sexual difference is the difference between freedom and subjection" (Pateman 1988, 6).

28. Joan Wallach Scott shows that the universalism of sexual difference won out over the universalism of abstract individualism. In her chapter "Sexularism" (2011, 91–116), she argues against the secularist promise of gender equality that there is no necessary connection between secularism and equality and, what is more, that modern sexual difference is a secular notion (grounded in nature, not religion) that troubles the promise of equality because abstract individuality and autonomy become coded masculine in the wake of the French Revolution. In *Only Paradoxes to Offer* (1996), Scott argues that the prevailing of sexual difference helped to bring about feminism and its paradoxical position within the political sphere, which forces political subjects to fight as women—and therefore to organize into a feminist movement—for the right not to be regarded as women.

29. The roots of the emergence of the second sex can be traced back to the Protestant Reformation and its influence on sexual politics in the sixteenth century. See Dabhoiwala 2012. Kord (1996, 36–42) points out that the new model has not yet become the dominant paradigm at the end of the eighteenth century. Krimmer (2004, 7, 9) diagnoses an "uneasy coexistence" of the two models and the ensuing "gender confusion so characteristic of the time around 1800." According to her, male authors were more interested in using the gendered body to stabilize positions, while female writers (who remain less well-known) continued to contest the new model.

30. See, for example, Adelbert von Chamisso's novella *Peter Schlemihl's Miraculous Story*, as discussed by Richard Block (2018, 29–54).

31. See Tobin 1996. See also Kuzniar (1996, 13) on how "the ontogenetic age gap between boy and adult male can be inscribed onto the phylogenetic spread between the ancients and the moderns."

32. It even seems justified to say that Goethe suppresses female same-sex desire because, as Gustafson (2002, 88) shows, it is part of the formula of attractions in *Wahlverwandtschaften* but never actually manifests in the story. Kuzniar (1996, 20–22) also deplores the lack of articulations of female same-sex desire in the age of Goethe.

33. Richard Sha (2008) argues that the very succession of two models of sexual difference (in degree and in kind) unsettles the claim to universality of the second model, especially during the period of its emergence.

34. See Pahl 2008; McAllister 2005; Gallas 2005, 141–58.

35. See Castle 1993; Jagose 2002, 12–13. Kleist actively addresses the invisibility of desire with his unusual take on the theater, which, as many (prominently Goethe) have complained, gives little to see onstage.

Chapter 1

1. *S* 576/5.1.2705: "If you kill each other, it is a mistake [*ein Versehen*]" (translation altered), *P* 145/24.2986: "my tongue pronounced one word to say another [*ich habe mich bloß versprochen*]" (translation altered), and *A* 100/2.4.1191: "done true to life but raised to the divine [*ins Göttliche verzeichnet*]."

2. See Dudenredaktion 2017, "ver," item 8.

3. See Adelung, Soltau, and Schönberger 1811, "ver," item 1.

4. The prefix also appears before adjectives or nouns to form a verb, which then expresses the transfer into a state that the adjective or noun determines, for example, *verdummen*: to become stupid, or *vergöttern*: to turn into a god.

5. See Grimm and Grimm 1984, "ver," items III.7 and III.8; Adelung, Soltau, and Schönberger 1811, "ver."

6. See ibid., "ver," item III.

7. We will discuss this structure of the overlap of opposites again under the heading "Doubles" in the second section of this chapter, titled "Mess."

8. My analysis of Kleist's mackles builds on the contributions of Gabriele Brandstetter and Rüdiger Campe on the repetition and relay of hypotyposes in *Penthesilea*. See Brandstetter 2001, 231; Campe 2008. See also Moser 2001, 103.

9. Regarding the masterstroke, see Schiller (2016, 3365), who describes naive or simple poetry as "a first jet, a happy inspiration [*ein glücklicher Wurf*], that needs no correction, when it turns out well, and which cannot be rectified if ill turned out."

10. Cf. Reuß 1992, 11. Reuß, however, confirms the originality of Odysseus's speech.

11. Compare Brandstetter's (2001, 232) similar analysis of repetition in a different scene.

12. This has prompted the august critique that he fails to make use of the capacities for mimesis specific to the theater and writes for an invisible theater. See Goethe's letter to Adam Müller, August 28, 1807, in Sembdner 1996, 162.

13. For a discussion of this scene, see the last subsection of this chapter: "Theatrical Metalepsis."

14. With regard to the essay on the marionette theater, Harst also analyzes how Kleist establishes distinctions that he then undermines. See Harst 2012, 38n43.

15. This allows Klotz (1996, 97, my translation) to riff on the biblical phrase "an eye for a tongue, a tongue for an eye."

16. The play's plaintiff, Mrs. Martha complaints that nobody will be able "to judge it back together again" (*J* 19 (Constantine)/6.419). Harst (2012, 182) shows that the various verbal descriptions of the jug do not form a coherent image when combined.

17. Riley 2000, 111–12. See also Judith Butler's queer theoretical work since *Gender Trouble*.

18. For the source of this section's title, see *J* 53/1505–6 (translation altered): "Suppose the matter here, / As I'm afraid it may, remains undisentangled." I have altered Swan's elegant translation of *unentworren* as "unsolved." "Undisentangled," while even clumsier than *unentworren*, renders its double negative and the sense of chaos that the word enacts.

19. Kleist titles the additionally supplied alternate version *Variant*, i.e., in a bit of transgender crossing of philology, literary production and theatricality, he uses a nonexistent masculine form of the technical term *Variante*. Reuß argues that, by including a variant, Kleist calls into question the traditional idea of the artwork (Kleist 2000, 430n56). Reuß also provides details regarding the incompleteness of both versions (ibid., 429–31).

20. For my reading of this orgasmic moment, see chapter 2.

21. Even if the similarity is not so strong that someone who wielded a door handle instead of a sword wouldn't make a rather bumbling spectacle.

22. For a complete analysis of this passage, see Pahl 2015.

23. "Es ist gehauen nicht und nicht gestochen, / Ein Vorfall, koboldartig, wie ein Märchen, / Und dennoch *ist* es, wie das Sonnenlicht."

24. I have translated *Vorfall* (literally "pre-fall" or "fall in front of") as "incident" because it derives from the Latin word *cadere*, "to fall."

25. In the French language, the proper name Sosie turned into a noun meaning doppelgänger after the success of Rotrou's *Les deux Sosies* (1638) and Molière's *Amphitryon* (1668).

26. He implicitly prides himself of his rhetorical versatility when he asks Amphitryon at the beginning of their conversation how he should pitch it to him

27. Grimm's dictionary notes that the somersaults are part of the gaiety of kobolds. See "Kobold" II.3 in Grimm and Grimm 1984, 11.1550.

28. Heine tells the story of Kobold Hüdeken who strangles and tears to pieces a boy who has bespattered Hüdeken with water. See Heine 1979, 24. At times, Kobolds look like manifestations of bad conscience, in particular in the wake of an infanticide. Some, for example, come as the revenants of unwanted babies carrying the knife that killed them still in their bodies.

29. See the eponymous fairy tale by the Brothers Grimm.

30. Indeed, the word category originally meant a public accusation or the disapproving judgment of the public. From the Greek *kata* (against) and *agora* (public assembly). Cf. Derrida 2009, 150–52.

Rumpelstilzchen is confident that nobody will be able to name "him" accurately, and when this nevertheless happens, "he" is outraged and destroys what the name refers to.

31. See Derrida 2009, 161: "I would say that definition, where it stops in the 'S is P,' in the definite article *le* or *la*, is always *bêtise*, the very definition of *bêtise*." See also ibid., 166–70.

32. Whether Sosias indeed plays a supporting role is also unclear. His drama dominates the first act of the play. According to the rules of the genre, Sosias should be the protagonist of the comedy. After Plautus, who produced the first comedy from the Amphitryon myth, Routrou turns the doubled Sosias into the eponymous hero of his play *Les Sosies* (1638) and Molière (1668) writes the part for himself: in the original production, he plays Amphitryon's servant and, masked as Sosias, uses the double function of author and actor to ridicule the ruling class. See Molière 2010, 1519. Virginia Scott (2000, 156) argues that Molière's satire is directed at King Louis XIV.

33. See Szondi 1973, 159–63; Theisen 2008, 153–64; Pahl 2015, 528–53.

34. See Hinderer 2001, 42, who gives Werther and Albert, Götz and Weislingen, Maria and Adelheid, Faust and Mephisto, Gretchen and Helena, Clavigo and Carlos, Stella and Cäcilie, Egmont and Alba, lphigenie and Thoas, Tasso and Antonio, and the Princess and Leonore Sanvitale as examples of antithetical characters in Goethe's works.

35. The first act of *The Schroffenstein Family* consists of two scenes, the first introducing the branch of the family that lives at Rossitz, the second introducing the branch that lives at Warwand. In *Penthesilea*, scenes 1 through 4 focus on the Greeks, and scenes 5 through 8 on the Amazons.

36. See Pahl 2015.

37. This is what Adam claims happened to him. See *J*, scene 1.

38. This also has the reverse effect that the comic double can suddenly appear as the serious and honest hero. Helmut Grugger (2010, 70–72) points out that it is Ruprecht who ponders oedipal self-blinding and that, beginning with the twelfth scene, he fashions himself as a sympathetic and insightful lover.

39. Knecht Ruprecht is the helper of Santa Claus (St. Nikolaus).

40. In chapter 5, I will elaborate on these different modes of seeing.

41. Katie might have three fathers: Gottschalk calls her his daughter as well (*K* 218/3.6.1700).

42. The historical facts also resist the construction of a neat sequence. While, roughly speaking, Kleist writes *The Broken Jug* before *Penthesilea*, their genesis overlaps in the complex actuality of life. Kleist starts to work on *The Broken Jug* in 1803 (perhaps already in 1802). In 1806, Kleist edits *The Broken Jug* and begins work on *Penthesilea*. *Penthesilea* is published in 1808, i.e., before *The Broken Jug* (1811), and Kleist revises *The Broken Jug* again after its unsuccessful staging by Goethe in 1808.

43. The two lines appear in the 1808 manuscript of *The Broken Jug* (see Kleist 1995, 334) as in the published text of 1811; the first completed manuscript circulates in early 1807 but is lost now. One can assume that Kleist wrote *Küsse, Bisse* in late 1807.

44. Cf. Gallas 2005, 119; Grugger 2010, 75.

45. See Peters 2003; Földényi 1999, 11.

46. Redecker (2018, 261) points out that Judith Butler describes the paradox of subject formation through interpellation as metalepsis, referring to the metaleptic temporality, in which the response to interpellation and thus constitution

of the subject already presumes the existence of the subject able, willing, or compelled to respond.

47. See Redecker 2018, 256–58, 261, 263–64. See also Pier 2016, paragraph 7: "Metalepsis has a complex history in that it has been regarded either as a variety of metonymy, a particular form of synonymy, or both. As metonymy, it has been identified (a): expression of the consequent understood as the precedent or vice versa and; (b) as a chain of associations ("a few ears of corn" for "a few years," the transfer of sense implying "a few harvests" and "a few summers"). Another possibility is to regard metalepsis in terms of an overlap between synonymy and homonymy in such a way as not to respect the semantic demarcation between distinct signifiers, resulting in the use of an inappropriate synonym."

48. Ilse Graham (1977, 243) concludes her superb study of Kleist with an analysis of what, in an enviable formulation, she describes as "Kleist's journeying into the physical regions of his medium." Jacobs (1989, 114) adds that by literalizing a simile, Penthesilea's suicide makes it henceforth impossible to extricate the literal from the figurative.

49. I use the word "fabulously" here with all the resonances and connotations that secure its place in the gay idiom.

50. We might read this also as a parodic reference to preformation theory.

51. We will discuss hypotyposis in chapter 3.

52. Medieval mystics certainly supplied ecstatically lubricated descriptions of the virtuous soul.

53. Theobald here skirts the image of the lactating father that we will discuss in chapter 3, in the section titled "Mammalogic," but, strictly speaking, it is not the father but his love that gives the breast here.

54. Kleist sent the first number of his journal *Phöbus* (which included the "organic fragment" of *Penthesilea*) to Goethe with the words "I present it to you 'on the knees of my heart' " (Kleist 1982, 178–79). The formulation derives from the apocryphal Prayer of Manasseh 1.1: "Now therefore I bow the knee of mine heart, beseeching thee of grace" (KJV).

55. See Graf 2010 for a historical overview of the construction of a tasteful and taste-shaping theater in the eighteenth century.

56. Fischer-Lichte 2001, 32–33.

57. See also Fischer-Lichte 2002, 165–70, 198–201.

58. See Kleist's letter to Marie von Kleist, June 1807: "The real work of art is not that which is offered to the senses, but which the mind, aroused by the senses, thinks to itself within" (Kleist 1982, 171).

59. Goethe was among the first to find Kleist's tragedy comical (see Sembdner 1996, 213). He didn't realize that he might have been the butt of what he thought was unintentional comedy. See also Griffiths 2009; Angress 1977, 120ff.

60. This sexualization is also present, but in more modest form, in the scene with Homburg—his shirt is unbuttoned and when he reaches for the wreath he strips the Princess of a piece of clothing (a glove).

61. See Chaouli 1996 for the disgust that Penthesilea evokes.

62. Not only because Kleist's play kills Achilles, whom the Greeks, according to the prophecy, need to win the Trojan War, but also because his *Penthesilea* presents a different organization of gender, desire, and reproduction.

63. Comical characters typically have a strong appetite; some even derive their names from the food they prefer (Hans Wurst, Pickelhering). See Bartl 2015.

64. Her tragedy lies in the fact that she appears comical (or mad or sexy) even in her most powerful desires and heroic achievements (she has killed the invincible Achilles). Even a sophisticated reader like Chaouli (1996, 139) claims to see that she "scribbles madly" with "her teeth" "all over his body" when in fact her action is precise, economical, and powerful: "the tooth [*den Zahn*] she sinks into his ivory breast" (*P* 128/23.2670).

Chapter 2

1. I include *The Broken Jug* in this list because Kleist flattens the ontological hierarchy between things and characters.

2. Note the different terminology in Bersani 1986 and Edelman 2004. While Edelman opposes "the drive" to "desire," Bersani means by "desire's mobility" something similar to what Edelman calls "pulsations of the drive."

3. See Bersani 1986; Bersani and Dutoit 1998, 2004.

4. Allemann (2005, 12–19) identifies anticipation as a structuring principle of the overdrama, but he also describes the paralyzing effect of such anticipation (36). He sees mainly retroactive effects in *The Broken Jug*, describing them as anticipation turned backward (105), but considers this play a failure for this very reason. Cf. Peters 2003, chapter 4.

5. Allemann draws a clear line between reality and dream, which is untenable, given Kleist's thorough entangling of dissimulation or illusion and sincerity or truth.

6. Cf. Gailus 2010; Gustafson 1989. For discussions of Kleist's language skepticism, see Holz 1962, 26, 93; Kommerell 1991, 244; Lindsay 1977; Seeba 1981.

7. With a somewhat different vector of inquiry (future-oriented and concerned with providing a theory for a possible praxis of radical social change), Redecker (2018) shows the same phenomenon when she calls our attention to Masterman's explication of Kuhn's notion of the paradigm shift. Masterman (1970, 69) explains that the articulation of a new paradigm begins "with some trick, or embryonic technique, or a picture, and the insight that this is applicable in this field." She underscores that this beginning "is intuitive; it does not go by rules" (85). The success of the new paradigm depends on its currency and on the capability of other operations to fall into line with it. This retroactive proof means that a trick, technique, gesture, or device that will have established itself as a new paradigm may already be in use under the old paradigm without being recognized as new.

8. For an analysis of *Augenblick* as historical moment, see Plug 1997.

9. Campe draws our attention to the remarkable *hysteron proteron* of the two examples Kleist offers in "On the Gradual Fabrication of Thoughts while Speaking": first Mirabeau's response to the royal order to leave the Jeu de Peaume that initiates (even consummates, as Mirabeau himself describes it) the French Revolution, and then the speech of the fox in La Fontaine's fable "The Animals Sick of the Plague," which saves not only the fox's own head but also the king's (Campe 2012a, 14). Historically, the latter comes before the former. The two examples also exemplify the two peripetic temporalities: the dramatic turn and the continuity (17).

10. See Luhmann 1998, chapters 12 and 13; Illouz 1997, chapter 4.

11. Only Herrmann pursues a larger idea or an actual cause: liberty for Germania.

12. See my discussion of Kleist's camp humor in chapter 4.

13. Cf. Allemann 2005, 170–73, for a discussion of this scene.

14. Cf. Allemann 2005, 166. What some might find excessive is indeed divine law for Penthesilea: "She must choose / The one sent by the god to stand against her [*Den ihr der Gott im Kampf erscheinen läßt*]" (*P* 100/15.2146–47). Allemann (2005, 168) interprets this law emphasizing the role of splendor/appearance.

15. See Kleist 2004, 409: "the indecency of the whole procedure." See also Campe 2012a, 9.

16. Including the experiment of the *Berliner Abendblätter*. See Peters 2003.

17. In *The Broken Jug* the shivers and leaps are also figured as *Fraktur*. See my discussion below.

18. Its setting during the Dutch war of independence from Spain connects the story to *The Broken Jug*, set in the independent Netherlands. Napoleon's dynastic politics in the Netherlands (he turned the Batavian Republic into the Kingdom of the Netherlands and installed his brother as king) links both to Kleist's time.

19. The essay's title echoes the phrase *L'appétit vient en mangeant*, which Kleist uses in French in the body of the text (see Campe 2012b, 10).

20. Peters uses the word *übersetzen*, which means both "ferry" and "translate."

21. See my discussion in the previous chapter.

22. For a synopsis of *The Broken Jug* see the beginning of the "Mess" section of chapter 1.

23. The problem for women consists in their supposed sexual passivity, which Fichte (2000, 266) deduces with flimsy reasoning in §2. For Fichte, female sexual activity is an impossibility.

24. I am referring here to the conservative Christian slogan "God made Adam and Eve, not Adam and Steve."

25. Stephens (1999, 465) also critiques Allemann's exclusively sanguine notion of the anticipatory vision. In addition, Stephens helpfully differentiates between textual anticipation and the conscious anticipations of a character's imagination.

26. See, in particular, Bersani 1986, 38–39. Also: "The immobilization of fantasmatic structures can only have a violent dénouement. That is, the oppressive, expressive, destabilizing, exciting representation must be evacuated; the masochistic origin of sexuality means that the extreme logic of sexual pleasure is its explosive end. Masochism is both relieved and fulfilled by death" (46).

27. For how repetition serves life, see Bersani 1986, 39; for how it serves pleasure see ibid., 63–64: "The possibility of exploiting the shattering effects of sexuality in order to maintain the tensions of an eroticized, de-narrativized, and mobile consciousness has been neglected, or refused, in favor of a view of pleasure as nothing more than the reduction of all tension and the evacuation of all excitement."

28. See, for example, Grugger 2010, 86.

29. Note that the name of Adam's clerk, Licht (light), aligns him with the values of the Enlightenment.

30. See the discussion above of Kleist's anecdote "Improbable Realities" ("Unwahrscheinliche Wahrhaftigkeiten").

31. Samuel Taylor Coleridge (2014, chapter 14) coined the phrase "willing suspension of disbelief" in 1817.

32. The text announces its linguistic practice in the first dialogue: "ADAM: I fell . . . / LICHT: Nonfiguratively [*unbildlich*], you crashed? / ADAM: Just so. The figure I cut / Might not have been a pretty one" (*J* 4/1.14–15).

33. As the most prominent examples of the genre of the analytic drama, Pütz (1970, 202ff.) cites Sophocles's *Oedipus Tyrannos* and Kleist's *The Broken Jug*.

34. Allemann (2005, 95) argues that *Jug* follows the conventional comedy pattern of a guardian figure opposing a love union and creating various complications until the play ends in the wedding tableau.

35. See Sedgwick 1985. Adam's clubfoot not only evokes Oedipus but also the devil—an analogy that Mrs. Bridget carries to extremes in her testimony. In folklore, Knecht Ruprecht functions as a version of the devil in that he is used as a bogeyman to scare children into good behavior.

36. For parental abuse, see *J* 43/9.1199, *J* 46/9.1293–97, and *J* 447/7.1352–53.

37. "EVE: Jesus Christ! I cry. Ruprecht comes!" (*J* 83/Variant.2221).

38. See her extensive play with the signifiers *scheiden* (cut off, break apart) and *entscheiden* (decide) in *J* 6.419–22.

39. Walter protests the evacuation of the courtroom. The stage directions are imprecise as to who actually leaves and who remains. It is clear that Ruprecht and Martha stay, as they are being asked for additional information during the ensuing dialogue between Walter and Adam.

40. The 2010 production, directed by Jan Bosse, at the Maxim Gorki Theater in Berlin, for example, played scene 10 during the break. Some spectators went outside; others remained in the auditorium to watch the exchange between Walter and Adam.

41. See the *Hagestolz* entry in *Deutsches Wörterbuch*.

42. For the history of the bachelor, see Baumgartner 1997; Snyder 1999, chapter 1.

43. Hoffmann's novella was published in 1821. So, Kleist might reference here the comedy *Die Hagestolzen* (1793) by his rival August Wilhelm Iffland, who had been the director of the National Theater Berlin since 1796. Goethe deemed it Iffland's best play (Eckermann 1836, 1.141)—if that was known to Kleist, it certainly was reason enough to work the signifier into his not-so-subtle net of intrigues and accusations around Iffland's own sexual preferences (cf. Weigel 2011).

44. For an analysis of the surge in sodomy trials in the Netherlands around the time of the setting of Kleist's play, see van der Meer 1994. It would be worthwhile to read the court proceedings of *The Broken Jug* as a sodomy trial in disguise.

45. Most of these references also express a Francophobe sentiment. Walter prefers wine "von unserm Rhein" to French wine (*J* 50/10.1421–22). During Kleist's time, Prussia subsidized the cultivation of silk moths in order to prevent the drain of currency to France or Italy (where most of the silk had to be imported from). Niersteiner and Limburger allude to the apprehension (near Limburg) and conviction (by a judge from Nierstein) of the so-called Schinderhannes, a criminal who was idealized as a kind of Robin Hood stealing from the rich and fighting against the French.

46. "ADAM: Nierstein. By God, well done. A taster's tongue. / From Nierstein, yes, in deed, it is, Your Grace, / As sure as if I'd fetched it thence myself. / WALTER: I drank it, at the press, three years ago" (*J* 53/10.1510–12).

47. Derks 1990 supplies ample evidence for the codes of homosexual culture in Germany around 1800.

48. In fact a lot of effort is spent, social norms and cultural mechanisms are set in place, to produce this desire and to not allow it to wane—no matter the age of the Adam in question.

49. "Two minutes and it's done!" (*J* 82/Variant.2185).

50. Kleist blurs the line that separates the action of the play from the drama of interpretation in that he anticipates audience interpretations and has his characters and their actions be implicitly informed by these interpretations. Cf. Müller-Seidel 1971, 172.

51. The phrase "*Ein Schein, nach allen Regeln*" (*J* 82/Variant.2180) makes it obvious that Kleist plays here with the different meanings of *Schein*. It can be translated into theater terms as "an illusion, according to the rules" or into the language of bureaucracy as "a proper document"

52. Despite Goethe's aestheticizing educational efforts, the audience at Goethe's theater in Weimar apparently preferred the cut to the chase. Kleist cut the play and added the variant after it flopped in Weimar.

53. See for example J 82/Variant.2198–2200.

54. I think Kleist invites this slippage from medical to marriage certificate (*Trauschein*).

55. If the jug figures Eve, then Adam, looking like the jug, may stand in for Eve. In addition to refusing heterosexual complementarity, Adam replicating Eve also disturbs the normative sequence, which posits woman as derivative of man. Similarly, while, according to Genesis, god created Eve out of Adam's rib for his disport, Kleist's Eve declares, "that God created Ruprecht / . . . for [her] delight" (*J* 77/Variant.2021–22).

56. See essays 11, 12, 14, and 80 of Lessing's *Hamburg Dramaturgy* (Lessing 1962).

57. See my discussion of camp in chapter 4.

58. Cf. Jagose 2002 and her analysis of the heteronormative bent of the logic of consistency and consequence.

59. See the beginning of the section titled "Yes, Yes" in this chapter.

60. Eve bends over Ruprecht, embraces and cradles him like the Virgin Mary does with the body of the Crucified. *Lieber Mensch* echoes Pontius Pilate's *Ecce homo*.

61. "I mumble inarticulately, drawl out my conjunctions, use unnecessary appositions, and avail myself of all other dilatory tricks to gain the time required for fabricating my idea in the workshop of Reason" (Kleist 1982, 219).

Chapter 3

1. Katie's rival and double Kunigunde is described as "a piece of mosaic, assembled from all three realms of nature" (*K* 249/5.3.2446–47).

2. This analysis builds on the work of Simon Richter (2014, 22), who began to elaborate a sense of "a language that originates from the breast and is based on lack" by moving into the picture men with breasts and women without. Richter importantly unsettles the presumed femininity of the breast, which still drives the

wonderfully informative but in its guiding question ("Who owns the breast?") conservatively feminist work of Marilyn Yalom (1997, 3). I hope to take Richter's work further by offering more substantial and more detailed descriptions of the structure and possible manifestations of breast language and breast logic, in particular, by mobilizing the notion of cleavage. I also broaden the scope by attending to the overlay of the different logics and grammars originating from phallus, mamma, and anus.

3. In the way Jessica Benjamin (1995, 96, 98), drawing on Donald Winnicott, sees "a symbolic space within a social, differentiated maternal dyad" and argues for "demystify[ing] the ostensibly undifferentiated perfection . . . of the preoedipal maternal dyad as an idealized appearance produced by the Oedipal discourse."

4. Against the standard denigration of the imaginary, Luce Irigaray (1985) has exposed the unacknowledged dependence of the patriarchal order on the imaginary in the form of women reflecting and enhancing man's image of himself. Drawing on Melanie Klein and Julia Kristeva, Mary Jacobus (1995) affirms a maternal imaginary. Others emphasize jouissance by playfully, but in a revolutionary spirit, ignoring the symbolic law and flying with what Hélène Cixous calls *écriture de la différence sexuelle*, what Kristeva calls the "semiotic," or what Lacan calls *lalangue*.

5. While, in her important piece "The Lesbian Phallus," Judith Butler (1993) dissociates the phallus from masculinity, she later describes the symbolic as "the realm of the Law that regulates desire in the Oedipus complex" and explores the possibilities for "change within kinship relations" (Butler 2000, 18). Italian feminists have developed a female countersymbolic under the heading of entrustment, which in some instantiations had the disadvantage of centering the maternal but in others have taken a more queer turn. See also Loftus (1996, 207–33), who calls for a "multiplication . . . of the symbolic order" by refusing or undoing the Lacanian separation of body and sign, penis and phallus (what he calls the designing of the body; 224).

6. For an explanation of the use of the underscore between the singular and the plural of breast, see the beginning of the first section of this chapter, titled "Cleavage."

7. For the sexual foundation of the sign, see Waltz 1993, 109. See Halle 2004, 15–18, for the "heterocoital imperative" (15) of the "heterosexual sign system" (16). For a critical analysis of the desire to have the last word, see Mieszkowski 2014b.

8. Lacan insisted on the difference between penis and phallus, and one can make the argument that the phallus does not really signify power and autonomy but the lack thereof. See Luepnitz 2003, 226: "Lacan observed that many human beings use the penis to cover their pervasive sense of bodily lack, and so he chose the term 'phallus' to refer to our wish for completeness." She also clarifies that "the phallus is not what men have and women lack; we might say that it is what men believe they have and what women are considered to lack" (227). But this distinction was too hairsplitting for Gallop (1988, 124), who comes to the conclusion, "phallus/penis: same difference."

9. See my discussion in chapter 5 in the section titled "Dagger, the Feeling Thing."

10. See Richter (2014, 23, 167) regarding the metonymic logic of breast language.

11. Paul B. Preciado (2018) calls for the resexualization of the anus to counter dominant heterocentric sexuality, which, as Preciado maintains, has excluded this body zone as dirty and abject.

12. Using the advertising for the Hitchcock film *The Birds* ("The Birds is coming") to elucidate the effect of jouissance, Edelman (2004, 133) quips, "The catchphrase fucks with the copula." He elaborates that "the slogan alludes to a fissure that sunders the syntax of social reality just as . . . it seems to sunder the agreement of subject and verb."

13. See Edelman (2004, 133), who describes "the narrative teleology of the subject" as "always constituted at the expense of jouissance, at the cost of the violent involuntarity, the pulsive pressure of a coming, in the throes of which the subject of meaning could only come apart too."

14. See Edelman 2004, 133: "turning meaning, wherein we think we live, into chaos and filth and death."

15. The real produces anxiety, hence the need for protection from the real. Cf. Lacan 1988, 164: "There is an anxiety-provoking image which summarizes what we can call the revelation of that which is least penetrable in the real, of the real lacking any possible mediation, of the ultimate real, of . . . the object of anxiety *par excellence*."

16. In English and German, the word bosom (*Busen*) serves as a synonym for breast that, in one of its meanings, is used with an erotic connotation referring specifically to a woman's breast, and is more frequently used metaphorically, meaning the seat of emotion and a place of intimacy.

17. See Klein 1986, 143: "In the earliest phase the persecuting and the good objects (breasts) are kept wide apart in the child's mind. When, along with the introjection of the whole and real object, they come closer together, the ego has over and over again recourse to that mechanism—so important for the development of the relations to objects—namely, a splitting of its imagos into loved and hated, that is to say, into good and dangerous ones."

18. See *P* 13/2.242. According to myth, the Greeks had been told by the seer Calchas that Troy would not fall without Achilles's help.

19. "In the very first months of the baby's existence it has sadistic impulses directed, not only against its mother's breast, but also against the inside of her body: scooping it out, devouring the contents . . ."

20. Note the O. It is a pictogram, not only for nothingness or the hole, but also for the perfect roundness of the breast image.

21. Richter 2014, 101: "While the woman's body is encouraged to flow, if within the narrow channels of maternal domesticity, the man's body must be disciplined to forms of extreme containment. . . . He becomes, as it were, a solid citizen, autonomous and self-complete." See also Koschorke 1999; Theweleit 1987, 229–362.

22. See, for example, Johann: "It must get out of this breast" (*S* 470/1.1.337, my translation) and Ruprecht: "It wells up in me like a burst of blood . . . Off pops a button from my chest" (*J* 35/7.963–65).

23. I thank Christina Speech Hinz for alerting me to this omission.

24. Strahl's cleavage is confounding in the sense that it does not offer up an easy distinction between a good and a bad breast.

25. This analysis of Kleist's text swells is indebted to Richter's (2014, 104–36) chapter on Christoph Martin Wieland, which gives a beautiful account of how

Kleist's mentor created breast-giving literature. Unlike Kleist, Wieland is interested only in the erotic female breast.

26. Interestingly, Meroë's question, "You won't escape [*entweichen*], then?," can also be read as "You won't de-soften (i.e., "You won't harden"), then?"

27. According to Adelung (1811), *Troßknecht* is not only a job title but was also used in the figurative sense to denote a spineless and slovenly person.

28. The prince is introduced into the play as a sleepwalker, and he never quite seems to wake to full presence of mind—except, perhaps, for the moment when he receives the death sentence.

29. Thereby text assumes a role that the characters are unable or unwilling to play.

30. Penthesilea uses speech to forge a dagger out of feeling and kills herself with this speech. See my analysis in chapter 5.

31. According to Catholic legend, Ursula negotiated a postponement of the marriage with a Hunnic pagan prince, arranged by her Christian royal father, in order to travel to Rome. With ten ladies in waiting, each attended by a thousand maidens, she embarked on a voyage across the North Sea and up the Rhine. On her continued refusal to marry, the total of eleven thousand virgins were massacred by the Huns near Cologne.

Together with her plan to join the Ursulines, Katie thus abandons affiliation with a story of sexualized violence and mass killing but also with the female bear, the animal of sexualized revenge in Kleist's *The Battle of Herrmann* (*ursula* is Latin and means "little she-bear").

32. See, for example, Kleist's letter to his sister Ulrike from March 13, 1803.

33. Freud had dated their emergence to the anal stage, i.e., at two to four years of age, and Karl Abraham had introduced the oral-sadistic stage with the appearance of teeth, at around five to twelve months.

34. "I believe that oral-sadistic impulses towards the mother's breast are active from the beginning of life" (Klein 1986, 180).

35. See Klein 1986, 125: "Full identification with the object based on the libidinal attachment, first to the breast, then to the whole person, goes hand in hand with anxiety for it (of its disintegration), with guilt and remorse, with a sense of responsibility for preserving it intact against persecutors and the id, and with sadness relating to expectations of the impending loss of it. These emotions, whether conscious or unconscious, are in my view among the essential and fundamental elements of the feeling we call love."

36. Klein (1986, 120) clarifies that the child inflicts in fantasy injuries on its parents "primarily from hate and secondarily in self-defence." Revenge thus rationalizes and covers over the original hatred.

37. Surrounded by nonmetaphorical (literal and metonymical) language, the metaphor the scribe starts with—the marble heart that denotes courage—slides toward the less metaphorical meaning of a marble chest that resists the horns of the aurochs.

38. Thusnelda prefaces her expression of gratitude with the lines "You clothe me in honour, Ventidius, / Only to see me stripped of it again" (*BH* 8/1.2.88–89), hinting at the Romans' aggressive intentions and thus slyly undermining her reassurance of Ventidius.

39. Retroactively, though, great importance will be attached to the curl.

40. As in Penthesilea's case, where Achilles stands in for Otrere.

41. Agnes and Ottokar belong to different branches of the same family. Their initials suggest that they present the beginning and end—the alpha and omega—of the Schroffensteins' future.

42. Here the kinship is biological and the weapon is a sword, whereas in *Prince Frederick of Homburg* the kinship is adoptive and the weapon is a bullet (*PH* 310/3.5.985–86) and in *Amphitryon* the kinship is symbolic (man's relation to his god) and the weapon is a fantasized sting (*A* 122/3.5.1952).

43. Meanwhile the parental generation proves more infantile as it attacks the children for their more mature behavior.

44. See Klein 1986, 150: "In the baby, processes of introjection and projection, since they are dominated by aggression and anxieties which reinforce each other, lead to fears of persecution by terrifying objects." By setting up the feud within the family, Kleist blurs the border between external and internal.

45. Krimmer (2004, 120–29) reads Kleist's first play as an attempt to come to terms with his sister's gender defiance.

46. "It is finished [*Es ist vollbracht*]," John 19:30 (Luther 2017, 134).

47. As if by contagion, Rupert also uses touch (he touches his own hair) to help him with the recognition.

48. His chestiness and recklessness are driven by the imaginary order of the glorious breast.

49. See Lacan and Miller 2011, 13: "Il n'y a pas de rapport sexuel."

50. Hederich (1996, 34) notes that Thetis tried to protect her son from having to fight in the Trojan War by rearing Achilles as a girl.

51. Földényi (1999, 312) defines paradise in Kleist as "the future past." This formulation suggests that paradise participates in the undoing of continuous time, be it linear or circular. The phrase presents time as discontinuous or torn and the torn pieces of time as jumbled: "future" comes before "past." Yesterday, as Ventidius was anticipating paradise, he was already in paradise. Today this paradise lies behind him, yet he presses forward: "Welcome, / Sweet Iris to my Juno, / Who is to open Elysium to me!—" (*BH* 109/5.17.2373–75).

52. See Detering (1994, 122–25), who argues that the homoeroticism of the scene negates bourgeois convention, including genre conventions, thus abolishing the idyll.

53. Paradise is thus the aggressor here.

54. See also *P* 8/1.103: "So, word for word, your messenger reported." Anal-grammar differs from mammalogic—which also fosters doubling—in that its doubles are interchangeable, whereas the doubles of mammalogic are incompatible but nevertheless stick to one another.

55. *P* 145/24.2981–82. *Verreißen* means "to offer a scathing critique."

56. Ventidius and the bear occupy a liminal space between the back of the stage and backstage. While the stage directions for scene 18 list Ventidius as visible behind the gate, they don't mention the bear, even though Ventidius's speech—spoken from behind—suggests that the bear is right next to him.

57. In chapter 5, I elaborate on the teichoscopy of feeling. Through the lens of Lacan's (1978, 79–90) remarks on anamorphosis, we can interpret this scene as Ventidius looking at Thusnelda from the different angle of a compromised position and seeing a monster instead of a goddess (Juno). We find a similarly

terrifying epiphany in Achilles's vision of Penthesilea with hounds, elephants, and bladed chariots. Both suddenly face the real, which means death.

58. See Lessing's theory of catharsis as serving emotional moderation in essay 78 of his *Hamburg Dramaturgy*.

59. For a provocative and far-reaching theory of the dildo, see Preciado 2018.

60. Borgard (2015) observes that the setting of the scene, behind Herrmann's tent, locates the tent in the space of the auditorium and thus asks the audience to identify with the brutish Teuton leader.

61. *Sich sträuben* translates as "to bristle" and evokes the attribute *haarsträubend* (hair-raising).

62. See Borchers 1974, 31; Luther 2017, 23 (Gospel of Matthew 16:19).

63. Pfeiffer (1989, 104–31) analyzed the fantasy of the fragmented body in Kleist and connected it to the organization of gender and the regulation of sexuality.

Chapter 4

1. Theisen (2008) notes the Shakespearean mixture of tragic and comic elements in *Penthesilea*. See also Fetscher 2000. Griffiths (2009) offers an excellent analysis of the elements of double-edged comedy in the tragedy *Penthesilea*. Stephens (1983, 197) finds that *The Schroffenstein Family* fails aesthetically and as tragedy because the parodistic element "runs riot" in the end. Klotz (1996, 73–74) brings to the fore the subterranean humor of the she-bear scene in *The Battle of Herrmann*.

2. See Feil's (2005, 482) explanation, drawing on Freud, of queer comedy as both integrating and disintegrating: "Freud differentiates wit from humor by indicating that wit involves the assumption of the paternal function in order to subordinate someone else through mockery. . . . This gratifies the joker as 'an outlet for aggressive tendencies.' . . . Humor, on the other hand, involves the subject's internalization of both parental and infantile roles, mocking her/himself through this process. . . . While this may involve self-denigration . . . , [it also alters] the function of the superego so that it 'is in fact repudiating reality and serving an illusion' . . . [thus] becoming an agency of pleasure and pride."

3. "A couple of honest chicken dogs, who had been turned by the School of Hard Knocks into sly old dogs, and who snatched up everything the moment it showed its face on the earth, pounced one day on a little bird. The bird perplexed because he suddenly found himself out of his element, cringed, hopping now here, now there, and just when his opponents felt themselves triumphant, suddenly, in his extremity, he began to beat his wings and vaulted into the air: and there they stood, their eyes like oysters, those heroes of the meadow, with tails jammed between their legs, and gaping after him. // Esprit, when you soar: how the sages stand there and watch!" (Kleist 1982, 229).

4. For the New Year in 1800, Kleist presented his gender-bending sister, Ulrike von Kleist, with this wish: "You amphibian, that ever lives in two elements, waver no more and finally choose a safe gender [*ein sichres Geschlecht*]. One cannot swim and fly [*fliegen*] at the same time; therefore, leave the water and try it in the air; shake your wings and fly [*fleuch*]!" (Kleist 2005, 20, my translation). His expression *sichres Geschlecht* has often been read as "definite gender," but, given her gender nonconformity, it seems to me to make more sense that he wishes for

her to be safe—especially since the very encouragement to choose a gender recognizes her resistance against the idea that sex is a given and that gender should align with sex. Note that the German makes no difference between sex and gender and that *Geschlecht* can also mean "family" or "race." *Fleuch* can mean "fly" or "flee."

5. Even Klotz (1996, 80), who is very aware of the comical elements in Kleist, overlooks the humor in *Penthesilea* when he maintains that "it is Kleist's only stage play that does not have any traces of comedy, neither intentional nor unintentional ones."

6. For an exemplary analysis of the tragic in Kleist's comedies, see Szondi 1978, 248.

7. Even Newton (1979, 109), who knows a trick or two, admits being confused by camp queens' "tendency to laugh at situations that to me were horrifying or tragic."

8. For a brief introduction to camp, see Dynes et al. 1990, 189–90. Lassen 2011, 24–34, offers a helpful history that focuses on camp as political strategy. For further reading, see Cleto 1999; Meyer 1994. Esther Newton's (1979) pioneering study significantly contributed to the ethnography (and ethnicization) of gay and lesbian communities in the United States in the 1970s. Susan Sontag's (1999) "Notes on 'Camp'" is probably the best-known discussion of camp. Even though her "Notes" essay is clearly informed by queer culture, infused with queer-cultural examples, and structured by quotes from Oscar Wilde, Sontag downplays and comes close to repudiating the homosexual contribution to camp in her explicit arguments. As a result, Sontag has been pointedly criticized by many queer theorists for having depoliticized camp and sold out to the mainstream (especially by Meyer 1994; see in particular 5, 10). Despite Sontag's partly homophobic, partly compartmentalizing (see Pellegrini 2007) flattening of camp, I find that many of her observations in this essay of 1964 still feel fresh and relevant.

9. See Pellegrini 2007, 170: "Camp responds to the experience of homosexual stigmatization by sending up and theatricalizing the stigma, thereby ameliorating its impact."

10. I will not reproduce here discussions about the degree of lesbian versus gay suffering and the primacy or derivativeness of lesbian versus gay camp, because I find them unhelpful.

11. See Pellegrini 2007, 178. See also Newton 1979, 111: "Only by fully embracing the stigma itself can one neutralize the sting and make it laughable."

12. Dollimore 1991, 311, 230: "As a style, and even more as a politics, the transgressive reinscriptions practiced by such writers have proved controversial, especially when grounded in the celebration of a perverse inauthenticity disturbingly implicated in authenticity itself." While Ross (1989) warns of the antiliberatory and apolitical effect of camp, Dollimore (1991), Meyer (1994), Padva (2000), and others elaborate on the political force of queer camp.

13. According to one online dictionary, "camp" means "tasteless." S.v. "se camper," *Douglas Harper Online Etymology Dictionary*, accessed April 4, 2017, http://www.etymonline.com/index.php?term=camp&allowed_in_frame=0.

14. Klotz (1996, 66) references many of Kleist's "highly defamiliarizing variations" on "archetypes of world theater."

15. It is an example of Kleist's peculiar irony and of how he twists together verbal and physical comedy that the device that was invented to make a loud noise is asked to play a silent part. See *A* 74/1.2.258. Regarding commedia dell'arte and gender, see Krimmer 2004, 28: "The trousers' role is a fairly recent phenomenon when compared to the deeply rooted tradition of men in women's parts. . . . It was only after women had proven themselves as actresses in the commedia dell'arte that they also began to play men's roles on stage."

16. See Feil 2005, 481: "Camp transforms the meanings of 'low' cultural taste as a strategy to redefine the 'low' social identity of queerness."

17. See Ross 1989, 151: "Camp involves a rediscovery of history's waste."

18. Feil (2005, 480) offers the absurdly excessive violence and queer camp aesthetic of the early films by John Waters as an example of a campy reveling in displeasure and violence.

19. For the influence of the Reformation on sexual politics, see Dabhoiwala 2012; for that of the French Revolution, see Joan Wallach Scott 1996.

20. Also known as the Twin Battle of Jena and Auerstedt.

21. Frederick the Great compensated for the years of suffering from the tyranny of his father, King Frederick William I—who executed his son's apparent lover, Lieutenant Hans Hermann von Katte, and forced him to marry a woman of the father's choosing—by not only living his homosexuality instead of producing heirs but also surpassing his father, the so-called Soldier King, in military adventurousness (Blanning 2016, 77).

The hero of Kleist's *Prince Frederick of Homburg* (note that the Prussian king and his father as well as Kleist's hero and his elective father share the same first name) is not only thirsty for military fame but also haunted by a father who keeps rising from the dead (his biological father is dead and his elective father is pronounced dead but then reappears) to threaten him with death (after manipulating his erotic desire). Crown Prince Frederick of Prussia thought that his father's guards had come to lead him to being executed when instead they led him to watch the execution of his beloved Katte, after which he suffered a nervous breakdown and gave in to his father's manipulations.

22. See the first section of the introduction.

23. Vinken (2011) also passes heavy criticism on readings of Kleist as warmongering nationalist. She argues that Kleist's *The Battle of Herrmann* exposes the dishonesty of the bourgeois nationalist ideology of the family.

24. When Carl Schmitt (2007, 7) called Kleist "the real poet of national resistance" and described *The Battle of Herrmann* as "the greatest partisan poem of all times," he missed Kleist's joke. He didn't realize that guerrilla warfare and camp humor have some tactics in common: they come from behind and attack by indirection. When Kleist performs—and he does so in all of his texts—the gradual disintegration of the structure he sets up in the beginning, by increasingly blurring its distinctions and identifications, these are instances of his guerrilla warfare in and through literature against the recently established binary organization of sex/gender and the patriarchic and heteronormative symbolic order.

25. See my discussion of Bernhard Greiner and Wolf Kittler in the section of this chapter titled "Stentor" as well as my discussion of Manfred Schneider and Anthony Stephens in the section titled "Partial."

26. "Bassa Manelka!" and "Bassa Teremtetem!": distorted versions of swear-words, typically used by Hungarian hussars, that seem to mean something like "Be fucked by your Creator!" See Földényi 1999, 40.

27. See the last section, "From Behind," of the previous chapter.

28. See the *Trommelschläger* entry in Grimm and Grimm 1984.

29. It is noteworthy that, with the curse words, Kleist evokes a (Hungarian) minority within the (German) minority of scattered soldiers after the lost battle. Földényi (1999, 42) describes the Hungarian people as isolated within the dominant Austro-German culture, ignored, rendered invisible, and pronounced insignificant to the point that the only reaction they have left is to curse, but their curses, too, disappear in the unwillingness of the dominant culture to translate them.

30. This is an emotionally abusive tactic. As a reader of Kleist, one cannot win or, if one does, it is a victory over oneself.

31. Bohrer (2004, 194) mentions the "Anecdote from the Recent War" as an example of Kleist's "striking [*frappierend*] style" that seems to want to wound the reader.

32. Sophocles 2003, l. 332–33. The standard German translations, including Hölderlin's translation of 1804, render the Greek *deina* as *ungeheuer* (tremendous). The standard English translation—"wondrous"—doesn't convey the same ambiguity of admiration and terror.

33. Kleist knows, of course, that the earth doesn't stand but revolves around the sun.

34. King Frederick William III showed a fatal indecisiveness as Napoleon was preparing to march on Berlin, and the Prussian troops deployed to Jena, led by General Prince Hohenlohe, were utterly surprised when Napoleon attacked them in the early morning of October 14, 1806.

35. Lacan refers to the limit of the real with the Greek signifier *Atè* as that which "human life can only briefly cross" (Lacan 2013, 262–63). Antigone serves as Lacan's example of a particularly strong relation to the real: she frightens us with her atrocious intransigence and stuns us with her splendid beauty.

36. As such, the drummer strikes one as exceptional in Kleist's universe. Other warriors—Ventidius and Achilles, for example—do not preserve their integrity and separate identity in the face of death. They both try to connect and communicate with the objects of their desire asking for clemency and compassion—"Penthesilea! My bride! What are you doing?," exclaims Achilles, and Ventidius complains, "Ah! Such suffering! Woe is me! O Thusnelda!" (*P* 127/23.2664, *BH* 111/5.19.2421). Unlike Antigone and the drummer, they thus both stay within the realm of the human. And they are both torn apart. Other characters—sons yearning for love—get to enjoy the clemency of a reprieve. Their world is senselessly rattled by death and destruction but such encounter with the real does not lead to isolation but to the almost miraculous forging of new bonds. In Kleist's novella *The Earthquake in Chili*, Jeronimo, about to kill himself in his prison cell, receives unexpected deliverance by way of a major earthquake. With almost all the institutions of power destroyed (at least in their architectonic form), the survivors, who gather in a meadow outside the burning city of St. Jago, receive a renewed chance at paradise. They are free to engage in romantic relationships that were hitherto prohibited and to form

new, more communal kinship relations. In another novella, *The Foundling*, the plague rattles the existing sociality and introduces queer family arrangements (families that are not based on biological reproduction) that bring strange desires to the fore. Yet in both cases, the interval of hope closes before the story ends. Both stories lead to the smashing of the skull of a son. Meanwhile the "Anecdote from the Recent War" comes from beyond the interval of hope and makes fun of it.

37. It is worth pointing out again that Antigone has something queer about her. As a child of incest who insists on sibling love at the expense of heterosexual exogamy, Antigone—even if perhaps "not quite a queer heroine," according to Butler (2000, 72, 76)—does "emblematize a certain heterosexual fatality" in that, while being the one "who concludes the oedipal drama, [she] fails to produce heterosexual closure for that drama." She refuses all intimacy, even company, with living humans, rejecting the polis and its leader Creon, her fiancé Haemon, and the help of her sister Ismene.

38. Consider the practices of resistance of demonstrators mooning the police or punk musicians flashing a browneye at the bourgeois world.

39. See chapter 3 above.

40. See Herder 1993, 509. Many of Kleist's texts undermine the apparent anti-Napoleonic German nationalism with their campy performances of French (or Romance) language and culture drag. See Vinken 2011, esp. the chapter "How German Is It?" See also Essen 1999; Campe 2012b, 9–10.

41. The joke conjures up the image of a body stripped of its skin. The somewhat unusual, certainly antiquated (already at Kleist's time) use of *abziehen* when referring to the stripping of trousers (*zog er sich die Hosen ab*) supports this image, because in most contexts the word means "flaying." Bettine Menke (2007, 649) describes the flashing of the browneye as "a display of grotesque corporeality" against the "new bodily canon," emerging in the eighteenth century, of the beautiful body as individual, complete, well-contoured, and with all orifices closed. Lessing's highly influential insistence that Laocoon's mouth may not be represented in sculpture as open needs to be mentioned as the fulcrum of this German Hellenism in the wake of Winckelmann.

42. *Götz von Berlichingen* (1773) is the first major success of Goethe's *Sturm und Drang* period. The *Sturm und Drang* authors claimed Shakespeare as their forefather.

43. Another face-off in this theater of nationalized oppositions takes place between the organically developed honor code that Götz personifies, on the one hand, and the universal and abstract norms of Roman law, the phoniness of the nobility (associated with French courtly society), and the deceitfulness of Roman Catholic clerics, on the other.

44. During the Middle Ages and into the seventeenth century, the Imperial Knights were free agents without representation in the Imperial Diet; the emperor of the Holy Roman Empire was their immediate overlord. By the seventeenth century, their honor code and right to self-defense were on the decline in favor of an abstract, generalized law and the state's monopoly on the use of force. Götz von Berlinchingen's iron hand prosthesis serves as an overdetermined symbol for both the denaturalization of personal power and Götz's stubborn and overcompensating attachment to it.

45. On the "original vicariousness of sovereign power," see Agamben, Chiesa, and Mandarini 2011, 139. For Kleist's work on the deputy structure, especially in *Katie*, see Scholze 2015.

46. In "The Kent Seminar," Laplanche (1992) explains his theory of the "enigmatic signifier." He maintains that adults—i.e., subjects divided between the conscious and the unconscious—send divided messages. Their gestures have a more or less obvious and conscious meaning, but they also carry an unconscious, that is to say, repressed meaning. Laplanche maintains that what the subject "has repressed is mostly sexual" (21). The infant, who does not understand the sexual and does not yet have an unconscious, receives messages from adult caregivers that it perceives to have additional meanings, but these meanings remain largely enigmatic to the infant. Laplanche gives the example of breastfeeding. For the mother, the breast is an erogenous zone. That is to say, for a woman, giving the breast is a gesture that inevitably carries a latent sexual meaning, even if the mother is not aware of it. The child has no idea what the sexual fantasies of the mother are, but s/he perceives that there is an implicit message hidden in the explicit gesture. Laplanche explains that "the enigmatic signifier is doubly enigmatic, not only in the usual meaning of puzzling or interrogative, rich in meaning, but also enigmatic in the precise sense that the meaning remains hidden, not only for the one who receives the message but also for the one who sends it" (22–23). The "signifier" does not need to be verbal: "Every gesture of the adult is a signifier for the child" (22).

47. The comment complicates any attribution of nationalism to the author.

48. In *Beobachter an der Spree*, the joke reads: "Mich im Hintern schießen zu lassen, damit der Balg ganz bleibe."

49. Wolf Kittler (1987), drawing on Carl Schmitt: "Heinrich von Kleist quickly joined in this anti-French propaganda." See also Maass 1957; Seeba 2005.

50. See Greiner 2000; Riedl 2009, 42–43; Angress 1977; Fischer 2001.

51. In traditional terms, it is not correct to call the shift from idea to body a metonymical shift. See my discussions of metalepsis in chapters 1 and 3.

52. See Kleist 2000, 4.

53. See Hahn 2004, esp. his reference to Samuel Moreland's invention of a megaphone called a tuba stentoro-phonica (112).

54. See Dean 2008 for an argument about the ethical dimension of the death drive.

55. Dynes et al. (1990, 189–90) advise that "camp tolerantly views everyone as imperfect, but eminently salvageable."

56. Tim Dean (2003) argues that Lacan's theory of the partial death drive provides a useful source for queer theory.

57. Despite Braunstein's (2003, 104–6) overly purist warnings, we can speak of jouissance as a satisfaction (of the death drive), provided we understand that the meaning of "satisfaction" has shifted away from its common use.

58. Conventionally, psychoanalysts identify a limited number of partial objects. Dean (2003, 246) clarifies that "Lacan invokes the oral, anal, and scopic drives that Freud discusses in 'Instincts and their vicissitudes,' . . . adding to Freud's incomplete list the vocatory drive (in which the voice is taken as an object)." Since the object-cause of desire exceeds our ability to identify it in language, according to Lacan, I see no reason not to extend the list to include skin.

59. See Copjec 2002, 20: "What is at issue in the intersection of freedom and death is not biological death, but the death drive. It is to the latter that we owe the possibility of an ethical act that does not alienate freedom or incur additional guilt."

60. When he finally had a chance to treat his suicide as a theatrical creation, the partializing quality of the death drive was lost in the complete conflation of play and earnest.

61. Guiscard claims that he is immune to the plague (*G* 371/10.477–81).

62. Greiner (2001, 141) points out that the anachronism of the name Istanbul, instead of Constantinople, undermines Guiscard's confidence in his victory.

63. See Greiner (2001, 142) for an equation of the lost fatherland with the lost paradise. Armin's call is undermined by the fact that Italy is not exactly the original home of the Normans. A return is rendered rather complicated by the fact that "home" has multiplied by virtue of historical migration and expansion of territory—from Norway, to Normandy, to Apulia and Calabria.

64. Reuß, Staengle, and Baumann (2000, 4) point out that the German word for frankincense, *Weihrauch*, is ambivalent in itself. It combines the holy (*Weihe*) with the profane (*Rauch*: fume, reek).

65. Both are stock characters in the commedia dell'arte. The Zanni is a clown or buffoon. The Capitano is a pretentious military man or just an arrogant boaster.

66. Hence the phrase "the night of the guerilla war" in the previously cited passage from Kittler 1987. Guerrilla warfare aims at disabling vision.

67. Kittler (1987, 250) provides a rather naive reading of the surefootedness of feeling and its relation to gender in Kleist.

68. Up until the scene when she has the bear lacerate Ventidius, Thusnelda voices understanding for the Romans. Kittler's (1987, 250) description of the song of the bards as "harangues of hatred" notwithstanding, its emotional valence is actually very ambiguous: the song struggles to move from forgiveness to hatred. Only Herrmann separates hatred from forgiveness by assigning them different and mutually exclusive objects—love is reserved for the Teutons (even the Teuton traitors) and hate for the Romans.

69. *BH* 105/5.14.2287 (translation altered): "This the enemy that makes my bosom swell!"

70. For a discussion of Thusnelda's dildo, see the section "From Behind" in chapter 3.

71. Large oak trees were venerated as sacred by the Germanic peoples.

72. Septimus claims prisoner of war status and Herrmann willfully disregards the law of war when he orders Septimus slain (see 100–102/5.13.2189–2227).

73. See chapter 1. Mackles result from a slight shift (*Verrückung*) of the printing plates during the printing process.

74. In the section of this chapter titled "Shoot for the Moon."

75. Regarding references to Schiller, especially his *Wallenstein*, in *Guiscard*, see Samuel 1981, 330, 337, 346.

76. For Schiller, grace is feminine and dignity is masculine.

77. See the section titled "From Behind" in chapter 3.

78. Kleist's mentor Wieland believed that with *Guiscard* Kleist would be able to "fill the gaping hole in our contemporary literature [*die große Lücke in unserer dermaligen Literatur auszufüllen*]" and become the modern equivalent to Aeschylus, Sophocles, and Shakespeare. See Sembdner 1996, 81–82.

79. Ross (1989, 152) speaks of the "necrophilic economy which underpins the camp sensibility, not only in its amorous resurrection of deceased cultural forms, but also in its capacity to promise immortality to the tastemaking intellect." While we usually think of styles or objects being thus resurrected in a campy fashion, Kleist extends this operation to figures of the human—especially heroes, rulers, and aristocrats: relics from epic and tragic art who, in the real life of his time, have been reduced to irrelevance (with Kleist's old, titled family experiencing this decline firsthand).

80. Act 2, scene 5, features the account of the Elector's death. Scene 6 is devoted to the family's emotional response. In scene 7 they hear rumors of his well-being, and in scene 8 these rumors are confirmed.

81. Another example is the reported death and presumed resurrection of Count F in *The Marquise of O* (Kleist 2004, 284–86).

82. As already mentioned above in a footnote to the Introduction, Kant (2000, 125) considers the dynamically sublime "the more attractive, the more fearful it is, provided only that we are in security."

83. Sublimity and exaltation (*Erhabenes* and *Erhebung*) figure both (reactionary) ennoblement and (revolutionary) uprising.

84. Kleist's Guiscard fragment can be read as structured by the parallel oppositions inside-outside and silent-loud (*lautlos-laut*). For Reuß (see Reuß, Staengle, and Baumann 2000, especially 5, 9), the tent of the commander figures the inside, which is called to come out or to express itself (*sich äußern*), just like the voice of the people is asked to either speak clearly and loudly or not at all. However, I see the fate (*Los*) of sound (*Laut*) here—the *Lautlos*—rather in the contagion of one sphere with the other, in the blurring of the inside with the outside and of quiet with thunder—to the point that there are no more two distinct spheres but only a dilating movement.

85. Find full quote in the "Slapstick" section earlier in this chapter.

86. For the emphasis on artificiality, see Sontag 1999, 280: "Camp sees everything in quotation marks." For her emphasis on sincerity, see the quotations "Camp rests on innocence" (283); "Without passion, one gets pseudo-Camp" (284); and "The essential element is seriousness" (283).

87. I thank Rochelle Tobias for this pun and for her feedback on an earlier version of this analysis. While Shakespeare is certainly the master, nobody ultimately masters a pun—it is always a chance offered by language—a chance that can backfire. See Bates 1999.

88. The mockery is again directed at the Enlightenment notion of embodiment, according to which the body and its gestures refer with one-to-one precision to the movements of the soul. Textuality, by definition, has no interiority, therefore its gestures are signs without referents. They add to the wealth of "empty" gestures in Kleist's theater. See Fischer-Lichte 2001.

89. The original publication features four dots to mark the first ellipsis. This suggests an exact reference between dots and letters in all three cases if one adlibs: "Sie mögten ihn in den Popo schießen, damit das Fell kein Loch bekäme." This neat reference is humorously unsettled by the fact that, as Menke (2007, 651) points out, common German parlance uses the much lengthier descriptive phrase "four letters" (*vier Buchstaben*) to render this first ellipsis (as in "Setz dich auf deine vier Buchstaben!").

Chapter 5

1. Anita Sokolsky (1987) argues that only the retrospective interpretations of sentimentality produced the ideology of expression and that the culture of sentimentality itself exceeds and escapes this ideology.

2. This is to say that it naturalizes feeling and desire in general as well as specific, culturally sanctioned feelings and desires while excluding others as unnatural.

3. Since "heterosexuality annexes to itself the cultural force of sequence," the teleological force of narrative has been described as heterosexualizing (Jagose 2002, 147n4). Cf. Roof 1996; Morrison 1993.

4. As Christian Moser (1993) does.

5. One that is largely in line with the new theory of emotion that Lisa Feldman Barrett (2017) has recently developed using the methods and criteria of the natural sciences (psychology and neuroscience).

6. Cf. Barrett 2017, x–xi. She calls it the "classical view of emotion." Her scientific method doesn't allow her to get into view historical differences, so the "classical view" encompasses everything from Plato and "the Buddha" to modern science up until her discovery.

7. See also ibid., 133, 419.

8. "Not all cultures understand emotions as internal mental states. Himba and Hadza emotion concepts, for example, appear to be more focused on actions. This is also true of certain Japanese emotion concepts. The Ifaluk of Micronesia consider emotions as transactions between people. To them, anger is not a feeling of rage, a scowl, a pounding fist, or a loud yelling voice, all within the skin of one person, but a situation in which two people are engaged in a script—a dance, if you will—around a common goal. In the Ifaluk view, anger does not 'live' inside either participant" (Barrett 2017, 83).

9. This shows an affinity of Kleist's strategies with what is now discussed under the heading "imperceptible politics." See Papadopoulos, Stephenson, and Tsianos 2008, 73: "Imperceptible politics is practised in the present." "But at the same time, it is imaginary and outside of the present historical chronotope."

10. See the section titled "Open Breast Closed" in chapter 3.

11. For Hegel's theory of tragedy, see the chapter "True Spirit: Ethical Life" in *Phenomenology of Spirit* (e.g., Hegel 1977) and Hegel 2014, 431–36. For the term "tragic collision," see Bradley 1909, 114–56. Hegel repeatedly uses the term "collision [*Kollision*]" in section b of "True Spirit. Ethical Life."

12. Achilles is often compared to the sun in this text. With her remark, Prothoë thus makes not only a general statement about rationality and female interiority but also a specific one about things that should be hidden from Achilles.

13. The same awareness of the ontological and epistemological status of a literary text applies when I question (as I did above) the objectivity of Achilles's perception.

14. Note that with this teichoscopy Kleist makes explicit what I have identified earlier as the general characteristic of Kleistian teichoscopies, namely that they create concrete scenes and concrete feelings out of indistinguishable and unidentifiable chaos. This teichoscopic episode begins with the girl on the hill responding to the request to report whether she sees Penthesilea: "We don't see anything! / We can't make out a single plume down there, / Only the shadow of a thundercloud / Racing across the wide plain, and the surge / Of scattered groups

of warriors pressing on" (*P* 46/ 7.1010–15). Then, Amazon authority figures spin ideas and formulate more targeted questions ("HIGH PRIESTESS: What . . . is she trying to do? / CAPTAIN: . . . what's left and worth her conquering?" [*P* 46–47/7.1025–28]), which in turn enables the girl on the lookout to make out a shape in the chaos—the luminous vision of Achilles. The use of teichoscopy creates a vision based on anticipatory and interpretive notions.

15. Here teichoscopy interrupts but cannot detract attention from a conversation between the Captain and the High Priestess about Penthesilea's emotional state.

16. Achilles only physically repeats what Penthesilea has already experienced when her dying mother, Otrere, sent her into war and seemed to be more interested in Achilles than in her daughter. The mother's death left Penthesilea feeling empty, compounded by the mother's withdrawal of attention right before her death. Cf. Klein 1986, 91.

17. At the most literal, Prothoë might be encouraging Penthesilea to contract her vaginal muscles around his penis in an orgasm, but this still remains in the realm of metaphor in that it shifts the site of penetration from breast to vagina and denies any violence.

18. Cf. Cullens and von Mücke (1997, 130), who read the play as exhibiting the (discursive) production of what they see as specifically modern sexuality, i.e., of sexuality as a traumatic experience. In particular, they point out the substitution of the erotic scene, everyone involved in the secret trial expects to hear, by a description of violence. Strahl and Katie thus seem to act out the Freudian child's interpretation of the parental intercourse as an act of violence and offense rather than pleasure.

19. See my discussion of Allemann's analysis in chapter 2.

20. The count, for example, remembers her flimsy little shirt while Katie denies having worn such a thing—even though a few lines later she corroborates his account using the same word for her nightshirt (*Hemdchen*) as he did (*K* 236/4.2.2126, 237/4.2.2142).

21. Theobald, who plays the role of the father, paints a vivid picture of Katie and his enthusiasm for her has all the characteristics of a vision, as defined by Allemann (including radiance), even though without the dramatological import. See *K* 164–65/1.1.62–106.

22. *K* 165/1.1.73–88. This was the bourgeois recognition of Katie or her recognition by the citizens of the city.

23. The maid Marianna gave Katie the idea of marrying a knight. It's obviously a maid's fantasy based on a fairy-tale topos.

24. Interestingly, Kunigunde sends Katie into the fire, thereby initiating the trial by fire.

25. The Emperor reveals "the whole secret" in great, forensic detail to the "four walls" (*K* 248/5.2.2431–42). The phrase alludes to the fourth wall of the theater and to the idea, introduced by Diderot, that actors play as if they had no spectators. This theatrical practice allows for the unburdened disclosure of secrets and thus for plays to serve as allegories of the soul.

26. The heat of the fever drives his insides out as in the old, more fluid, humor-based anatomy developed by Galen. The phrase "on the tip of his tongue [*lag nun auf seiner Zunge*]" makes feelings and words physical.

27. In her hand she holds a rolled-up portrait of Strahl, which she has recovered from the burning castle.

28. Katie exclaims: "Guard me, ye heavenly! What's happening to me?" (*K* 226/3.14.1888, translation altered).

29. *Entwurf* means "sketch" or "draft." The word thus references the scene of writing as well as the theater where the stage director might use the draft of a scene as a basis for improvisation.

30. Reeve (1991, 113) interprets his kneeling as humbling himself in front of Katie.

31. The truth value of Katie's vision is slightly unsettled by other things she says, as well.

32. While the lovebug is known in the United States, the phrase "in love with me like a beetle [*verliebt ja, wie ein Käfer, bist Du mir*]" makes no obvious sense in German.

33. One station in this transformation is reached when he decides to follow her creed: "Her faith is firmly grounded as a tower!— / So be it! I resign myself" (*K* 234/4.2.2077, translation altered). Katie believes in love and converts Strahl, presenting a modern version of the legend of Saint Catherine, whose eloquence and acumen convinced her Pagean persecutors of the Christian belief.

Chapter 6

1. See Fischer-Lichte 2002, 252–57.

2. Letter to Heinrich von Collin, December 8, 1808. See Kleist 1982, 181–82.

3. See Kleist's letter to Marie von Kleist from late autumn 1807: "Now I am curious what you will think of my Kate of Heilbronn, for she is the reverse side of Penthesilea, her opposite pole, a being quite as great in her complete submission as the other is in her self-assertion" (Kleist 1982, 175).

4. See also Halberstam's (1998, 115) critique of this focus as producing discrimination within the lesbian "community": "When white lesbians continue to invest exclusively in this construction of lesbian sex as elusive, apparitional, silent, and intangible, other hyper-visible lesbian sexualities with highly complex relations to silence and exposure are totally discounted."

5. "We use the term imperceptible politics to designate everyday cultural and practical practices of escape" (Papadopoulos, Stephenson, and Tsianos 2008, 72).

6. The Amazons are called "daughters of Mars" (*P* 81/14.1632, 100/15.2145, 126/23.2602), "of Mars begotten" (*P* 89/15.1825), or "daughters of Ares [*Arestöchter*]" (*P* 56/9.1218, translation altered).

7. The oedipal law does regulate the Amazons' sexual relations with men. A heavy emphasis is placed on the incest requirement, which is one side of the double bind of the oedipalized incest taboo: the Amazons—daughters of Mars—are ritualistically named "brides of Mars" (*P* 97/15.2056). The Amazon law softens this father-daughter incest requirement by calling for arbitrary substitutes for Mars. The Amazons cannot have lasting relationships with these substitutes (foreign men) because they are all married to Mars, their father. Alternatively, one could say that men must remain foreign to them.

8. Kleist's use of the word *Geschlecht* oscillates between the older sense of "family" or "tribe" and the modern sense of "gender" or "sex."

9. Penthesilea confesses, "I loved her" (*P* 101/15.2172) and "Nothing seemed more sacred / Than to fulfill and honor her last wish" (*P* 101/15.2162–63).

10. Note that the passage circles around his name without mentioning it but features the names of Otrerë und Prothoë (*P* 100/15.2141–43).

11. See my discussion of Penthesilea's suicide monologue in the previous chapter.

12. See my analysis of their play fight in Pahl 2015.

13. This figuration might be confusing since a version of male homosexuality goes by the name "Greek love" in Kleist's days, but it is important to keep in mind that, in this tragedy, the Greek camp—with Odysseus as its ideological leader—stands for the heteronormative (and patriarchal) organization of society.

14. As we have already seen, these models are by no means pure and thus do not simply or straightforwardly function as the opposite of bourgeois sexual culture. Otrerë betrays the values of female same-sex love, many Amazons parrot bourgeois ideas at times, and by the middle of the play, Achilles presumes the Greek organization of gender and sexuality to be in line with the natural order of things and considers everything else as unnatural. He thus reflects the naturalizing impulse of the late eighteenth century—the turn to nature as foundational principle, after religion and aristocracy have lost their legitimizing power due to the Enlightenment and the French Revolution.

15. According to Greek myth, Thetis herself was raped by Peleus in the presence of the gods (Hederich 1996). Only Eris, the goddess of strife, was not invited to this "wedding." The Olympian gods and many narrators and commentators on the myth clearly meant to "forget" the discord at the heart of this relationship (that Thetis did not want Peleus). But Eris crashed the party and threw a golden apple into the crowd, which resulted in a competition between Hera, Athena, and Aphrodite over who was the fairest and then caused the Trojan War, a struggle over the most beautiful woman, Helena. Homer's *Iliad* continues to reproduce such agonistic and hierarchical gender norms, beginning with the squabble between the two leaders Agamemnon and Achilles, who feel their honor compromised when the other wants to rob them of their prize—a young, beautiful woman—and continuing on the divine level with the wedded strife between Zeus and Hera and the celebration of Zeus's superiority. In this context, women fight with their physical beauty and with ruses while men use their physical strength and their position of authority.

With *Penthesilea*, Kleist displaces and queers this scenario. See Jacobs (1989, 86, 88), who analyzes how "the entire action of *Penthesilea* progresses as a carefully placed wedge in the design of Homer's text" and its assumption "that man is man, and woman woman." Cf. Cixous (1986, 118, 120), who sees that Penthesilea and Achilles "must mutually destroy the warrior in themselves, the enemy that society has inscribed in their memory; they must kill warring power to liberate loving power," thereby "muddling clear oppositions." See also Brandstetter 1997, 76, 113, for a discussion of Penthesilea's death wish as motivated by the hope to transcend the boundaries of gender.

16. Achilles fell in love with Penthesilea and with the daughter of the King of Troy (Hederich 1996, 36).

17. Odysseus uses the metaphor of fire and water to articulate this binary logic most forcefully (*P* 8/1.125–26).

18. Note the increase in homophobia during the Napoleonic Wars, discussed above, in the introduction.

19. Christian Moser (1993, 149) has identified a curious and politically ambiguous quality of Kleist's writing, namely that he entraps his readers, provoking them to use moral prejudices that violate others' bodies. We become guilty of such an imaginary violation if we jump to conventional conclusions about the gender identity and the sexual orientation of Achilles and Penthesilea.

20. See the conclusion of chapter 3 on how Penthesilea gives Achilles cleavage.

21. See the analyses of Laqueur (1990) and Butler (1990, 1–34) of the social constructedness of biological differences, which lends significance to in themselves insignificant bodily differences.

22. Tanaïs is also the Phoenician name for Diana, the goddess of the hunt, who serves as an important reference point of the play.

23. See also Gallas (2005, 195), who highlights the identification between Achilles, Penthesilea, and Hector around the attack on the breast and the wound in the neck.

24. This dissolution of the boundary of the body also undoes the difference between interiority and exteriority, to the point where it makes little sense to diagnose these wounds as external manifestations of an internal emotion.

25. Grosz argues against the coupling of sexual desire and death (that pervades our imaginary in the form of the praying mantis devouring her mate) and for a sexual culture that emphasizes the salutary dissolution of the organically organized body.

26. Its syntax follows the rules of analgrammar, developed in chapter 3. At the same time, what I describe in this section shows overlaps of the analgrammatic with queer versions of the mammatangential and the phallic order: noncleaving (to the) breasts and ejaculating eyes.

27. "The situation is quite different when the mind or spirit [*Geist*] has thought everything out before anything is spoken. In the act of mere expression it is thus left behind" (Kleist 1982, 221).

28. See Kaiser (2011, 99–102) for an excellent analysis of the various iterations of Katie's formula of ignorance as progressively performing her becoming imperceptible.

29. Solomon 3:6 (New International Version): "Who is this coming up from the wilderness / like a column of smoke, / perfumed with myrrh and incense?" Nitschke (2013, 215–16) also notes the erotic relation of father to daughter.

30. With regard to a politics of becoming imperceptible and yet impossible to be ignored, compare Scheifele's (1992, 106) suggestion that Penthesilea would like to become dust in order to be able to perpetually irritate.

31. Joan's father accuses her of a pact with the devil. Kunigunde thinks that the devil must have guided Katie through the burning castle (*K* 228/3.15).

32. Wetter means "weather." Strahl connotes "thunderbolt" (*Blitzstrahl*). See also chapter 3, near the end of the section "Breast Image and Breast Language: Glorious and Overflowing."

33. The stage directions specify: "*She sinks down. The Countess receives* [*empfängt*] *her*" (*K* 259/5.14, translation altered). Given the reorganization of kinship relations in this final act, it makes sense to read the rather unusual word choice *empfängt* here as an indication of the maternal tie—of Katie being conceived by the Countess.

34. See also the section "Breast Image and Breast Language: Glorious and Overflowing" in chapter 3.

35. In this play, the heterosexual couple formation is repeatedly disturbed by a third. While Strahl has the flamboyant cherub as his mate, Katie couples with Kunigunde, Eleonore, the Countess, or the girls at home. This structure of relationality is reflected in the fact that the word repetitions we find in *Katie* are word triplets—for example, "Trust, trust, trust!" (*K* 200/2.9.1166, my translation), "Mother! Mother! Mother" (*K* 200/2.9.1181), and "Nein, nein, nein" (*K* 4.2.2097). Compare to the analysis of same-sex syntax in the section titled "Abreast," earlier in this chapter.

36. Her question "Are your young limbs now quite restored to vigour?" exudes a vague eroticism (*K* 240/4.6.2213).

37. Kleist finishes both texts in 1807.

38. This is an aspect of the parallel between Penthesilea and Katie that Kleist asserts. For both of them, the male love object is more or less explicitly an arbitrary signifier.

39. See the section "From Behind" in chapter 3.

40. The scene of New Year's Eve vanishes as soon as the knight touches Katie. See *K* 201/2.9.1233, 237/4.2.2138–39.

41. McAllister (2005, 113) reads Kunigunde as a parodically exaggerated cypher for the aesthetics of Romanticism (the fragment, the conglomerate aesthetics of the novel) and argues that Kleist creates her to mock the gender politics of Romanticism, in particular the Romanticist use of a female image for male self-reflection and self-definition.

42. Most notably in *Penthesilea*, when Achilles is torn apart by Penthesilea and her hounds.

43. See Cixous 1981, 41–44. Catherine's offense was her creed; with her superior intelligence and eloquence she managed to convince fifty philosophers and the emperor's wife to convert to Christianity.

44. Clark translates *Molch* (newt) as "salamander." This choice makes sense given the fire imagery of the play, including Katie's "ordeal by fire" and the veil in the colors of fire that Kunigunde wears as she enters the grotto (*K* 239/4.4, stage directions).

45. I am referring to the fact that Katie broke both her legs when she threw herself out the window and to her current state of being shaken and trembling from the encounter with Kunigunde in the bath.

46. Reeve (1991, 118–19) also interprets this scene in sexual terms but fails to recognize its lesbian implications.

47. In the episode of the burning castle Kunigunde also directs Katie to the "centre room" (*K* 223/3.12.1832).

48. It would be easy, and in keeping with the tradition of court appearances in the theater, to assign the jury members a group name (like Councilmen of Heilbronn). Hence, the fact that their individual names are provided feels marked and, considering their extravagance (Otto von der Flühe, Wenzel von Nachtheim, Hans von Bärenklau), even excessive.

49. That K and K's contact happens in an artificial cave ironizes the efforts of the bourgeois theater to naturalize the stage as a place of interiority. See also Scholze (2015, 119), who points out that Kunigunde's affiliation with the grotto contributes to her grotesque quality.

BIBLIOGRAPHY

Adelung, Johann Christoph, Dietrich Wilhelm Soltau, and Franz Xaver Schönberger. 1811. *Grammatisch-kritisches Wörterbuch der hochdeutschen Mundart: Mit beständiger Vergleichung der übrigen Mundarten, besonders aber der Oberdeutschen*. Vienna: Ph. Bauer.

Agamben, Giorgio, Lorenzo Chiesa, and Matteo Mandarini. 2011. *The Kingdom and the Glory*. Stanford, Calif.: Stanford University Press.

AG Feministisch Sprachhandeln der Humboldt-Universität zu Berlin. 2014–15. *Was tun? Sprachhandeln – aber wie? W_Ortungen statt Tatenlosigkeit!* 2nd ed. http://feministisch-sprachhandeln.org/wp-content/uploads/2015/04/sprachleitfaden_zweite_auflage.pdf

Ahmed, Sara. 2010. "Killing Joy: Feminism and the History of Happiness." *Signs* 35, no. 3: 571–92.

———. 2004. *The Cultural Politics of Emotion*. New York: Routledge.

Allan, Seán, and Elystan Griffiths. 2011. "Introduction. Heinrich von Kleist: Performance and Performativity." In "Performance and Performativity in the Works of Heinrich von Kleist," edited by Seán Allan and Elystan Griffiths, special issue, *German Life and Letters* 64, no. 3: 327–487.

Allemann, Beda. 2005. *Heinrich von Kleist: Ein dramaturgisches Modell*. Edited by Eckart Oehlenschläger. Bielefeld: Aisthesis

Angress, R. K. 1977. "Kleist's Treatment of Imperialism: 'Die Hermannsschlacht' and 'Die Verlobung in St. Domingo.' " *Monatshefte* 69, no. 1: 17–33.

Arntzen, Helmut. 1968. *Die ernste Komödie: Das deutsche Lustspiel von Lessing bis Kleist*. Munich: Nymphenburger Verlagshandlung.

Babuscio, Jack. 1993. "Camp and the Gay Sensibility." In *Camp Grounds: Style and Homosexuality*, edited by David Bergman, 19–38. Amherst: University of Massachusetts Press.

Bächtold-Stäubli, Hanns, and Eduard Hoffmann-Krayer, eds. 1927–42. *Handwörterbuch des deutschen Aberglaubens*. 10 vols. Berlin: De Gruyter.

Barad, Karen. 2014. "Diffracting Diffraction: Cutting Together-Apart." *Parallax* 20, no. 3: 168–87.

Barrett, Lisa Feldman. 2017. *How Emotions Are Made: The Secret Life of the Brain*. Boston: Houghton Mifflin Harcourt.

Bartl, Andrea. 2015. *Die deutsche Komödie: Metamorphosen des Harlekin*. Stuttgart: Reclam.

Bates, Catherine. 1999. "The Point of Puns." *Modern Philology* 96, no. 40: 421–38.

Baumgartner, Katrin. 1997. *Hagestolz und alte Jungfer: Entwicklung, Instrumentalisierung und Fortleben von Klischees und Stereotypen über Unverheiratetgebliebene*. Münster: Waxmann.

Benjamin, Jessica. 1995. *Like Subjects, Love Objects: Essays on Recognition and Sexual Difference*. New Haven, Conn.: Yale University Press.

Bergoffen, Debra B. 1996. "Phallic Queerings." *Philosophy Today* 40, no. 1: 206–10.

Berlant, Lauren, and Sianne Ngai. 2017. "Comedy Has Issues." *Critical Inquiry* 43 (winter): 233–49.

Bersani, Leo. 2015. *Thoughts and Things*. Chicago: University of Chicago Press.

———. 1996. *Homos*. Cambridge, Mass.: Harvard University Press.

———. 1986. *The Freudian Body: Psychoanalysis and Art*. New York: Columbia University Press.

Bersani, Leo, and Ulysse Dutoit. 2004. *Forms of Being: Cinema, Aesthetics, Subjectivity*. London: British Film Institute.

———. 1998. *Caravaggio's Secrets*. Cambridge, Mass.: MIT Press.

Blanning, Tim. 2016. *Frederick the Great, King of Prussia*. New York: Random House.

Bloch, Ruth. 1978. "Untangling the Roots of Modern Sex Roles: A Survey of Four Centuries of Change." *Signs* 4, no. 2: 237–57.

Block, Richard O. 2018. *Echoes of Queer Messianism: From Frankenstein to Brokeback Mountain*. Albany: State University of New York Press.

Bohrer, Karl Heinz. 2004. *Imaginationen des Bösen: Zur Begründung einer ästhetischen Kategorie*. Munich: Hanser.

———. 1994. *Suddenness: On the Moment of Aesthetic Appearance*. New York: Columbia University Press.

Booth, Mark. 1983. *Camp*. London: Quartet.

Borchers, Walter. 1974. *Der Osnabrücker Domschatz*. Osnabrück: Wenner.

Borgard, Roland. 2015. "Off Cage: Kleists Herrmannsbärin." Talk at the conference *Unarten: Kleist und das Gesetz der Gattung* at Kleist Museum, Frankfurt/Oder, September 26.

Boyle, Nicholas. 1987. *Goethe: Faust Part One*. Landmarks of World Literature. Cambridge: Cambridge University Press.

Bradley, A. C. 1909. *Oxford Lectures on Poetics*. London: Macmillan.

Brandstetter, Gabriele. 2007. "Kleists Choreographien." In *Kleist-Jahrbuch 2007*, edited by Günter Blamberger, Gabriele Brandstetter, Ingo Breuer, Wolfgang de Bruyn, Sabine Doering, and Klaus Müller-Salget, 25–37. Stuttgart: J. B. Metzler.

———. 2001. "Inszenierte Katharsis in Kleists Penthesilea." In *Gewagte Experimente und Kühne Konstellationen: Kleists Werk zwischen Klassizismus und Romantik*, edited by Christine Lubkoll and Günter Oesterle, 225–48. Würzburg: Königshausen & Neumann.

———. 2000. "Eine Tragödie von der Brust heruntergehustet: Darstellung von Katharsis in Kleists Penthesilea." In *Heinrich von Kleist und die Aufklärung*, edited by Timothy J. Mehigan, 186–210. Rochester, N.Y.: Camden House.

———. 1999. "Duell im Spiegel: Zum Rahmenspiel in Kleists Amphitryon." In *Kleist-Jahrbuch 1999*, edited by Günter Blamberger, 109–27. Stuttgart: J. B. Metzler.

———. 1997. "*Penthesilea*: 'Das Wort des Greuelrätsels.' Die Überschreitung der Tragödie." In *Interpretationen: Kleists Dramen*, edited by Walter Hinderer, 75–115. Stuttgart: Reclam.

Braunstein, Nestor A. 2003. "Desire and Jouissance in the Teachings of Lacan." In *The Cambridge Companion to Lacan*, edited by Jean-Michel Rabaté, 102–14. Cambridge: Cambridge University Press.

Brodsky, Claudia. 2013. "Kleist and Kant: Meaning and Förmlichkeit." In *Heinrich von Kleist: Style and Concept: Explorations of Literary Dissonance*, edited by Dieter Sevin and Christoph Zeller, 201–10. Berlin: De Gruyter.

Butler, Judith. 2006. *Precarious Life: The Powers of Mourning and Violence*. London: Verso.

———. 2004. *Undoing Gender*. New York: Routledge.

———. 2000. *Antigone's Claim: Kinship between Life and Death*. New York: Columbia University Press.

———. 1997. *The Psychic Life of Power: Theories in Subjection*. Stanford, Calif.: Stanford University Press.

———. 1993. "The Lesbian Phallus and the Morphological Imaginary." In *Bodies That Matter*, 28–57. New York: Routledge.

———. 1990. *Gender Trouble: Feminism and the Subversion of Identity*. New York: Routledge.

Butler, Judith, and Athena Athanasiou. 2013. *Dispossession: The Performative in the Political*. PCVS-Polity Conversations Series. Cambridge: Polity.

Butler, Judith, and Joan Wallach Scott. 1992. *Feminists Theorize the Political*. New York: Routledge.

Calhoon, Kenneth S. 2013. *Affecting Grace: Theatre, Subject, and the Shakespearean Paradox in German Literature from Lessing to Kleist*. German and European Studies. Toronto: University of Toronto Press.

———. 1989. "Sacrifice and the Semiotics of Power in *Der zerbrochene Krug*." *Comparative Literature* 41, no. 3: 230–51.

Campe, Rüdiger. 2013. "Kants Krise und Kleists Verfahren." Public Lecture at Freie Universität Berlin, July 4.

———. 2012a. *The Game of Probability: Literature and Calculation from Pascal to Kleist*. Translated by Ellwood H. Wiggins. Stanford, Calif.: Stanford University Press.

———. 2012b. "Verfahren: Kleists allmähliche Verfertigung der Gedanken beim Reden." *Sprache und Literatur* 110: 2–21.

———. 2010. "Zeigen statt Sagen: Kleists hier und jetzt und die Figur des Zeigens." In *Zeigen: Die Rhetorik des Sichtbaren*, edited by Gottfried Boehm, Sebastian Egenhofer, and Christian Spies, 439–55. Munich: Fink.

———. 2008. "Zweierlei Gesetz in Kleists Penthesilea: Naturrecht und Biopolitik." In *Penthesileas Versprechen: Exemplarische Studien über die literarische Referenz*, 7–18. Freiburg: Rombach.

———. 1990. *Affekt und Ausdruck: Zur Umwandlung der literarischen Rede im 17. und 18. Jahrhundert*. Tübingen: Niemeyer.

Campe, Rüdiger, and Julia Weber. 2014. *Rethinking Emotion: Interiority and Exteriority in Premodern, Modern, and Contemporary Thought*. Berlin: De Gruyter.

Castle, Terry. 1993. *The Apparitional Lesbian: Female Homosexuality and Modern Culture*. Gender and Culture. New York: Columbia University Press.

Cavarero, Adriana. 2013. "Recritude: Reflections on Postural Ontology." *Journal of Speculative Philosophy* 27, no. 3: 220–35.

Chaouli, Michel. 1996. "Devouring Metaphor: Disgust and Taste in Kleist's *Penthesilea*." *German Quarterly* 69, no. 2: 125–43.

Christiansen, Adrienne E., and Jeremy J. Hanson. 1996. "Comedy as Cure for Tragedy: ACT UP and the Rhetoric of AIDS." *Quarterly Journal of Speech* 82: 157–70.

Cixous, Hélène. 1986. "Sorties: Out and Out: Attacks/Ways Out/Forays." In *The Newly Born Woman*, by translated by Betsy Wing, 63–132. Minneapolis: University of Minnesota Press.

———. 1981. "Castration or Decapitation?" Translated by Annette Kuhn. *Signs* 7, no. 1: 41–55.

Cixous, Hélène, and Mireille Calle-Gruber. 1997. *Hélène Cixous, Rootprints: Memory and Life Writing*. Translated by Eric Prenowitz. London: Routledge.

Cleto, Fabio. 1999. *Camp: Queer Aesthetics and the Performing Subject: A Reader*. Ann Arbor: University of Michigan Press.

Coleridge, Samuel Taylor. 2014. *Biographia Literaria*. New, fully annotated critical ed. Edited by Adam Roberts. Edinburgh: Edinburgh University Press.

Comay, Rebecca. 2001. *Mourning Sickness: Hegel and the French Revolution*. Stanford, Calif.: Stanford University Press.

Copjec, Joan. 2002. *Imagine There's No Woman: Ethics and Sublimation*. Cambridge, Mass.: MIT Press.

Cullens, Chris, and Dorothea von Mücke. 1997. "*Das Kätchen von Heilbronn*: 'Ein Kind recht nach der Lust Gottes.'" In *Interpretationen: Kleists Dramen*, edited by Walter Hinderer. Stuttgart: Reclam.

———. 1989. "Love in Kleist's Penthesilea and Kätchen Von Heilbronn." *Deutsche Vierteljahrsschrift für Literaturwissenschaft und Geistesgeschichte* 63, no. 3: 461–93.

Dabhoiwala, Faramerz. 2012. *The Origins of Sex: The History of the First Sexual Revolution*. London: Allen Lane.

Dean, Tim. 2008. "An Impossible Embrace: Queerness, Futurity, and the Death Drive." In *A Time for the Humanities: Futurity and the Limits of Autonomy*, edited by James J. Bono, Tim Dean, and Ewa Plonowska Ziarek, 122–40. New York: Fordham University Press.

———. 2003. "Lacan and Queer Theory." In *The Cambridge Companion to Lacan*, edited by Jean-Michel Rabaté, 238–52. Cambridge: Cambridge University Press.

Deleuze, Gilles, and Félix Guattari. 1987. *A Thousand Plateaus: Capitalism and Schizophrenia*. Translated by Brian Massumi. Minneapolis: University of Minnesota Press.

Derks, Paul. 1990. *Die Schande der heiligen Päderastie: Homosexualität und Öffentlichkeit in der deutschen Literatur 1750–1850*. Berlin: Rosa Winkel.

Derrida, Jacques. 2009. *The Beast and the Sovereign*. Chicago: University of Chicago Press.

———. 1988. "Signature, Event, Context." In *Limited Inc.*, edited by Gerald Graff, translated by Samuel Weber and Jeffrey Mehlman, 1–23. Evanston, Ill.: Northwestern University Press.

Detering, Heinrich. 1994. *Das offene Geheimnis: Zur literarischen Produktivität eines Tabus von Winckelmann bis zu Thomas Mann*. Göttingen: Wallstein.

Dollimore, Jonathan. 1991. *Sexual Dissidence: Augustine to Wilde, Freud to Foucault*. Oxford: Oxford University Press.

Duden, Barbara. 1977. "Das schöne Eigentum: Zur Herausbildung des bürgerlichen Frauenbildes an der Wende vom 18. zum 19. Jahrhundert." *Kursbuch* 47: 125–40.

Dudenredaktion. 2017. *Duden, die deutsche Rechtschreibung*. Berlin: Dudenverlag.

Duggan, Lisa, and Kathleen McHugh. 1996. "A Fem(me)inist Manifesto." *Women and Performance* 8, no. 2: 153–59.

Dynes, Wayne R., Warren Johansson, William A. Percy, and Stephen Donaldson. 1990. *Encyclopedia of Homosexuality*. New York: Garland.

Eckermann, Johann Peter. 1836. *Gespräche mit Goethe in den letzten Jahren seines Lebens*. 3 vols. Leipzig: F. A. Brockhaus.

Edelman, Lee. 2004. *No Future: Queer Theory and the Death Drive*. Series Q. Durham, N.C.: Duke University Press.

Essen, Gesa von. 1999. "Germanen und Römer im Spiel der Masken: Heinrich von Kleists Hermannsschlacht." *Kleist-Jahrbuch*, 41–52.

Feil, Ken. 2005. "Queer Comedy." In *Comedy: A Geographic and Historical Guide*, edited by Maurice Charney, 477–92. Westport, Conn.: Praeger.

Fetscher, Justus. 2000. "Über das Komische in Kleists Trauerspiel Penthesilea." *Heilbronner Kleist-Blätter* 8: 50–67.

Fichte, Johann. 2000. "Outline of Family Right." In *Foundations of Natural Right*, edited by Frederick Neuhouser and translated by Michael Baur, 268–71. Cambridge: Cambridge University Press.

Fischer, Bernd. 2001. "Fremdbestimmung und Identitätspolitik in *Die Hermannsschlacht*." In *Kleists Erzählungen und Dramen: Neuen Studien*, edited by Paul Michael Lützeler and David Pan, 165–78. Würzburg: Könighausen & Neumann.

Fischer-Lichte, Erika. 2002. *History of European Drama and Theatre*. New York: Routledge.

———. 2001. "Theatralität: Zur Frage nach Kleists Theaterkonzeption." In *Kleist-Jahrbuch 2001*, edited by Günter Blamberger, Sabine Doerning, and Klaus Müller-Salget, 25–37. Stuttgart: J. B. Metzler.

———. 1998. "Inszenierung und Theatralität." In *Inszenierungsgesellschaft—ein einführendes Handbuch*, edited by Herbert Willems and Martin Jurga, 81–90. Berlin: VS Verlag für Sozialwissenschaften.

Földényi, F. László. 1999. *Heinrich von Kleist: Im Netz der Wörter*. Munich: Matthes & Seitz.

Foucault, Michel. 1990. *The History of Sexuality*. Translated by Robert Hurley. New York: Vintage.

Gailus, Andreas. 2010. "Language Unmoored: On Kleist's 'The Betrothal in St. Domingue.'" *Germanic Review* 85: 20–43.

———. 2006. *Passions of the Sign: Revolution and Language in Kant, Goethe, Kleist*. Baltimore: Johns Hopkins University Press.

Gallas, Helga. 2007. "Kleists Welt im Vergleich zur Dominanz des *Imaginären* in der Romantik und zur Inflation des *Realen* in der Postmoderne." In *Heinrich von Kleist: Freiburger Literaturpsychologische Gespräche. Jahrbuch für Literatur und Psychoanalyse,* Bd. 27, edited by Ortrud Gutjahr, 279–95. Freiburg: Könighausen & Neumann.

———. 2005. *Kleist: Gesetz, Begehren, Sexualität: Zwischen symbolischer und imaginärer Identifizierung.* Nexus, Vol. 77. Frankfurt a.M.: Stroemfeld.

Gallop, Jane. 1988. *Thinking through the Body.* New York: Columbia University Press.

Genette, Gérard. 2004. *Métalepse: De la figure à la fiction.* Paris: Presses Universitaires de Lorraine.

Goethe, Johann Wolfgang von. 1981. "Zum Shakespeares-Tag." In *Goethes Werke: Hamburger Ausgabe in 14 Bänden,* Neubearbeitung ed., edited by Erich Trunz, vol. 12: *Schriften zur Kunst—Schriften zur Literatur—Maximen und Reflexionen,* 224–27. Munich: Beck.

———. 1991. *Götz von Berlichingen: A Play.* Translated by Charles E. Passage. Prospect Heights, Ill.: Waveland.

Graf, Ruedi. 2010. *Das Theater im Literaturstaat: Literarisches Theater auf dem Weg zur Bildungsmacht.* Berlin: De Gruyter.

Graham, Ilse. 1977. *Heinrich von Kleist: Word into Flesh. A Poet's Quest for the Symbol.* Berlin: De Gruyter.

Green, Martin, and John Swan. 1994. *The Triumph of Pierrot: The Commedia dell'Arte and the Modern Imagination.* University Park: Pennsylvania State University Press.

Greiner, Bernhard. 2001. "'Die große Lücke in unserer dermaligen Literatur Auszufüllen': Die unausführbare Tragödie Robert Guiskard." In *Kleists Erzählungen und Dramen: Neue Studien,* edited by Paul Michael Lützeler and David Pan, 135–49. Würzburg: Königshausen & Neumann.

———. 2000. *Kleists Dramen und Erzählungen: Experimente zum "Fall" der Kunst.* Tübingen: Francke.

Griffiths, Elystan. 2012. "'Die Unverhoffte Wirkung': Revolutionary Violence, 'Beschränkung,' and the Rewriting of the Domestic Idyll in Kleist's Works." *German Life and Letters* 65, no. 4: 399–420.

———. 2009. "Gender, Laughter, and the Desecration of Enlightenment: Kleist's *Penthesilea* as 'Hundekomödie.'" *Modern Language Review* 104, no. 2: 453–71.

———. 2005. *Political Change and Human Emancipation in the Works of Heinrich von Kleist.* Studies in German Literature, Linguistics, and Culture. Rochester, N.Y.: Camden House.

Grimm, Jacob, and Wilhelm Grimm. 1984. *Deutsches Wörterbuch.* Munich: dtv.

Grosz, E. A. 1995. *Space, Time, and Perversion: Essays on the Politics of Bodies.* New York: Routledge.

Grugger, Helmut. 2010. *Dramaturgie des Subjekts bei Heinrich von Kleist.* Würzburg: Königshausen & Neumann.

Gumbrecht, Hans Ulrich, and Friederike Knüpling. 2014. *Kleist Revisited.* Munich: Fink.

Gustafson, Susan E. 2002. *Men Desiring Men: The Poetry of Same-Sex Identity and Desire in German Classicism.* Detroit: Wayne State University Press.

———. 1989. "'Die allmähliche Verfertigung der Gedanken beim Reden': The Linguistic Question in Kleist's *Amphitryon.*" *Seminar* 25, no. 2: 104–26.

Gutjahr, Ortrud. 2011a. *"Das Käthchen von Heilbronn" und "Penthesilea" von Heinrich von Kleist: Extreme Ähnlichkeiten in Roger Vontobels Inszenierungen am Schauspielhaus Hamburg*. Reihe Theater und Universität im Gespräch, Bd. 13. Würzburg: Königshausen & Neumann.

———. 2011b. "Das unkalkulierbare Andere: Geschlechter-Szenen auf dem Schauplatz des Krieges in Heinrich von Kleists Penthesilea." In *Geschlechter-SpielRäume: Dramatik, Theater, Performance und Gender*, edited by Gaby Pailer and Franziska Schößler, 95–120. Amsterdam: Rodopi.

———, ed. 2008a. *Heinrich von Kleist (Freiburger literaturpsychologische Gespräche). Jahrbuch für Literatur und Psychoanalyse*, vol. 27, edited by Ortrud Gutjahr. Würzburg: Königshausen & Neumann.

———. 2008b. "Unheimliche Heimkehr: Der Schauplatz des Anderen in Heinrich von Kleists Amphitryon." In *Heinrich von Kleist (Freiburger literaturpsychologische Gespräche). Jahrbuch für Literatur und Psychoanalyse*, vol. 27, edited by Ortrud Gutjahr, 95–120. Würzburg: Königshausen & Neumann.

———. 2006. *Penthesilea von Heinrich von Kleist: Geschlechter Szenen in Stephan Kimmigs Inszenierung am Thalia Theater Hamburg*. Reihe Theater und Universität im Gespräch, Bd. 3. Würzburg: Königshausen & Neumann.

Hahn, Torsten. 2004. "Rauschen, Gerücht und Gegensinn: Nachrichtenübermittlung in Heinrich von Kleists *Robert Guiskard*." In *Kontingenz und Steuerung: Literatur als Gesellschaftsexperiment 1750–1830*, vol. 2 of *Studien zur Kulturpoetik*, edited by Torsten Hahn, Erich Kleinschmidt, and Nicolas Pethes, 101–21. Würzburg: Königshausen & Neumann.

Halberstam, Judith. 1998. *Female Masculinity*. Durham, N.C.: Duke University Press.

Halle, Randall. 2004. *Queer Social Philosophy: Critical Readings from Kant to Adorno*. Urbana: University of Illinois Press.

Haraway, Donna Jeanne. 1991. "The Promise of Monsters: A Regenerative Politics for Inappropriate/d Others." In *Cultural Studies*, edited by Lawrence Grossberg et al., 295–337. New York: Routledge.

Harst, Joachim. 2012. *Heilstheater: Figur des barocken Trauerspiels zwischen Gryphius und Kleist*. Munich: Fink.

Hederich, Benjamin. 1996. *Gründliches mythologisches Lexikon*. Darmstadt: Wissenschaftliche Buchgesellschaft.

Hegel, Georg Wilhelm Friedrich. 2014. *Lectures on the Philosophy of Art: The Hotho Transcript of the 1823 Berlin Lectures*. Translated by Robert F. Brown. Oxford: Oxford University Press.

———. 1977. *Phenomenology of Spirit*. Translated by Arnold V. Miller. Oxford: Oxford University Press.

Heimböckel, Dieter. 2003. *Emphatische Unaussprechlichkeit: Sprachkritik im Werk Heinrich von Kleists: Ein Beitrag zur Literarischen Sprachskepsistradition der Moderne*. Göttingen: Vandenhoeck & Ruprecht.

Heine, Heinrich. 1979. "Zur Geschichte der Religion und Philosophie in Deutschland." In *Historisch-kritische Gesamtausgabe der Werke*, edited by Manfred Windfuhr, 9–120. Hamburg: Hoffmann und Campe.

Henke, Burkhard, Susanne Kord, and Simon Richter. 2000. *Unwrapping Goethe's Weimar: Essays in Cultural Studies and Local Knowledge*. Rochester, N.Y.: Camden House.

Herder, Johann Gottfried. 1993. "Von deutscher Art und Kunst." In *Schriften zur Ästhetik und Literatur 1767–1781*, vol. 2 of *Herder: Werke in 10 Bänden*, edited by Günter Arnold and Gunter Grimm, 445–562. Frankfurt a.M.: Deutscher Klassiker Verlag.

Hinderer, Walter. 2011. *Vom Gesetz des Widerspruchs: Über Heinrich von Kleist.* Würzburg: Königshausen & Neumann.

———. 2001. "Immanuel Kants Begriff der negativen Größen, Adam Müllers Lehre vom Gegensatz und Heinrich von Kleists Ästhetik der Negation." In *Gewagte Experimente und kühne Konstellationen: Kleists Werk zwischen Klassizismus und Romantik*, edited by Christine Lubkoll and Günter Oesterle, 35–62. Würzburg: Königshausen & Neumann.

———. 1981. *Kleists Dramen: Neue Interpretationen.* Stuttgart: Reclam.

Hoffmann, E. T. A. 1885. *Weird Tales.* Vol. 1. Translated by John Thomas Bealby. New York: Charles Scribner's Sons.

Hoff-Purviance, Linda. 1982. "The Form of Kleist's *Penthesilea* and the *Iliad.*" *German Quarterly* 55, no. 1: 39–48.

Hölderlin, Friedrich. 1978. "Antigone." In *Sämtliche Werke: Frankfurter Ausgabe. Historisch-Kritische Ausgabe, Bd. 16. Sophokles*, edited by D. E. Sattler and Anja Ross. Frankfurt a.M.: Roter Stern.

Holz, Hans Heinz. 1962. *Macht und Ohnmacht der Sprache: Untersuchung zum Sprachverständnis und Stil Heinrich von Kleists.* Frankfurt a.M.: Aisthesis Verlag.

Honegger, Claudia. 1991. *Die Ordnung der Geschlechter: Die Wissenschaften vom Menschen und das Weib, 1750–1850.* Frankfurt a.M.: Campus.

Horn, Anette, and Peter Horn. 2013. *"Ich bin dir wohl ein Rätsel": Heinrich von Kleists Dramen.* Beiträge zur Kulturwissenschaft, Bd. 30. Oberhausen: Athena.

Horst, Eleanor ter. 2003. *Lessing, Goethe, Kleist, and the Transformation of Gender: From Hermaphrodite to Amazon.* New York: Peter Lang.

Hull, Isabel V. 1996. *Sexuality, State, and Civil Society in Germany, 1700–1815.* Ithaca, N.Y.: Cornell University Press.

Illouz, Eva. 1997. *Consuming the Romantic Utopia: Love and the Cultural Contradictions of Capitalism.* Berkeley: University of California Press.

Irigaray, Luce. 1985. *Speculum of the Other Woman.* Translated by Gillian C. Gill. Ithaca, N.Y.: Cornell University Press.

Isherwood, Christopher. 2013. *The World in the Evening.* New York: Farrar, Straus and Giroux.

Jacobs, Carol. 1989. *Uncontainable Romanticism: Shelley, Brontë, Kleist.* Baltimore: Johns Hopkins University Press.

Jacobus, Mary. 1995. *First Things: The Maternal Imaginary in Literature, Art, and Psychoanalysis.* New York: Routledge.

Jagose, Annamarie. 2007. "'Critical Extasy': Orgasm and Sensibility in 'Memoirs of a Woman of Pleasure.'" *Signs: Journal of Women in Culture and Society* 32, no. 2: 459.

———. 2002. *Inconsequence: Lesbian Representation and the Logic of Sexual Sequence.* Ithaca, N.Y.: Cornell University Press.

James, William. 1977. *A Pluralistic Universe.* Cambridge, Mass.: Harvard University Press.

Janvier, Louis Joseph. 1977. *Les Constitutions d'Haiti (1801–1885).* Vol. 1. Port-au-Prince: Éditions Fardin.

Jauss, Hans Robert. 1981. "Von Plautus bis Kleist: 'Amphiyon' im dialogischen Prozeß der Arbeit am Mythos." In *Kleists Dramen: Neue Interpretationen*, edited by Walter Hinderer, 114–43. Stuttgart: Reclam.

Kaiser, Brigit Mara. 2011. *Figures of Simplicity: Sensation and Thinking in Kleist and Melville*. Albany: State University of New York.

Kant, Emmanuel. 2006. *Anthropology from a Pragmatic Point of View*. Edited and translated by Robert B. Louden. Cambridge: Cambridge University Press.

———. 2000. *Critique of Judgment*. Translated by J. H. Bernard. New York: Prometheus.

———. 1990. *Critique of Pure Reason*. Translated by J. M. D. Meiklejohn. Buffalo: Prometheus.

Karlyn, Kathleen Rowe. 1995. *The Unruly Woman: Gender and the Genres of Laughter*. Austin: University of Texas Press.

Katz, Jonathan Ned. 1995. *The Invention of Heterosexuality*. New York: Dutton.

Kittler, Wolf. 1987. *Die Geburt des Partisanen aus dem Geist der Poesie: Heinrich von Kleist und die Strategie der Befreiungskriege*. Reihe Litterae. Freiburg: Rombach.

Klein, Melanie. 1986. *The Selected Melanie Klein*. Edited by Juliet Mitchell. New York: The Free Press.

Klein, Melanie, and Joan Riviere. 1964. *Love, Hate and Reparation*. New York: Norton.

Kleist, Heinrich von. 2009. *Selected Prose of Heinrich von Kleist*. Translated by Peter Wortsmann. New York: Archipelago Books.

———. 2005. "Sämtliche Gedichte." In *Sämtliche Werke "Brandenburger Ausgabe (BKA)."* Edited by Roland Reuß and Peter Staengle. Vol. 3. Frankfurt a.M.: Stromfeld/Roter Stern.

———. 2004. *Selected Writings*. Translated by David Constantine. Indianapolis: Hackett.

———. 2000. "Robert Guiskard. Fragment aus dem Trauerspiel: Robert Guiskard, Herzog der Normänner." In *Sämtliche Werke "Brandenburger Ausgabe (BKA)."* Edited by Roland Reuß and Peter Staengle. Vol. I/2. Frankfurt a.M.: Stromfeld/Roter Stern.

———. 1995. "Der Zerbrochne Krug." In *Sämtliche Werke "Brandenburger Ausgabe (BKA)."* Edited by Roland Reuß and Peter Staengle. Vol. I/3. Frankfurt a.M.: Stromfeld/Roter Stern.

———. 1982. *An Abyss Deep Enough: Letters of Heinrich von Kleist, with a Selection of Essays and Anecdotes*. Edited and translated by Philip B. Miller. New York: Dutton.

Klotz, Volker. 1996. *Radikaldramatik: Szenische Vor-Avantgarde: Von Holberg zu Nestroy, von Kleist zu Grabbe*. Bielefeld: Aisthesis.

Kommerell, Max. 1991. "Die Sprache und das Unaussprechliche: Eine Betrachtung über Heinrich von Kleist." In *Geist und Buchstabe der Dichtung: Goethe, Schiller, Kleist, Hölderlin*, 243–317. Frankfurt a.M.: Klostermann.

Kord, Susanne. 1996. *Sich einen Namen machen: Anonymität und weibliche Autorschaft 1700–1900*. Stuttgart: Metzler.

Koschorke, Albrecht. 1999. *Körperströme und Schriftverkehr: Mediologie des 18. Jahrhunderts*. Munich: Wilhelm Fink.

Koselleck, Reinhardt. 2004. "Historical Criteria of the Modern Concept of Revolution." In *Futures Past: On the Semantics of Historical Time*. New York: Columbia University Press.

Koser, Julie. 2016. *Armed Ambiguity: Women Warriors in German Literature and Culture in the Age of Goethe*. Evanston, Ill.: Northwestern University Press.

Krafft-Ebing, R. von. 1898. *Psychopathia Sexualis: Mit besonderer Berücksichtigung der conträren Sexualempfindung: Eine klinisch-forensische Studie*. Stuttgart: Verlag von F. Enke.

Krimmer, Elisabeth. 2010. "The Revolutionary and Napoleonic Wars." In *The Representation of War in German Literature: From 1800 to the Present*, 19–65. Cambridge: Cambridge University Press.

———. 2008. "The Gender of Terror: War as (Im)Moral Institution in Kleist's 'Hermannsschlacht' and 'Penthesilea.'" *German Quarterly* 81, no. 1: 66.

———. 2004. *In the Company of Men: Cross-Dressed Women around 1800*. Detroit: Wayne State University Press.

———. 2003. "'Die Allmähliche Verfertigung des Geschlechts beim Anziehen': Epistemologies of the Body in Kleist's *Die Familie Schroffenstein*." In *Body Dialectics in the Age of Goethe*, vol. 55 of *Amsterdamer Beiträge zur neueren Germanistik*, edited by Marianne Henn and Holger Pausch, 347–63. New York: Rodopi.

Krimmer, Elisabeth, and Patricia Anne Simpson. 2011. *Enlightened War*. Studies in German Literature Linguistics and Culture, Vol. 98. Rochester, N.Y.: Boydell & Brewer.

Kuzniar, Alice, ed. 1996. *Outing Goethe and His Age*. Stanford, Calif.: Stanford University Press.

Lacan, Jacques. 2013. *The Ethics of Psychoanalysis 1959–1960*. Edited by Jacques-Alain Miller; translated with notes by Dennis Porter. Hoboken, N.J.: Taylor and Francis.

———. 1982. *On Feminine Sexuality: The Limits of Love and Knowledge*. The Seminar of Jacques Lacan, Vol. 20. Edited by Juliet Mitchell and Jacqueline Rose, translated by Jacqueline Rose. New York: Norton.

———. 1988. *The Ego in Freud's Theory and in the Technique of Psychoanalysis, 1954–1955*. The Seminar of Jacques Lacan, Vol. 2. Translated by Sylvana Tomaselli. New York: Norton.

———. 1985. "Conférence à Genève sur le symptôme." *Les Block-Notes de la psychanalyse*, no. 5: 5–23.

———. 1978. *The Four Fundamental Concepts of Psycho-Analysis*. Edited by Jacques-Alain Miller; translated by Alan Sheridan. New York: Norton.

Lacan, Jacques, and Jacques-Alain Miller. 2011. *Le séminaire de Jacques Lacan*. Livre 19: *Ou pire*. Paris: Seuil.

Landgraf, Edgar. 2011. *Improvisation as Art*. New Directions in German Studies. New York: Bloomsbury.

Laplanche, Jean. 1992. *Seduction, Translation and the Drives: A Dossier*. Edited by John Fletcher and Martin Stanton; translated by Martin Stanton. ICA Documents, Vol. 11, 21–40. London: Institute of Contemporary Arts.

Laqueur, Thomas Walter. 2003. *Solitary Sex: A Cultural History of Masturbation*. New York: Zone Books.

———. 1990. *Making Sex: Body and Gender from the Greeks to Freud*. Cambridge, Mass.: Harvard University Press.

Lassen, Christian. 2011. *Camp Comforts: Reparative Gay Literature in Times of AIDS*. Bielefeld: Transcript Verlag.

Lessing, Gotthold Ephraim. 1962. *Hamburg Dramaturgy*. Introduction by Victor Lange. New York: Dover.

Lindsay, J. M. 1977. "Faulty Communication in the Works of Kleist." *German Life and Letters* 31: 57–67.

Loftus, Brian. 1996. "Biopia: Bisexuality and the Crisis of Visibility in a Queer Symbolic." In *Representing Bisexualities: Subjects and Cultures of Fluid Desires*, edited by Maria Pramaggiore and Donald E. Hall, 207–33. New York: NYU Press.

Luepnitz, Deborah. 2003. "Beyond the Phallus: Lacan and Feminism." In *The Cambridge Companion to Lacan*, 221–37. Cambridge: Cambridge University Press.

Luhmann, Niklas. 1998. *Love as Passion*. Stanford, Calif.: Stanford University Press.

Lundberg, Christian O. 2012. *Lacan in Public: Psychoanalysis and the Science of Rhetoric*. Tuscaloosa: University of Alabama Press.

Luther, Martin. 2017. *Die Bibel: Mit Apokryphen*. Edited by Evangelische Kirche in Deutschland. Stuttgart: Deutsche Bibelgesellschaft.

Lyon, John. 2008. "Kleist's *Prinz Friedrich von Homburg* and the Crisis of Masculinity." *Germanic Review* 83, no. 2: 167–87.

Maass, Joachim. 1957. *Kleist, die Fackel Preußens*. Munich: K. Desch.

MacLeod, Catriona. 1998. *Embodying Ambiguity: Androgyny and Aesthetics from Winckelmann to Keller*. Kritik. Detroit: Wayne State University Press.

———. 1996. "The 'Third Sex' in an Age of Difference: Androgyny and Homosexuality in Winckelmann, Friedrich Schlegel, and Kleist." In *Outing Goethe and His Age*, edited by Alice Kuzniar, 194–214. Stanford, Calif.: Stanford University Press.

Marso, Lori Jo. 2018. "Feminist Cringe Comedy: Dear Dick, The Joke Is on You." *Politics and Gender*, August 6, 1–23. doi:10.1017/S1743923X18000387.

Masterman, Margaret. 1970. "The Nature of a Paradigm." In *Criticism and the Growth of Knowledge: Proceedings of the International Colloquium in the Philosophy of Science, 1965*, edited by Imre Lakatos and Alan Musgrave, 59–90. Cambridge: University of Cambridge Press.

Mayer, Hans. 1982. *Outsiders: A Study in Life and Letters*. Translated by Denis Sweet. Cambridge, Mass.: MIT Press.

McAllister, Grant Profant. 2005. *Kleist's Female Leading Characters and the Subversion of Idealist Discourse*. New York: Peter Lang.

Meer, Theo van der. 1994. "Sodomy and the Pursuit of the Third Sex in the Early Modern Period." In *Third Sex, Third Gender*, edited by Gilbert Herdt, 137–212. New York: Zone Books.

Meister, Jan Christoph, and Peter Hühn, eds. 2012. *The Living Handbook of Narratology*. Hamburg: Hamburg University Press.

Menke, Bettine. 2007. "Holes and Excesses: On Wit and the Joke in Kleist's 'Anecdote from the Last War.' " *MLN* 122, no. 3: 647–64.

———. 2000. "*Penthesilea*: Das Bild des Körpers und seine Zerfällung." In *Erotik und Sexualität im Werk Heinrich von Kleists*, 117–36. Heilbronn: Kleist-Archiv Sembdner.

———. 1997. "Körper-Bild und -Zerfällung, *Staub*: Über Heinrich von Kleists *Penthesilea*." In *Körper—Gedächtnis—Schrift: Der Körper als Medium kultureller Erinnerung*, edited by Claudia Öhlschläger, 122–58. Berlin: Erich Schmidt.

Meyer, Moe. 1994. *The Politics and Poetics of Camp*. New York: Routledge.

Mieszkowski, Jan. 2014a. "Almost Nearly: The Languages of Approximation." *Seminar: A Journal of Germanic Studies* 50, no. 3: 258–75.

———. 2014b. "The Next Word (or Something Like It)." *MLN* 129, no. 3: 606–20.

———. 2009. "Who's Afraid of Anacoluthon?" *MLN* 124, no. 3: 648.

———. 2000. "Breaking the Laws of Language: Freedom and History in Kleist's *Prinz Friedrich von Homburg*." In *Studies in Romanticism* 39, no. 1: 111.

Miller, D. A. 1993. "Sontag's Urbanity." In *Lesbian and Gay Studies Reader*, edited by Henry Abelove, Michèle Aina Barale, and David M. Halperin, 91–101. New York: Routledge.

Milton, John. 1974. *Samson Agonistes*. London: Oxford University Press.

Mizejewski, Linda. 2014. *Pretty/Funny: Women Comedians and Body Politics*. Austin: University of Texas Press.

Molière. 2000. *Oeuvres complètes*. Edited by Georges Forestier and Claude Bourqui. Paris: Gallimard.

Morrison, Paul. 1993. "End Pleasure." *GLQ: A Journal of Lesbian and Gay Studies* 1, no. 1: 53–78.

Moser, Christian. 2001. "Prüfungen der Unschuld: Zeuge und Zeugnis bei Kleist und Rousseau." In *Heinrich von Kleist und die Aufklärung*, edited by Tim Mehigan, 92–112. Columbia, S.C.: Camden House.

———. 1993. *Verfehlte Gefühle: Wissen, Begehren, Darstellen bei Kleist und Rousseau*. Epistemata. Reihe Literaturwissenschaft. Vol. 94. Würzburg: Königshausen & Neumann.

Müller-Seidel, Walter. 1971. *Versehen und Erkennen: Eine Studie über Heinrich von Kleist*. Cologne: Böhlau-Verlag.

Nealon, Christopher. 2004. "Camp Messianism, or, the Hopes of Poetry in Late-Late Capitalism." *American Literature* 76, no. 3: 579–602.

Nessel, Sabine, and Winfried Pauleit. 2004. "Alle müssen sich bewegen: Pathos der Politik und Hüftschwung bei Elvis." *Ästhetik und Kommunikation* 35, no. 124: 73–78.

Neumann, Gerhard. 2007. "Rituale der Liebe." In *Die neue Kraft der Rituale*, edited by Axel Michaels, 45–65. Heidelberg: Winter Verlag.

Newton, Esther. 1979. *Mother Camp: Female Impersonators in America*. Chicago: University of Chicago Press.

Ngai, Sianne. 2012. *Our Aesthetic Categories: Zany, Cute, Interesting*. Cambridge, Mass.: Harvard University Press.

———. 2005. *Ugly Feelings*. Cambridge, Mass.: Harvard University Press.

Nietzsche, Friedrich. 2000. *Basic Writings*. Translated and edited by Walter Kaufmann. New York: Modern Library.

Nietzsche, Friedrich Wilhelm. 1967. *Werke*. Kritische Gesamtausgabe. Edited by Giorgio Colli and Mazzino Montinari. Berlin: De Gruyter.

Nitschke, Claudia. 2013. "Kleist: Romantische Komplikationen." In *Der öffentliche Vater: Konzeptionen paternaler Souveränität in der deutschen Literatur (1755–1921)*, 199–234. Berlin: De Gruyter.

Padva, Gilad. 2000. "Priscilla Fights Back: The Politicization of Camp Subculture." *Journal of Communication Inquiry* 24, no. 2: 216.

Pahl, Katrin. 2015. "What a Mess." *MLN* 130, no. 3: 528–53.

———. 2012. *Tropes of Transport: Hegel and Emotion*. Evanston, Ill.: Northwestern University Press.

———. 2011. "Doublings and Couplings: The Feeling Thing in Valéry and Kleist." *Zeitschrift für Medien- und Kulturforschung* 1: 177–84.

———. 2008. "'Geliebte, sprich!'—wenn Frauen sich haben." In *Penthesileas Versprechen: Exemplarische Studien über die literarische Referenz*, edited by Rüdiger Campe, 151–87. Freiburg: Rombach.

Papadopoulos, Dimitris, Niamh Stephenson, and Vassilis Tsianos. 2008. *Escape Routes: Control and Subversion in the Twenty-First Century*. Chicago: University of Chicago Press.

Pateman, Carole. 1988. *The Sexual Contract*. London: Polity.

Patterson, Michael. 1990. *The First German Theatre: Schiller, Goethe, Kleist, and Büchner in Performance*. Theatre Production Studies. New York: Routledge.

Pellegrini, Ann. 2007. "After Sontag: Future Notes on Camp." In *A Companion to Lesbian, Gay, Bisexual, Transgender, and Queer Studies*, edited by E. Haggerty and M. McGarry, 168–93. Oxford: Blackwell.

Peters, Sibylle. 2003. *Heinrich von Kleist und der Gebrauch der Zeit: Von der MachArt der Berliner Abendblätter*. Würzburg: Königshausen & Neumann.

Pewny, Katharina. 2011. "Der Penis als Dildo Oder: Das letzte Spektakel der Männlichkeit (in der Performancekunst)." In *GeschlechterSpielRäume: Dramatik, Theater, Performance und Gender*, edited by Gaby Pailer and Franziska Schößler, 329–40. Amsterdam: Rodopi.

Pfau, Thomas. 2005. *Romantic Moods: Paranoia, Trauma, and Melancholy, 1790–1840*. Baltimore: Johns Hopkins University Press.

Pfeiffer, Joachim. 1996. "Friendship and Gender: The Aesthetic Construction of Subjectivity in Kleist." In *Outing Goethe and His Age*, edited by Alice Kuzniar, 215–27. Stanford, Calif.: Stanford University Press.

———. 1989. *Die zerbrochenen Bilder: Gestörte Ordnungen im Werk Heinrich von Kleists*. Würzburg: Königshausen & Neumann.

Pier, John. 2016. "Metalepsis." In *The Living Handbook of Narratology*, edited by Peter Hühn. Hamburg: Hamburg University. http://www.lhn.uni-hamburg.de/article/metalepsis-revised-version-uploaded-13-july-2016.

Plautus. 2011. *Amphitryon*. Translated by Wolfgang de Melo. Loeb Classical Library, Book 60, 1–132, Cambridge: Harvard University Press.

Plug, Jan. 1997. "The Borders of a Lip: Kleist, Language, and Politics." *Studies in Romanticism* 36, no. 3: 391–425.

Preciado, Paul B. 2018. *Countersexual Manifesto*. Translated by Kevin Gerry Dunn. New York: Columbia University Press.

Pütz, Peter. 1970. *Die Zeit im Drama: Zur Technik dramatischer Spannung*. Göttingen: Vandenhoeck & Ruprecht.

Redecker, Eva von. 2018. *Praxis und Revolution: Eine Sozialtheorie radikalen Wandels*. Frankfurt a.M.: Campus.

Reeve, William C. 1991. *Kleist's Aristocratic Heritage and "Das Käthchen von Heilbronn."* Montreal: McGill-Queen's University Press.

Reuß, Roland. 1992. "'Im Geklüft': Zur Sprache von Kleists 'Penthesilea.'" *Brandenburger Kleist-Blätter* 5: 3–27.

Reuß, Roland, Peter Staengle, and Hans-Heinrich Baumann. 2000. "*'Lautlos': Kritik der Rede in Kleists 'Robert Guiskard.'*" *Brandenburger Kleist-Blätter* 13: 3–11.

Richter, Simon. 2014. *Missing the Breast*. Literary Conjugations. Seattle: University of Washington Press.

Riedl, Peter Philipp. 2011. "Gewaltinszenierungen: Formen des Spiels im Spiel in Kleists Dramen." *German Life and Letters* 64, no. 3: 354–73.

———. 2009. "Texturen des Terrors: Politische Gewalt im Werk Heinrich von Kleists." *Publications of the English Goethe Society* 78, nos. 1–2: 32–46.

Riley, Denise. 2000. *The Words of Selves*. Stanford, Calif.: Stanford University Press.

Rinck, Monika. 2015. "Helden und Köter und Fraun: Rede zur Verleihung des Kleist-Preises." In *Kleists Jahrbuch 2016*, 11–18. Stuttgart: J. B. Metzler.

Riviere, Joan. 2015. "Womanliness as a Masquerade." In *Female Sexuality: The Early Psychoanalytic Controversies*. Edited by Russell Grigg, Dominique Hecq, and Craig Smith, 172–82. London: Karnac Books.

Roof, Judith. 1996. *Come as You Are: Sexuality and Narrative*. Between Men—Between Women. New York: Columbia University Press.

Ross, Andrew. 1989. "Uses of Camp." In *No Respect: Intellectuals and Popular Culture*, 135–70. London: Routledge.

Rousseau, Jean-Jacques. 1979. *Emile, or On Education*. Translated by Allan Bloom. New York: Basic Books.

Rubin, Gayle. 1975. "The Traffic in Women: Notes on the 'Political Economy' of Sex." In *Toward an Anthropology of Women*, edited by Rayna Reiter, 157–210. New York: Monthly Review Press.

"Rumpelstilzchen." 2004. In *Kinder- und Hausmärchen gesammelt durch die Brüder Grimm*, edited by Heinz Rölleke, 250–53. Frankfurt a.M.: Insel Verlag.

Samuel, Richard. 1981. "Heinrich von Kleists *Robert Guiskard* und seine Wiederbelebung 1807–1808." *Kleist-Jahrbuch 1981/1982*, 315–48.

Sandburg, Carl. 1936. *The People, Yes*. New York: Harcourt, Brace and Company.

Schede, Hans-Georg. 2008. *Heinrich von Kleist*. Reinbek bei Hamburg: Rowohlt.

Scheifele, Sigrid. 1992. *Projektionen des Weiblichen: Lebensentwürfe in Kleists Penthesilea*. Epistemata: Würzburger Wissenschaftliche Schriften. Reihe Literaturwissenschaft, Bd. 86. Würzburg: Königshausen & Neumann.

Schiebinger, Londa. 1986. "Skeletons in the Closet: The First Illustrations of the Female Skeleton in Eighteenth-Century Anatomy." *Representations* 14 (spring): 42–82.

Schiller, Friedrich. 2016. "Idyl." In *The Works of Frederick Schiller*, 3359–75. Dinslaken: anboco.

———. 2005a. "*On Grace and Dignity.*" Translated by Jane Veronica Curran. In *Schiller's 'On Grace and Dignity' In Its Cultural Context: Essays and a New Translation*. Edited by Jane Veronica Curran and Christophe Fricker, 123–70. Rochester, N.Y.: Camden House.

———. 2005b. "Über das Gegenwärtige Teutsche Theater" (1782). In *Sämtliche Werke: Vermischte Schriften*. Berlin: Aufbau.

———. 1993. "On Naïve and Sentimental Poetry." In *Essays*, edited by Daniel O. Dahlstrom and Walter Hinderer, 179–201. New York: Continuum.

———. 1959. *The Maiden of Orleans, a Romantic Tragedy*. Translated by John T. Krumpelmann. Studies in the Germanic Languages and Literatures, Vol. 24. Chapel Hill: University of North Carolina Press.

Schmitt, Carl. 2007. *Theory of the Partisan: Intermediate Commentary on the Concept of the Political*. Translated by G. L. Ulmen. New York: Telos.

Schneider, Manfred. 2001. "Die Welt im Ausnahmezustand: Kleists Kriegstheater." In *Kleist-Jahrbuch 2001*, edited by Günter Blamberger, Sabine Doerning, and Klaus Müller-Salget, 104–19. Stuttgart: J. B. Metzler.

Scholze, Philipp. 2015. *Zwischen den Knien der Autorität: Mythos, Liebe, Macht in Heinrich von Kleists "Das Käthchen Von Heilbronn."* Göttingen: Vandenhoeck & Ruprecht.

Scott, Joan Wallach. 2011. *The Fantasy of Feminist History*. Durham, N.C.: Duke University Press.

———. 1996. *Only Paradoxes to Offer*. Cambridge, Mass.: Harvard University Press.

Scott, Virginia. 2000. *Molière: A Theatrical Life*. Cambridge: Cambridge University Press.

Sedgwick, Eve Kosofsky. 1997. "Paranoid Reading and Reparative Reading, or, You're So Paranoid, You Probably Think This Essay Is about You." In *Touching Feeling: Affect, Pedagogy, Performativity*, 123–52. Durham, N.C.: Duke University Press.

———. 1985. *Between Men: English Literature and Male Homosocial Desire*. Gender and Culture. New York: Columbia University Press.

Seeba, Hinrich C. 2005. "Die Filzlaus im Leib Germaniens: Kleists *Hermannsschlacht* als Programm ethnischer Säuberung." In *Beiträge zur Kleist-Forschung* 19: 45–60.

———. 1981. "Identitätskrise und Sprachskepsis in Kleists *Familie Schroffenstein*." In *Kleists Aktualität*, edited by Walter Müller-Seidel, 104–50. Darmstadt: Wissenschaftliche Buchgesellschaft.

Seeba, Hinrich C., and Ernst Osterkamp. 1988. "'Historia in Absentia': Zur Aussparung von Hermanns Schlacht bei Kleist." *Kleist-Jahrbuch* 1988/89: 242–52.

Sembdner, Helmut. 1996. *Heinrich von Kleist's Lebensspuren: Dokumente und Berichte der Zeitgenossen*. Munich: Hanser.

Sha, Richard. 2008. *Perverse Romanticism: Aesthetics and Sexuality in Britain, 1750–1832*. Baltimore: Johns Hopkins University Press.

Simpson, Patricia Anne. 2006. *The Erotics of War in German Romanticism*. Lewisburg: Bucknell University Press.

Snyder, Katherine V. 1999. *Bachelors, Manhood, and the Novel, 1850–1925*. Cambridge: Cambridge University Press.

Sokolsky, Anita. 1987. "The Resistance to Sentimentality: Yeats, de Man, and the Aesthetic Education." *Yale Journal of Criticism: Interpretation in the Humanities* 1, no. 1: 67–86.

Sontag, Susan. 1999. "Notes on Camp." In *Against Interpretation and Other Essays*, 275–92. New York: Anchor Books.

Sophocles. 2003. *Antigone*. Translated by David Franklin and John Harrison. Cambridge Translations from Greek Drama. Cambridge: Cambridge University Press.

Stephens, Anthony R. 1999. *Kleist: Sprache und Gewalt*. Reihe Litterae, Bd. 64. Freiburg: Rombach.

———. 1983. "The Illusion of a Shaped World: Kleist and Tragedy." *AUMLA: Journal of the Australasian Universities Language and Literature Association* 60, no. 60: 197–219.

Szondi, Peter. 1978. "Versuch über das Tragische." In *Schriften 1*. Frankfurt a.M.: Insel.

———. 1973. "*Fünfmal Amphitryon: Plautus, Molière, Kleist, Giraudoux, Kaiser*." In *Lektüren und Lektionen: Versuche über Literatur, Literaturtheorie und Literatursoziologie*, edited by Peter Szondi, 153–84. Frankfurt a.M.: Suhrkamp.

———. 1961. "Amphitryon: Kleists 'Lustspiel nach Molière.' " *Euphorion* 55: 249–59.

Theisen, Bianca. 2008. " 'Helden und Köter und Fraun': Kleists Hundekomödie." In *Penthesileas Versprechen: Exemplarische Studien über die literarische Referenz*, edited by Rüdiger Campe, 153–64. Freiburg: Rombach.

Theweleit, Klaus. 1987. *Male Fantasies*. Vol. 1, *Women. Floods. Bodies. History*. Minneapolis: University of Minnesota Press.

Tobin, Robert Deam. 2015. *Peripheral Desires: The German Discovery of Sex*. Philadelphia: University of Pennsylvania Press.

———. 2000. *Warm Brothers: Queer Theory and the Age of Goethe*. Philadelphia: University of Pennsylvania Press.

———. 1996. "In and against Nature: Goethe on Homosexuality and Heterosexuality." *Outing Goethe and His Age*, edited by Alice Kuzniar, 94–110. Stanford, Calif.: Stanford University Press.

Trinh T. Minh-ha. 1986–87. "She, the Inappropriate/d Other." *Discourse* 8 (fall/winter): 1–132.

Vinken, Barbara. 2011. *Bestien: Kleist und die Deutschen*. Berlin: Merve.

Vogel, Juliane. 2018. *Aus dem Grund: Auftrittsprotokolle zwischen Racine und Nietzsche*. Reihe Bild und Text. Munich: Wilhelm Fink.

———. 2002. *Die Furie und das Gesetz: Zur Dramaturgie der "grossen Szene" in der Tragödie des 19. Jahrhunderts*. Reihe Litterae, Bd. 94. Freiburg: Rombach.

Waltz, Matthias. 2001. "Ethik der Welt—Ethik des Realen." In *Jacques Lacan—Wege zu seinem Werk*, 97–129. Stuttgart: Klett-Cotta.

———. 1993. *Ordnung der Namen: Die Entstehung der Moderne: Rousseau, Proust, Sartre*. Frankfurt a.M.: Fischer.

Weckel, Ulrike. 1998. *Ordnung, Politik und Geselligkeit der Geschlechter im 18. Jahrhundert*. Göttingen: Wallstein.

Weigel, Alexander. 2011. "Theaternot, Theaterkritik, Theatertraum: Heinrich von Kleist und das Theater seiner Zeit." *German Life and Letters* 64: 437–54.

Wellbery, David E. 1997. "*Der zerbrochne Krug*: Das Spiel der Geschlechterdifferenz." In *Interpretationen: Kleists Dramen*, edited by Walter Hinderer, 11–32. Stuttgart: Reclam.

Wild, Christopher J. 2003. *Theater der Keuschheit, Keuschheit des Theaters: Zu einer Geschichte der (Anti-)Theatralität von Gryphius bis Kleist*. Freiburg: Rombach.

Yalom, Marilyn. 1997. *A History of the Breast*. New York: Random House.

INDEX